CAMBRIDGE TEXTS IN THE
HISTORY OF POLITICAL THOUGHT

ASTELL
Political Writings

CAMBRIDGE TEXTS IN THE HISTORY OF POLITICAL THOUGHT

Series editors

RAYMOND GEUSS
Lecturer in Social and Political Sciences, University of Cambridge

QUENTIN SKINNER
Professor of Political Science in the University of Cambridge

Cambridge Texts in the History of Political Thought is now firmly established as the major student textbook series in political theory. It aims to make available to students all the most important texts in the history of western political thought, from ancient Greece to the early twentieth century. All the familiar classic texts will be included but the series does at the same time seek to enlarge the conventional canon by incorporating an extensive range of less well-known works, many of them never before available in a modern English edition. Wherever possible, texts are published in complete and unabridged form, and translations are specially commissioned for the series. Each volume contains a critical introduction together with chronologies, biographical sketches, a guide to further reading and any necessary glossaries and textual apparatus. When completed, the series will aim to offer an outline of the entire evolution of western political thought.

For a list of titles published in the series, please see end of book.

ASTELL

Political Writings

EDITED BY
PATRICIA SPRINGBORG

Reader in Government,
University of Sydney

Published by the Press Syndicate of the University of Cambridge
The Pitt Building, Trumpington Street, Cambridge CB2 1RP
40 West 20th Street, New York, NY 10011–4211, USA
10 Stamford Road, Oakleigh, Melbourne 3166, Australia

First published 1996

Printed in Great Britain at the University Press, Cambridge

A catalogue record for this book is available from the British Library

Library of Congress cataloguing in publication data

Mary Astell, political writings / edited by Patricia Springborg.
p.   cm. – (Cambridge texts in the history of political thought)
Includes bibliographical references and index.
ISBN 0 521 41800 3 (hb)   0521 42845 9 (pb)
1. Astell, Mary, 1668–1731.   2. Political science–England–
History.   3. Political science–Early works to 1700.
I. Springborg, Patricia.   II. Series.
JA84.G7M37   1996
305.42–dc20   95–37464 CIP

ISBN 0 521 41800 3 hardback
ISBN 0 521 42845 9 paperback

Dedication

This volume is dedicated to those who by their inspiration and assistance made it possible, especially Christine Ambrose, Dick Ashcraft, Conal Condren, Ros Conyngham, Kathy Dempsey, Jim Farr, Lindsay Gardiner, Mark Goldie, Philip Hamburger, Bridget Hill, Isobel Horton, Ann Kelly, Shareen Matthews, John McCrystal, Carole Pateman, John Pocock, Maria Robertson, Lois Schwoerer, Quentin Skinner, Johann and Margaret Sommerville, Patricia Harris Stäblein, Robert, Ziyad and George Springborg. The institutions to which I owe such a debt include the Department of Government, Fisher Library and the Vice-Chancellor's Publication Fund of the University of Sydney; the State Libraries of New South Wales and Victoria; the Australian Research Council; the Folger Shakespeare Library; the Woodrow Wilson International Center for Scholars, Washington, D.C.; the Rare Book Collection of the Library of Congress; the John D. and Catherine T. MacArthur Foundation; and the Brookings Institution. Last, but not least, it is dedicated to the memory of Mary Astell herself, a seminal political theorist, philosopher and theologian, for too long sunk in obscurity.

Contents

Acknowledgements

Besides the general debt to individuals and institutions expressed in the Dedication, I owe acknowledgement of specific tasks. Immense thanks to Maria Robertson, Louise Chappell, Ros Conyngham, Isobel Horton, Shareen Matthews, of the Department of Government, University of Sydney, and Christine Ambrose and Kathy Dempsey, senior research assistants, who entered the text, checked and rechecked it. To Kathy Dempsey special thanks are owed for her excellent drafts of the Chronology and Biographical Notes and preparation of the Index. The Vice-Chancellor's Publication Fund of the University of Sydney and the Research Council of Australia, through ARC Small Grant FIO.26994 93/94/95 covered research expenses specific to this project, for which I am greatly indebted. To the Librarians of Fisher Library, University of Sydney; the State Library of New South Wales, in particular Sue Thomas; the State Library of Victoria; the Rare Book Librarian of the Library of Congress; Georgiana Ziegler, Betsy Walsh and the unfailingly helpful staff of the Folger Shakespeare Library, I am indebted for provision of the editions, often the very ones Astell used, from which I worked. My grateful thanks to those who provided support for full-time research, 1993–5: the University of Sydney, The Folger Institute, the Woodrow Wilson International Center for Scholars, the Brookings Institution, Washington, D.C., and the John D. and Catherine T. MacArthur Foundation for a Research and Writing Grant which the Brookings Institution administered. To my programme directors at these institutions, Lena Orlin at the Folger Institute; Jim Morris, Michael Lacey and

Ann Sheffield, at the Woodrow Wilson Center; John Steinbruner at Brookings and Kate Early at the MacArthur Foundation, I am truly thankful for support and kind understanding as I juggled my projects. To my patient and unfailingly courteous editor at Cambridge University Press, Richard Fisher, and copy editor, Pauline Leng, I am deeply grateful. Professor Quentin Skinner of Christ's College and Mark Goldie, Vice-Master at Churchill College, Cambridge; John Pocock, the Johns Hopkins University; Johann Sommerville, University of Wisconsin, and Margaret Sommerville; and the late and much lamented Dick Ashcraft of UCLA; all generously assisted me by reading drafts and on points of information.

Facsimile title-pages of the first editions of *Reflections upon Marriage, A Fair Way with the Dissenters* and *An Impartial Enquiry* are reproduced by kind permission of the Folger Shakespeare Library.

It was my intention, by providing for Mary Astell the sort of critical edition with which canonical theorists are typically furnished, to accord her the status that is only her due. Any faults in the presentation of this edition that may remain are entirely my own. My husband, Robert Springborg, and sons, Ziyad and George, have been exemplary in the support they have shown for this, among my projects the one that most clearly represents a public service. It is dedicated to them all and to the memory of Mary Astell, who died poor as she lived, and of whom few personal traces survive, in the form of manuscripts, or even a likeness of a once-celebrated woman.

Note

(*q.v.*) following a name indicates an entry in the Biographical notes.

Introduction

Mary Astell's life

Born on 12 November, 1666 to Peter Astell, a member of the Company of Hostmen at Newcastle upon Tyne, and his wife the former Mary Errington, Mary Astell is an unlikely candidate for the role of England's first feminist (Hill, 1986). Her father, although described as a gentleman, began as an apprentice to the Company of Hostmen, which enjoyed a virtual monopoly of the cartage of coal and grindstones. He did not complete his apprenticeship until Mary was eight years old and died when she was twelve, leaving the family debt-ridden. In the 1660s and 1670s 83 per cent of North Country women, and in the 1680s and 1690s 72 per cent, were illiterate; as calculated from signatures to court records, unable even to write their names (Cressy, 1977, 1980). Mary Astell, lacking formal education, found a family mentor in Ralph Astell, curate of St Nicholas church, Newcastle, author of 'New-castle's heartie Congratulations' to the King, the poem *Vota Non Bella* (1666), which had established his Royalist credentials. According to George Ballard, the eighteenth-century source on contemporary learned women, Astell mastered French, gained some knowledge of Latin and 'under his [Ralph's] tuition made considerable progress in philosophy, mathematics and logic' (*Memoirs of Several Ladies of Great Britain*, p. 382).

From her uncle Mary Astell may also have learned her Tory (*q.v.*) politics. A Royalist family tradition had been attested in the epitaph for her grandfather, William Astell, which, after recounting his sufferings for Charles I (*q.v.*), declared his reward union in death, not with his God, but with his master – 'Triumphant Charles he's gone to see' (Smith, 1916, 5; Kinnaird, 1979, 69, n.63). With few exceptions, the gentry of the North in any case tended to Royalism and even in some cases Catholicism (Hill, 1986, 5). Mary Astell's mother, Mary Errington, was from an old Catholic gentry family of Newcastle (Estcourt and Payne, 1885, 180; cited Perry, 1986, 39), which may well account for Mary's relative leniency towards Popery, compared with Presbyterianism (*q.v.*) her bent for Neoplatonism in the ecstatic tradition and her Jacobite (*q.v.*) sympathies.

In worldly terms Mary Astell's was a rather uneventful life, broken in its scholarly solitude by the period of political pamphleteering from 1697 to 1709, then lived out quietly to its close in 1731, when she died of breast cancer. At twenty years of age she had left Newcastle for London, and there she lived, mainly in Chelsea, a single woman associating with a small group of like-minded intellectual women, High Church (*q.v.*) prelates and their wives. These included Lady Catherine Jones (*q.v.*), daughter of the Earl of Ranelagh, Paymaster-General of the Navy, who was her patron. The correspondence between John Norris (*q.v.*) and Mary Astell, the *Letters Concerning the Love of God* (1695), is dedicated to her; and she is also the addressee of Mary Astell's *magnum opus*, *The Christian Religion as Profess'd by a Daughter of the Church* (1705). Lady Mary Wortley Montagu (*q.v.*), to whose *Embassy Letters: The Travels of an English Lady in Europe, Asia and Africa* (1724, 1725), Mary Astell added a Preface, Lady Anne Coventry and Lady Elizabeth Hastings were among the titled women of her acquaintance; while Elizabeth Elstob, Anglo-Saxon scholar and correspondent of George Ballard and the learned Bishop Francis Atterbury (*q.v.*), with whom Astell corresponded, numbered among the scholars who were also Chelsea neighbours (Hill, 1986, 7–9). At the height of her political activity Mary Astell belonged among the clientele of the Tory print shop of her publisher, Richard Wilkin, at the King's Head in St Paul's Church Yard. It is reported that she received a number of important guests at the Chelsea house where she lived, and that when she had no inclination to receive them, 'she would look out at the window and jestingly tell them (as Cato did Nasica), "Mrs. Astell is not at home," and in good earnest keep them out' (Ballard, *Memoirs of Several Ladies of Great Britain*, p. 385).

From her earliest writings Mary Astell showed herself to be a competent theologian, engaging ecclesiastics and known religious writers of her day. The first of her ecclesiastical correspondents, William Sancroft (*q.v.*), Archbishop of Canterbury and later nonjuror (*q.v.*), was also her earliest patron, assisting her when she first arrived in London, perhaps financially, as we know from the prefatory letter to the *Collection of Poems* (1689) Astell dedicated to him (Hill, 1986, 183–4). The exchange of letters between Mary Astell and the Cambridge Platonist (*q.v.*) John Norris, rector of Bemerton, begun in 1693, so impressed her correspondent that he undertook to have them published, warning of 'a diffidence in some who from the excellency of these writings may be tempted to question whether my correspondent be a woman or not' (Norris, 1695, in Hill, 1986, 191). John Evelyn, in his *Numismata: Or a Discourse of Medals, Antient and Modern* (1697, p. 265), listed her among other learned women he had omitted from his catalogue, absolving himself as follows: 'nor without the highest ingratitude for the satisfaction I still receive by what I read of Madam Astell's besides what lately she has proposed to the virtuous of her sex, to show by her own example what great things and excellencies it is capable of' (cited by Ballard, *Memoirs of Several Ladies of Great Britain*, p. 387).

Among prominent people Astell won immediate fame, or notoriety, as the case may be, for her *A Serious Proposal to the Ladies for the Advancement of their True and Greatest Interest* (1694), a call for a female educational academy along Platonist lines and her first major published work. Bishop Gilbert Burnet (*q.v.*) had no objection to women's education in principle, but he did intervene to warn Princess Anne (later Queen Anne (*q.v.*)) against supporting Mary Astell's proposal for a women's academy because of the language in which it was couched: 'a Monastery or if you will (to avoid giving offence . . . by names which tho' innocent in themselves have been abus'd by superstitious practices) we will call it a Religious Retirement'. Burnet feared that the language of *A Serious Proposal* smacked too much of a Catholic nunnery, and would bring disrepute as being Popish (Ballard, *Memoirs of Several Ladies of Great Britain*, p. 383).

Francis Atterbury, Bishop of Rochester, echoed concerns about the unladylike forthrightness of Astell's general style in a letter to Dr Smalridge that is quite revealing of both his and Astell's characters. Ballard (p. 387), quotes it at length, with his own comment in parentheses:

> I happened about a fortnight ago to dine with Mrs Astell. She spoke to me of my sermon (which I suppose by what follows, is that which he preached and afterwards printed, against Bishop Hoadly's (*q.v.*) *Measures of Submission*) and desired me to print it; and after I had given the proper answer, hinted to me that she should be glad of perusing it, I complied with her, and sent her the sermon the next day. Yesterday she returned it with this sheet of remarks, which I cannot forbear communicating to you, because I take them to be of an extraordinary nature, considering they came from the pen of a woman. Indeed one would not imagine a woman had written them. There is not an expression that carries the least air of her sex from the beginning to the end of it. She attacks my very home you see, and artfully enough, under a pretence of taking my part against other divines, who are in Hoadly's measures. Had she had as much good breeding as good sense, she would be perfect; but she has not the most decent manner of insinuating what she means, but is now and then a little offensive and shocking in her expressions; which I wonder at, because a civil turn of words is what her sex is always mistress of. She, I think is wanting in it. But her sensible and rational way of writing makes amends for that defect, if indeed anything can make amends for it. I dread to engage her, so I only wrote a general civil answer to her, and leave the rest to an oral conference. Her way of solving the difficulty about swearing to the Queen is somewhat singular.

Mary Astell showed rare political acumen, as Bishop Atterbury notes, for which she was to become equally celebrated in her day. John Locke (*q.v.*) owned Astell's *Reflections upon Marriage*, as the catalogue of his library attests, and like most of his contemporaries also attributed to her the works of Judith Drake (Harrison and Laslett, 1971, items 1104, 1105 and 1914). Mary Astell was subjected to the rough and tumble of Grub Street by the greatest polemicists of her day, Jonathan Swift (*q.v.*), Daniel Defoe (*q.v.*) and Richard Steele (*q.v.*); an honour she could perhaps have done without. Daniel Defoe confessed himself to be an admirer – a sentiment that was not reciprocated. He emulated her educational work, *A Serious Proposal*, which became a model for his own 'An Academy for Women' in *An Essay upon Projects* (1697). Bishop Berkeley thought her ideas in the *Proposal* worth plagiarizing in the *Ladies Library* which Steele edited, to the extent of some one hundred pages; and Steele redoubled the insult by making her the object of satire in the *Tatler*, nos. 32 and 63 (Norton, 1961, 59–60; Perry 1986, 100). The attack on *A Serious Proposal to the Ladies* (1694) in *Tatler*, no. 32, from White's Chocolate-house, 22 June, 1709, had initially been attributed to Swift or Addison, his amanuensis (Nichols, *Tatler*, 1786, II, 449 ff.). But this was impossible given that Swift had not yet returned from Ireland and could not therefore have collaborated with Addison at this point. Astell herself, in the Preface to the 1722 edition of *Bart'lemy Fair* (p. A2a) exposed the satire as the work of Steele, appearing 'a little after [the first edition of] the Enquiry [*Bart'lemy Fair*] appear'd' and as a response to it.

Astell, who was satirized in the *Tatler* as 'erect[ing] a monastery or religious retirement', was similarly satirized on the stage, for instance as the prototype of a character in Mrs Centlivre's play, *The Basset Table* (1760; see Norton, 1961, 59–60). For women did not spare her either. Aphra Behn made fun of her. Lady Damaris Masham (*q.v.*), daughter of the Cambridge Platonist Ralph Cudworth (*q.v.*) and Locke's confidante, thought her metaphysics to have dangerous implications, leading 'to as wild an Enthusiasm [*q.v.*] as any that has been yet seen; and which can End in nothing but Monasteries and Hermitages; with all those Sottish and Wicked Superstitions which have accompanied them where-ever they have been in use' (*A Discourse Concerning the Love of God*, p. 120). Masham, like Defoe and Steele, sought to salvage Astell's proposal for female academies with her own educational project, set out in her *Occasional Thoughts in Reference to a Vertuous or Christian Life* (1705). Commentators believe that this work was directed to answering Astell's 1705 rebuttal of Masham's earlier *Discourse Concerning the Love of God* (1696) in *The Christian Religion* (see Hutton, 1993, 36–7). But if, as the Preface states, Masham's work published in 1705 had been written two years earlier, this could only have been accomplished by last-minute textual interpolations. It is more likely that Masham is responding to Astell's *A Serious Proposal, Part II* (1697), in which Astell mounts a vigorous rebuttal of critics of her original project, and specifically Masham, while setting out to destroy the entire system of Masham's patron, Locke.

Astell, Tory historiography and Whig natural rights

Mary Astell, probably under commission from her printer, Richard Wilkin, wrote three Tory tracts. The first two, *Moderation truly Stated* (1704) and *A Fair Way with the Dissenters* (1704), were associated with the Occasional Conformity (*q.v.*) Bill, introduced in the first weeks of Anne's reign, to deprive Nonconformists (*q.v.*) of the subterfuge of occasional attendance at Church of England services in order to qualify for office. The third, *An Impartial Enquiry into the Causes of Rebellion and Civil War in this Kingdom* (1704), was occasioned by White Kennett's (*q.v.*) sermon commemorating the death of Charles I (*q.v.*) on 31 January, 1704. Kennett ranked with Benjamin Hoadly and William Fleetwood as among the most significant Whig (*q.v.*) bishops of the age (Goldie, 1978, 46, 206). The publication of his contentious 1704 commemorative sermon stirred a reaction in print to which Astell's *An Impartial Enquiry* belongs, entering the Tory canon as a classic.

That Mary Astell's defence of monarchy in the Age of Anne should have taken the form of *An Impartial Enquiry into the Causes of the Rebellion and Civil War* a half century earlier is not suprising. Goldie (1978, 192) remarks:

> The baleful presence of the great rebellion hung over a generation whose fathers had experienced it at first hand. It stalked through the pamphlets, diaries were full of anecdotes of the Interregnum; and the cult of the royal Martyr flourished.

'Forty-one' was a catch-cry in the Restoration Tory armory for the first Stuart shipwreck of the state caused by the Civil War, the execution of Charles I and the establishment of the republic in 1649 (Skinner, 1972; Goldie, 1978; Scott, 1988). Parallels were commonplace between 1641 and the Exclusion Crisis (*q.v.*) of 1679–81 in which Shaftesbury (*q.v.*) and the Whigs attempted to prevent James, Duke of York (later James II), from inheriting the throne. The Allegiance Debate of 1689, which addressed the tangle of conflicting oaths undertaken to the Commonwealth, to the Stuarts, and, subsequently, to William III, saw the republication of texts originally associated with the regicide of Charles I in 1649. These were parallels that Astell, following her authority on the history of the Rebellion, Lord Clarendon (*q.v.*), drew in her pamphlet *An Impartial Enquiry*. Prompted by the publication of White Kennett's memorial sermon on Charles I's death, it convicted the Whig bishop for damning with faint praise 'the Royal King and Martyr', depicted in Tory iconography 'as a mythological but appealing figure' (Skinner, 1972, 85).

Astell's text has diverse targets, drawing strong parallels between the constitutional crisis of 1641 and the Exclusion Crisis of 1679–81 (p. 15), looking forward to the continuing problems posed by the Pretender and anticipating Whig exploitation of Jacobitism. White Kennett's speech, like so many tracts of the day, spoke of one revolution in terms of another. Astell's rebuttal did likewise. It rehearsed popular Tory views on the unholy alliance of revolutionary doctrines in the Roman Catholic and Calvinist (*q.v.*)/Whig traditions, containing a particularly zealous version of the Tory litanies of Popish and Presbyterian defenders of popular sovereignty (Goldie, 1978, 22–3). Astell emphasized the degree to which Presbyterians inflated fears of Popery and the French alliance to keep alive the spectre of the Pretender, destabilize the monarchy and fuel the fires for their own causes of popular sovereignty and consent. For, from the Engagement Controversy (*q.v.*) of 1649 and the Exclusion Crisis of 1679 to the death of Anne in 1714, the greatest problem was stability: to persuade the people that the revolution ushered in by the Civil Wars of the 1640s was finished (Skinner, 1972, 79). The problem with the Whigs, in Astell's eyes, was that they – Algernon Sidney, Locke and Defoe among them – had sought to persuade people that it was not finished, fomenting a state of emergency for party political purposes. The debate over Occasional Conformity and the legitimacy of Dissent turned on these issues.

The plethora of conflicting oaths of allegiance produced in the seventeenth century created a specific problem of loyalty (Goldie, 1978, 74). More generally it called into question the principle of hereditary right. On these questions the great constitutional debates were waged, summarized in the battle between Sir Robert Filmer (*q.v.*) and Locke. The Engagement Controversy of 1649 had been waged over allegiance to the regicidal Commonwealth. Those who in 1689 were required to swear allegiance to William and Mary had earlier solemnly sworn fealty to James II and to the Restoration oaths which renounced the taking of arms against kings 'upon any pretence'. The Abjuration Oath included in the Act of Settlement of 1701, which guaranteed the Hanoverian succession, renounced

James and his heirs as being incapacitated because of their Catholicism: the sacred doctrine of hereditary right was brushed aside (Goldie, 1978, 71, 74, 83, 347). Nonjurors, those who would not swear in 1689, were not necessarily Jacobites, but rather men who put a strict construction on earlier oaths to the Stuart Royal House (Goldie, 1978, 130). Among them Mary Astell numbered her closest friends – Archbishop Sancroft, Lord Clarendon, Henry Dodwell (*q.v.*), and Bishop George Hickes (*q.v.*) – some of whom, like Astell herself, may have harboured Jacobite sympathies.

Both Goldie (1980a, 504) and Ashcraft (1986, 1992a, 1992b) have observed the shifting nature of political allegiances in the 1680s. Many of those who supported the Stuarts early in the decade failed to do so after 1688. Ashcraft (1992b, 102) notes that keeping a Catholic off the throne was an imperative among the radicals of the 1680s, in particular among the group which coalesced around Anthony Ashley Cooper, first Earl of Shaftesbury, to which Locke belonged. Shaftesbury's own position shifted from initial support of Charles II's restoration to active opposition, once the King's embrace of toleration proved to be a chimera and the characteristic Royalist and Tory forces came into play. Recent commentators (Thompson, 1988, 275–94; Wootton, 1992b, 92–3; Ashcraft 1992, 101) note a corresponding shift in programme from republicanism compatible with monarchy, expressed in a peculiar mixture of ancient constitution and natural rights, to the language of popular sovereignty, as Shaftesbury and his adherents sought a constituency for the new social order. Doctrines of resistance that had grown up in the Catholic Church in the interstices of disputes over temporal powers between the Pope and the Emperor or his princes were redeployed. Henry Foulis (*q.v.*), Astell's source, in *The History of the Romish Treasons* (pp. 75 ff.), had noticed the indebtedness of Whig advocates of popular sovereignty to the Scholastics and Jesuits, a claim which Astell repeated, targeting Locke (*An Impartial Enquiry*, pp. 24–8). Filmer, who correctly linked lineal patriarchy and the power of kings, had made the connection earlier, noting in *Patriarcha* (1680) the ammunition provided to Presbyterians by Catholic counter-reformation supporters of the right of resistance such as Francisco Suarez and Cardinal Robert Bellarmine (*q.v.*). Bellarmine, Filmer claimed, 'makes God the author of a democratical estate' (Sommerville, 1982, 24), a more radical claim than later could be pressed even against Locke and the Whigs.

The unholy alliance alleged between Papists and Presbyterians had been given some substance by James II's effort to base his support on both Catholics and Dissenters (*q.v.*). In the event it was James II's Popery, against which significant numbers of Tories as well as Whigs had taken a stand, on which the Revolution of 1688 turned (Goldie, 1980a, 504). The successive revolutions of 1649 and 1688 had briefly ushered in the juristic absurdity of a kingdom without a king, a hiatus that republicans had leapt to fill. While Harrington's (*q.v.*) classical republicanism invoked the memory of the radical democracy of the ancient Israelites more frequently than that of the Greeks, thus perpetuating the legacy of the Civil War sects, Locke's doctrine of consent suggested the alternative of Parliament as a constituent assembly. It was this trajectory along which Whig thought of the 1680s moved (Goldie, 1980b; cf. McNally, 1989) and to which Astell so passionately responded.

Astell and Locke

Mary Astell was a defender of sacral monarchy and hereditary right and, therefore, was opposed to the Williamite settlement and the propagandists who facilitated it (Schwoerer, 1977). She was hostile to the latitudinarianism (*q.v.*) or Low Church (*q.v.*) Anglicanism it represented, and the toleration of Dissenters which promised to be its mainstay; a toleration promulgated by Daniel Defoe, James Tyrrell and Samuel Johnson (*q.v.*), but particularly by Locke (*An Impartial Enquiry*, pp. 18–20). For all its uncompromising brashness, Locke's *Two Treatises* quickly did duty in legitimizing William III's revolution (1988, pp. 45–66; Goldie, 1980b, 517–21). In each of Astell's works the principal, but largely unacknowledged, target is Locke. We can be almost sure of this because of the extensive and hostile debate over religious doctrine conducted between Astell and Locke's companion Lady Damaris Masham. Both of Masham's books, *A Discourse Concerning the Love of God* (1696) and *Occasional Thoughts in Reference to a Vertuous or Christian Life* (1705), were written in defence of Locke's *Reasonableness of Christianity* (1695), and more or less targeted at his respondents, Norris and Astell

(Smith, 1916, 111–12; Perry, 1986, 87–8). Astell's idealist *A Serious Proposal* (1694) had been initially taken for the work of Masham, as typical of the daughter of Ralph Cudworth (Ballard MS 41:133, cited Smith, 1916, 113). But when in 1695 the Astell–Norris letters were published, they were quickly followed by Masham's critique of Norris's *Practical Discourses* (1691), with clear allusion to the Astell–Norris correspondence in her *Discourse Concerning the Love of God* (1696). Norris replied directly to Masham's pamphlet in the fourth volume of the second edition of his *Practical Discourses* of 1698, assuming it to be the work of Locke; an assumption that Astell also made. It is true that in 1693, while living in the Masham household, Locke had written *Remarks upon some of Mr Norris' Books, wherein he asserts P. Malebranche's Opinion of Seeing All Things in God* (1693), addressed to Norris and Astell as Neoplatonists, and followers of Descartes (*q.v.*). But published posthumously, Astell could not have known of it.

Astell's long and carefully thought-out reply to Masham, *The Christian Religion as Profess'd by a Daughter of the Church* (1705), examined the doctrines of Locke's *Reasonableness of Christianity* (1695), the anonymous *The Ladies Religion* (1697) and Masham's *Discourse*, as if all three were by Locke. She discussed the *Two Treatises* by name, referring sarcastically to the '*Fundamental, Sacred and unalterable Law of Self-Preservation*, as some call it' (*Two Treatises of Government*, Book II, Section 149, cited Astell, *The Christian Religion*, p. 139). The argument that self-preservation motivates individuals to contract is cited at many points in Astell's political works, whether in response to Locke, Defoe or Kennett. Even more salient is Astell's rebuttal of Locke's argument for consent, where she turns to a distinction between authorization and designation familiar from Scholastic debates over popular sovereignty. Promulgated in the seventeenth century by Suarez and Bellarmine, the very Papal theoreticians to whom the Independents (*q.v.*) were said to defer, this distinction derived the power of kings from an act of translation from the people. However, it did not allow that the people empowered the king, which only God could do, distinguishing between divine authorization and the power of the people to name a specific incumbent to the role (Sommerville, 1982, 530–1; 1986, 22–3).

This distinction, standard in English academic circles before the Civil War, was specifically endorsed by Filmer and attacked by

Locke, to whom Astell threw it back. Citing the *Two Treatises* explicitly in *The Christian Religion* (Book II, Section 23, cited Astell, *The Christian Religion*, p. 139), she points out that the argument quite simply assumes what is requiring to be proved, that the people have the power to give that which the theory demands, namely their consent; an assumption that rests on erroneous theories of popular sovereignty that have ever been a threat to monarchy, as she sets out to demonstrate from Papist and Presbyterian sources. Astell's argument that the social contract has its analogue in the marriage contract (Pateman, 1988, 1989) was consistent with Scholastic distinctions commonplace in pre-Civil War England. If the polity is not founded on consent, nor is marriage, consent through contract being the necessary but not the sufficient condition for entry into an estate divinely authorized but to which individual incumbents are named, as registered in marriage vows and coronation oaths.

In *The Christian Religion* Astell reexamined the doctrines of the *Essay Concerning Human Understanding* and its implications explored in Locke's correspondence with the Bishop of Worcester, Edward Stillingfleet (*q.v.*) (Locke, 1823 IX, pp. 24–59). One of Locke's chief objections to Cambridge Platonism was its inaccessibility to those of 'vulgar capacities'. In the *Reasonableness of Christianity* (p. 279), he had declared condescendingly: 'you may as soon hope to have all Day-Labourers and Tradesmen, the Spinsters and Dairy Maids perfect Mathematicians, as to have them perfect in *Ethicks* this way'. Astell, who refers to this passage in two places in *The Christian Religion* (p. 301; pp. 402–3), gave a pointed reply, declaring that her theology comprised only '*plain Propositions and short Reasonings about things familiar to our Minds, as* need not *amaze* any part of Mankind, no not the *Day Labourer and Tradesmen, the Spinsters and Dairy Maids*, who may very easily *comprehend* what a Woman cou'd write' (pp. 402–3; see Perry, 1986, 92–3).

Astell's response should not be interpreted to mean that, unlike Locke, she considered differences of class, rank and gender inconsequential in everyday life. These were realities that her providentialist philosophy admitted, and did not attempt to veil with notions of contractual equality. She acknowledges that, when she marries, a woman 'Elects a Monarch for Life . . . giv[ing] him an Authority she cannot recall however he misapply it'; and that 'how much soever Arbitrary Power may be dislik'd on a Throne, not *Milton* himself wou'd cry up Liberty to poor *Female Slaves*, or plead for the Lawfulness of Resisting a Private Tyranny' (*Reflections*, 1706 pp. 31, 27). She does not rule out, although she could hardly condone, the marriage–monarchy homology as it is employed even by her friend and correspondent John Norris. On the possibility of 'strict friendship between Man and Wife', Norris once wrote of the husband: 'the greatest Monarch in the World may find Opportunities to descend from the Throne of Majesty to the familiar Caresses of a dear Favourite: and unking himself a while for the more glorious Title of Friend' (*Collection of Miscellanies*, pp. 311–14, cited Hill, 1986, 38). It is precisely these considerations that prompt her feminist cry: '*If all Men are born free*, how is it that all Women are born slaves? as they must be if the being subjected to the *inconstant, uncertain, unknown arbitrary Will* of Men, be the *perfect Condition of Slavery?*' (*Reflections*, 1706, p. xi) – a cry directed to Locke of the *Two Treatises*.

Martyn Thompson (1976, 184), writing on the reception of Locke's *Two Treatises* points out that the work was overshadowed by its more famous contemporaries: James Tyrrell's *Patriarcha non monarcha* (1680), Algernon Sidney's *Discourses Concerning Government* (written before 1683, but published 1698), and Samuel von Pufendorf's (*q.v.*) *De jure naturae et gentium* (1672) and *De officio hominis et civis* (1673). Benjamin Hoadly's *The Original and Institution of Civil Government, Discuss'd* (1710) produced Lockian arguments, for which it was commended in Parliament, with only one reference to Locke's *Two Treatises* and that to the 'criticism of "Some Branches" of patriarchal thought' in the first treatise (Thompson, 1976, 184). Charles Leslie's (*q.v.*) *The New Association, Part II* (1703) and the anonymous *An Essay Upon Government* (1705), are believed to have delivered the first systematic criticisms, and then of the link between patriarchalism and divine right, which is the subject of the first treatise. Leslie, who observed Locke's hand in the work of William Molyneux (*The Case of Ireland's being bound by Acts of Parliament in England, Stated*, 1698), mounted against him the Lockian argument that Irish Parliaments had 'consented' to English rule by swearing allegiance to William and Mary in 1692 and 1695 (Leslie, *Considerations of Importance to Ireland*, (1698), p. 3, cited Thompson, 1976, 187, 189). But by 1703, Leslie was arguing that the notion of consent, argued by the 'Great *L—k* in his

Two Discourses of Government' was 'Nonsense' (*The New Association, Part II*, A Supplement, p. 4). These were arguments that Leslie pursued in *Cassandra. Num. I* (1704–5, p. 4) and his weekly, *Rehearsal* (no. 36, 31 March–7 April, 1705; no. 37, 7 April–14 April; nos. 38, 55, 56, 58, 59, 60, 61 and 66, 1705; Thompson, 1976, 187, 189), in what was to become a virtual crusade.

Do we have reason to believe that Mary Astell, who as early as 1696 was attuned to Locke's views in the form of Damaris Masham's response to the Astell–Norris letters (Perry, 1986, 87), and who had written her extensive response in *The Christian Religion* by 1705, was rebutting Locke's *Two Treatises* explicitly in *An Impartial Inquiry?* In *A Fair Way with the Dissenters* (p. 15), Astell makes reference to *The New Association* (1702, *Part II*, 1703) by Leslie. Had she read *The New Association, Part II*, she could not have failed to notice the reference to Locke, were she not otherwise aware of the arguments of the *Two Treatises*. There Leslie challenged Locke and his like to extend to the family the freedom from patriarchal tyranny he suggests for the state. Leslie's argument made in the Supplement to *The New Association, Part II*, dated 25 March, 1703 (pp. 6–7), is to be found in Astell's famous 1706 Preface to *Reflections upon Marriage*, and anticipated in the main body of that work published two years earlier than Leslie's (1700, pp. 29, 32, 38–41, 92–5). Astell points to the hypocrisy of Independents and Radicals who promote tyranny in private while deploring it in public. Although the Protestant Civil War Sects, and even the radical Milton, championed women's equality as believers, they were not prepared to tear down biblically sanctioned patriarchialism, the foundation of their faith.

Astell may be the first systematic commentator on the *Two Treatises of Government*, having personal reasons that Leslie did not have for her investigation of Locke's political views. She drops many hints and references into her polemic that Locke is her target, but one of the most telling is her reference to Anthony Ashley Cooper, first Earl of Shaftesbury and Locke's patron, who in 1673, as Lord Chancellor, delivered the famous speech, *Delenda est Carthago*, against the Dutch threat, with Locke, it is said, prompting him from behind his chair (Laslett, 1988, p. 30). Astell refers sarcastically to Shaftesbury as: 'a Leading Peer among the *Whiggs*, and who consequently wou'd be thought a Great Patriot and Friend to

Liberty, and very much in the Interest of his Country, [who] took the freedom to say in the House of Lords, *Delenda est Carthago*' (*An Impartial Enquiry*, p. 22).

Locke had explicitly attacked the Tory alternative to resistance, passive obedience, which he characterized in a famous disquisition on Isaiah 65:25 in Chapter 19 of the *Second Treatise:* 'Who would not think it an admirable peace betwixt the Mighty and the Mean when the Lamb, without resistance yielded his Throat to be torn by the imperious Wolf?' Locke answered his own rhetorical question thus: 'no doubt *Ulysses*, who was a prudent Man, preach'd up *Passive Obedience*, and exhorted [his Companions] to a quiet Submission, by representing to them of what concernment Peace was to Mankind' (Chapter 19, Section 228, p. 417). Not coincidentally, the words of Isaiah resonated once again in the title of Leslie's pamphlet *The Wolf Stripp'd of his Shepherd's Cloathing* (1704) and in the conclusion to Astell's celebrated 1706 Preface to *Reflections upon Marriage*. There she mocks Locke with her reference to 'those Halcyon, or if you will *Millennium* Days, in which the Wolf and the Lamb shall feed together, and a Tyrannous Domination which Nature never meant [i.e., that of men], shall no longer render useless if not hurtful, the Industry and Understandings of half Mankind!'

Most of Astell's references to 'liberty', 'property' and 'natural rights', like those for 'self-preservation', seem to be veiled references to Locke as a member of Shaftesbury's party, or to Defoe as a member of Locke's, characterized by her as sycophantic schemers, peddling theories for political advantage. Thus in *A Fair Way with the Dissenters* (p. 2) she speaks scathingly of 'little Scriblers and Busiebodies, who, either for Bread, and to deserve their Wages of the Party, or out of an innate Love to Mischief, alarm the Mob, and impose upon the Ignorant and Careless Reeader [*sic*]'.

A long disquisition on Locke in *Moderation truly Stated* (pp. 11–13), after naming him, puts into his mouth all the most heinous arguments for toleration of dissent, presenting him as a defender of party above all, who to effect the balance will throw Presbyterians into the scales, 'and if this is not sufficient, we can add *Independents, Anabaptists* [*q.v.*], *Socinians* [*q.v.*], and what not, to make a dead weight upon occasion' and deny 'the Prince a Prerogative' (p. 12). Apparently representative of '*Low Church-Men*', Locke is painted as a Machiavellian for whom toleration, because of the possibilities of party manoeuvring that it allows, is 'a most essential part of the Constitution' (pp. 12–13):

> If any body does but dream that it is struck at, or if he has so good faculty as to smell out Designs against it and Consequences at the Distance of some Ages, and which no body but himself or his Echo's hear a Word of, whoop the Government is almost shatter'd to pieces, and we're within a hair's breadth of being once more in a State of Nature!

This particular Locke, the man of party, who has his 'echos', Defoe undoubtedly among them, had long been lost to view and has only recently been resuscitated by scholarship. Locke, who in the 1680s had mounted arguments for popular sovereignty reminiscent of counter-reformation Catholicism, as Foulis and likeminded Tories never tired of pointing out, had in the 1690s become a politically complacent civil servant, advisor to government and friend of the great. More specifically, as we now know from the recently published fragment to Clarke (1690, published in Farr and Roberts, 1985), he had for party reasons come to support an oath of allegiance to William as the only test of consent. He thus qualified in Astell's eyes for the caricature of the classical Whig, a self-interested, scheming opportunist (*Moderation truly Stated*, pp. 27–8).

Marriage of Crown and Commonwealth

Marriage between Crown and Commonwealth was an ancient image for political association. But regicide had problematized the inviolability of the subject–sovereign relation and hereditable rights more generally, which underwent a new theorization in the seventeenth century. Relations between husbands and wives, parents and children, were also theorized anew. Robert South had noted in 1679 (*Sermons Preached upon Several Occasions: Six Sermons*, 1737, 5.8, cited Hill, 1986, 39): 'It is but too frequent a complaint, that neither are men so good husbands, nor women so good wives, as they were before that *Accursed Rebellion* had made that fatal leading breach in the conjugal tie between the *best of Kings* and the *happiest of People*.' Thomas Hobbes (*q.v.*), in order to close the divide between public and private spheres, since Aristotle held to describe different social orders, construed the partnership between sovereign and subjects as a contractual one, extending the logic of contract to relations between husband and wife, parents and children (Hinton, 1967; Shanley, 1979; Pateman, 1988, 1989), which consistency demanded of him. Locke, whose reliance on Aristotelian and Scholastic arguments is greater than usually credited, did not take this step, for which he was convicted by Astell and Leslie. If the marriage contract was not a contract among equals, nor was that with the sovereign, and they noted the general reluctance among contractarians to admit arguments against domestic tyranny, on the grounds of consent, that they pressed against the state. The whole edifice of social contract was aimed at denying hereditary right on which the Stuart case turned – the rest simply decoration, as Astell, in *Reflections upon Marriage*, pointed out.

The settlement of 1688, which involved William of Orange accepting the Crown while James still lived, reenacted the violation of hereditary right as the basis for subject–sovereign relations of 1649, under a different ruse (Hill, 1986, 39). Hobbes and Locke, apologists for a settlement in each case (as the lesser evil, in the case of Hobbes), had sought legitimation in the best terms that were available – social contract and consent. Astell correctly saw the continuity between the theories of Hobbes and Locke, despite the great disparities in their views. The analogue between marriage contract and social contract, which they promulgated, was to dominate liberal political thought of the modern period, but in the late seventeenth and early eighteenth centuries it had as yet few adherents (Goldie, 1978, 235 ff.). Gilbert Burnet, a central figure in William's machinations for the Crown, an anti-republican Whig who had earlier endorsed passive obedience, in the summer of 1689 had functioned as an official propagandist for William of Orange. In his *An Enquiry into the Measures of Submission* (1689), his most radical work, he declared men to be born free, their liberty constrained only by contract, with governments enlisted as guarantors of rights and property. In his *Enquiry into the Present State of Affairs*, a few months later, 'published by authority', however, no mention of contract was made. The Convention's draft Declaration of Rights of 1689 mentioned as grounds for the 'abdication' of James, the violation of an 'original contract', but this phrase, suggesting a politically dangerous precedent, never appeared in the final Declaration, or in the subsequent Bill of Rights (Goldie, 1978, 73–4; 1980a, 477). Lois Schwoerer (1977, 851–3) has shown how in the revision process, in which Burnet participated, of the earlier *Declaration of His Highness William Henry, Prince of Orange*, which promulgated the rationale for William's intervention, the future King showed himself fully aware of the extent to which he would be held hostage to Parliament by virtue of doctrines of consent. He chose instead to emphasize a mandate as 'Dutch Deliverer', saviour of Protestantism and the Anglican Church, restorer of English native liberties. Astell's many sarcastic references to these claims throughout *An Impartial Enquiry*, are directed at William and his propagandists.

Throughout the reign of Anne the doctrine of social contract was subject to ridicule on several grounds: as being theoretically incoherent, historically incorrect, biblically unorthodox and practically unviable. Mary Astell, with characteristic economy, by rejecting the marriage contract/social contract homology, attempted to kill two birds with one stone: the doctrine of resistance and the doctrine of subordination through consent. In more than one way she turned Locke against himself, using the Scholastic arguments he used against slavery against the social contract in general: people may choose the person of the governor but they cannot empower him, because 'None can give what they have not' (*An Impartial Enquiry*, p. 34; and *The Christian Religion*, citing Locke, *Two Treatises*, Book II, Section 149 (1988, 367)).

Astell subscribed to the providentialist argument against natural right and could show by the exclusion of women from the latter proof positive of Locke's error. The submission of women to their husbands, like the submission of citizens to their sovereigns, far from being a case of free individuals contracting into subordination, a far-fetched idea on the face of it, was rather a case of divinely ordained hierarchy. Women submitted to their husbands as part of the divinely ordained social order: the same social order in which citizens submitted to the necessity of government – just because the social world, like the cosmos itself, was not a harmoniously balanced self-regulating mechanism, but required government, divine and civil. It was required of women that they should submit humbly and obediently to the rule of their husbands, for whose arbitrary government there were no rational claims, just as the citizen should passively obey and promise non-resistance to civil government, constitutional and just at best, but arbitrary and despotic at worst. Earthly life was a testing time, pain and hardship were part of the test; so were high-handed and arbitrary governors. Mary Astell's passions are roused against the notion that *Reason* could command obedience to husbands, any more than *Reason* is the grounds for obedience to civil government. On the ground of Reason all of humankind is equal, since mind and soul are not subject to the gendered, class, or racial hierarchies that govern bodies in the civil space.

Mary Astell's *Reflections upon Marriage* is a truly political work whose target is less the injustice of traditional Christian marriage than the absurdity of voluntarism on which social contract theory is predicated. Protestant, Catholic and even pagan writers up to and including the seventeenth century of our era seem to have agreed on the submission of wives to husbands as essential to the institution of marriage. The consent of wives to husbands was the necessary but not sufficient condition for entry into the marital estate. The act of marriage, in the voluminous writings that survive on almost every aspect of the institution, was considered to be complex and could not be reduced to either 'promising' or 'consent' as the moderns would have it. Just as marriage in antiquity, and in Mediterranean families today, involved a commitment between families, the conveyancing of the wife as a property transaction, and the induction of the bride into a new lineage, with new household authorities and new gods; so the Medieval and early Christian marriage, whether Catholic or Protestant, comprised promises between the parties and separate vows to God undertaken by the parties to the agreement. These vows sealed the entry of husband and wife into an estate in which the ideal was friendly association based on the rule of husband over the wife.

From all that we know, this is more or less what the idea of 'state', as derived from the notion of 'estate', entailed in the early modern period (Hexter, 1973). To the extent that the 'estate' of a prince was his property, the enjoyment of which involved the exercise of a carefully detailed, divinely sanctioned, schedule of rights and duties; to the same extent the estate of marriage, like the 'religious estate', or membership of a religious order, involved a grid of rights and duties commanded by God and executed by members of natural hierarchies. Hobbes and Locke made a categorial mistake in deriving the authority of husbands from the contract itself, but they did it in order to draw the political analogue they desired, a theory of social contract capable of empowering a sovereign. It was the genius of Mary Astell to be among the first to point this out. Her line of argument in *Reflections upon Marriage* is to show the absurdity of contractarian voluntarism when it is extended into the private realm, something that Hobbes and Locke never fully allowed anyway. Hobbes had avoided the logic of his own conclusions by modelling marriage on the contract between victor and vanquished in the aftermath of political conquest or civil war, to avoid the ramifications of peacetime contract within the family. Locke took his escape by making consent, for which there were institutional forms of ratification in the public sphere, all but meaningless in the private. If Hobbes and Locke used an idiosyncratic interpretation of the institution of marriage to buttress a novel view of the political estate, Mary Astell reinstated the traditional interpretation of marriage in order to undo them. To marry and accept the obligations of the estate, or not to marry, were the choices she offered. They were the same choices that were offered by political thinkers down to John Stuart Mill, who in his most personal reflections did not envisage democratizing the institution of marriage even to the extent that he was prepared to see democratization of the polity. Like Mill so much later, Astell could wish for the reform of morals and manners which would remove the tyranny from which women suffered, without requiring that marriage as an institution be revolutionized (a position with which Harriet Taylor, Mill's wife, seriously disagreed). Her protests from the heart represent a call for the removal of unnecessary injustices from which women suffer, but a rejection of war-born radical contractarianism which had found its way into the theories of Hobbes and Locke.

Chronology of Principal Events
in Mary Astell's Life

1666   Mary Astell born on 12 November at Newcastle upon Tyne

1672   Charles II's Declaration of Indulgence for Protestant Dissenters

1673   Declaration of Indulgence revoked and the Test Act, banning Catholics from holding office, passed

1678   Sancroft becomes Archbishop of Canterbury
Astell's father dies

1679   Exclusion Bill to exclude James II from the throne debated

1681   Oxford Parliament meets
Oxford Parliament dissolved

1683   The Rye House Plot resulted in leading Whigs being executed for their alleged plot to kill Charles II

1684   Astell's mother dies

1685   Charles II dies and is replaced by James II
James II's Parliament

1686   Astell moves to London, living mostly in Chelsea

1687   James II's Declaration of Indulgence for liberty of conscience

1688   James II dissolves Parliament
Birth of a son to James, a possible Catholic heir
Invasion of Prince William of Orange and his wife Mary, James' own daughter
James flees to France

1689   Convention Parliament meets and offers the Crown jointly
        to William and Mary
        Coronation of King William III and Queen Mary II
        Nine Years War against France begins
        Bill of Rights, regulating the English succession, nominated
        Mary's sister Anne and her children as the next in line
        Toleration Act, allowing freedom of worship for Protestant
        dissenters, passed
        Astell presents her 'A Collection of Poems' to Archbishop
        Sancroft
1690   Secession of nonjurors from the Church of England
1693   Astell begins her correspondence with John Norris
1694   Queen Mary II dies childless
        Astell's *A Serious Proposal to the Ladies, for the Advance-
        ment of Their True and Greatest Interest. By a Lover of her
        Sex* first published
1695   The letters written between Astell and John Norris are
        published as *Letters Concerning the Love of God Between the
        Author of the Proposal to the Ladies and Mr John Norris,
        Wherein his Discourse Shewing That it Ought to be Entire and
        Exclusive of all Other Loves is Further Clear and Justified*
        Second edition, corrected, of Astell's *A Serious Proposal to
        the Ladies* published
1696   The Fenwick conspiracy, a plan by James II and King
        Louis XIV of France to assassinate King William,
        uncovered
        Third edition, corrected, of Astell's *A Serious Proposal to
        the Ladies* published
1697   Astell's *A Serious Proposal to the Ladies, Part II, Wherein
        a Method is Offer'd for the Improvement of their Minds* pub-
        lished. It was dedicated to the Princess of Denmark who
        later became Queen Anne
        Also Astell's *A Serious Proposal to the Ladies, for the
        Advancement of Their True and Greatest Interest, in 2 parts.
        By a Lover of her Sex* published
1700   Queen Anne's only child, William, dies
        Astell's *Some Reflections upon Marriage, Occasion'd by the
        Duke and Duchess of Mazarine's* [Mancini (*q.v.*)] *Case;
        which is also consider'd*, published anonymously. (No copies

of a second edition have been found, although it is believed to have been published in 1703 or 1704)

1701   The Act of Settlement establishes the Dowager Electress Sophia of Hanover, a grand-daughter of James I, as next in line after Anne

James II dies in exile

Louis XIV of France nominates the son of James II, James III, known as the Old Pretender, as heir

1702   King William III dies unexpectedly in an accident

Queen Anne, daughter of James II and the last of the Stuarts, succeeds him

1704   The following works by Astell are published:

Moderation truly Stated: Or a Review of a Late Pamphlet entitul'd Moderation a Vertue [James Owen (*q.v.*)]. *With a Prefatory Discourse to Dr D'Avenant Concerning His Late Essays on Peace and War*

A Fair Way with the Dissenters and their Patrons. Not writ by Mr L—y, or any other Furious Jacobite [q.v.] whether Clergyman or Layman; but by a very moderate Person and Dutiful Subject to the Queen

An Impartial Enquiry into the Causes of Rebellion and Civil War in this Kingdom in an Examination of Dr Kennet's Sermon, Jan. 31, 1703–4 and Vindication of the Royal Martyr

1705   An octavo volume of Astell's entitled *The Christian Religion as Profess'd by a Daughter of the Church of England* published anonymously

Also a second edition of Astell's *Some Reflections Upon Marriage . . ., corrected by the author with some few things added* published

1706   Astell engaged in controversy with Atterbury

Third edition of Astell's *Some Reflections upon Marriage . . .* published under the title of *Reflections upon Marriage, To which is added a Preface in Answer to Some Objections*

1707   The first Parliament of Great Britain meets

1709   Astell's *Bart'lemy Fair or an Enquiry after Wit in which due Respect is had to a Letter Concerning Enthusiasm. To my Lord XXX by Mr Wotton (q.v.)*, published

1711   Occasional Conformity Act passed

1714   The Electress Sophia dies

Queen Anne also dies, and is succeeded by the Lutheran King George I, Sophia's next descendant in line

1715   First Parliament of George I

1719   Occasional Conformity Act repealed

1722   Atterbury's plot to launch an armed invasion of Britain on behalf of the Old Pretender discovered

Atterbury exiled and Robert Walpole seals his position as the King's number one minister, a position he held for twenty years

Astell's *An Enquiry after Wit wherein the Trifling Arguing and Impious Raillery of the Late Earl of Shaftesbury in his Letter Concerning Enthusiasm and Other Profane Writers are Fully Answered, and Justly Exposed* published as a second edition to *Bart'lemy Fair*

1727   George I dies and is succeeded by his son George II

1730   Three of Astell's works are republished:

A fourth edition of *Reflections upon Marriage with Additions* was published in London and a fifth edition of the same was published in Dublin

A third edition of *Letters Concerning the Love of God*

A third edition of *The Christian Religion as Profess'd by a Daughter of the Church of England*

1731   Astell dies of breast cancer on 9 May

Bibliographic Essay

The contribution of Tory women publicists to political debate under Queen Anne is a much neglected subject. Of the scholarly articles that treat Astell, still not great in number, McCrystal (1992b) is balanced. The 1916 biography by Smith remains the most accurate and informative, and the longer and livelier 1986 biography by Perry, relies on it. The useful anthology by Bridget Hill (1986) has a general introduction which sets the scene; and the MA thesis of John McCrystal (1992a) is one of the accounts most sensitive to the ambiguities of Astell's position (see also Springborg, 1995).

Astell's contemporaries, among whom Damaris Masham, Steele, Swift and the later Ballard number, provide a spectrum of views of her. No modern account can fail to pass through its filter. Norton's bibliographic essay (1961) provides a useful guide. Recent, and not so recent, essays on her female contemporaries and their environment (Blanchard, 1929; Anderson, 1936; Needham, 1949; Thomas, 1958; George, 1973; Higgins, 1973; Butler, 1978; Smith, 1982; Mack, 1984; Myers, 1985; Pateman, 1988, 1989), and especially the essays on Masham (O'Donnell, 1987, 1984; Hutton, 1993), are invaluable.

Enmeshed as she is in the political and theological debates of her day, Astell's views are not comprehensible without some knowledge of the historical terrain. On both fronts John Locke is a central figure. Astell was a hostile critic of his latitudinarianism and of his contractarianism. Her *magnum opus*, *The Christian Religion*, a considered response to Locke's *The Reasonableness of Christianity*, is central to an understanding of the integrity of Astell's overall corpus. In *A Fair Way with the Dissenters*, Astell takes a second work on the subject by Defoe, Locke's popularizer, *More Short-Ways With the Dissenters* (1704), as the object of her critique; and in *An Impartial Enquiry* White Kennett (*A Compassionate Enquiry*) is a surrogate for Locke. The Cambridge Platonists, Ralph Cudworth and John Norris – the latter her interlocutor in *Letters Concerning the Love of God* – form the historical context for her religious views. The textual apparatus of the Laslett (1988) edition of Locke, Harrison and Laslett (1971) on Locke's library and the Yoltons' bibliographical survey (1985) of writings on Locke remain indispensable. Revisionist Locke scholarship, in particular the important studies of Mark Goldie (1978, 1980a, 1980b, 1991) and Richard Ashcraft (1986, 1992a, 1992b), faithfully represent the Locke whom Astell encounters. On the subject of sex and subjection in early modern Europe, the reader cannot do better than Margaret Sommerville's magisterial survey (1995).

Select Bibliography

The references here are to works indispensable for Astell's political writings. Further references can be found in the Notes and Biographical Notes.

Primary texts

Anon. 1704. *A Ladies Religion: In a Letter to the Honourable My Lady Howard. The Second Edition. To which is added, A Second Letter to the same Lady, concerning the Import of Fear in Religion,* 'by a Divine of the Church of England'. London.

Astell, Mary. 1689. *A Collection of Poems Humbly Presented and Dedicated to the most Reverend Father in God William* [Sancroft] *by Divine Providence Lord Archbishop of Canterbury*, Rawlinson MSS Poet. 154:50, Oxford: Bodleian Library. Excerpted in Bridget Hill, *The First English Feminist: 'Reflections Upon Marriage' and other Writings by Mary Astell*, Aldershot, Hants.: Gower/Maurice Temple Smith, 1986, pp. 183–4. Published in full as Appendix D to Ruth Perry, *The Celebrated Mary Astell: An Early English Feminist*. University of Chicago Press, 1986, pp. 400–54.

1694. *A Serious Proposal to the Ladies for the Advancement of their True and Greatest Interest*. London. Second edition corrected, 1695, London. Fourth edition, 1701, London.

1695. *Letters Concerning the Love of God, between the Author of the Proposal to the Ladies and Mr John Norris*. London.

1697. *A Serious Proposal to the Ladies, Part II, Wherein a Method is Offer'd for the Improvement of their Minds*. London.

1697. *A Serious Proposal to the Ladies for the Advancement of their True and Greatest Interest*. Parts I and II. London.

1700. *Some Reflections upon Marriage, Occasion'd by the Duke & Dutchess of Mazarine's Case* ... London. Second edition c. 1703–4 (no known copies extant).

1704. *A Fair Way with the Dissenters and their Patrons*. London.

1704. *An Impartial Enquiry into the Causes of Rebellion and Civil War in this Kingdom in an Examination of Dr Kennett's Sermon, Jan. 31, 1703/4 and Vindication of the Royal Martyr*. London.

1704. *Moderation truly Stated: Or A Review of a Late Pamphlet, Entitul'd, Moderation a Vertue, or, The Occasional Conformist Justified from the Imputation of Hypocrisy* ... London.

1705. *The Christian Religion as Profess'd by a Daughter of the Church of England in a Letter to the Right Honourable T. L., C. I.* London.

1706. *Reflections upon Marriage, To which is added a Preface in Answer to Some Objections*. Third edition. London.

1709. *Bart'lemy Fair: Or an Enquiry after Wit in which due Respect is had to a Letter Concerning Enthusiasm. To my Lord XXX by Mr. Wotton* [pseud.] London. The 1722 edition appeared under the title, *An Enquiry after Wit, wherein the Trifling Arguing and Impious Raillery of the Late Earl of Shaftesbury in his letter concerning Enthusiasm and other Profane Writers are fully answered and justly exposed*.

1730. *Reflections upon Marriage, To which is added a Preface in Answer to Some Objections*. Fourth edition. London.

Ballard, George. (1752) 1985. *Memoirs of Several Ladies of Great Britain Who have been Celebrated for their Writings or Skill in the Learned Languages, Arts and Sciences*. Ruth Perry, ed. Detroit: Wayne State University Press.

Baxter, Richard. 1653. *Christian Concord*. London.

1659. *Five Disputations of Church-Government, and Worship* ... London.

Burnet, Gilbert. 1689. *An Enquiry into the Measures of Submission to the Supream Authority: And of the Grounds upon which it may be Lawful or necessary for Subjects, to defend their Religion, Lives and Liberties. In Six Papers by Gilbert Burnet, DD* London.

1689. *An Enquiry into the Present State of Affairs*.

1704. *The Bishop of Salisbury's Speech in the House of Lords, upon the Bill against Occasional Conformity*.

Cawdrey, Daniel. 1657. *Independencie a Great Schism.*

Centlivre, S. 1760. 'Basset Table'. In *Works.* London.

Church of England. (1604) 1675. *A Collection of Articles Injunctions, Canons, Orders, Ordinances and Constitutions Ecclesiastical . . .* London.

    1687. *Certain Sermons or Homilies Appointed to be Read in Churches in the Time of Queen Elizabeth of Famous Memory: And now Reprinted for the Use of Private Families.* London.

Cocqueau, Léonard (F. Leonardus Coquaeus Aurelius). 1610. *Eremita Augustinianus, examen praefationis monitoriae, Iacobi I, Magnae Britanniae . . . in quo examine resellitur & apologia ipsa regis, & summi pontificis brevia ad Catholicos Anglos defenduntur.*

Cook, John. 1649. *King Charles His Case: Or, An Appeal to All Rational Men, Concerning His Tryal at the High Court of Justice: Being for the Most Part, That Which Was Intended to Have Been Delivered at the Bar, if the King had Pleaded to the Charge.*

Defoe, Daniel. 1697. 'An Academy for Women'. In *An Essay upon Projects.* London.

    1698. *An Enquiry into the Occasional Conformity of Dissenters.* London.

    1700/1. *The True Born Englishman: A Satyr . . .* London.

    1701. *The Legion Memorial.* Reprinted 1702 with *The Memorial, Alias Legion, Answered . . .* London.

    1702. *The Legionites Plot.* London.

    1702. *A New Test of the Church of England's Loyalty.* London.

    1702. *The Shortest Way with the Dissenters: Or Proposals for the Establishment of the Church.* London.

    1704? *The Legions Humble Address to the Lords.* London.

    1704. *More Short-Ways with the Dissenters.* London.

    1704. *A New Test of the Church of England's Honesty.* London.

Dennis, John. 1702. *The Danger of Priestcraft to Religion and Government: With some Politick Reasons for Toleration. Occasion'd by a Discourse of Mr Sacheverel's [q.v.] Intitul'd, The Political Union, etc. . . .* London.

Drake, Judith. 1696. *An Essay In Defence of the Female Sex.* London.

Dugdale, Sir William. 1681. *A Short View of the late Troubles in England.* Oxford.

Edwards, Thomas. 1644. *Antapologia: or a full Answer to the Apologeticall Narration of Mr Goodwin, Mr Nye, Mr Sympson, Mr Burroughes, Mr Bridge, Members of the Assembly of Divines.* London.

1646. *Gangraena: Or a Catalogue and Discovery of many Errours, Heresies, Blasphemies, and Pernicious Practices of the Sectaries of this Time, Vented and Acted in England in These Four Last Years ...* London.

1646. *The Second Part of Gangraena: Or a Fresh and Further Discovery of the Errours ... of the Sectaries of this Time ...* London.

1646. *The Third Part of Gangraena: Or A New and Higher Discovery of the Errours ... of the Sectaries of these Times ...* in response, *inter alia* to William Dell's *Right Reformation ... In a Sermon ... Preached to the Honourable House of Commons, November 25, 1646.* London.

Filmer, Robert (1680) 1991. *Patriarcha and Other Writings.* Johann Sommerville, ed. Cambridge University Press.

Foulis, Henry. 1674. *The History of the Wicked Plots and Conspiracies of Our Pretended Saints: Representing the Beginning, Constitution and designs of the Jesuite. With the Conspiracies, Schisms, Perjury, Seditions, and Rebellions, Hypocrisie, Sacriledge, Vilifying Humour of Some Presbyterians: Proved by a Series of Authentik Examples, as they have been acted in Great Britain, from the Beginning of that Faction to this Time.* Second edition, Oxford.

1681. *The History of the Romish Treasons and Usurpations: Together with a Particular Account of Many Gross Corruptions and Impostures in the Church of Rome, Highly dishonourable and injurious to Christian Religion.* Second edition, London.

Glanvill, Joseph. (1678) 1681. *The Zealous and Impartial Protestant.* London.

Grotius, Hugo. (1625) 1641. *Appendix ad interpretationem locorum Novi Testamenti quae de Antichristo agunt aut agere putantur ...* Amsterdam.

Hoadly, Benjamin. 1705. *The Measures of Submission to the Civil Magistrate Considered.*

1710. *The Original and Institution of Civil Government, Discuss'd.* London.

Hobbes, Thomas. 1991. *Leviathan.* Richard Tuck, ed. Cambridge University Press.

Hooper, George. 1704. *A Sermon preach'd before the Lords Spiritual and Temporal in Parliament Assembled, in the Abbey-Church of Westminister, on Monday Jan. 31st 1703/4, the Fast-Day for the Martyrdom of King Charles the 1st. By George Lord Bishop of St Asaph.* London.

Hyde, Edward, first Earl of Clarendon. 1702. *The History of the Rebellion and Civil Wars in England, begun in the Year 1641. With the Precedent Passages, and Actions, that Contributed Thereunto, and the Happy End, and Conclusion Thereof by the King's Blessed Restoration, and Return upon the 29th of May, in the Year 1660.* Oxford.

Kennett, White. 1704. *A Compassionate Enquiry into the Causes of the Civil War: In a Sermon Preached in the Church of St. Botolph Aldgate, On January 31, 1704. the Day of the Fast of the Martyrdom of King Charles I.* London.

1715. *The Witchcraft of the Present Rebellion.*

Leslie, Charles. 1698. *Considerations of Importance to Ireland.*

1702. *The New Association of those Called Moderate-Church-man, with the Modern-Whigs and Fanaticks to Under-mine and Blow-up the present Church and Government* ... Third corrected edition, London.

1703. *The New Association. Part II. With farther Improvements ... An Answer to some Objections in the Pretended D. Foe's Explication in 'the Reflections upon the Shortest Way'* ... with 'A Supplement', dated 25 March, 1703, entitled, 'With a short Account of the *Original of Government:* Compared with the *Schemes* of the *Republicans* and *Whigs*'. London and Westminster.

1703. *Reflections Upon Some Scandalous and Malicious Pamphlets, viz. I, The Shortest Way with the Dissenters* ... London.

1704. *The Bishop of Salisbury's Proper Defence from a Speech Cry'd about the Streets in his Name, and Said to have been spoken by him in the House of Lords, upon the Bill against Occasional Conformity.* London and Westminster.

1704. *A Vindication of the Royal Martyr King Charles I: From the Irish Massacre in ... 1641, cast upon Him in the Life of Richard Baxter ... and since the Abridgment by E. Calamy.* London.

1704. *The Wolf Stript of his Shepherd's Cloathing. In Answer to a Late Celebrated Book Intituled Moderation a Vertue.* London.

1704–5. *Cassandra. (But I Hope not) Telling What Will Come of It: In Answer to The Occasional Letter. Num. I. Wherein The New-Associations, etc., Are Considered.* London and Westminster.

1707. *The Second Part of the Wolf Stript of his Shepherds Cloathing.* London.

1708. *A View of the Times their Principles and Practices in the First Volume of the Rehearsals.* London.

Lilly, William. 1651. *Monarchy and no Monarchy.*

Locke, John. (1689) 1823. *Essay Concerning Human Understanding.* In *The Works of John Locke*, London, I–IV, vol. I.

    (1690) 1988. *John Locke's Two Treatises of Government.* Peter Laslett, ed. Cambridge University Press.

    (1693) 1823. 'Remarks upon some of Mr Norris's Books, wherein he asserts P. Malebranche's Opinion of seeing all Things in God'. In *The Works of John Locke*, London, IX, pp. 247–59.

    (1695) 1823. 'The Reasonableness of Christianity, as Delivered in the Scriptures'. In *The Works of John Locke*, London, VII, pp. 1–158.

    (1690) 1985. Minute to Edward Clarke, Bodleian MS Locke e 18. Published in James Farr and Clayton Roberts, 'John Locke on the Glorious Revolution: A Rediscovered Document'. *Historical Journal* 28: 385–98.

Malebranche, Nicolas. 1678. *De la recherche de la verité: ou l'on traitte de la nature de l'esprit de l'homme, & de l'usage qu'il en doit faire pour éviter l'erreur dans les sciences.* Fourth revised and enlarged edition, 1700, Paris.

    1694, 1695. *Malebranche's Search After Truth: Or a Treatise of the Nature of the Humane Mind.* 2 volumes, London.

    1700. *Father Malebranche his Treatise Concerning the Search after Truth: The Whole Work Complete . . .* T. Taylor, trans. Second corrected edition, London.

Mancini, Hortense, n.d. Duchess of Mazarin. *Memoires de Madame la Duchesse de Mazarin.* Cologne.

    1676. *The Memoires of the Dutchess Mazarine. Written in French by her Own Hand, and Done into English by P. Porter, Esq; Together with the Reasons of her Coming into England. Likewise, A Letter containing a True Character of her Person and Conversation.* London.

    1713. *Memoirs of the Dutchess of Mazarine: Written in her Name by the Abbott of St Réal, with a Letter Containing a True Character of Her Person and Conversation . . .*

Masham, Damaris. 1696. *A Discourse Concerning the Love of God.* London.

    1705. *Occasional Thoughts in Reference to a Virtuous or Christian Life.* London.

Milton, John. 1649. *Ikonoklastes in Answer to a Book Intitl'd Eikon Basilike, The Portrature of his Sacred Majesty in his Solitudes and Sufferings.* London.

Molyneux. 1698. *The Case of Ireland's Being Bound by Acts of Parliament in England, Stated*. Dublin.

Nicholls, William. 1701. *The Duty of Inferiours Towards their Superiours, in Five Practical Discourses*. London.

Norris, John. 1691. *Practical Discourses on Some Divine Subjects*. London. Second edition, 1692.

1695. *Letters Concerning the Love of God Between the Author of the Proposal to the Ladies and Mr John Norris*. London. Second edition, 1705, corrected by the author and with some few things added.

1717. *A Collection of Miscellanies*. London.

Owen, James. 1703. *Moderation a Vertue: Or, The Occasional Conformist Justify'd from the Imputation of Hypocrisy*. London.

1704. *Moderation still a Vertue: In Answer to Several Bitter Pamphlets: Especially Two, Entituled Occasional Conformity a most Unjustifiable Practice*, and *The Wolf Stripp'd of his Shepherd's Cloathing*. London.

Owen, John. 1651. *The Advantage of the Kingdome of Christ in the Shaking of the Kingdoms of the World . . . in a sermon preached to the Parliament, Octob. 24*. Oxford.

Parsons, Robert. 1594. *A Conference abovt the Next Svccession to the Crowne of Ingland . . .* London.

1609. *A Quiet and Sober Reckoning with M. Thomas Morton*.

Prynne, William. 1644. *A Full Reply to Certaine Breife Observations and anti-Queries . . . Together with Certaine Breife Animadversions on Mr John Goodwins Theomachia*. London.

Pufendorf, Samuel Von, 1672. *De jure naturae et geritium*. Lund.

1673. *De officio hominis et civis*. Lund.

Rutherford, Samuel. 1649. *Free Disputation* [*against Pretended Liberty of Conscience*].

St Evremont. 1698. *Plaidoyez de Mr Herard pour Monsieur le Duc de Mazarin contre Madame la Duchesse de Mazarin son epouse; et le factum pour Madame la Duchesse de Mazarin contre Monsieur le Duc de Mazarin son mari par Mr de St Evremont*.

Sacheverell, Henry. 1708. *The Nature and Mischief of Prejudice and Partiality Stated in a Sermon Preach'd at St Mary's in Oxford at the Assizes held there, March 9, 1703/4*. Second edition, London.

1710. *The Doctrine of Passive Obedience and Nonresistance, as Established in the Church of England . . .* London.

Sidney, Algernon. (written before 1683) 1698. *Discourses Concerning Government*. London.

South, Robert. (1679) 1737. *Sermons Preached upon Several Occasions: Six Sermons*. 6 volumes. London.

Tyrrell, James. 1680. *Patriarcha Non Monarcha, Englished on the Patriarch Unmonarch'd*. London.

Ward, Edward. 1703. *The Secret History of the Calves' Head Clubb*, London and Westminster.

Wesley, Samuel. (1703) 1704. *A Letter from a Country Divine to his Friend in London, concerning the Education of Dissenters in their Private Academies* ... Second edition, London.

Whiston, William. 1696. *A New Theory of the Earth, From its Original, to the Consummation of all Things...*

Secondary texts

Anderson, Paul Bunyan. 1936. 'Mistress Delariviere Manley's Biography', *Modern Philology*, 33, 3, 261–78.

Ashcraft, Richard. 1986. *Revolutionary Politics and Locke's Two Treatises of Government*. Princeton University Press.

1992a. 'The Radical Dimensions of Locke's Political Thought: A Dialogic Essay on Some Problems of Interpretation'. *History of Political Thought*, 13, 4, 703–72.

1992b. 'Simple Objections and Complex Reality: Theorizing Political Radicalism in Seventeenth-century England'. *Political Studies*, 40, 99–117.

Backscheider, Paula R. 1989. *Daniel Defoe: His Life*. Baltimore: Johns Hopkins University Press.

Bingham, Edwin R. 1947. 'The Political Apprenticeship of Benjamin Hoadly'. *Church History*, 16, 154–65.

Blanchard, Rae. 1929. 'Richard Steele and the Status of Women'. *Studies in Philology*, 26, 3, 325–55.

British Biographical Archive, 1984. Microfiche edition. Laureen Ballie, managing ed. London: K. G. Saur Ltd.

Butler, Melissa. 1978. 'Early Liberal Roots of Feminism: John Locke and the Attack on Patriarchy'. *American Political Science Review*, 72, 1, 135–50.

Concise Encyclopaedia of Western Philosophy and Philosophers. 1975. J. O. Urmson, ed. London: Hutchinson.

Cressy, David. 1977. 'Literacy in Seventeenth Century England: More Evidence'. *Journal of Interdisciplinary History*, 8, 141–50.

    1980. *Literacy and Social Order: Reading the Writing in Tudor and Stuart England.* Cambridge University Press.

Dictionary of National Bibliography From the Earliest Times to 1900. 1953. Oxford University Press.

Diamond, Craig W. 1982. 'Public Identity in Restoration England'. Ph.D Dissertation, Johns Hopkins University, Baltimore, Md.

Dzelzainis, Martin, ed. 1991. *John Milton Political Writings.* Cambridge University Press.

Encyclopaedia Britannica. 1910. Eleventh edition. Cambridge University Press.

Encyclopaedia of Philosophy. 1967. Paul Edwards, ed. in chief. New York: Macmillan.

Estcourt, Edgar E. and J. O. Payne. 1885. *The Catholic Nonjurors of 1715.* New York: Catholic Publication Society.

European Authors, 1000–1900: A Biographical Dictionary of European Literature. 1967. Stanley J. Kuntz and Vineta Colby, eds. New York: H. W. Wilson Co.

Farr, James and Clayton Roberts. 1985. 'John Locke on the Glorious Revolution: A Rediscovered Document'. [Bodleian MS Locke e.18, fo.4v] *The Historical Journal*, 28, 385–98.

George, Margaret. 1973. 'From "Goodwife" to "Mistress": The Transformation of the Female in Bourgeois Culture'. *Science and Society*, 37, 152–77.

Goldie, Mark. 1978. 'Tory Political Thought 1689–1714.' Ph.D dissertation, University of Cambridge.

    1980a. 'The Roots of True Whiggism, 1688–1694'. *History of Political Thought*, 1, 195–236.

    1980b. 'The Revolution of 1689 and the Structure of Political Argument'. *Bulletin of Research in the Humanities*, 83, 473–564.

    1991. 'The Theory of Religious Intolerance in Restoration England'. In O. P. Grell, J. I. Israel and N. Tyacke, eds. *From Persecution to Toleration.* Oxford University Press.

Harrison, John and Laslett, Peter. 1971. *The Library of John Locke.* Second edition, Oxford: Clarendon Press.

Hexter, John H. 1976. 'The Predatory Vision: Niccolo Machiavell, *Il Principe* and *lo Stato*'. In J. H. Hexter, *The Vision of Politics on the Eve of the Reformation.* New York: Basic Books, pp. 150–78.

Higgins, Patricia. 1973. 'The Reactions of Women, with Special Reference to Women Petitioners'. In *Politics, Religion and the English Civil War*. Brian Manning, ed. London: Edward Arnold.

Hill, Bridget. 1986. *The First English Feminist: 'Reflections Upon Marriage' and Other Writings by Mary Astell*. Aldershot, Hants: Gower Publishing.

Hinton, R. W. K. 1967, 1968. 'Husbands, Fathers and Conquerors'. 2 parts. *Political Studies*, 15, 3, 291–300; 16, 1, 55–67.

Hutton, Sarah. 1993. 'Damaris Cudworth, Lady Masham: between Platonism and Elightenment'. *British Journal for the History of Philosophy*, 1, 1, 29–54.

Jones, J. R. 1987. *Charles II: Royal Politician*. London: Allen & Unwin.

Jolley, Nicholas. 1975. 'Leibniz on Hobbes, Locke's *Two Treatises* and Sherlock's *Case of Allegiance*'. *Historical Journal*, 18, 21–35.

Kiernan, Thomas. 1966. *Who's Who in the History of Philosophy*. London: Vision Press.

Kinnaird, Joan K. 1979. 'Mary Astell and the Conservative Contribution to English Feminism'. *Journal of British Studies*, 19: 53–79.

Kenyon, J. P. 1978. *Stuart England*. London: Penguin Books.

McCrystal, John William. 1992a. 'An Inadvertant Feminist: Mary Astell (1666–1731)'. MA thesis, Department of Political Studies, Auckland University.

1992b. 'A Lady's Calling: Mary Astell's Notion of Women'. *Political Theory Newsletter*, 4, 156–70.

Mack, Phyllis. 1984. 'Women as Prophets during the English Civil War'. In Margaret Jacob and James Jacob, eds. *The Origins of Anglo-American Radicalism*. London: George Allen & Unwin, pp. 214–31.

McNally, David. 1989. 'Locke, Levellers and Liberty: Property and Democracy in the Thought of the First Whigs'. *History of Political Thought*, 10, 17–40.

Miller, John. 1973. *Popery and Politics 1660–1688*. Cambridge University Press.

Monod, Paul Kléber. 1989. *Jacobitism and the English People 1688–1788*. Cambridge University Press.

Myers, Mitzi. 1985. 'Domesticating Minerva: Bathusa Makin's "Curious" Argument for Women's Education'. *Studies in Eighteenth Century Culture*, 14, 173–92.

National Union Catalog. 1840 – 679 vols. Chicago, Ill.: American Library Association.

Needham, Gwendolyn B. 1949. 'Mary de la Rivière Manley, Tory Defender', *Huntington Library Quarterly*, 12, 3, 253–88.

New Encyclopaedia Britannica. 1991. (Macropaedia and Micropaedia). Encyclopaedia Britannica Inc., University of Chicago.

New Schaff-Herzog Encyclopedia of Religious Knowledge. 1908. 12 volumes. New York and London: Funk and Wagnalls Co.

Norton, J. E. 1961. 'Some Uncollected Authors XXVII: Mary Astell, 1666–1731'. *The Book Collector*, 10, 1, 58–60.

O'Donnell, Sheryl. 1978. 'Mr Locke and the Ladies: The Indellible Words on the Tabula Rasa'. *Studies in Eighteenth Century Culture*, 8, 151–64.

    1984. ' "My Idea in Your Mind": John Locke and Damaris Cudworth Masham'. In Ruth Perry and Martine Brownley, eds, *Mothering the Mind.* New York: Homes & Meier, pp. 26–46.

Overton, J. H. 1903. *The Nonjurors: Their Lives, Principles and Writings:* New York: Thomas Whittaker.

Oxford Dictionary of the Christian Church. F. L. Cross and E. A. Livingstone, eds. Second edition. Oxford University Press.

Oxford English Dictionary. 1989. Eleventh edition. Oxford University Press.

Pateman, Carole. 1988. *The Sexual Contract.* Cambridge: Polity Press.

    1989. 'God Hath Ordained to Man a Helper: Hobbes, Patriarchy and Conjugal Right'. *British Journal of Political Science*, 19, 445–64.

Perry, Ruth. 1986. *The Celebrated Mary Astell: An Early English Feminist.* University of Chicago Press.

Phillipson, Nicholas. 1993. 'Politeness and Politics in the Reigns of Anne and the Early Hanoverians'. In J. G. A. Pocock, Gordon J. Schochet and Lois G. Schwoerer, eds. *The Varieties of British Political Thought, 1500–1800.* Washington, D.C., Folger Institute, pp. 211–45.

Scaltsas, Patricia Ward. 1990. 'Women as Ends – Women as Means in the Enlightenment'. In *Women's Rights and the Rights of Man.* A. J. Arnaud and E. Kingdom, eds. Aberdeen University Press, pp. 138–48.

Schochet, G. J. 1975. *Patriarchalism and Political Theory.* Oxford: Blackwell.

Schwoerer, Lois, G. 1977. 'Propaganda in the Revolution of 1688–89'. *American Historical Review*, 82, 843–74.

1990. 'Locke, Lockean Ideas and the Glorious Revolution'. *Journal of the History of Ideas*, 51, 4, 531–48.

1993. 'The Right to Resist: Whig Resistance Theory, 1688 to 1694'. In Nicholas Phillipson and Quentin Skinner, eds, *Political Discourse in Early Modern Britain*. Cambridge University Press, 232–52.

Scott, Jonathan. 1988. 'Radicalism and Restoration: The Shape of the Stuart Experience'. *The Historical Journal*, 31, 2, 453–67.

Shanley, Mary Lyndon. 1979. 'Marriage Contract and Social Contract in Seventeenth Century English Political Thought'. *Western Political Quarterly*, 32, 79–91.

Skinner, Quentin. 1972. 'Conquest and Consent: Thomas Hobbes and the Engagement Controversy'. In G. E. Aylmer, ed. *The Interregnum: The Quest for Settlement 1646–1660*. London.

Smith, Alan G. R. 1984. *The Emergence of a Nation State: The Commonwealth of England 1529–1660*. London and New York: Longman.

Smith, Hilda. 1982. *Reason's Disciples*. Urbana: University of Illinois Press.

Smith, Florence M. 1916. *Mary Astell*. New York: Columbia University Press.

Sommerville, Johann P. 1982. 'From Suarez to Filmer: A Reappraisal'. *Historical Journal*, 25, 525–40.

Sommerville, Johann P., ed. 1991. Introduction to *Sir Robert Filmer, 'Patriarcha' and Other Writings*. Cambridge University Press.

Sommerville, Margaret. 1995. *Sex and Subjection: Attitudes to Women in Early Modern Society*. London: Edward Arnold.

Springborg, Patricia. 1995. 'Mary Astell (1666–1731), Critic of Locke'. *American Political Science Review*, 89, 2, September 1995, 621–33.

Squadrito, K. M. 1987. 'Mary Astell's Critique of Locke's View of Thinking Matter', *Journal of the History of Philosophy*, 25, 433–40.

Thomas, Rev. D. R. 1874. *History of the Diocese of St Asaph*. London.

Thomas, Keith. 1958. 'Women and the Civil War Sects'. *Past and Present*, 13, 42–62.

Thompson, Martyn P. 1976. 'The Reception of Locke's *Two Treatises of Government*, 1690–1705'. *Political Studies*, 24, 184–91.

1980. 'Revolution and Influence: A Reply to Nelson on Locke's *Two Treatises of Government*'. *Political Studies*: 28, 100–8.

Tuck, Richard. 1987. Review of Michael Mendle, *Dangerous Positions: Mixed Government, the Estates of the Realm, and the Answer to the XIX Propositions* (Birmingham: University of Alabama Press, 1985), *Journal of Modern History* 59, 3, 570–2.

Wootton, David. 1992. 'John Locke and Richard Ashcraft's *Revolutionary Politics*'. *Political Studies*, 40, 79–98.

Worden, Blair, ed. 1986. *Stuart England*. Oxford: Phaidon Press Ltd.

Yolton, Jean S. and Yolton, John W. 1985. *John Locke: A Reference Guide*. Boston, Mass.: G. K. Hall & Co.

Francis   Williams

· S O M E ·

REFLECTIONS

U P O N

Marriage,

Occasion'd by the

Duke & Dutchess

O F

Mazarine's CASE;

Which is also consider'd.

L O N D O N:

Printed for *John Nutt* near *Stationers-Hall*, 1700.

Note on the Text

The *Reflections*, published first in 1700, the prefatory Advertisement suggests, were occasioned by a book which 'came but late to hand', undoubtedly translations of the proceedings of the famous Mazarin divorce case mentioned in Astell's subtitle. In the opening sentences of the first edition (1700, p. 1) she declares: 'Curiosity . . . having induced me to read the Account of an unhappy Marriage, I thought an Afternoon would not be quite thrown away in pursuing such *Reflections* as it occasioned.' This ingenuous beginning gives little hint of the inflammatory material to come. True, in the Advertisement, the anonymous author, as if to absolve herself, declares she has 'no other Design than to Correct some Abuses, which are not the less because Power and Prescription seem to Authorize them'. On the first page of the fourth edition, Astell added a further protest: 'I am so far from designing a Satire upon Marriage, as some pretend, either unkindly or ignorantly, through want of *Reflection* in that Sense wherein I use the Word' (1730, pp. 1–2). But a satire of the manners and mores governing early eighteenth-century marriage was certainly what she had produced, and the Mazarin divorce was no more than a convenient peg to hang it on.

Marriage and divorce were hotly debated subjects in the seventeenth century. One of the more famous, if arcane, works which argued for the permissibility of divorce was John Selden's *Uxor Hebraica* (1646). At least as controversial was John Milton's (*q.v.*) defence of divorce, following his brief ill-starred

It should be noted that the facsimile title-page on p. 1 is from the first (1700) edition, not the third (1706), which is printed here. This is not available for reproduction.

marriage of 1643. These are not arguments which Astell repeats, believing, as she does, marriage to be an indestructable union sanctified by the Church. Instead, she makes the furore over the Mazarin divorce the occasion for an assessment of the role of women in society, their inequality and the realities that women face when they enter marriage; realities of social hierarchy and unequal power that individuals face in society at large. Astell, with her famous question '*If all Men are born free*, how is it that all Women are born slaves?' mocks Hobbes, Locke, Dennis, Sidney, Tyrrell and those who would maintain that individuals contract out of freedom in the state of nature, into servitude in the state. As it stands her *Reflections upon Marriage* is perhaps the first articulated critique of the analogue between the marriage contract and the social contract on which early modern natural rights theories so heavily depend. It is in particular a protest against those who would claim freedom for men and servitude for women as the consequence of the marriage contract, the position put most forcefully by Gilbert Burnet in *An Enquiry into the Measures of Submission to the Supream Authority* (1689). In this, his most radical work, a particular target for Astell perhaps, Burnet (p. 53) both subscribed to the doctrine that all men are born free, and to the subordination of women.

By 1700 Astell had already developed a coherent thesis on the incongruity of Whig arguments for consent, equality, the right to resist tyranny, and the power of oaths and covenants to secure rights. In the first edition of the *Reflections* she used the institution of marriage to demonstrate it. There are innumerable references to 'the Wits', 'men of Sense', 'Understanding', 'the Original State', 'Natural Right', 'Liberty', which cue us to the Whigs and the Shaftesbury circle, including Locke. Astell points to the arbitrariness of views which ascribe freedom as a birthright for men and subjection as natural for women. Her conclusion is not the liberation of women but the rather more dismal prospect of obedience to authority as a duty for everyone, freedom and equality being virtues of the celestial realm. Her social criticism derives, ironically, from assumptions she shares with Filmer, the author of *Patriarcha* (1680), a number of whose arguments she replicates. Filmer had in fact produced a short tract, 'In Praise of the Vertuous Wife'. His purpose, like that of Astell, was to refute claims made by the radical sects – and later of Whigs – to natural equality and freedom in the Original State, out of which individuals are said to contract into civil society.

4

Displaying considerable erudition, Filmer had examined the claim that 'men are born free' from sources as early and as diverse as the Bible, the *Corpus iuris civilis* (i.i.4; Filmer, *Patriarcha*, pp. 64–5) to Hugo Grotius' (*q.v.*) *De jure belli ac pacis* (1625; Filmer, *Patriarcha*, pp. 64–5), claiming to show that in no case did they mean what they appear to say. Marshalling his legal expertise, Filmer argued that the right to freedom implied specific freedoms, cases of manumission and the like, and not an unconditional right. Everything remained as it was, citizens bound to 'Render unto Caesar' (Matthew 22:21) had open to them the paths of active or passive obedience, depending on the wisdom of the prince, and a continuing obligation to the Magna Carta as the source of their liberty (Filmer, *Patriarcha*, p. 4). Astell takes a leaf out of Filmer's book: if these authoritative sources did not sanction an unconditional freedom, they did not sanction unconditional servitude – that of women – either.

Filmer had become tainted in Astell's day by imitators such as William Nicholls, whose *The Duty of Inferiours Towards their Superiours* (1701), patriarchalist in the modern sense, she cites. This fact tends to obscure the continuum of argument on constitutional matters from Filmer to Augustan Tories, among whom Astell numbers. We have cause to note that in the Preface to the third edition Astell's focus sharpens considerably, and Locke is clearly in her sights. Between 1700 and 1706 Charles Leslie, in the Supplement to *The New Association, Part II* (1703), had launched what is believed to have been the first published attack on the *Two Treatises*. We should not be surprised to find that Astell's arguments reproduce, and improve upon, those for which Leslie is more famous. Moreover, Leslie's arguments are already anticipated in the main body of the *Reflections* (1700, p. 27), even in Astell's famous remarks lampooning the Independents' hypocrisy, and that of Milton, who would refuse liberty to 'poor *Female Slaves*' and 'the Lawfulness of Resisting a Private Tyranny'.

A collation of the editions of the *Reflections* is difficult because of structural changes made between the five editions published in Astell's lifetime. The third edition (1706) is usually favoured for what is known as the famous '1706 Preface', and is reproduced here because it has become more or less standard. Of the second edition (1703), believed to have made only minor typographical changes to the first, no copies are extant. But by the fourth edition (1730) the Preface is relegated to an Appendix because of being 'extended to an uncommon

Length', as the Advertisement claims. In fact the differences between the Appendix to edition four and the Preface to the third edition are very minor, mainly punctuation and the addition of a few words. The major changes in the fourth edition occur in the first twenty pages where Astell revises the introductory ten pages of the first and the third editions; and in the last five pages, which she adds (1730, pp. 128–32), reflecting more expansively on the examples of the Countess Mazarin, her uncle the Cardinal and the corrupt culture of the court they represent. In the fourth, as in the first and second editions, an Advertisement, incorporated as the first page of the Preface of the third edition, and unchanged from edition to edition, constitutes the only prefatory material. The typefaces of Astell's Preface, in italics in the original, with roman type for emphases, have been reversed, in accordance with modern practice. S and double s, etc., are modernized, otherwise punctuation and spelling are preserved as Astell has written them. Errata entered on p. xxvi of the third edition are indicated in square brackets in the text and flagged with the abbreviation *err*. In this as in the other texts the original pagination is indicated in bold in square brackets. In the case of *Reflections upon Marriage*, roman numerals are used according to convention, for the Preface, which is in fact not paginated in the 1706 edition, and arabic numerals for the body of the text. From p. 80 on, the 1706 edition is mispaginated in the original, omitting 81 and 82, going from 80 on left facing to 83 on the right-facing page. In addition, p. 87 in this sequence is mispaginated as 78, probably a further typographical error.

[i] The Preface

These Reflections being made in the Country, where the Book that occasion'd them came but late to Hand,[1] the *Reader* is desir'd to excuse their Unseasonableness as well as other Faults; and to believe that they have no other Design than to Correct some Abuses, which are not the less because Power and Prescription seem to Authorize them. If any is [*err.*, are] so needlessly curious as to enquire from what Hand they come, they may please to know, that it is not good Manners to ask, since the Title-Page does not tell them: We are all of us sufficiently Vain, and without doubt the Celebrated Name of *Author*, which most are so fond of, had not been avoided but for very good Reasons: To name but one; *Who will care to pull upon themselves an Hornet's Nest?* 'Tis a very great Fault to regard rather who it is that Speaks, than what is Spoken; and either to submit to Authority, when we should only yield to Reason; or if Reason press too hard, to think to ward it off by Personal Objections and Reflections. Bold Truths may pass while the Speaker is *Incognito*, but are not endur'd when he is known; few Minds being strong enough to bear what Contradicts their Principles and Practices without Recriminating when they can. And tho' to tell the Truth be the most Friendly Office, yet whosoever is so hardy as to venture at it, shall be counted an Enemy for so doing.

[ii] *Thus far the old Advertisement, when the Reflections first appear'd, A.D. 1700.*

---

[1] Probably *The Arguments of Mons. Herard for the Duke of Mazarin against the Dutchess, his Spouse, and the Factum for the dutchess by Mons. St Evremont*, trans. from French (1699).

But the *Reflector* who hopes *Reflector* is not bad English, now *Governor* is happily of the Feminine Gender, had as good or better have said nothing; For People by being forbid, are only excited to a more curious Enquiry. A certain Ingenious [*err.* Ingenuous] Gentleman[2] (as she is inform'd) had the Good-Nature to own these Reflections, so far as to affirm that he had the Original *M.S.* in his Closet, a Proof she is not able to produce; and so to make himself responsible for all their Faults, for which she returns him all due Acknowledgment. However, the Generality being of Opinion, that a Man would have had more Prudence and Manners than to have Publish'd such unseasonable Truths, or to have betray'd the *Arcana Imperii* of his Sex, she humbly confesses, that the Contrivance and Execution of this Design, which is unfortunately accus'd of being so destructive to the Government, of the Men I mean, is entirely her own. She neither advis'd with Friends, nor turn'd over Antient or Modern Authors, nor prudently submitted to the Correction of such as are, or such as *think* they are good Judges, but with an *English* Spirit and Genius, set out upon the Forlorn Hope, meaning no hurt to any body, nor designing any thing but the Publick Good, and to retrieve, if possible, the Native Liberty, the Rights and Privileges of the Subject.

Far be it from her to stir up Sedition of any sort, none can abhor it more; and she heartily wishes that our Masters wou'd pay their Civil and Ecclesiastical Governors the same Submission, which they themselves exact from their Domestic Subjects. Nor can she [iii] imagine how she any way undermines the Masculine Empire, or blows the Trumpet of Rebellion to the Moiety of Mankind. Is it by exhorting Women, not to expect to have their own Will in any thing, but to be entirely Submissive, when once they have made choice of a Lord and Master, tho' he happen not to be so Wise, so Kind, or even so Just a Governor as was expected? She did not indeed advise them to think his Folly Wisdom, nor his Brutality

---

[2] Astell does not disclose his identity. She uses the terms 'ingenious' or 'ingenuous' frequently of her interlocutors, as of William Nicholls and William Whiston (*q.v.*), who would not have been candidates. The term *arcana imperii* (state secrets) is employed by Sir Robert Filmer in the first chapter of his *Patriarcha* (1680) (see *Patriarcha and Other Writings*, ed. J. Sommerville, Cambridge University Press 1991, p. 3), as Locke tells us in the *First Treatise* (Chapter 2, Section 6, 1988 p. 145), and the tone of the whole passage suggests that she may have Locke in mind.

that Love and Worship he promised in his Matrimonial Oath, for this required a Flight of Wit and Sense much above her poor Ability, and proper only to Masculine Understandings. However she did not in any manner prompt them to Resist, or to Abdicate the Perjur'd Spouse, tho, the Laws of GOD and the Land make special Provision for it, in a case wherein, as is to be fear'd, few Men can truly plead Not Guilty.

'Tis true, thro' Want of Learning, and of that Superior Genius which Men as Men lay claim to, she was ignorant of the *Natural Inferiority* of our Sex, which our Masters lay down as a Self-Evident and Fundamental Truth.[3] She saw nothing in the Reason of Things, to make this either a Principle or a Conclusion, but much to the contrary; it being Sedition at least, if not Treason to assert it in this Reign. For if by the Natural Superiority of their Sex, they mean that *every* Man is by Nature superior to *every* Woman, which is the obvious meaning, and that which must be stuck to if they would speak Sense, it wou'd be a Sin in *any* Woman to have Dominion over *any* Man, and the greatest Queen ought not to command but to obey her Footman, because no Municipal Laws can supersede or change the Law of Nature; so that if the Dominion of the Men be such, the *Salique Law*, as unjust as *English Men* have ever thought it, ought to take place [iv] over all the Earth, and the most glorious Reigns in the *English, Danish, Castilian,* and other Annals, were wicked Violations of the Law of Nature!

If they mean that *some* Men are superior to *some* Women this is no great Discovery;[4] had they turn'd the Tables they might have

---

[3] William Nicholls, *The Duty of Inferiours towards their Superiours, in Five Practical Discourses* (London, 1701), 'Discourse IV, The Duty of Wives to their Husbands'.

[4] Astell may well be referring to theories of Nicolas Malebranche (*q.v.*), *De la recherche de la verité: ou l'on traitte de la nature de l'esprit de l'homme, & de l'usage qu'il en doit faire pour éviter l'erreur dans les sciences*, fourth revised and enlarged edition (Paris, 1678). Malebranche deals with the structure of mind and sex differences in Part II, 'Concerning the Imagination', 1.1, 'Of the Imagination of Women'. See the 1700 translation by Thomas Taylor, *Father Malebranche his Treatise Concerning the Search after Truth . . .* second corrected edition (London). Discussing the greater excitability of women, Taylor, p. 64, accurately translates Malebranche (*De la recherche* pp. 105–6): But though it be certain, that this Delicacy of the Fibres of the Brain is the principal Cause of all these Effects; yet it is not equally certain, that it is universally to be found in all Women. Or if it be to be found, yet their Animal Spirits are sometimes so exactly proportion'd to the Fibres of their Brain, that there are Women to be met with, who have a greater solidity of Mind than some Men. 'Tis in a certain Temperature of the Largeness and Agi-

seen that *some* Women are Superior to *some* Men. Or had they been pleased to remember their Oaths of Allegiance and Supremacy, they might have known that *One* Woman is superior to *All* the Men in these Nations, or else they have sworn to very little purpose. And it must not be suppos'd, that their Reason and Religion wou'd suffer them to take Oaths, contrary to the Law of Nature and Reason of things.

By all which it appears, that our Reflector's Ignorance is very pitiable, it may be her Misfortune but not her Crime, especially since she is willing to be better inform'd, and hopes she shall never be so obstinate as to shut her Eyes against the Light of Truth, which is not to be charg'd with Novelty, how late soever we may be bless'd with the Discovery. Nor can Error, be it as Antient as it may, ever plead Prescription against Truth. And since the only way to remove all Doubts, to answer all Objections, and to give the Mind entire Satisfaction, is not by *Affirming*, but by *Proving*, so that every one may see with their *own* Eyes, and Judge according to the best of their *own* Understandings, She hopes it is no Presumption to insist on this Natural Right of Judging for her self, and the rather, because by quitting it, we give up all the Means of Rational Conviction. Allow us then as many Glasses as you please to help our Sight, and as many good Arguments as you can afford to Convince our Understandings: But don't exact of us we beseech you, to affirm that we see such things as are only the Discovery of [v] Men who have quicker Senses; or that we understand and Know what we have by Hear-say only; for to be so excessively Complaisant is neither to see nor to understand.

That the Custom of the World has put Women, generally speaking, into a State of Subjection, is not deny'd; but the Right can no more be prov'd from the Fact, than the Predominancy of Vice can justifie it. A certain great Man has endeavour'd to prove by Reasons not contemptible, that in the Original State of things the Woman

tation of the Animal Spirits, and Conformity with the Fibres of the Brain, that the strength of parts consists: And Women have sometimes that just Temperature. There are Women Strong and constant, and there are Men that are Weak and Fickle. There are Women that are Learned, Couragious, and capable of every thing. And on the contrary, there are Men that are Soft Effeminate, incapable of any Penetration, or dispatch of any Business. In Fine, when we attribute any Failures to a certain Sex, Age, or Condition, they are only to be understood of the generality; it being ever suppos'd, there is no general Rule without Exception.'

was the Superior, and that her Subjection to the Man is an Effect of the Fall, and the Punishment of her Sin.[5] And that Ingenious Theorist Mr *Whiston*[6] asserts, That before the Fall there was a greater equality between the two Sexes. However this be 'tis certainly no Arrogance in a Woman to conclude, that she was made for the Service of GOD, and that this is her End. Because GOD made all Things for Himself, and a Rational Mind is too noble a Being to be Made for the Sake and Service of any Creature. The Service she at any time becomes oblig'd to pay to a Man, is only a Business by the Bye. Just as it may be any Man's Business and Duty to keep Hogs; he was not Made for this, but if he hires himself out to such an Employment, he ought conscientiously to perform it. Nor can anything be concluded to the contrary from St. *Paul's* Argument, *I Cor. 11*. For he argues only for Decency and Order, according to the present Custom and State of things. Taking his Words strictly and literally, they prove too much, in that *Praying and Prophecying in the Church* are allow'd the Women, provided they do it with their Head Cover'd, as well as the Men; and no inequality can be inferr'd from hence, neither from the Gradation the Apostle there uses, that *the Head of every Man is Christ, and that the Head of the* [vi] *Woman is the Man, and the Head of Christ is GOD*;[7] It being evident from the Form of Baptism, that there is no natural Inferiority among the Divine Persons, but that they are in all things Coequal. The Apostle indeed adds, that *the Man is the*

---

[5] This could be a reference to Thomas Hobbes, *Leviathan*, Richard Tuck, ed (Cambridge University Press, 1991, p. 140): 'If there be no Contract the Dominion is in the Mother. For in the condition of meer Nature, where there are no Matrimoniall lawes, it cannot be known who is the Father, unlesse it be declared by the Mother: and therefore the right of Dominion over the Child dependeth on her will.' Hobbes' case for the superior claims of the mother compared with the father to authority over the child is likely to have been one of the features of his argument that so enraged Nicholls (*Duty of Inferiours*, p. 49), to whom Astell is responding. See below n.10.

[6] William Whiston is probably Astell's source here. His *A New Theory of the Earth, From its Original, to the Consummation of all Things* (1696) claims in the title to vindicate the 'Mosaick History of the Creation' as 'perfectly agreeable to Reason and Philosophy'. A peculiar mishmash of the Bible and classical sources, leaning heavily on Herodotus, it does claim to show that 'The Lives of the *Antediluvians* were more universally equal' (Book III, Chapter 3, Section 42); and that 'the Female was then very different from what she is now; particularly she was in a state of greater Equality with the Male' (Book IV, Chapter 2, Section 25), (pp. 186, 272).

[7] 1 Corinthians 11:3.

Glory of God, and the Woman the Glory of the Man,[8] Etc. But what does he infer from hence? he says not a word of Inequality, or natural Inferiority, but concludes, that a Woman ought to Cover her head, and a Man ought not to cover his, and that *even Nature itself teaches* us, that *if a Man have long hair it is a shame unto him.*[9] Whatever the Apostle's Argument proves in this place nothing can be plainer, than that there is much more said against the present Fashion of Men's wearing long Hair, than for that Supremacy they lay claim to. For by all that appears in the Text, it is not so much a Law of Nature, that Women shou'd Obey Men, as that Men shou'd not wear long Hair. Now how can a Christian Nation allow Fashions contrary to the Law of Nature, forbidden by an Apostle and declared by him to be a shame to Man [*err.* Men]? Or if Custom may make an alteration in one Case it may in another, but what then becomes of the Nature and Reason of things? Besides, the Conclusion the Apostle draws from his Argument concerning Women, *viz.* that they *shou'd have power on their heads because of the Angels,*[10] is so very obscure a Text, That that Ingenious Paraphrast[11] who pleads so much for the *Natural Subjection* of Women, Ingenuously confesses, that he does not understand it. Probably it refers to some Custom among the *Corinthians*, which being well

---

[8] 1 Corinthians 11:7

[9] 1 Corinthians 11:14.

[10] 1 Corinthians 11:10.

[11] William Nicholls (*Duty of Inferiours*, pp. 87–8), in fact sets out to show that submission of wives to their husbands is not merely customary, but founded in 'a higher State of natural Perfection and Dignity, and thereupon . . . a just Claim of Superiority, which every thing which is of more worth has a Right to, over that which has less'. When it comes to it, Nicholls has to admit that the prominence given in the Gospel to the submission of wives means 'not but that the violation of some other Conjugal Duties, were great Sins; but This was a more spreading one' – attaching the foundation of Law and Order. Having conceded the prudential rationale, he nevertheless buttresses his natural law claim to female inferiority by producing a long litany of woman's natural weaknesses, beginning: 'There is more of natural Imbecility in the Woman, than the Man, as well in respect of her Bodily, as in her Intellectual Capacities' (pp. 85–6). This must have been particularly galling in an author who otherwise shared Astell's political and religious beliefs, defending Divine Right of Kings against Hobbes and Hobbists (p. 49): 'the *Leviathan* (as Mr. *Hobbs* calls the secular Power) has never an occasion so much to exert his force, as upon the Principles and Scholars of the wicked Book which goes under that name; a Book which destroys all ties of Conscience between Prince and Subjects, and lays all Governments open to whatsoever powerful or crafty Villains can attempt against them.'

known to them the Apostle only hints at it, but which we are ignorant of, and therefore apt to mistake him. 'is like that the False Apostle whom St *Paul* writes against had led *Captive* some of their [vii] Rich and Powerful but *silly Women*,[12] who having as mean an Opinion of the Reason GOD had given them, as any Deceiver cou'd desire, did not like the noble minded *Bereans, search the Scriptures whether those things were so*,[13] but lazily took up with having Men's Persons in admiration, and follow'd their Leaders Blindfold, the certain Rout to Destruction. And it is also probable that the same cunning Seducer, imploy'd these Women to carry on his own Designs and putting them upon what he might not think fit to appear in himself, made them guilty of Indecent Behaviour in the Church of *Corinth*. And therefore St *Paul* thought it necessary to reprove them so severely in order to humble them, but this being done, he takes care in the Conclusion to set the matter on a right Foot, placing the two Sexes on a Level, to keep Men as much as might be, from taking those advantages which People who have strength in their hands, are apt to assume over those who can't contend with them. For, says he, *Nevertheless*, or notwithstanding the former Argument, *the Man is not without the Woman, nor the Woman without the Man, but all things of GOD.*[14] The Relation between the two Sexes is mutual, and the Dependance Reciprocal, both of them Depending intirely upon GOD, and upon Him only; which one wou'd think is no great Argument of the natural Inferiority of either Sex.

Our *Reflector* is of Opinion that Disputes of this kind, extending to Human Nature in general, and not peculiar to those to whom the Word of GOD has been reveal'd, ought to be decided by natural Reason only. And that the Holy Scriptures shou'd not be Interessed [*sic*] in the present Controversy, in which it determines nothing, any more than it does between the *Copernican* and *Ptolomean* Systems.[15] The Design of those Holy [viii] Books being to make us

---

[12] See II Timothy 3:6.

[13] See Acts 17:11.

[14] I Corinthians 11:11–12.

[15] Probably a reference to William Whiston's, *New Theory* (pp. 38 ff.). The jibe that Astell ('Our *Reflector*') has paid insufficient attention to Scripture on the question of the natural inferiority of women and answered from natural Reason, Astell cannot let pass, and so she musters impressive scriptural evidence to the contrary.

excellent Moralists and Perfect Christians, not great Philosophers. And being writ for the Vulgar as well as for the Learned, they are accommodated to the common way of Speech and the Usage of the World; in which we have but a short Probation, so that it matters not much what part we Act, whether of Governing or Obeying, provided we perform it well with respect to the World to come.

One does not wonder indeed, that when an Adversary is drove to a Nonplus and Reason declares against him, he flies to Authority, especially to Divine, which is infallible, and therefore ought not to be disputed. But Scripture is not always on their side who make parade of it, and thro' their skill in Languages and the Tricks of the Schools, wrest it from its genuine sense to their own Inventions. And Supposing, not granting, that it were apparently to the Woman's [*err.* 'Women's] Disadvantage, no fair and generous Adversary but wou'd be asham'd to urge this advantage. Because Women without their own Fault, are kept in Ignorance of the Original, wanting Languages and other helps to Criticise on the Sacred Text, of which they know no more, than Men are pleas'd to impart in their Translations. In short, they shew their desire to maintain their Hypotheses, but by no means their Reverence to the Sacred Oracles who engage them in such Disputes. And therefore the blame be theirs, who have unnecessarily introduc'd them in the present Subject, and who by saying that the *Reflections* were not agreeable to Scripture, oblige the Reflector to shew that those who affirm it must either mistake her Meaning, or the Sense of Holy Scripture, or both, if they think what they say, and do not find fault merely because they resolve to do so. For had she ever writ any thing contrary to those sacred Truths, she wou'd be the first in pronouncing its Condemnation.

[ix] But what says the Holy Scripture? It speaks of Women as in a State of Subjection, and so it does of the *Jews* and *Christians* when under the Dominion of the *Chaldeans* and *Romans*, requiring of the one as well as of the other a quiet submission to them under whose Power they liv'd. But will any one say that these had a *Natural Superiority* and Right to Dominion?[16] that they had a superior

---

[16] Astell returns to Nicholls' tract and its catalogue of instances of female natural inequality, in order to deny the thesis and assert rather the position of Whiston (*New Theory*, pp. 38 ff.), that the subordination of women is a matter of convention, or government, necessitated by the Fall. The paradox of women's position,

Understanding, or any Pre-eminence, except what their greater Strength acquir'd? Or that the other were subjected to their Adversaries for any other Reason but the Punishment of their sins, and in order to their Reformation? Or for the Exercise of their Vertue, and because the Order of the World and the Good of Society requir'd it?

If Mankind had never sinn'd, Reason wou'd always have been obey'd, there wou'd have been no struggle for Dominion, and Brutal Power wou'd not have prevail'd. But in the laps'd State of Mankind, and now that Men will not be guided by their Reason but by their Appetites, and do not what they *ought* but what they *can*, the Reason, or that which stands for it, the Will and Pleasure of the Governor is to be the Reason of those who will not be guided by their own, and must take place for Order's sake, altho' it shou'd not be conformable to right Reason. Nor can there be any Society great or little, from Empires down to private Families, without a last Resort, to determine the Affairs of that Society by an irresistible Sentence. Now unless this Supremacy be fix'd somewhere, there will be a perpetual Contention about it, such is the love of Dominion, and let the Reason of things be what it may, those who have least Force, or Cunning to supply it, will have the Disadvantage. So that since Women are acknowledg'd to have least Bodily strength, their being commanded to obey is in pure kindness to them and [x] for their Quiet and Security, as well as for the Exercise of their Vertue. But does it follow that Domestic Governors have more Sense than their Subjects, any more than that other Gover-

as minds and souls equal to men, but as bodies subject to their dictates, is nowhere more delicately expressed than in the passage beginning: 'in the laps'd State of Mankind, and now that Men will not be guided by their Reason but by their Appetites, and do not what they *ought*, but what they *can*, the Reason, or that which stands for it, the Will and Pleasure of the Governor is to be the Reason of those who will not be guided by their own and must take place for Order's sake, altho' it shou'd not be conformable to right Reason'. In *Moderation truly Stated: Or a Review of a late Pamphlet, Entitul'd Moderation a Vertue* (London, 1704), p. 59, Astell made the prudential argument for order even more forcefully: 'In a word, Order is a Sacred Thing, 'tis that Law which God prescribes Himself, and inviolably observes. Subordination is a necessary consequence of Order, for in a State of Ignorance and [De]pravity such as ours is, there is not any thing that tends more to Confusion than Equality. It does not therefore become the gross of Mankind to set up for that which is best in their own conceit; but humbly to observe where GOD has Delegated his Power, and submit to it, *as unto the Lord and not to Man*'.

nors have? We do not find that any Man thinks the worse of his own Understanding because another has superior Power; or concludes himself less capable of a Post of Honour and Authority, because he is not Prefer'd to it. How much time wou'd lie on Men's hands, how empty wou'd the Places of Concourse be, and how silent most Companies did Men forbear to Censure their Governors, that is in effect to think themselves Wiser. Indeed Government wou'd be much more desirable than it is, did it invest the Possessor with a superior Understanding as well as Power. And if mere Power gives a Right to Rule, there can be no such thing as Usurpation; but a Highway-Man so long as he has strength to force, has also a Right to require our Obedience.[17]

[17] This would appear to be a direct reference to one of the most central passages of Locke's *Second Treatise* (Section 119, 1988, pp. 347–8), where having established that 'man is born free', Locke sets out the conditions on which one can be bound to a civil authority: '119. *Every Man* being, as has been shewed, *naturally free*, and nothing being able to put him into subjection to any Earthly Power, but only his own Consent; it is to be considered, what shall be understood to be *a sufficient Declaration of* a Mans *Consent, to make him subject* to the Laws of any Government. There is a common distinction of an express and a tacit consent, which will concern our present Case. No body doubts but an *express Consent*, of any Man, entring into any Society, makes him a perfect Member of that Society, a Subject of that Government. The difficulty is, what ought to be look'd upon as a *tacit Consent*, and how far it binds, *i.e.* how far any one shall be looked on to have consented, and thereby submitted to any Government, where he has made no Expressions of it at all. And to this I say, that every Man, that hath any Possession, or Enjoyment, of any part of the Dominions of any Government, doth thereby give his *tacit Consent*, and is as far forth obliged to Obedience to the Laws of that Government, during such Enjoyment, as any one under it; whether this his Possession be of land, to him and his Heirs for ever, or a Lodging only for a week; or whether it be barely travelling freely on the Highway; and in Effect, it reaches as far as the very being of any one within the Territories of that Government.

The function of Locke's argument in the very fluid situation leading up to 1688 was not lost on Mary Astell – it was to disentangle political obligation from dynastic allegiance and break the knot of conflicting oaths undertaken to the Commonwealth, to the Stuarts and, subsequently, to William III. The image of the highwayman was perhaps unfortunate, a sign of rogue government of which Astell made the most. If a highwayman travelling through a territory was deemed, as Locke suggested, by the use of its roads to assent to its form of government, right gives way to might: 'And if mere Power gives a Right to Rule, there can be no such thing as Usurpation; but a Highway-Man so long as he has strength to force, has also a Right to require our Obedience' (*Some Reflections upon Marriage, Occasion'd by the Duke & Duchess of Mazarine's Case*, third edition (London, 1706), p. x)). Astell also invoked the image of the highwayman against Milton '(who was a better Poet than Divine or Politician)', and whose defence of contract in the *Ikonoklastes in Answer to a Book Intitl'd 'Eikon Basilike': The Portraiture of*

Again, if Absolute Sovereignty be not necessary in a State, how comes it to be so in a Family? or if in a Family why not in a State; since no Reason can be alledg'd for the one that will not hold more strongly for the other? If the Authority of the Husband so far as it extends, is sacred and inalienable, why not of the Prince? The Domestic Sovereign is without Dispute Elected, and the Stipulations and Contract are mutual, is it not then partial in Men to the last degree, to contend for, and practise that Arbitrary Dominion in their Families, which they abhor and exclaim against in the State?[18] For if Arbitrary Power is evil in itself, and an improper Method of Governing Rational and Free Agents it ought not to be Practis'd any where; Nor is it less, but rather more mischievous in Families than in Kingdoms, by how much *100000* Tyrants are worse than one.[19] What tho' a Husband can't [xi] deprive a Wife of Life with-

---

his Sacred Majesty in his Solitudes and Sufferings (London, 1649, p. 237) Astell rebuts: 'And if a Thief meets me on the High-way and goes off with my Purse, therefore he has a Right to it, and GOD Approves the Action!' (*Moderation truly Stated*, p. 80). Finally, in *An Impartial Enquiry, into the Causes of Rebellion and Civil War in this Kingdom* (London, 1704) deftly casting her argument against resistance and Lockian self-preservation, Astell uses the image again: 'He who robs upon the High-Way, has his *Prospects*, and *Persuasions*, and *Necessities*; and when he resists the Officers of Justice, he only *means Self-Preservation*' (p. 54).

18 Charles Leslie, in his 'Supplement', dated 25 March, 1703, 'With a short Account of the *Original of Government*: Compared with the *Schemes* of the *Republicans* and *Whigs*' to *The New Association: Part II. With farther Improvements . . . An Answer to some* Objections *in the Pretended* D. Foe's *Explication in 'the Reflections upon the Shortest Way'* (London and Westminster), gives what is believed to be the first systematic commentary on Locke's *Two Treatises* (Thompson, 1980). There Leslie (pp. 6–7) makes precisely the argument against Locke that Astell makes here, drawing the conclusion that she implies: 'These Men whose chief *Topick* is the *Liberty* of the *People*, and against *Arbitrary Power*, are the most *Absolute* of any other in their *Families*, and so [7] Proportionably, as they rise *Higher* . . . And can any Believe, that a *Tyrant* in a *Family* would not prove the same upon a *Throne*? It has ever prov'd so. And I desire no other *Test* for these Publick *Patrons* for *Liberty*, than to look into their *Conversation* and their *Families*. Then let any Man *Believe* them if he *Can*; and *Trust* them, if he *please*.'

19 Charles Leslie had used this form of words to argue against popular sovereignty (*Rehearsals*, I, no. 51, 21 July 1705 *A View of the Times their Principles and Practices in the First Volume of the Rehearsals* (London, 1708); cited Monod, 1989, 19; Schwoerer, 1993, 236): 'To cure the *Tyranny* of a *King*, by setting up the *People*, is setting 10000 *Tyrants* over us, instead of *One*. It is *Hell* broke *Loose*, worse than the worst of the *Devils*. And besides, it Admits of no *Remedy*. We have no *Prospect* of the *End*. There is nothing but Eternal *Revolution* and *Confusion*, in Advancing the Power of the *People*. One *Party* WORRYING *Another*; and *Another* UNDER-MINING, and then WORRYING *That*. For each *Party* are equally the *People*. As it is now in *Poland*. And as it was in *England*, before the *Restoration* 1660.'

out being responsible to the Law, he may however do what is much more grievous to a generous Mind, render Life miserable, for which she has no Redress, scarce Pity which is afforded to every other Complainant. It being thought a Wife's Duty to suffer everything without Complaint. If *all Men are born free*, how is it that all Women are born slaves?[20] as they must be if the being subjected to the *inconstant, uncertain, unknown, arbitrary Will* of Men, be the *perfect*

It is noteworthy that Astell gives the number of tyrants as 100,000. But Leslie gives it as 10,000, referring perhaps to the figure mentioned by Aristotle in the *Politics* (2.1.12, 1262a1–10) with reference to Plato's communal *Republic*, where he argues that it were better to have a nephew who was truly a nephew than parents who numbered anywhere from 2,000 to 10,000.

[20] I thank John Pocock for his verbal query about the status of the word 'slave' here. My answer is that it must be ironic. Astell denied Locke's claim to one's property in one's person; a claim that applied in his day only to men. In Locke this right is crucially important in the negative: as the incapacity of individuals (men) to incur hereditable impediments to their freedom or voluntarily to enter into slavery. To the extent that a positive right was entailed it was part of a package tailored by Locke to undermine hereditable monarchy. Since Astell denied property in one's person, vouched for in Locke by the right to real property (a right to which women were denied) she could not technically argue the slavery of women compared with the freedom of men. Nor does she seriously attempt to do so. This marks a difference between her work and that of Judith Drake, often attributed to her, who seriously advances a comparison between early modern married women and 'our Negroes in our Western Plantations'. See Judith Drake, *An Essay in Defence of the Female Sex* (1696) p. 22.

Astell's famous aphorism would seem to be made with direct reference to Locke's *Two Treatises*. The *First Treatise* sets out to rebut Sir Robert Filmer's *Patriarcha*, founded, Locke claims (Book I, Chapter 1, Section 2, 1988, p. 142), on two principles, the first '*That all Government is absolute Monarchy*'; the second '*That no Man is Born free.*' To the refutation of these principles the entire *First Treatise* is dedicated. The principle that 'men are born free' is asserted in the *Second Treatise* at Sections 4, 22, 87, 95, 113 etc. Locke was by no means the only thinker of his day to make the case for liberty as a birthright, renowned among the radical sects (Thomas, 1958, 50). Charles Leslie's *New Association*, responding to Lockian ideas, inveighs against 'that *Whig-Principle* (strenuously Asserted in this *Pamphlet*) That all Men are Born *Free*' (p. 10), referring to the pamphlet, *The Danger of Priest-craft to Religion and Government* (London, 1702) by John Dennis (1657–1734). Locke's contemporary Gilbert Burnet, author of the 1689 tract, *An Enquiry into the Measures of Submission to the Supream Authority: And of the Grounds upon which it may be Lawful or necessary for Subjects, to defend their Religion, Lives and Liberties* (London), was also a possible source for Astell. The most liberal of all his writings, published before Locke's *Two Treatises* (1690), this work appears to be the source for Astell's later sarcastic reference to '*my Lord of Salisbury*' in *A Fair Way with the Dissenters and their Patrons* (London, 1704, p. 16). Burnet's work begins by specifically excluding women from the natural right to freedom enjoyed by men, allowing voluntary enslavement, also permitted by Hobbes, but denied by Locke and Astell (*An Enquiry*, p. 53).

Condition of Slavery?[21] and if the Essence of Freedom consists, as our Masters say it does, in having a *standing Rule to live by?*[22] And why is Slavery so much condemn'd and strove against in one Case, and so highly applauded and held so necessary and so sacred in another?

'is true that GOD told *Eve* after the Fall that *her Husband shou'd Rule over her:*[23] And so it is that he told *Esau* by the mouth of *Isaac* his Father, that he shou'd serve his *younger Brother*, and shou'd in time, and when he was strong enough to do it, *break the Yoke from off his Neck.*[24] Now why one Text shou'd be a Command any more than the other, and not both of them be Predictions only; or why the former shou'd prove *Adam's* natural Right to Rule,[25] and much

---

[21] Astell echoes two different sections of Locke's *Two Treatises*. The first is Book II, Section 22 (1988, pp. 283–4): 'A Liberty to follow my own Will in all things, where the Rule prescribes not; and not to be subject to the inconstant, uncertain, unknown, Arbitrary Will of another Man.' The second is Book II, Section 149 (1988, p. 367): 'For no Man, or Society of Men, having a Power to deliver up their *Preservation*, or consequently the means of it, to the Absolute Will and arbitrary Dominion of another; whenever any one shall go about to bring them into such a Slavish Condition, they will always have a right to preserve what they have not a Power to part with; and to rid themselves of those who invade this Fundamental, Sacred and unalterable law of *Self-Preservation*, for which they enter'd Society.'

In *The Christian Religion as Profess'd by a Daughter of the Church of England* (London, 1705, p. 133), Astell quotes this passage from the *Two Treatises* with acknowledgement '139. Suppose our Enemy is a Persecutor, and does invade that *Fundamental, Sacred and unalterable Law of Self-Preservation*, as some call it. *(Two Treatises of Government, B.2, S.149)*.'

[22] This is clearly a paraphrase of Locke's *Second Treatise*, Book II Section 22 (1988, pp. 283–4): '*Freedom* then is not what Sir *R. F.* tells us, *O. A.*55 [244]. *A Liberty for every one to do what he lists, to live as he pleases, and not to be tyed by any Laws*: But *Freedom of Men under Government*, is, to have a standing Rule to live by, common to every one of that Society, and made by the Legislative Power erected in it.'

[23] Genesis 3:16.

[24] Genesis 27:40.

[25] This is Robert Filmer's argument, of which Locke's is simply the reverse. Astell attacks both of them for deducing a right from a fact – in Locke's case the fact from which the subordination of women is inferred is their lack of property. The title of Adam to sovereignty is Filmer's claim that Locke submits to extensive scrutiny in the *First Treatise*, Chapters, 5, 6, etc. His conclusion, after a review of the relevant biblical passages, 'viz. 1 *Gen.* 28. and 3. *Gen.* 16', is worth noting (Locke, *First Treatise*, Chapter 5, Section 49, 1988, p. 176): 'one whereof signifies only the Subjection of the Inferior Ranks of Creatures to Mankind, and the other the Subjection that is due from a Wife to her Husband, both far enough from that which Subjects owe the Governours of Political Societies'.

less every Man's, any more than the latter is a Proof of *Jacob's* Right to Rule, and of *Esau's* to Rebel, one is yet to learn? The Text in both Cases foretelling what wou'd be; but, [*err.* in] neither of them determining what ought to be.

But the Scripture commands *Wives to submit themselves to their own Husbands.* True; for which St. *Paul* gives a Mystical Reason (Eph 5.22, etc) and St *Peter* a Prudential and Charitable one (1 St. Pet. 3.) but neither of them derive that Subjection from the Law of Nature. Nay St *Paul*, as if he [xii] foresaw and meant to prevent this Plea, giving directions for their Conduct to Women in general, *I Tim. 2*, when he comes to speak of *Subjection*, he changes his Phrase from *Women* which denotes the whole Sex, to *Woman* which in the New Testament is appropriated to a Wife.

As for his not suffering Women to speak in the Church, no sober Person that I know of pretends to it. That Learned Paraphrast indeed, who lays so much stress on the *Natural Subjection*, provided this Prerogative be secur'd, is willing to give up the other.[26] For he endeavours to prove that Inspir'd Women as well as Men us'd to speak in the Church, and that St. *Paul* does not forbid it, but only takes care that the Women shou'd signifie their Subjection by wearing a Veil. But the Apostle is his own best Expositor, let us therefore compare his Precepts with his Practice, for he was all of a piece, and did not contradict himself. Now by this Comparison we find, that tho' he forbids Women to teach in the Church, and this for several Prudential Reasons, like those he introduces with an *I give my Opinion, and now speak I not the Lord*, and not because of any Law of Nature, or Positive Divine Precept, for that the words *they are Commanded* (1 Cor. 14.24.)[27] are not in the Original, appears from the *Italic* Character, yet he did not found this Prohibition on any suppos'd want of Understanding in Woman, or of ability to Teach; neither does he confine them at all times to *learn in silence*. For the Eloquent *Apollos* who was himself a Teacher, was instructed by *Priscilla* as well as by her Husband *Aquila*, and was improv'd by them both in the Christian Faith.[28] Nor does St. *Paul* blame her for this, or suppose that she *Usurp'd Authority* over that great *Man*, so far from this, that as she is always honourably mention'd [xiii]

[26] Probably William Nicholls, but it could also be Filmer.
[27] Hill (1986, 77 n.3) notes that this citation is in fact to 1 Corinthians 14:34
[28] Acts 18, 24 and 26.

in Holy Scripture, so our Apostle in his Salutations, *Rom 16.* places her in the Front, even before her Husband, giving to her as well as to him, the Noble Title of his *Helper in Christ Jesus*, and of one *to whom all the Churches of the Gentiles* had great Obligations.[29]

But it will be said perhaps, that in 1 *Tim. 2. 13*, etc. St *Paul* argues for the Woman's subjection from the Reason of things. To this I answer, that it must be confess'd that this (according to the vulgar Interpretation) is a very obscure place, and I shou'd be glad to see a Natural, and not a Forc'd Interpretation given of it by those who take it Literally. Whereas if it be taken Allegorically, with respect to the Mystical Union between Christ and his Church, to which St. *Paul* frequently accommodates the Matrimonial Relation, the difficulties vanish. For the Earthly *Adam's* being *Form'd* before *Eve*, seems as little to prove her Natural Subjection to him, as the Living Creatures, Fishes, Birds and Beasts being Form'd before them both, proves that Mankind must be subject to these Animals. Nor can the Apostle mean that *Eve* only sinned; or that she only was *Deceiv'd*, for if *Adam* sinn'd wilfully and knowingly, he became the greater Transgressor. But it is very true that the Second *Adam*, the Man Christ Jesus, *was first form'd*, and then his Spouse the Church. He was not in any respect *Deceiv'd*, nor does she pretend to Infallibility. And from this second *Adam*, promis'd to *Eve* in the Day of our first Parent's Transgression, and from Him only, do all their Race, Men as well as Women, derive their Hopes of Salvation. Nor is it promis'd to either Sex on any other Terms besides Perseverance in *Faith, Charity, Holiness and Sobriety.*

If the Learned will not admit of this Interpretation I know not how to contend with them. For Sense [xiv] is a Portion that GOD Himself has been pleas'd to distribute to both Sexes with an Impartial Hand, but Learning is what Men have engross'd to themselves, and one can't but admire their great Improvements! For after doubting whether there was such a thing as Truth, and after many hundred years Disputes about it, in the last Century an extraordinary Genius arose,[30] (whom yet some are pleas'd to call a Visionary)

---

[29] Romans 16:3–4.
[30] The quotation that follows comes from Nicolas Malebranche's *De la recherche de la verité* (1678). It represents a variation of Malebranche's general thesis on the 'presumptuous *Pride* of some of the *Learned*', as stated in his Preface ('L'orgueil de certains Sçavans', p. ix, Fourth edition, p. v), and more specifically in Part II,

enquir'd after it, and laid down the best Method of finding it. Not to the general liking of the Men of Letters, perhaps, because it was wrote in a vulgar Language, and was so natural and easy as to debase Truth to Common Understandings, shewing too plainly that Learning and true Knowledge are two very different things. 'For it often happens (says that Author) that Women and Children acknowledge the Falsehood of those Prejudices we contend with, because they do not dare to judge without examination, and they bring all the attention they are capable of to what they reade. Whereas on the contrary, the Learned continue wedded to their own Opinions, because they will not take the trouble of examining what is contrary to their receiv'd Doctrines.'

Sciences indeed have been invented and taught long ago, and, as Men grew better advis'd, new Modell'd. So that it is become a considerable piece of Learning to give an account of the Rise and Progress of the Sciences, and of the various Opinions of Men concerning them. But Certainty and Demonstration are much pretended to in this present Age, and being obtain'd in many things, 'tis hop'd Men will never Dispute them away in that which is of greatest Importance, the Way of Salvation. And because there is not any thing more certain than what is delivered in the Oracles of GOD, we come now to consider what they offer in favour of our Sex.

[xv] Let it be premis'd, (according to the Reasoning of a very Ingenious Person in a like Case) that One Text for us, is more to be regarded than many against us. Because that *One* being different from what Custom has establish'd, ought to be taken with Philosophical Strictness; whereas the *Many* being express'd according to the vulgar Mode of Speech, ought to have no greater stress laid on them, than that evident Condescension will bear.[31] One place then

---

Chapter 1 'Concerning the Imagination': 'But this is enough to be said of Women and Children, That as they are not concern'd with searching after Truth and the Instruction of others; so their Errors do not occasion much Prejudice; since little credit is given to things by them advanc'd.' See T. Taylor's translation, *Father Malebranche his Treatise Concerning the Search after Truth*, p. 64, which accurately translates Malebranche (*De la recherche*, p. 106). Mary Astell's version is a somewhat free rendering of Taylor and of the other available English translation, *Malebranche's Search After Truth: Or a Treatise of the Nature of the Humane Mind*, 2 vols. (London, 1694, 1695), vol. I, p. 162, which translates the same passage.

[31] This could be William Nicholls, it could be Filmer and it could even be Locke, of whom she uses the phraseology 'according to the Reasoning of a very Ingenious Person in a like Case' elsewhere. All of them could be accused of philosophically

were sufficient, but we have many Instances wherein Holy Scripture considers Women very differently from what they appear in the common Prejudices of Mankind.

The World will hardly allow a Woman to say any thing well, unless as she borrows it from Men, or is assisted by them: But GOD Himself allows that the Daughters of *Zelophehad spake right*, and passes their Request into a Law.[32] Considering how much the Tyranny shall I say, or the superior Force of Men, keeps Women from Acting in the World, or doing any thing considerable, and remembring withal the conciseness of the Sacred Story, no small part of it is bestow'd in transmitting the History of Women famous in their Generations: Two of the Canonical Books bearing the Names of those great Women whose Vertues and Actions are there recorded. *Ruth* being call'd from among the *Gentiles* to be an Ancestor of the Messiah, and *Esther* being rais'd up by GOD to be the great Instrument of the Deliverance and Prosperity of the Jewish Church.

The Character of *Isaac*, tho' one of the most blameless Men taken notice of in the Old Testament, must give place to *Rebecca's*, whose Affections are more Reasonably plac'd than his, her Favourite Son being the same who was GOD's Favourite. Nor was the Blessing bestow'd according to his but to her Desire; so that if [xvi] you will not allow, that her Command to *Jacob* superseded *Isaac's* to *Esau*, his desire to give the Blessing to this Son, being evidently an effect of his Partiality: You must at least grant that she paid greater deference to the Divine Revelation, and for this Reason at least, had a Right to oppose her Husband's Design; which it seems *Isaac* was sensible of when upon his Disappointment he *trembled so exceedingly*.[33] And so much notice is taken even of *Rebecca's* Nurse that we have an account where she Died and where she was Buried.[34]

GOD is pleas'd to record it among His Favours to the Ingrateful Jews, that He sent before them His Servants *Moses, Aaron*, and *MIRIAM*; who was also a Prophetess, and Instructed the Women how to bear their part with *Moses* in his Triumphal Hymn. Is she to be blam'd for her Ambition? and is not the High Priest *Aaron* also? who has his share in the Reproof as well as in the Crime; nor

privileging a given text, although each of them different texts, and considering the rest custom.

[32] Numbers 27:2.
[33] Genesis 25, 26, 27.
[34] Genesis 24:59 and 35:8.

cou'd she have mov'd Sedition if she had not been a considerable Person, which appears also by the Respect the People paid her, in deferring their Journey till she was ready.[35]

Where shall we find a nobler piece of Poetry than *Deborah's* Song? or a better and greater Ruler than that Renowned Woman whose Government so much excell'd that of the former Judges? And tho' she had a Husband, she her self Judg'd *Israel* and consequently was his Sovereign, of whom we know no more than the Name.[36] Which Instance, as I humbly suppose, overthrows the pretence of *Natural Inferiority*. For it is not the bare Relation of a Fact, by which none ought to be concluded, unless it is conformable to a Rule, and to the Reason of things: But *Deborah's* Government was confer'd on her by GOD Himself. Consequently the Sovereignty of a Woman is not contrary to the [xvii] Law of Nature; for the Law of Nature is the Law of GOD, who cannot contradict Himself; and yet it was GOD who Inspir'd and Approv'd that great Woman, raising her up to Judge and to Deliver His People *Israel*.

Not to insist on the Courage of that valiant Woman who deliver'd *Thebez* by slaying the Assailant;[37] nor upon the preference which GOD thought fit to give to *Sampson's* Mother, in sending the Angel to her, and not to her Husband, whose vulgar Fear she so prudently answer'd, as plainly shews her superior Understanding:[38] To pass over *Abigail's* wise conduct, whereby she preserv'd her Family and deserv'd *David's* acknowledgments, for restraining him from doing a Rash and unjustifiable Action; the Holy Penman giving her the Character of a *Woman of good Understanding*, whilst her Husband has that of a Churlish and Foolish Person, and a Son of *Belial*:[39] To say nothing of the wise *Woman* (as the Text calls her) of *Tekoah*;[40] or of her of *Abel* who has the same Epithet, and who by her Prudence deliver'd the City and appeas'd a dangerous Rebellion:[41] Nor of the Queen of *Sheba* [err. Sheba] whose Journey to hear the Wisdom of *Solomon*, shews her own good Judgment and great share in that excel-

---

[35] Numbers 12.
[36] Judges 4 and 5.
[37] Judges 9:53.
[38] Judges 13.
[39] I Samuel 25.
[40] II Samuel 14.
[41] II Samuel 20:16–22.

lent Endowment.[42] *Solomon* does not think himself too Wise to be Instructed by his Mother, nor too great to Record her Lessons, which if he had follow'd he might have spar'd the trouble of Repentance, and been deliver'd from a great deal of that Vanity he so deeply Regrets.[43]

What Reason can be assign'd why the Mothers of the Kings of *Judah*, are so frequently noted in those very short accounts that are given of their Reigns, but the great Respect paid them, or perhaps their Influence on the Government, and share in the Administrations. [xviii] This is not improbable, since the wicked *Athaliah* had power to carry on her Intrigues so far as to get possession of the Throne, and to keep it for some Years.[44] Neither was there any necessity for *Asa's* removing his Mother (or Grandmother) from being Queen, if this were merely Titular, and did not carry Power and Authority along with it.[45] And we find what Influence *Jezabel* had in *Israel*, indeed to her Husband's and her own Destruction.[46]

It was a *Widow-Woman* whom GOD made choice of to sustain his Prophet *Elijah at Zarephah*.[47] And the History of the *Shunamite* is a noble Instance of the Account that is made of Women in Holy Scripture. For whether it was not the Custom in *Shunem* for the Husband to Dictate, or whether her's was conscious of her superior Vertue, or whatever was the Reason, we find it is she who Governs, *dwelling* with great Honour and Satisfaction *among her own People*. Which Happiness she understood so well, and was so far from a troublesome Ambition, that she desires no Recommendation to *the King or Captain of the Host* when the Prophet offer'd it, being already greater than they cou'd make her. The Text calls her a *Great Woman*, whilst her Husband is hardly taken notice of, and this no otherwise than as performing the Office of a Bailiff. It is *her* Piety and Hospitality that are Recorded, *She* invites the Prophet to *her House*; who converses with and is entertain'd by *her*. She gives her Husband no account of *her* Affairs any further than to tell him *her* Designs that he may see them Executed. And when he desires to know the reason of her Conduct, all the Answer she affords is,

---

[42] I Kings 10.
[43] I Kings 2.
[44] II Kings 11:1–3.
[45] I Kings 15:13.
[46] I Kings 16:31–3; 18:4; 19:2; 21.
[47] I Kings 17:9.

Well, or as the Margin has it from the Hebrew, *Peace*.[48] Nor can this be thought assuming, since it is no more than what the Prophet encourages, for all his Addresses are [xix] to *her*, he takes no Notice of her Husband. His Benefits are confer'd on *her*, 'tis *she* and *her Household* whom he warns of a Famine, and 'tis *she* who appeals to the King for the Restitution of *her House and Land*.[49] I wou'd not infer from hence that Women generally speaking, ought to govern in their Families when they have a Husband, but I think this Instance and Example is a sufficient Proof, that if by Custom or Contract, or the Laws of the Country, or Birth-right (as in the Case of Sovereign Princesses) they have the supreme Authority, it is no Usurpation, nor do they Act contrary to Holy Scripture, nor consequently to the Law of Nature. For they are no where that I know of forbidden to claim their Just Right: The Apostle 'tis true wou'd not have them *usurp* Authority where Custom and the Law of the strongest had brought them into Subjection, as it has in these parts of the World. Tho' in remoter Regions, if Travellers rightly inform us, the Succession to the Crown is entail'd on the Female Line.

GOD Himself who *is no Respecter of Persons, with whom there is neither Bond nor Free, Male nor Female, but they are all one in Christ Jesus*, did not deny Women that Divine Gift the Spirit of Prophecy, neither under the Jewish nor Christian Dispensation. We have nam'd two great Prophetesses already, *Miriam* and *Deborah*, and besides other Instances, *Huldah* the Prophetess was such an Oracle that the good King *Josiah*, that great Pattern of Vertue, sends even the High Priest himself to consult her, and to receive directions from her in the most arduous Affairs.[50] *It shall come to pass*, saith the Lord, *that I will pour out my Spirit upon all Flesh, and your Sons and your Daughters shall Prophesy*,[51] which was accordingly fulfill'd by the Mission of the Holy [xx] Ghost on the day of *Pentecost*, as St. *Peter* tells us. And besides others, there is mention of four Daughters of *Philip*, Virgins who did Prophesy.[52] For as in the Old, so in the New Testament, Women make a considerable Figure; the Holy Virgin receiving the greatest Honour that Human Nature is capable of, when the Son of

---

[48] II Kings 4.
[49] II Kings 8:1–6.
[50] II Kings, 22:14.
[51] Joel 2:28.
[52] Acts 21:9.

GOD vouchsafed to be her Son and to derive his Humanity from her only. And if it is a greater Blessing *to hear the Word of* GOD *and keep it*, who are more considerable for their Assiduity in this than the Female Disciples of our Lord? *Mary* being Exemplary and receiving a noble Encomium from Him, for her Choice of the better Part.

It wou'd be thought tedious to enumerate all the excellent Women mention'd in the New Testament, whose humble Penitence and ardent Love, as *Magdalen's*; their lively Faith and holy Importunity, as the *Syrophenician's*; extraordinary Piety and Uprightness, as *Elizabeth's*; Hospitality, Charity and Diligence, as *Martha's, Tabitha's*; etc. (see St. *Luc.* 8)[53] frequent and assiduous Devotions and Austerities, as *Anna's*;[54] Constancy and Courage, Perseverance and ardent Zeal, as that of the Holy Women who attended our Lord to His Cross, when His Disciples generally forsook, and the most Courageous had deny'd, Him; are Recorded for our Example. Their Love was stronger than Death, it follow'd our Saviour into the Grave. And as a Reward, both the Angel and even the Lord Himself appears first to them, and sends them to Preach the great Article of the Resurrection to the very Apostles, who being as yet under the Power of the Prejudices of their Sex, esteem'd the Holy Women's *Words as idle Tales and believed them not.*[55]

Some Men will have it, that the Reason of our Lord's appearing first to the Women, was their being [xxi] least able to keep a Secret; a Witty and Masculine Remarque and wonderfully Reverent! But not to dispute whether those Women were Blabs or no, there are many Instances in Holy Scripture of Women who did not betray the Confidence repos'd in them. Thus *Rahab* tho' formerly an ill Woman, being Converted by the *Report* of those Miracles, which tho' the *Israelites saw*, yet they *believ'd not in* GOD, *nor put their Trust in his Word*, She acknowledges the GOD of Heaven, and as a Reward of her faithful Service in concealing *Joshua's* Spies, is with her Family exempted from the Ruine of her Country, and also has the Honor of being nam'd in the Messiah's Genealogy.[56] *Michal* to save *David's* Life exposes her self to the Fury of a Jealous and

---

[53] As Hill (1986, 85 n.4) points out, Mary Astell's references should read Luke 8:2; Mark 7:25–30; Luke 1:5–57; Luke 10:38 and 40; Acts 9:36.
[54] Luke 2:36–8.
[55] Luke 24:11.
[56] Joshua 2 and 6:22–5.

Tyrannical Prince.[57] A Girl was trusted by *David's* Grave Councellors to convey him Intelligence in his Son's Rebellion; and when a Lad had found it out and blab'd it to *Absalom*, the King's Friends confiding in the Prudence and Fidelity of a Woman were secur'd by her.[58] When our Lord escap'd from the Jews, he trusted Himself in the hands of *Martha* and *Mary*.[59] So does St. *Peter* with another *Mary* when the Angel deliver'd him from *Herod*, the Damsel *Rhoda* too was acquainted with the Secret.[60] More might be said, but one wou'd think here is enough to shew, that whatever other Great and Wise Reasons Men may have for despising Women, and keeping them in Ignorance and Slavery, it can't be from their having learnt to do so in Holy Scripture. The Bible is for, and not against us, and cannot without great violence done to it, be urg'd to our Prejudice.

However, there are strong and prevalent Reasons which demonstrate the Superiority and Pre-eminence of the Men. For in the first place, Boys have much Time and Pains, Care and Cost bestow'd on their [xxii] Education, Girls have little or none. The former are early initiated in the Sciences, are made acquainted with Antient and Modern Discoveries, they Study Books and Men, have all imaginable encouragement; not only Fame, a dry Reward now adays, but also Title, Authority, Power, and Riches themselves which purchase all things, are the Reward of their Improvement. The latter are restrain'd, frown'd upon, and beat, not *for* but *from* the Muses; Laughter and Ridicule that never-failing Scare-Crow is set up to drive them from the Tree of Knowledge. But if in spite of all Difficulties Nature prevails, and they can't be kept so ignorant as their Masters wou'd have them, they are star'd upon as Monsters, Censur'd, Envy'd, and every way Discourag'd, or at the best they have the Fate the Proverb assigns them, *Vertue is prais'd and starv'd.* And therefore since the coursest Materials need the most Curing, as every Workman can inform you, and the worst Ground the most elaborate Culture, it undeniably follows, that Men's Understandings are superior to Women's, for after many Years Study and Experience they become Wise and Learned, and Women are not Born so!

[57] II Samuel 3.
[58] II Samuel 17:17–20.
[59] Luke 10:38 and 39.
[60] Acts 12:12–14.

Again, Men are possess'd of all Places of Power, Trust and Profit, they make Laws and exercise the Magistracy, not only the sharpest Sword, but even all the Swords and Blunderbusses are theirs, which by the strongest Logic in the World, gives them the best Title to every thing they please to claim as their Prerogative; who shall contend with them? Immemorial Prescription is on their side in these parts of the World, Antient Tradition and Modern Usage! Our Fathers have all along both Taught and Practis'd Superiority over the weaker Sex, and consequently Women are by Nature inferior to Men, as was to be Demonstrated. [xxiii] An Argument which must be acknowledg'd unanswerable, for as well as I love my Sex, I will not pretend a Reply to *such* Demonstration!

Only let me beg to be inform'd, to whom we poor Fatherless Maids, and Widows who have lost their Masters, owe Subjection? It can't be to all Men in general, unless all Men were agreed to give the same Commands; do we then fall as Strays to the first who finds us? By the Maxims of some Men, and the Conduct of some Women one wou'd think so. But whoever he be that thus happens to become our Master, if he allows us to be Reasonable Creatures, and does not merely Compliment us with that Title, since no Man denies our Readiness to use our Tongues, it wou'd tend, I shou'd think, to our Master's advantage, and therefore he may please to be advis'd to teach us to improve our Reason. But if Reason is only allow'd us by way of Raillery, and the secret Maxim is that we have none, or little more than Brutes, 'tis the best way to confine us with Chain and Block to the Chimney-Corner, which probably might save the Estates of some Families and the Honor of others.

I do not propose this to prevent a Rebellion, for Women are not so well united as to form an Insurrection. They are for the most part Wise enough to Love their Chains, and to discern how very becomingly they set.[61] They think as humbly of themselves as their Masters can wish, with respect to the other Sex, but in regard to their own, they have a Spice of Masculine Ambition, every one wou'd Lead, and none will Follow. Both Sexes being too apt to Envy, and too backward in Emulating, and take more delight in

---

[61] Their chains 'set' in the 1706 Preface, but 'fit' in the 1700 Appendix (p. 175) and the 1730 Appendix (p. 175).

detracting from their Neighbour's Vertue than in improving their own. And therefore as to those Women who find themselves born for Slavery and are so sensible of their own Meanness as to conclude it impossible to attain to [**xxiv**] any thing excellent, since they are, or ought to be best acquainted with their own Strength and Genius, She's a Fool who wou'd attempt their Deliverance or Improvement. No, let them enjoy the great Honor and Felicity of their Tame, Submissive and Depending Temper! Let the Men applaud, and let them Glory in, this wonderful Humility! Let them receive the Flatteries and Grimaces of the other Sex, live unenvy'd by their own, and be as much Belov'd as one such Woman can afford to Love another! Let them enjoy the Glory of treading in the Footsteps of their Predecessors, and of having the Prudence to avoid that audacious attempt of soaring beyond their Sphere! Let them Huswife or Play, Dress and be pretty entertaining Company! Or which is better, relieve the Poor to ease their own Compassions, reade Pious Books, say their Prayers and go to Church, because they have been Taught and Us'd to do so, without being able to give a better Reason for their Faith and Practice! Let them not by any means aspire at being Women of Understanding, because no Man can endure a Woman of Superior Sense, or wou'd treat a reasonable Woman civilly, but that he thinks he stands on higher ground, and that she is so Wise as to make exceptions in his Favour, and to take her Measures by his Directions; they may pretend to Sense indeed, since mere Pretences only render one the more Ridiculous! Let them in short be what is call'd very Women, for this is most acceptable to all sorts of Men; or let them aim at the Title of *Good Devout* Women, since some Men can bear with this; but let them not Judge of the Sex by their own Scantling. For the great Author of Nature and Fountain of all Perfection, never design'd that the Mean and Imperfect, but that the most Compleat and [**xxv**] Excellent of His Creatures in every Kind, shou'd be the Standard to the rest.

To conclude, if that GREAT QUEEN who has subdu'd the Proud, and made the pretended Invincible more than once fly before her; who has Rescu'd an Empire, Reduc'd a Kingdom, Conquer'd Provinces in as little time almost as one can Travel them, and seems to have Chain'd Victory to her Standard; who disposes of Crowns, gives Laws and Liberty to *Europe*, and is the chief Instrument in the Hand of the Almighty to pull down and to set up the Great Men of the Earth; who

Conquers everywhere for others, and no where for her self but in the Hearts of the Conquer'd, who are of the number of those who reap the benefit of her Triumphs; whilst she only reaps for her self the Lawrels of Disinteressed Glory, and the Royal Pleasure of doing Heroically; if this Glory of her own Sex and Envy of the other, will not think we need, or does not hold us worthy of, the Protection of her ever Victorious Arms, and Men have not the Gratitude for her sake at least, to do Justice to her Sex, who has been such a universal Benefactress to theirs: Adieu to the Liberties not of this or that Nation or Region only, but of the Moiety of Mankind! To all the great things that Women might perform, Inspir'd by her Example, Encourag'd by her Smiles, and supported by her Power! To their Discovery of New Worlds for the Exercise of her Goodness, New Sciences to publish her Fame, and reducing Nature itself to a Subjection to her Empire! To their destroying those worst of Tyrants Impiety and Immorality, which dare to stalk about even in her own Dominions, and to devour Souls almost within view of her Throne, leaving a stench behind them scarce to be corrected even by the Incense of her Devotions! To the Women's tracing a new Path to Honor, [xxvi] in which none shall walk but such as scorn to Cringe in order to Rise, and who are Proof both against giving and receiving Flattery! In a word, to those Halcyon, or if you will *Millennium* Days, in which the Wolf and the Lamb shall feed together, and a Tyrannous Domination which Nature never meant, shall no longer render useless if not hurtful, the Industry and Understandings of half Mankind!

[i] Some Reflections upon Marriage

Curiosity, which is sometimes an occasion of Good, and too frequently of Mischief, by disturbing either our Own, or our Neighbour's Repose, having put me upon reading the *Duke and Dutchess of Mazarine's Case;*[1] I thought an Afternoon wou'd not be quite thrown away in pursuing some Reflections that it occasion'd. The Name of *Mazarine* is considerable enough to draw the Eyes of the Curious, and when one remembers what a noise it had [*err.* once] made in *Europe*, what Politick Schemes have been laid, what vast Designs brought about by the Cardinal that bore it; how well his measures were concerted for the Grandeur of that Nation into which he was transplanted, and that he wanted neither Power nor Inclination to establish his own Family and make it as considerable as [2] any Subject's could possible be, and what Honours and Riches he had heap'd together in order to this; one cannot but enquire how it comes about that he should be so defeated in this last design? and that those to whom he intrusted his Name and Treasure, should make a figure so very different from what might have been expected from them? And tho' one had not Piety enough to make a Religious

---

[1] The considerable literature on the Mazarin divorce, running in some cases to several editions, includes the *Memoires de Madame la Duchesse de Mazarin* (Cologne, n.d.). The *Memoires* have two English editions: *The Memoires of the Dutchess Mazarine. Written in French by her Own Hand, and Done into English by P. Porter, Esq; Together with the Reasons of her Coming into England. Likewise, A Letter containing a True Character of her Person and Conversation* (London, 1676); and the *Memoirs of the Dutchess of Mazarine: Written in her Name by The Abbott of St Réal, with a Letter Containing a True Character of Her Person and Conversation* (n.p., 1713).

Reflection, yet Civil Prudence would almost enforce them to say, that *Man being in Honour has no Understanding, but is compar'd unto the Beasts that perish.* He Blesseth his Soul, and thinks himself a happy Man, imagining his House will endure for ever, and that he has establish'd his Name and Family. But how wise soever he may be in other respects, in this he acts no better than the Ignorant and Foolish. For as he carries nothing away with him when he dies, so neither will his Pomp and Glory descend as he intended. Generous and Worthy Actions only can secure him from Oblivion, or what is worse, being remembred with Contempt; so little reason have we to Envy any Man's Wealth and Greatness, but much to Emulate his Wisdom and Vertue.

The Dutchess of *Mazarine's* Name has spread perhaps as far as her Uncle's and [3] one can't help wishing that so much Wit and Beauty, so much Politeness and Address, has been accompany'd and supported by more valuable and lasting Qualities; one cannot but desire that her Advocate instead of recriminating had clear'd the imputations laid on her, and that she her self, who says enough in her Memoirs to shew she was unfortunate, had said more to prove her self discreet. They must be highly ill-natur'd who do not pity her ill Fortune at the same time that they must blame her Conduct, and regret that such a Treasure should fall into his hands who was not worthy of it, nor knew how to value and improve it; that she who was capable of being a great Ornament to her Family and Blessing to the Age she liv'd in, should only serve (to say no worse) as an unhappy Shipwrack to point out the dangers of an ill Education and unequal Marriage.

Monsieur *Mazarine* is not to be justified, nor Madam his Spouse excus'd. It is no question which is most Criminal, the having no Sense, or the abuse of a liberal Portion; nor any hard matter to determine who is most to be pity'd he whom Nature never qualify'd for great things, who therefore can't be very sensible of great Misfortunes; or she, who being capable of every thing must therefore [4] suffer more and be the more lamented. To be yok'd for Life to a disagreeable Person and Temper; to have Folly and Ignorance tyrannize over Wit and Sense; to be contradicted in every thing one does or says, and bore down not by Reason but Authority; to be denied ones most innocent desires, for no other cause but the Will and Pleasure of an absolute Lord and Master, whose Follies a

Woman with all her Prudence cannot hide, and whose Commands she cannot but despise at the same time she obeys them; is a misery none can have a just Idea of, but those who have felt it.

These are great Provocations, but nothing can justify the revenging the Injuries we receive from others, upon our selves: The Italian Proverb shews a much better way;[2] *If you would be reveng'd of your Enemies, live well.* Had *Madam Mazarine's* Education made a right Improvement of her Wit and Sense, we should not have found her seeking Relief by such imprudent, not to say scandalous Methods, as the running away in Disguise with a spruce Cavalier, and rambling to so many Courts and Places, nor diverting her self with such Childish, Ridiculous, or Ill-natur'd Amusements, as the greatest part of the Adventures in her Memoirs are made up of. True Wit consists not meerly in doing [5] or saying what is out of the way, but in such surprizing things as are fit and becoming the person from whom they come. That which stirs us up to Laughter most commonly excites our Contempt; to please and to make Merry are two very different Talents. But what Remedies can be administred, what Relief expected, when Devotion, the only true Support in Distress, is turn'd into Ridicule? Unhappy is that Grandeur which makes us too great to be good; and that Wit which sets us at a distance from true Wisdom. Even Bigotry it self, as contemptible as it is, is preferable to Prophane Wit; for *that* only requires our Pity, but *this* deserves our Abhorrence.

A Woman who seeks Consolation under Domestic troubles from the Gaieties of a Court, from Gaming and Courtship, from Rambling and odd Adventures, and the Amusements meer [*err.* mixt] Company affords, may Plaister up the Sore, but will never heal it; nay, which is worse, she makes it Fester beyond a possibility of Cure. She justifies the Injury her Husband has done her, by shewing that whatever other good Qualities she may have, Discretion, one of the Principal, is wanting. She may be Innocent, but she can never prove she is so, all that Charity can do for her when she's Censur'd is [6] only to be silent, it can make no Apologies for suspicious Actions. An ill Husband may deprive a Wife of the comfort and quiet of her Life; may give her occasion of exercising her

---

[2] Proverb given in the Italian in the first edition (*Some Reflections upon Marriage, Occasion'd by the Duke & Dutchess of Mazarine's Case* (London, 1700), p. 5): '*Vuoi far vendetta del tuo nemico governati bene*'; but not in the fourth (1730, p. 6).

Virtue, may try her Patience and Fortitude to the utmost, but that's all he can do: 'tis her self only can accomplish her Ruin. Had Madam *Mazarine's* Reserve been what it ought to be, Monsieur *Herard*[3] needed not to have warded off so carefully, the nice Subject of the Lady's Honour, nor her Advocate have strain'd so hard for Colours to excuse such Actions as will hardly bear 'em; a Man indeed shews the best side of his Wit, tho' the worst of his Integrity, when he has an ill Cause to manage. Truth is bold and vehement; she depends upon her own strength, and so she be plac'd in a true Light, thinks it not necessary to use Artifice and Address as a Recommendation; but the prejudices of Men have made them necessary: their Imagination gets the better of their Understanding, and more judge according to Appearances, than search after the Truth of Things.

What an ill Figure does a Woman make with all the Charms of her Beauty and Sprightliness of her Wit, with all her good Humour and insinuating Address; tho' she be the best Economist in the World, the most entertaining Conversation; if she [7] remit her Guard, abate in the Severity of her Caution and Strictness of her Vertue, and neglect those Methods which are necessary to keep her not only from a Crime, but from the very suspicion of one.

Are the being forbid having Comedies in her House, an ill natur'd Jest, dismissing of a Servant, imposing Domestics, or frequent changing them, sufficient Reasons to Authorize a Woman's leaving her Husband and breaking from the strongest Bands, exposing her self to Temptations and Injuries from the Bad, to the contempt, or at the best to the pity of the Good, and the just Censure of all? A Woman of sense one would think should take little satisfaction in the Cringes and Courtship of her Adorers, even when she is single; but it is Criminal in a Wife to admit them: interested Persons may call it Gallantry, but with the modest and discreet it is like to have a harder Name, or else Gallantry will pass for a scandalous thing, not to be allow'd among Vertuous Persons.

---

[3] Astell refers to the published arguments for the defence on either side, bound together: *Plaidoyez de Mr Herard pour Monsieur le Duc de Mazarin contre Madame la Duchesse de Mazarin son epouse; et le factum pour Madame la Duchesse de Mazarin contre Monsieur le Duc de Mazarin son mari par Mr de St Evremont* (1698). Astell probably read it in the English edition: *The Arguments of Mons. Herard for the Duke of Mazarin Against the Dutchess, his Spouse, and the Factum for the Dutchess by Mons. St Evremont*, trans. from French (1699) (see Hill, 1986, 91).

But Madam *Mazarine* is dead, may her Faults die with her; may there be no more occasion given for the like Adventures, or if there is, may the Ladies be more Wise and Good than to take it! Let us see then from whence the mischief proceeds, and try if it can be prevented; for certainly [8] Men may be very happy in a Married State; 'tis their own fault if they are at any time otherwise.[4] The wise Institutor of Matrimony never did any thing in vain; we are the Sots and Fools if what he design'd for our Good, be to us an occasion of falling. For Marriage, notwithstanding all the loose talk of the Town, the Satyrs of Ancient or Modern pretenders to Wit, will never lose its due praise from judicious Persons. Tho' much may be said against this or that Match, tho' the Ridiculousness of some, the Wickedness of others and Imprudence of too many, too often provoke our wonder or scorn, our indignation or pity, yet Marriage in general is too sacred to be treated with Disrespect, too venerable to be the subject of Raillery and Buffonery. It is the Institution of Heaven, the only Honourable way of continuing Mankind, and far be it from us to think there could have been a better than infinite Wisdom has found out for us.

But upon what are the Satyrs against Marriage grounded? Not upon the State itself, if they are just, but upon the ill Choice, or foolish Conduct of those who are in it, and what has Marriage, considered in its self, to do with these? Let every Man bear his own Burden: If through inordinate Passion, Rashness, [9] Humour, Pride, Covetousness, or any the like Folly, a Man makes an Imprudent Choice, Why should Marriage be exclaim'd against? Let him blame himself for entring into an unequal Yoke, and making Choice of one who perhaps may prove a Burthen, a Disgrace and Plague, instead of a Help and Comfort to him. Could there be no such thing as an happy Marriage, Arguments against Marriage would hold good, but since the thing is not only possible, but even very probable, provided we take but competent Care, Act like Wise Men and Christians, and acquit our selves as we ought, all we have to say against it serves only to shew the Levity or Impiety of our own Minds; we only make some flourishes of Wit, tho' scarce without

---

[4] This sentence in the first edition is cast in the singular, beginning 'Man' (*Reflections*, 1700, p. 8).

Injustice; and tho' we talk prettily it is but very little to the purpose.

Is it the being ty'd to *One* that offends us? Why this ought rather to recommend Marriage to us, and would really do so, were we guided by Reason, and not by Humour or brutish Passion. He who does not make Friendship the chief inducement to his Choice, and prefer it before any other consideration, does not deserve a good Wife, and therefore should not complain if he goes without one. Now we can never grow weary of our Friends; the [10] longer we have had them the more they are endear'd to us; and if we have One well assur'd, we need seek no further, but are sufficiently happy in Her. The love of Variety in this and in other cases, shews only the ill Temper of our own Minds, in that we seek for *settled* Happiness in this present World, where it is not to be found, instead of being Content with a competent share, chearfully enjoying and being thankful for the Good that is afforded us, and patiently bearing with the Inconveniences that attend it.

The Christian Institution of Marriage provides the best that may be for Domestic Quiet and Content, and for the Education of Children; so that if we were not under the tye of Religion, even the Good of Society and civil Duty would oblige us to what that requires at our Hands. And since the very best of us are but poor frail Creatures, full of Ignorance and Infirmity, so that in Justice we ought to tolerate each other, and exercise that Patience towards our Companions to Day, which we shall give them occasion to shew towards us to Morrow, the more we are accustom'd to any one's Conversation, the better shall we understand their Humour, be more able to comply with their Weakness and less offended at it. For he who would have every [11] one submit to his Humours and will not in his turn comply with them, tho' we should suppose him always in the Right, whereas a Man of this temper very seldom is so, he's not fit for a Husband, scarce fit for Society, but ought to be turn'd out of the Herd to live by himself.

There may indeed be inconveniences in a Married Life; but is there any Condition without them? And he who lives single that he may indulge Licentiousness and give up himself to the conduct of wild and ungovern'd Desires, or indeed out of any other inducement, than the Glory of GOD and the Good of his Soul, through the prospect he has of doing more Good, or because his frame and disposition of Mind are fitted for it, may rail as he pleases against Matrimony, but can never justifie his own Conduct, nor clear it from the imputation of Wickedness and Folly.

But if Marriage be such a blessed State, how comes it, may you say, that there are so few happy Marriages? Now in answer to this, it is not to be wonder'd that so few succeed, we should rather be surpriz'd to find so many do, considering how imprudently Men engage, the Motives they act by, and the very strange Conduct they observe throughout.

[12] For pray, what do Men propose to themselves in Marriage? What Qualifications do they look after in a Spouse? What will she bring is the first enquiry? How many Acres? Or how much ready Coin? Not that this is altogether an unnecessary Question, for Marriage without a Competency, that is, not only a bare Subsistence, but even a handsome and plentiful Provision, according to the Quality and Circumstances of the Parties, is no very comfortable Condition. They who marry for Love as they call it, find time enough to repent their rash Folly, and are not long in being convinc'd, that whatever fine Speeches might be made in the heat of Passion, there could be no *real Kindness* between those who can agree to make each other miserable. But as an Estate is to be consider'd, so it should not be the *Main*, much less the *Only* consideration, for Happiness does not depend on Wealth, *that* may be wanting, and too often is, where *this* abounds. He who Marries himself to a Fortune only, must expect no other satisfaction than that can bring him, but let him not say that Marriage but that his own Covetous or Prodigal Temper, has made him unhappy. What Joy has that Man in all his Plenty, who must either run from home to possess it, [13] contrary to all the Rules of Justice, to the Laws of GOD and Man, nay, even in opposition to Good nature, and Good breeding too, which some Men make more account of than all the rest; or else be forc'd to share it with a Woman whose Person or Temper is disagreeable, whose presence is sufficient to sour all his Enjoyments, so that if he has any remains of Religion, or Good manners, he must suffer the uneasiness of a continual watch, to force himself to a constrain'd Civility!

Few Men have so much Goodness as to bring themselves to a liking of what they loath'd, meerly because it is their Duty to like; on the contrary, when they Marry with an indifferency, to please

their Friends or encrease their Fortune, the indifferency proceeds
to an aversion, and perhaps even the kindness and complaisance of
the poor abus'd Wife shall only serve to encrease it. What follows
then? There is no content at home, so it is sought elsewhere, and
the Fortune so unjustly got, is as carelessly squander'd. The Man
takes a loose, what shou'd hinder him? He has all in his hands, and
Custom has almost taken off that small Restraint Reputation us'd
to lay. The Wife finds too late what was the Idol the Man adored
[14] which her Vanity perhaps, or it may be the Commands and
importunities of Relations, wou'd not let her see before; and now
he has got *that* into his possession, she must make court to him for
a little sorry Alimony out of her own Estate. If Discretion and Piety
prevails upon her Passions she sits down quietly, contented with
her lot, seeks no Consolation in the Multitude of Adorers, since he
whom only she desir'd to please, because it was her duty to do so,
will take no delight in her Wit or Beauty: She follows no Diversion
to allay her Grief, uses no Cordials to support her Spirit, that may
sully her Vertue or bring a Cloud upon her Reputation, she makes
no appeals to the mis-judging Croud, hardly mentions her Misfortunes to her most intimate Acquaintance, nor lays a load on her
Husband to ease her self, but wou'd if it were possible conceal his
Crimes, tho' her Prudence and Vertue give him a thousand Reproaches without her Intention or knowledge; and retiring from the
World, she seeks a more solid Comfort than it can give her, taking
care to do nothing that Censoriousness or even Malice itself can
misconstrue to her prejudice. Now she puts on all her Reserves,
and thinks even innocent Liberties scarce [15] allowable in her Dis-
consolate State; she has other Business to mind: Nor does she in
her Retirements reflect so much upon the hand that administers
this bitter Cup, as consider what is the best use she can make of it.
And thus indeed Marriage, however unfortunate in other respects,
becomes a very great Blessing to her. She might have been exposed
to all the Temptations of a plentiful Fortune, have given up her
self to Sloth and Luxury, and gone on at the common rate even of
the better sort, in doing no hurt, and as little good: But now her
kind Husband obliges her to *Consider*, and gives opportunity to
exercise her Vertue; he makes it necessary to withdraw from those
Gaieties and Pleasures of Life, which do more mischief under the
Shew of Innocency, than they cou'd if they appear'd attended with

a Crime, discomposing and dissolving the Mind, and making it uncapable of any manner of good, to be sure of any thing Great and Excellent. Silence and Solitude, the being forc'd from the ordinary Entertainments of her Station, may perhaps seem a desolate condition at first, and we may allow her, poor weak Woman! to be somewhat shock'd at it, since even a wise and courageous Man perhaps would not keep his ground. We [16] would conceal if we could for the Honour of the Sex, Men's being baffled and dispirited by a smaller Matter, were not the Instances too frequent and too notorious.

But a little time wears off all the uneasiness, and puts her in possession of Pleasures, which till now she has unkindly been kept a stranger to. Affliction, the sincerest Friend, the frankest Monitor, the best Instructer, and indeed the only useful School that Women are ever put to, rouses her understanding, opens her Eyes, fixes her Attention, and diffuses such a Light, such a Joy into her Mind, as not only Informs her better, but Entertains her more than ever her *Ruel*[5] did tho', crouded by the Men of Wit. She now distinguishes between Truth and Appearances, between solid and apparent Good; has found out the instability of all Earthly Things, and won't any more be deceiv'd by relying on them; can discern who are the Flatterers of her Fortune, and who the Admirers and Encouragers of her Vertue; accounting it no little blessing to be rid of those Leeches, who only hung upon her for their own Advantage. Now sober Thoughts succeed to hurry and impertinence, to Forms and Ceremony, she can secure her Time, and knows how to [17] Improve it; never truly a Happy Woman till she came in the Eye of the World to be reckon'd Miserable.

Thus the Husband's Vices may become an occasion of the Wife's Vertues, and his Neglect do her a more real Good than his Kindness could. But all injur'd Wives don't behave themselves after this Fashion, nor can their Husbands justly expect it. With what Face can he blame her for following his Example, and being as extravagant on the one Hand, as he is on the other? Tho' she cannot justifie

---

[5] 'A bedroom, where ladies of fashion in the seventeenth and eighteenth centuries, especially in France, held a morning reception for persons of distinction; hence, a reception of this kind' *Oxford English Dictionary*. Also an obsolete verb 'to fall', from O.F. 'rueler, roeler, rouler', 'to roll' (*ibid.*), and perhaps involving a pun in this context.

her Excesses to GOD, to the World, nor to her self, yet surely in respect of him they may admit of an excuse. For to all the rest of his Absurdities, (for Vice is always unreasonable,) he adds one more, who expects that Vertue from another which he won't practise himself.

But suppose a Man does not Marry for Money, tho' for one that does not, perhaps there are thousands that do; let him Marry for Love, an Heroick Action, which makes a mighty noise in the World, partly because of its rarity, and partly in regard of its extravagancy, and what does his Marrying for Love amount to? There's no great odds between his Marrying for the Love of Money, or for the Love of Beauty, the Man does not act according to Reason [18] in either Case, but is govern'd by irregular Appetites. But he loves her Wit perhaps, and this you'll say is more Spiritual, more refin'd; not at all if you examine it to the Bottom. For what is that which now adays passes under the name of Wit? A bitter and ill-natur'd Raillery, a pert Repartee, or a confident talking at all, and in such a multitude of Words, it's odds if something or other does not pass that is surprizing, tho' every thing that surprizes does not please; some things being wonder'd at for their Ugliness, as well as others for their Beauty. True Wit, durst one venture to describe it, is quite another thing, it consists in such a Sprightliness of Imagination, such a reach and turn of thought, so properly exprest, as strikes and pleases a judicious Tast. For tho' as one says of Beauty, *'tis in no Face but in the Lover's Mind*, so it may be said of some sort of Wit, it is not in him that speaks, but in the Imagination of his Hearer, yet doubtless there is a true Standard-Wit, which must be allow'd for such by every one who understands the Terms, I don't say that they shall *equally* like it; and it is this Standard-Wit that always pleases, the Spurious does so only for a Season.

[19] Now what is it that strikes a judicious Tast? Not that to be sure which injures the absent, or provokes the Company, which poisons the Mind under pretence of entertaining it, proceeding from or giving Countenance to false Ideas, to dangerous and immoral Principles. Wit indeed is distinct from Judgment but it is not contrary to it; 'tis rather its Handmaid, serving to awaken and fix the Attention, that so we may Judge rightly. Whatever Charms, does so because of its Regularity and Proportion; otherwise, tho' it is extraordinary and out of the way, it will only be star'd on like

[*err.* as] a Monster, but can never be lik'd. And tho a thought is ever so fine and new, ever so well exprest, if it suits not with Decorum and good Manners, it is not just and fit, and therefore offends our Reason, and consequently has no Charms, nor should afford us any entertainment.

But it must not be suppos'd that Women's Wit approaches those heights which Men arrive at, or that they indulge those Liberties the other take. Decency lays greater restraints on them, their timorousness does them this one, and perhaps this only piece of Service, it keeps them from breaking thro' those restraints, and following their Masters and Guides in many of their daring and masculine Crimes. As the [20] World goes, your Witty Men are usually distinguish'd by the Liberty they take with Religion, good Manners, or their Neighbour's Reputation: But, GOD be thank'd, it is not yet so bad, as that Women should form Cabals to propagate Atheism and Irreligion.[6] A Man then cannot hope to find a Woman whose Wit is of a size with his, but when he doats on Wit it is to be imagin'd he makes choice of that which comes the nearest to his own.

Thus, whether it be Wit or Beauty that a Man's in Love with, there's no great hopes of a lasting Happiness; Beauty with all the helps of Art is of no long date, the more it is help'd the sooner it decays, and he who only or chiefly chose for Beauty, will in a little time find the same reason for another Choice. Nor is that sort of Wit which he prefers of a more sure tenure, or allowing it to last, it will not always please. For that which has not a real excellency and value in it self, entertains no longer than the giddy Humour which recommended it to us holds; and when we can like on no just, or on very little Ground, 'tis certain a dislike will arise, as lightly and as unaccountably. And it is not improbable that such a Husband may in a little time by ill usage provoke such a Wife to

---

[6] In the fourth edition a footnote to this passage, marked with an asterisk, reads 'This was wrote in the Beginning of the present Century.' There is no mention of it in the first edition and in the fourth Astell does not say by whom it was written. The whole passage with its emphasis on liberty, wit, manners and tolerance is highly reminiscent of the third Earl of Shaftesbury. But the charge against women caballing could have come from contemporary criticism of Astell's *A Serious Proposal to the Ladies For the Advancement of their True and Greatest Interest* (London, 1694) – from the pens of Defoe or Swift, for instance.

exercise her Wit, that is, [21] her Spleen on him, and then it is not hard to guess how very agreeable it will be to him.

In a word, when we have reckon'd up how many look no further than the making of their Fortune, as they call it; who don't so much as propose to themselves any satisfaction in the Woman to whom they Plight their Faith, seeking only to be Masters of her Estate,[7] that so they may have Money enough to indulge all their irregular Appetites; who think they are as good as can be expected, if they are but according to the fashionable Term, *Civil Husbands*; when we have taken the number of your giddy Lovers, who are not more violent in their Passion than they are certain to Repent of it; when to these you have added such as Marry without any Thought at all, further than that it is the Custom of the World, what others have done before them, that the Family must be kept up, the ancient Race preserv'd, and therefore their kind Parents and Guardians chuse as they think convenient, without ever consulting the Young ones Inclinations, who must be satisfied or pretend so at least, upon pain of their displeasure, and that heavy consequence of it, forfeiture of their Estate: These set aside, I fear there will be but a small remainder to [22] Marry out of better considerations, and even amongst the few that do, not one in a hundred takes care to deserve his Choice.

But do the Women never chuse amiss? Are the Men only in fault? that is not pretended; for he who will be just, must be forc'd to acknowledge, that neither Sex are always in the right. A Woman indeed can't properly be said to Choose, all that is allow'd her, is to Refuse or Accept what is offer'd. And when we have made such reasonable allowances as are due to the Sex, perhaps they may not appear so much in fault as one would at first imagine, and a generous Spirit will find more occasion to pity, than to reprove. But sure I transgress it must not be suppos'd that the Ladies can do amiss! he is but an ill-bred Fellow who pretends that they need amendment! They are no doubt on't always in the right, and most of all when they take pity on distressed Lovers! whatever they *say* carries an Authority that no Reason can resist, and all that they *do*

---

[7] In the first edition (*Reflections* 1700, p. 22) 'Fortune', rather than 'Estate' in the third and fourth (1730, p. 35).

must needs be Exemplary! This is the Modish Language, nor is there a Man of Honour amongst the whole Tribe that would not venture his Life, nay and his Salvation too in their Defence, if any but himself attempts to injure them. But I must ask [23] pardon if I can't come up to these heights, nor flatter them with [t]he having no faults,[8] which is only a malicious way of continuing and encreasing their Mistakes.

Women, it's true, ought to be treated with Civility; for since a little Ceremony and out-side Respect is all their Guard, all the privilege that's allow'd them, it were barbarous to deprive them of it; and because I would treat them civilly, I would not express my Civility at the usual rate. I would not under pretence of honouring and paying a mighty Deference to the Ladies, call them fools to their faces; for what are all the fine Speeches and Submissions that are made, but an abusing them in a well-bred way? She must be a Fool with a witness, who can believe a Man, Proud and Vain as he is, will lay his boasted Authority, the Dignity and Prerogative of his Sex, one Moment at her Feet, but in prospect of taking it up again to more advantage; he may call himself her Slave a few days, but it is only in order to make her his all the rest of his Life.

Indeed that mistaken Self-Love that reigns in the most of us, both Men and Women, that over-good Opinion we have of our selves, and desire that others should have of us, makes us swallow every thing [24] that looks like Respect, without examining how wide it is from what it appears to be. For nothing is in truth a greater outrage than Flattery and feign'd Submissions, the plain English of which is this, 'I have a very mean Opinion both of your Understanding and Vertue, you are weak enough to be impos'd on, and vain enough to snatch at the Bait I throw; there's no danger of your finding out my meaning, or disappointing me of my Ends. I offer you *Incense* 'tis true, but you are like to pay for't, and to make me a Recompence for your Folly in Imagining I would give my self this trouble, did I not hope, nay were I not sure, to find my own account in it. If for nothing else, you'll serve at least as an exercise of my Wit, and how much soever you swell with my Breath, 'tis I deserve the Praise for talking so well on so poor a

---

[8] The phraseology, 'the having no faults' (*Reflections*, 1700, p. 24), in the third edition (1706) printed strangely as 'he having no faults', is restored in the fourth edition (1730, p. 38).

Subject. We who make the Idols, are the greater Deities; and as we set you up, so it is in our power to reduce you to your first obscurity, or to somewhat worse, to Contempt; you are therefore only on your good behaviour, and are like to be no more than what we please to make you.' This is the Flatterer's Language aside, this is the true sense of his heart, whatever his Grimace may be before the Company.

[25] Not but that 'tis possible, and sometimes matter of Fact, to express our selves beyond the Truth in praise of a Person, and yet not be guilty of Flattery; but then we must Think what we Say, and Mean what we Profess. We may be so blinded by some Passion or other, especially Love, which in Civil and Goodnatur'd Persons is apt to exceed, as to believe some Persons more deserving than really they are, and to pay them greater Respect and Kindness than is in strictness due to them. But this is not the present Case, for our fine Speech-makers doat too much on themselves to have any great passion for another, their Eyes are too much fixt on their own Excellencies, to view another's good Qualities through a magnifying Glass; or at least, if ever they turn that end of their Perspective towards their Neighbours, 'tis only in respect and reference to themselves. They are their own Centres, they find a disproportion in every line that does not tend thither, and in the next visit they make, you shall hear all the fine things they had said repeated to the new Object, and nothing remembred of the former but her Vanity, or something else as Ridiculous, which serves for a foil, or a whet to Discourse. For let there be ever so many Wits in the [26] Company, Conversation would languish, and they would be at a loss, did not a little Censoriousness come in at a need to help them.

Let us then treat the Ladies as Civilly as may be, but let us not do it by Flattering them, but by endeavouring to make them such as may truly deserve our hearty Esteem and Kindness. Men ought really for their own sakes to do what in them lies to make Women Wise and Good, and then it might be hoped they themselves would effectually Study and Practise that Wisdom and Vertue they recommend to others. But so long as Men have base and unworthy Ends to serve, it is not to be expected that they should consent to such Methods as would certainly disappoint them. They would have their own Relations do well, it is their Interest; but it sometimes happens to be for their turn that another Man's should not,

45

and then their Generosity fails them, and no Man is apter to find fault with another's dishonourable Actions, than he who is ready to do, or perhaps has done the same himself.

And as Men have little reason to expect Happiness when they Marry only for the Love of Money, Wit or Beauty, as has been already shewn, so much less can a Woman expect a tolerable life, when she [27] goes upon these Considerations. Let the business be carried as Prudently as it can be on the Woman's side, a reasonable Man can't deny that she has by much the harder bargain. Because she puts her self entirely into her Husband's Power, and if the Matrimonial Yoke be grievous, neither Law nor Custom afford her that redress which a Man obtains. He who has Sovereign Power does not value the Provocations of a Rebellious Subject, but knows how to subdue him with ease, and will make himself obey'd; but Patience and Submission are the only Comforts that are left to a poor People, who groan under Tyranny, unless they are Strong enough to break the Yoke, to Depose and Abdicate, which I doubt wou'd not be allow'd of here. For whatever may be said against Passive-Obedience in another case, I suppose there's no Man but likes it very well in this; how much soever Arbitrary Power may be dislik'd on a Throne, not *Milton*[9] himself wou'd cry up Liberty

---

[9] The fourth edition (*Reflections*, 1730, p. 45) inserts the phrase 'nor B. H—, nor any of the Advocates of Resistance', referring undoubtedly to Benjamin Hoadly. The reference to Milton may be specifically to his writings on divorce prompted by his own shortlived marriage. See Milton, *The Doctrine and Discipline of Divorce, Restor'd, to the Good of both Sexes, from the Bondage of Canon Law and other Mistakes, to Christian Freedom, guided by the Rule of Charity; wherein also many Places of Scripture have recovered their long-lost Meaning; reasonable to be now thought of in the Reformation intended* 1[?] August 1643, second enlarged edition, 2 February 1643–4; 'the author J. M., *The Judgement of Martin Bucer concerning Divorce. Writt'n to Edward the Sixt, in his Second Book of the Kingdom of Christ. And now Englisht. Wherein a Late Book restoring the Doctrine and Discipline of Divorce is heer confirm'd and justify'd by the Authoritie of Martin Bucer. To the Parlament of England* (London, 1644); 'By the former Author, J. M.' *Tetrachordon: Expositions upon the foure chief Places in Scripture which treat of Marriage, or Nullities in Marriage*; and 'By the former Author, J.M.', *Colasterion: A Reply to a Nameles Answer against 'The Doctrine and Discipline of Divorce'. Wherein the trivial Author of that Answer is discover'd, the License conferred with, and the opinion which they traduce, defended.* (London 1645). Milton's views on divorce were attacked by writers against the sects as typical, as in Ephraim Pagitt's *Heresiography* (1645) and Thomas Edward's (*q.v.*) *Gangraena: Or a full Answer to the Apologeticall Narration of Mr Goodwin, Mr Nye, Mr Simpson, Mr Burroughes, Mr Bridge, Members of the Assembly of Divines* (London, 1644), where Edwards, tells the story of a Mrs Attaway who, abandoning her 'unsanctified' husband to take up with a pre-

to poor *Female Slaves*, or plead for the Lawfulness of Resisting a Private Tyranny.

If there be a disagreeableness of Humours, this in my mind is harder to be born than greater faults, as being a continual Plague, and for the most part incurable; other Vices a Man may grow weary [28] of, or may be convinced of the evil of them, he may forsake them, or they him, but his Humour and Temper are seldom, if ever put off, Ill-nature sticks to him from his Youth to his grey Hairs, and a Boy that's Humorous and Proud, makes a Peevish, Positive and Insolent Old Man. Now if this be the case, and the Husband be full of himself, obstinately bent on his own way with or without Reason, if he be one who must be always Admir'd, always Humour'd, and yet scarce knows what will please him, if he has Prosperity enough to keep him from considering, and to furnish him with a train of Flatterers and obsequious Admirers; and Learning and Sense enough to make him a Fop in Perfection; for a Man can never be a complete Coxcomb, unless he has a considerable share of these to value himself upon; what can the poor Woman do? the Husband is too wise to be Advis'd, too good to be Reform'd, she must follow all his Paces, and tread in all his unreasonable steps, or there is no Peace, no Quiet for her, she must obey with the greatest exactness, 'tis in vain to expect any manner of Compliance on his side, and the more she complies the more she may; his fantastical humours grow with her desire to gratifie them, for Age encreases Opiniatry in some, [29] as well as it does Experience in others. Of such sort of folks as these it was that *Solomon spake*, when he said, *Seest thou a Man wise in his own conceit, there is more hope of a Fool than of him*; That is, the profligate Sinner, such a one being always a Fool in *Solomon's* Language, is in a fairer way of being convinc'd of his Folly, and brought to Reason, than the Proud Conceited Man. That Man indeed can never be good at heart, who is full of himself and his own Endowments. Not that it

---

acher, justified herself by citing Milton's first pamphlet (see also Thomas, 1958, 42–62). On 13 August 1644, Herbert Palmer, preaching before Parliament (published as *The Glass of God's Providence towards his Faithful Ones: Held forth in a Sermon preached to the Two Houses of Parliament, at Margareta Westminster, August 13. 1644, being an Extraordinary Day of Humiliation* (London, 1644)), responded to Milton's second pamphlet, *The Judgment of Martin Bucer on Divorce, Dictionary of National Bibliography*, declaring that Milton's book ought to be burned (Oxford, 1917).

is necessary, because it is not possible for one to be totally ignorant of his own good Qualities. I had almost said he *ought* to have a Modest sense of 'em, otherwise he can't be duly thankful, nor make the use of them that is required, to the Glory of God, and the good of Mankind; but he views them in a wrong light, if he discerns any thing that may exalt him above his Neighbours, make him over-look their Merit, or treat them with Neglect or Contempt. He ought to behold his Advantages with fear and trembling, as Talents which he has freely receiv'd, and for which he is highly Accountable, and therefore they shou'd not excite his Pride, but his Care and Industry.

And if Pride and Self-conceit keep a Man who has some good Qualities, and is [30] not so bad as the most of his Neighbours, from growing better, it for certain confirms and hardens the Wicked in his Crimes, it sets him up for a Wit, that is, according to Modern acceptation, one who rallies all that is serious, a Contemner of the Priests first, and then of the Deity Himself. For Penitence and Self-condemnation are what his Haughtiness cannot bear, and since his Crimes have brought upon him the reproaches of his own Mind, since he will not take the regular way to be rid of them, which is by Humbling himself and making his Peace with Heaven, he bids defiance to it, and wou'd if he could believe there is no future State, no after Retribution, because he knows that a heavy lot is in justice due to him.

If therefore it is a Woman's hard Fate to meet with a disagreeable Temper, and of all others the Haughty, Imperious and Self-conceited are the most so, she is as unhappy as any thing in this World can make her. For when a Wife's Temper does not please, if she makes her Husband uneasie, he can find entertainments abroad, he has a hundred ways of relieving himself, but neither Prudence nor Duty will allow a Woman to fly out, her Business and Entertainment are at home, and tho' [31] he makes it ever so uneasie to her she must be content and make her best on't. She who Elects a Monarch for Life, who gives him an Authority she cannot recall however he misapply it, who puts her Fortune and Person entirely in his Powers; nay even the very desires of her Heart according to some learned Casuists, so as that it is not lawful to Will or Desire any thing but what he approves and allows; had need be very sure that she does not make a Fool her Head, nor a Vicious Man her Guide and Pattern, she had best stay till she can meet with one who has the Government of his own Passions, and has duly regulated his own desires, since he is to have such an absolute Power over hers. But he who doats on a Face, he who makes Money his Idol, he who is Charm'd with vain and empty Wit, gives no such Evidence, either of Wisdom or Goodness, that a Woman of any tolerable Sense shou'd care to venture her self to his Conduct.

Indeed, your fine Gentleman's Actions are now adays such, that did not Custom and the Dignity of his Sex give Weight and Authority to them, a Woman that thinks twice might bless her self, and say, is this the Lord and Master to whom I am to promise Love, Honour and Obedience? What can be the object of Love but [32] amiable Qualities, the Image of the Deity impress'd upon a generous and God-like Mind, a Mind that is above this World, to be sure above all the Vices, the Tricks and Baseness of it; a Mind that is not full of it self, nor contracted to little private Interests, but which in Imitation of that glorious Pattern it endeavours to Copy after, expands and diffuses it self to its utmost capacity in doing Good? But this fine Gentleman is quite of another Strain, he is the reverse of this in every Instance. He is I confess very fond of his own Dear Person, he sees very much in it to admire; his Air and Mien, his Words and Actions, every Motion he makes declares it; but they must have a Judgment of his size, every whit as Shallow, and a Partiality as great as his own, who can be of his Mind. How then can I Love? And if not Love, much less Honour. Love may arise from Pity or a generous Desire to make that Lovely which as yet is not so, when we see any hopes of Success in our Endeavours of improving it; but Honour supposes some excellent Qualities already, something worth our Esteem, but [*err.* and] alas there is nothing more contemptible than this trifle of a Man, this meer Outside, whose Mind is as base and Mean as his external Pomp is Glittering. His Office or Title apart, to which [33] some Ceremonious Observance must be paid for Order's sake, there's nothing in him that can command our Respect. Strip him of Equipage and Fortune, and such things as only dazle our Eyes and Imaginations, but don't in any measure affect our Reason, or cause a Reverence in our Hearts, and the poor Creature sinks beneath our Notice, because not supported by real Worth. And if a Woman can neither Love nor Honour, she does ill in promising to Obey, since she is like to have but a crooked Rule to regulate her Actions.

A meer Obedience, such as is paid only to Authority, and not out of Love and a sense of the Justice and Reasonableness of the Command, will be of an uncertain Tenure. As it can't but be uneasie to the Person who pays it, so he who recieves [*err.* is to receive] it will be sometimes disappointed when he expects to find it; for that Woman must be endow'd with a Wisdom and Goodness much above what we suppose the Sex capable of, I fear much greater than e're a Man can pretend to, who can so constantly conquer her Passions, and divest herself even of Innocent Self-Love, as to give up the Cause when she is in the right, and to submit her enlightned Reason, to the Imperious Dictates of a blind Will, and wild Imagination, even when [34] she clearly perceives the ill Consequences of it, the Imprudence, nay Folly and Madness of such a Conduct.

And if a Woman runs such a Risque when she Marries Prudently according to the Opinion of the World, that is, when she permits her self to be dispos'd of to a Man equal to her in Birth, Education and Fortune, and as good as the most of his Neighbours, (for if none were to Marry, but Men of strict Vertue and Honour, I doubt the World would be but thinly peopled) if at the very best her Lot is hard, what can she expect who is Sold, or any otherwise betray'd into mercenary Hands, to one who is in all, or most respects unequal to her? A Lover who comes upon what is call'd equal Terms, makes no very advantageous Proposal to the Lady he Courts, and to whom he seems to be an humble Servant. For under many sounding Compliments, Words that have nothing in them, this is his true meaning, he wants one to manage his Family, an House-keeper, a necessary Evil,[10] one whose Interest it will be not to wrong him, and in whom therefore he can put greater confidence than in any he can hire for Money. One who may breed his Children, taking all the care and trouble of their Education, to [35] preserve his Name and Family. One whose Beauty, Wit, or good Humour and agreeable Conversation, will entertain him at Home when he has been contradicted and disappointed abroad; who will do him that Justice the ill-

---

[10] The phrase 'a necessary Evil' in the third edition, replaces 'an upper Servant' in the first (1700, p. 36), and is omitted altogether in the fourth (1730, p. 54).

natur'd World denies him, that is, in any one's Language but his own, sooth his Pride and Flatter his Vanity, by having always so much good Sense as to be on his side, to conclude him in the right, when others are so Ignorant, or so rude as to deny it. Who will not be Blind to his Merit nor contradict his Will and Pleasure, but make it her Business, her very Ambition to content him; whose softness and gentle Compliance will calm his Passions, to whom he may safely disclose his troublesome Thoughts, and in her Breast discharge his Cares; whose Duty, Submission and Observance, will heal those Wounds other Peoples opposition or neglect have given him. In a word, one whom he can intirely Govern, and consequently may form her to his will and liking, who must be his of [*err.* for] Life, and therefore cannot quit his Service let him treat her how he will.

And if this be what every Man expects, the Sum of his violent Love and Courtship, when it is put into Sense and rendred Intelligible, to what a fine pass does [36] she bring her self who purchases a Lord and Master, not only with her Money, but with what is of greater Value, at the price of her Discretion? Who has not so much as that poor Excuse, Precedent and Example; or if she has, they are only such as all the World condemns? She will not find him less a Governor because she was once his Superior, on the contrary the scum of the People are most Tyrannical when they get the Power, and treat their Betters with the greatest Insolence. For as the wise Man long since observ'd, a Servant when he Reigns is one of those things for which the Earth is disquieted, and which no body is able to bear.

It is the hardest thing in the World for a Woman to know that a Man is not Mercenary, that he does not Act on base and ungenerous Principles, even when he is her Equal, because being absolute Master, she and all the Grants he makes her are in his Power, and there have been but too many instances of Husbands that by wheedling or threatning their Wives, by seeming Kindness or cruel Usage, have perswaded or forc'd them out of what has been settled on them. So that the Woman has in truth no security but the Man's Honour and Good-nature, a Security that in this present Age no wise Person would [37] venture much upon. A Man enters into Articles very readily before Marriage, and so he may, for he performs no more of them afterwards than he thinks fit. A Wife must

never dispute with her Husband, his Reasons are now no doubt
on't better than hers, whatever they were before; he is sure to perswade her out of her Agreement, and bring her, it must be suppos'd,
Willingly, to give up what she did vainly hope to obtain, and what
she thought had been made sure to her. And if she shews any
Refractoriness, there are ways enough to humble her; so that by
right or wrong the Husband gains his Will. For Covenants betwixt
Husband and Wife, like Laws in an Arbitrary Government, are of
little Force, the Will of the Sovereign is all in all. Thus it is in
Matter of Fact, I will not answer for the Right of it; for if the
Woman's Reasons upon which those Agreements are grounded are
not Just and Good, why did he consent to them? Was it because
there was no other way to obtain his Suit, and with an Intention
to Annul them when it shall be in his Power? Where then is his
Sincerity? But if her Reasons are good, where is his Justice in obliging her to quit them? He neither way acts like an equitable or honest
Man.

[38] But when a Woman Marrys unequally and beneath her self,
there is almost Demonstration that the Man is Sordid and Unfair,
that instead of Loving her he only Loves himself, trapans and ruines
her to serve his own Ends. For if he had not a mighty Opinion of
himself, (which temper is like to make an admirable Husband,) he
cou'd never imagine that his Person and good Qualities should make
compensation for all the advantages she quits on his account. If he
had a real Esteem for her or valu'd her Reputation, he wou'd not
expose it, nor have her Discretion call'd in Question for his sake;
and if he truly Lov'd her he would not reduce her to Straits and
a narrow Fortune, nor so much as lessen her way of Living to better
his own. For since GOD has plac'd different Ranks in the World,
put some in a higher and some in a lower Station, for Order and
Beauty's sake, and for many good Reasons; tho' it is both our
Wisdom and Duty not only to submit with Patience, but to be
Thankful and well-satisfied when by his Providence we are brought
low, yet there is no manner of Reason for us to Degrade our selves;
on the contrary, much why we ought not. The better our Lot is in
this World and the more we have of it, the [39] greater is our leisure
to prepare for the next; we have the more opportunity to exercise
that God-like Quality, to tast that Divine Pleasure, Doing good to
the Bodies and Souls of those beneath us. Is it not then ill Manners

to Heaven, and an irreligious contempt of its Favours, for a Woman to slight that nobler Employment, to which it has assign'd her, and thrust her self down to a meaner Drudgery, to what is in the very literal Sense a caring for the things of the World, a caring not only to please, but to maintain a Husband?

And a Husband so chosen will not at all abate of his Authority and Right to Govern, whatever fair Promises he might make before. She has made him her Head, and he thinks himself as well qualify'd as the best to Act accordingly, nor has she given him any such Evidence of her Prudence as may dispose him to make an Act of Grace in her Favour. Besides, great Obligations are what Superiors cannot bear, they are more than can be return'd; to acknowledge, were only to reproach themselves with ingratitude, and therefore the readiest way is not to own but overlook them, or rather, as too many do, to repay them with Affronts and Injuries.

[40] What then is to be done? How must a Man chuse, and what Qualities must encline a Woman to accept, that so our Marry'd couple may be as happy as that State can make them? This is no hard Question; let the Soul be principally consider'd, and regard had in the first Place to a good Understanding, a Vertuous Mind, and in all other respects let there be as much equality as may be. If they are good Christians and of suitable Tempers all will be well; but I should be shrewdly tempted to suspect their Christianity who Marry after any of those ways we have been speaking of, I dare venture to say, that they don't Act according to the Precepts of the Gospel, they neither shew the Wisdom of the Serpent, nor the Innocency of the Dove, they have neither so much Government of themselves, nor so much Charity for their Neighbours, they neither take such care not to Scandalize others, nor to avoid Temptations themselves, are neither so much above this World, nor so affected with the next, as they wou'd certainly be did the Christian Religion operate in their Hearts, did they rightly understand and sincerely Practise it, or Acted *indeed* according to the Spirit of the Gospel.

[41] But it is not enough to enter wisely into this State, care must be taken of our Conduct afterwards. A Woman will not want being admonish'd of her Duty, the custom of the World, Economy, every thing almost reminds her of it. Governors do not often suffer their Subjects to forget Obedience through their want of demanding it, perhaps Husbands are but too forward on this occasion, and

claim their Right oftner and more Imperiously than either Discretion or good Manners will justifie, and might have both a more chearful and constant Obedience paid them if they were not so rigorous in Exacting it. For there is a mutual Stipulation, and Love, Honour, and Worship, by which certain Civility and Respect at least are meant, are as much the Woman's due, as Love, Honour, and Obedience are the Man's, and being the Woman is said to be the weaker Vessel, the Man shou'd be more careful not to grieve or offend her. Since her Reason is suppos'd to be less, and her Passions stronger than his, he shou'd not give occasion to call that supposition in Question by his pettish Carriage and needless Provocations. Since he is the *Man*, by which very word Custom wou'd have us understand not only greatest strength of Body, but even greatest [42] firmness and force of Mind, he shou'd not play the *little* Master so much as to expect to be cocker'd, nor run over to that side which the Woman [*err.* Women] us'd to be rank'd in; for according to the Wisdom of the *Italians*,[11] *Will you? Is spoken to sick Folks.*

Indeed Subjection, according to the Common Notion of it, is not over easie, none of us whether Men or Women but have so good an Opinion of our own Conduct as to believe we are fit, if not to direct others, at least to govern our selves. Nothing but a sound Understanding, and Grace the best improver of natural Reason, can correct this Opinion, truly humble us, and heartily reconcile us to Obedience. This bitter Cup therefore ought to be sweetned as much as may be; for Authority may be preserv'd and Government kept inviolable, without that nauseous Ostentation of Power which serves to no end or purpose, but to blow up the Pride and Vanity of those who have it, and to exasperate the Spirits of such as must truckle under it.

Insolence 'tis true is never the effect of Power but in weak and cowardly Spirits, who wanting true *Merit* and Judgment to support themselves in that advantageous Ground on which they stand, are ever appealing to their Authority, and making a shew of it to maintain their Vanity and [43] Pride. A truly great Mind and such as

[11] The Italian is given here in the first edition (1700, p. 44), '*Volete? si dice a gli ammalati*'.

is fit to Govern, tho' it may stand on its Right with its Equals, and modestly expect what is due to it even from its Superiors, yet it never contends with its Inferiors, nor makes use of its Superiority but to do them Good. So that considering the just Dignity of Man, his great Wisdom so conspicuous on all occasions! the goodness of his Temper and Reasonableness of all his Commands, which make it a Woman's Interest as well as Duty to be observant and Obedient in all things! that his Prerogative is settled by an undoubted Right, and the Prescription of many Ages; it cannot be suppos'd that he should make frequent and insolent Claims of an Authority so well establish'd and us'd with such moderation! nor give an impartial By-stander (cou'd such an one be found) any occasion from thence to suspect that he is inwardly conscious of the badness of his Title; Usurpers being always most desirous of Recognitions and busie in imposing Oaths, whereas a Lawful Prince contents himself with the usual Methods and Securities.

And since Power does naturally puff up, and he who finds himself exalted, seldom fails to think he *ought* to be so, it is more suitable to a Man's Wisdom and Generosity, to be mindful of his great [44] Obligations than to insist on his Rights and Prerogatives. Sweetness of Temper and an Obliging Carriage are so justly due to a Wife, that a Husband who must not be thought to want either Understanding to know what is fit, nor Goodness to perform it, can't be suppos'd not to shew them. For setting aside the hazards of her Person to keep up his Name and Family, with all the Pains and Trouble that attend it, which may well be thought great enough to deserve all the respect and kindness that may be, setting this aside, tho' 'tis very considerable, a Woman has so much the disadvantage in *most*, I was about to say in *all* things, that she makes a Man the greatest Compliment in the World when she condescends to take him *for Better for Worse.* She puts her self intirely in his Power, leaves all that is dear to her, her Friends and Family, to espouse his Interests and follow his Fortune, and makes it her Business and Duty to please him! What acknowledgements, what returns can he make? What Gratitude can be sufficient for such Obligations? She shews her good Opinion of him by the great Trust she reposes in him, and what a Brute must he be who betrays that Trust, or acts any way unworthy of it? Ingratitude is one of the [basest Vices, and

if a Man's Soul is sunk]¹² **[45]** so low as to be guilty of it towards
her who has so generously oblig'd him, and who so intirely depends
on him, if he can treat her Disrespectfully, who has so fully testify'd
her Esteem of him, she must have a stock of Vertue which he shou'd
blush to discern, if she can pay him that Obedience of which he is
so unworthy.

Superiors indeed are too apt to forget the common Privileges of
Mankind; that their Inferiors share with them the greatest Benefits,
and are as capable as themselves of enjoying the supreme Good;
that tho' the Order of the World requires an *Outward* Respect and
Obedience from some to others, yet the Mind is free, nothing but
Reason can oblige it, 'tis out of the reach of the most absolute
Tyrant. Nor will it ever be well either with those who Rule or those
in Subjection, even from the Throne to every Private Family, till
those in Authority look on themselves as plac'd in that Station for
the good and improvement of their Subjects, and not for their own
sakes; not as the reward of their Merit, or that they may prosecute
their own Desires and fulfil all their Pleasure, but as the Representatives of GOD whom they ought to imitate in the Justice and Equity
of their Laws, in doing good and communicating Blessings to all
beneath **[46]** them: By which, and not by following the imperious
Dictates of their own will, they become truly Great and Illustrious
and Worthily fill their Place. And the Governed for their Part ceasing to envy the Pomp and Name of Authority, shou'd respect their
Governours as plac'd in GOD's stead and contribute what they can
to ease them of their real Cares, by a chearful, and ready compliance
with their good endeavours, and by affording them the Pleasure of
success in such noble and generous Designs.

For upon a due estimate things are pretty equally divided; those
in Subjection as they have a less Glorious, so they have an easier
task and a less account to give, whereas he who Commands has in
a great measure the Faults of others to answer for as well as his
own. 'Tis true he has the Pleasure of doing more good than a Private Person can, and shall receive the Reward of it when Time shall
be no more, in compensation for the hazards he runs, the difficulties

---

¹² This phrase to complete the sense, present in the first (1700, p. 47) and fourth
editions (1730, p. 67), appears to have been inadvertently dropped from the
bottom of the page by the printer. It is not noted in the Errata to the third edition
(1706, p. xxvi).

he at present encounters, and the large Account he is to make here-after, which Pleasure and Reward are highly desirable and most worthy our pursuit; but they are Motives which such as usurp on their Governors, and make them uneasie in the due discharge [47] of their Duty, never propose. And for those other little things that move their Envy and Ambition, they are of no Esteem with a just Considerer, nor will such as violently pursue, find their Account in them.

But how can a Man respect his Wife when he has a contemptible Opinion of her and her Sex? When from his own Elevation he looks down on them as void of Understanding, and full of Ignorance and Passion, so that Folly and a Woman are equivalent Terms with him? Can he think there is any Gratitude due to her whose utmost services he exacts as strict Duty? Because she was made to be a Slave to his Will, and has no higher end than to Serve and Obey him! Perhaps we arrogate too much to our selves when we say this Material World was made for our sakes; that its Glorious Maker has given us the use of it is certain, but when we suppose a thing to be made purely for our sakes, because we have Dominion over it, we draw a false Conclusion, as he who shou'd say the People were made for the Prince who is set over them, wou'd be thought to be out of his Senses as well as his Politicks. Yet even allowing that GOD who made everything in Number, Weight and Measure, who never acts [48] but for some great and glorious End, an End agreeable to His Majesty, allowing that He Created such a Number of Rational Spirits merely to serve their fellow Creatures, yet how are these Lords and Masters helpt by the Contempt they shew of their poor humble Vassals? Is it not rather an hindrance to that Service they expect, as being an undeniable and constant Proof how unworthy they are to receive it?

None of GOD's Creatures absolutely consider'd are in their own Nature Contemptible; the meanest Fly, the poorest Insect has its Use and Vertue. Contempt is scarce a Human Passion, one may venture to say it was not in Innocent Man, for till Sin came into the World, there was nothing in it to be contemn'd. But Pride which makes every thing serve its purpose, wrested this Passion from its only use, so that instead of being an Antidote against Sin, it is become a grand promoter of it, nothing making us more worthy of that Contempt we shew, than when poor, weak, dependent

Creatures as we are! we look down with Scorn and Disdain on others.

There is not a surer Sign of a noble Mind, a Mind very far advanc'd towards perfection, than the being able to bear [49] Contempt and an unjust Treatment from ones Superiors evenly and patiently. For inward Worth and real Excellency are the true Ground of Superiority, and one Person is not in reality better than another, but as he is more Wise and Good. But this World being a place of Tryal and govern'd by general Laws, just Retributions being reserv'd for hereafter, Respect and Obedience many times become due for Order's sake to those who don't otherwise deserve them. Now tho' Humility keeps us from over-valuing our selves or viewing our Merit thro' a false and magnifying *Medium*, yet it does not put out our Eyes, it does not, it ought not to deprive us of that pleasing sentiment which attends our Acting as we ought to Act, which is as it were a foretast of Heaven, our present Reward for doing what is Just and Fit. And when a Superior does a Mean and unjust Thing, as all Contempt of one's Neighbour is, and yet this does not provoke his Inferiors to refuse that Observance which their Stations in the World require, they cannot but have an inward Sense of their own real Superiority, the other having no pretence to it, at the same time that they pay him an outward Respect and Deference, which is such a flagrant Testimony of the sincerest Love of Order as [50] proves their Souls to be of the highest and noblest Rank.

A Man therefore for his own sake, and to give evidence that he has a Right to those Prerogatives he assumes, shou'd treat Women with a little more Humanity and Regard than is usually paid them. Your whissling Wits may scoff at them, and what then? It matters not, for they Rally everything tho' ever so Sacred, and rail at the Women commonly in very good Company. Religion, its Priests, and those its most constant and regular Professors, are the usual Subjects of their manly, mannerly and surprizing Jests. Surprizing indeed! not for the newness of the Thought, the brightness of the Fancy, or nobleness of Expression, but for the good Assurance with which such threadbare Jests are again and again repeated. But that your grave Dons, your Learned Men, and which is more, your Men of Sense as they wou'd be thought, should stoop so low as to make Invectives against the Women, forget themselves so much as to Jest with their Slaves, who have neither Liberty nor Ingenuity to make

Reprizals! that they shou'd waste their Time, and debase their good Sense which fits them for the most weighty Affairs, such as are suitable to their profound Wisdoms and exalted [51] Understandings![13] to render those poor Wretches more ridiculous and odious who are already in their Opinion sufficiently contemptible, and find no better exercise of their Wit and Satyr than such as are not worth their Pains, tho' it were possible to Reform them, this, this indeed may justly be wondred at!

I know not whether or no Women are allow'd to have Souls, if they have perhaps, it is not prudent to provoke them too much, lest silly as they are, they at last recriminate, and then what polite and well-bred Gentleman, tho' himself is concern'd, can forbear taking that lawful Pleasure which all who understand Raillery must tast, when they find his Jests who insolently began to peck at his Neighbour, return'd with Interest upon his own Head? And indeed Men are too Humane, too Wise to venture at it did they not hope for this effect, and expect the Pleasure of finding their Wit turn to such account; for if it be lawful to reveal a Secret, this is without doubt the whole design of those fine Discourses which have been made against the Women from our great Fore-fathers to this present Time! Generous Man has too much Bravery, he is too Just and too Good to assault a defenceless Enemy, and if he did inveigh against the Women it was only to do them Service! For since neither [52] his Care of their Education, his hearty endeavours to improve their Minds, his wholsome Precepts, nor great Example cou'd do them good, as his last and kindest Essay, he resolv'd to try what Contempt wou'd do, and chose rather to expose himself by a seeming want of Justice, Equity, Ingenuity and Good-nature, than suffer Women to remain such vain and insignificant Creatures as they have hitherto been reckon'd! And truly Women are some degrees beneath what I have thus far thought them, if they do not make the best use of his kindness, improve themselves, and like Christians return it.

Let us see then what is their Part, what must they do to make the Matrimonial Yoke tolerable to themselves as well as pleasing to their Lords and Masters? That the World is an empty and deceitful

---

[13] This passage, with its allusions to anti-clericalism, 'Wits . . . Dons . . . learned Men . . . Men of Sense . . . Slaves . . . Liberty . . . profound Wisdoms and exalted Understandings', seems to cue us to Locke and the Shaftesbury circle.

Thing, that those Enjoyments which appear'd so desirable at a distance, which rais'd our Hopes and Expectations to such a mighty
Pitch, which we so passionately coveted, and so eagerly pursued,
vanish at our first approach, leaving nothing behind them but the
Folly of Delusion, and the pain of disappointed Hopes, is a common
Outcry; and yet as common as it is, tho' we complain of being
deceiv'd this Instant, we do not fail of contributing to the [53] Cheat
the very next. Tho' in reality it is not the World that abuses us, 'tis
we abuse ourselves, it is not the emptiness of that, but our own
false Judgments, our unreasonable Desires and Expectations that
Torment us; for he who exerts his whole strength to lift a Straw,
ought not to complain of the Burden, but of his own disproportion-
ate endeavour which gives him the pain he feels. The World affords
us all the Pleasure a sound Judgment can expect from it, and
answers all those Ends and Purposes for which it was design'd, let
us expect no more than is reasonable, and then we shall not fail of
our Expectation.

It is even so in the Case before us; a Woman who has been
taught to think Marriage her only Preferment, the Sum-total of her
Endeavours, the completion of all her hopes, that which must settle
and make her Happy in this World, and very few, in their Youth
especially, carry a Thought steadily to a greater distance; She who
has seen a Lover dying at her Feet, and can't therefore imagine that
he who professes to receive all his Happiness from her, can have
any other Design or Desire than to please her; whose Eyes have
been dazled with all the Glitter and Pomp of a Wedding, and who
hears of [54] nothing but Joy and Congratulations; who is transported with the Pleasure of being out of Pupillage and Mistress not
only of her self but of a Family too: She who is either so simple or
so vain, as to take her Lover at his Word either as to the Praises he
gave her, or the Promises he made for himself; in sum, she whose
Expectation has been rais'd by Court-ship, by all the fine things
that her Lover, her Governess, and Domestic Flatterers say, will
find a terrible disappointment when the hurry is over, and when
she comes calmly to consider her Condition, and views it no more
under a false Appearance, but as it truly is.

I doubt in such a View it will not appear over-desirable, if she
regards only the present State of Things. Hereafter may make
amends for what she must be prepar'd to suffer here, then will be

her Reward, this is her time of Tryal, the Season of exercising and improving her Vertues. A Woman that is not Mistress of her Passions, that cannot patiently submit even when Reason suffers with her, who does not practise Passive Obedience to the utmost, will never be acceptable to such an absolute Sovereign as a Husband. Wisdom ought to Govern without Contradiction, but Strength however will be obey'd. There are but few of those wise Persons [55] who can be content to be made yet wiser by Contradiction, the most will have their *Will*, and it is right because it is their's. Such is the vanity of Humane nature that nothing pleases like an intire Subjection; what Imperfections won't a Man over-look where this is not wanting! Tho' we live like Brutes, we wou'd have Incense offer'd us that is only due to Heaven it self, wou'd have an absolute and blind Obedience paid us by all over whom we pretend Authority. We were not made to Idolize one another, yet the whole strain of Courtship is little less than rank Idolatry: But does a Man intend to give, and not to receive his share in this Religious Worship? No such matter; Pride and Vanity and Self-love have their Designs, and if the Lover is so condescending as to set a Pattern in the time of his Addresses, he is so Just as to expect his Wife shou'd strictly Copy after it all the rest of her Life.

But how can a Woman scruple intire Subjection, how can she forbear to admire the worth and excellency of the Superior Sex, if she at all considers it? Have not all the great Actions that have been perform'd in the World been done by Men? Have not they founded Empires and overturn'd them? Do not they make Laws and continually repeal and amend them? Their [56] vast Minds lay Kingdoms wast, no bounds or measures can be prescrib'd to their Desires. War and Peace depend on them, they form Cabals and have the Wisdom and Courage to get over all these [*err.* the] Rubs which may lie in the way of their desired Grandeur. What is it they cannot do? They make Worlds and ruine them, form Systems of universal nature and dispute eternally about them; their Pen gives worth to the most trifling Controversie; nor can a fray be inconsiderable if they have drawn their Swords in't. All that the wise Man pronounces is an Oracle, and every Word the Witty speaks a Jest. It is a Woman's Happiness to hear, admire and praise them, especially if a little Ill-nature keeps them at any time from bestowing due Applauses on each other! And if she aspires no further, she is thought to be in her proper Sphere of Action, she is as wise and as good as can be expected from her!

She then who Marrys ought to lay it down for an indisputable Maxim, that her Husband must govern absolutely and intirely, and that she has nothing else to do but to Please and Obey. She must not attempt to divide his Authority, or so much as dispute it, to struggle with her Yoke will only make it gall the more, but [57] must believe him Wise and Good and in all respects the best, at least he must be so to her. She who can't do this is no way fit to be a Wife, she may set up for that peculiar Coronet the ancient Fathers talk'd of, but is not qualify'd to receive that great reward, which attends the eminent exercise of Humility and Self-denial, Patience and Resignation, the Duties that a Wife is call'd to.

But some refractory Woman perhaps will say, how can this be? Is it possible for her to believe him Wise and Good who by a thousand Demonstrations convinces her and all the World of the contrary? Did the bare Name of Husband confer Sense on a Man, and the mere being in Authority infallibly qualifie him for Government, much might be done. But since a wise Man and a Husband are not Terms convertible, and how loth soever one is to own it, Matter of Fact won't allow us to deny, that the Head many times stands in need of the Inferior's Brains to manage it, she must beg leave to be excus'd from such high thoughts of her Sovereign, and if she submits to his Power, it is not so much Reason as Necessity that compels her.

Now of how little force soever this Objection may be in other respects, methinks it is strong enough to prove the [58] necessity of a good Education, and that Men never mistake their true Interest more than when they endeavour to keep Women in Ignorance. Cou'd they indeed deprive them of their Natural good Sense at the same time they deny them the due improvement of it, they might compass their End; otherwise Natural Sense unassisted may run in to a false Track and serve only to punish him justly, who wou'd not allow it to be useful to himself or others. If Man's Authority be justly establish'd, the more Sense a Woman has, the more reason she will find to submit to it; if according to the Tradition of our Fathers, (who having had *Possession* of the Pen, thought they had also the best *Right* to it,) Women's Understanding is but small, and Men's Partiality adds no Weight to the Observation, ought not the more care to be taken to improve them? How it agrees with the Justice of Men we enquire not, but certainly Heaven is abundantly more equitable than to enjoyn Women the hardest Task and give them the least Strength to perform it. And if Men Learned, Wise and Discreet as they are, who have as is said all the advantages of Nature, and without controversy have, or may have all the assistance of Art, are so far from acquitting themselves as they ought, from living according to that [59] Reason and excellent Understanding they so much boast of, can it be expected that a Woman who is reckon'd silly enough in her self, at least comparatively, and whom Men take care to make yet more so, can it be expected that she shou'd constantly perform so difficult a Duty as intire Subjection, to which corrupt Nature is so averse?

If the Great and Wise *Cato*,[14] a *Man*, a Man of no ordinary firmness and strength of Mind, a Man who was esteem'd as an Oracle, and by the Philosophers and great Men of his Nation equall'd even to the Gods themselves; If he with all his Stoical Principles was not able to bear the sight of a triumphant Conqueror, (who perhaps wou'd have Insulted and perhaps wou'd not,) but out of a Cowardly fear of an Insult, ran to Death to secure him from it;[15] can it be thought that an ignorant weak Woman shou'd have patience to bear a continual Out-rage and Insolence all the days of her Life? Unless you will suppose her a *very Ass*, but then remember what the *Italians* say, to Quote them once more, since being very Husbands they may be presum'd to have Authority in this Case,[16] *an Ass tho' slow if provok'd will kick.*[17]

---

[14] Cato 'Censorius', Marcus Porcius (234–149 BC) of peasant stock, rose to the consulship on the basis of his legal ability and his reputation for probity. During his term he supported a stern policy of moral and economic reconstruction. His patriotism, to the point of hatred for things Greek – he spoke against the embassy of Athenian philosophers in 155 BC – made him a favourite among English ancient constitutionalists and common law advocates opposed to civil lawyers.

[15] Astell refers to Cato's attack on Sulpicius Galba, 149 BC, with whom he had had a long-running enmity dating to Galba's opposition to Aemilius Paullus' triumph.

[16] The Italian of the proverb which follows, '*L'afino pur pigro, Stimulator tira quelche calcio*', is inserted here in the first edition (1700, p. 63) and the fourth (1730).

[17] Astell's example of Cato is a curious one, suggesting the subordination of woman to be an unbearable outrage of her nature of the sort that Cato would have experienced had he submitted to Galba's triumph. Was her resort to the Italian proverb about the ass brought to mind by the sentence from Job quoted by Leslie in his discussion of Whig theories of natural equality, and specifically Locke's? – 'Men are Born *Free*, as *Job* says, *Like a wild Asses Colt*; and Consequently cannot be

We never see or perhaps make sport with the ill Effects of a bad Education, till it come to touch us home in the ill conduct [60] of a Sister, a Daughter, or Wife. Then the Women must be blam'd, their Folly is exclaim'd against, when all this while it was the wise Man's Fault, who did not set a better Guard on those who according to him stand in so much need of one. A young Gentleman, as a celebrated Author tells us,[18] ought above all things to be acquainted with the State of the World, the Ways and Humours, the Follies, the Cheats, the Faults of the Age he is fallen into, he should by degrees be inform'd of the Vice in Fashion, and warn'd of the Application and Design of those who will make it their Business to corrupt him, shou'd be told the Arts they use and the Trains they lay, be prepar'd to be Shock'd by some and caress'd by others; warn'd who are like to oppose, who to mislead, who to undermine, and who to serve him. He shou'd be instructed how to know and distinguish them, where he shou'd let them see, and when dissemble the Knowledge of them and their Aims and Workings. Our Author is much in the right, and not to disparage any other Accomplishments which are useful in their kind, this will turn to more account than any Language or Philosophy, Art or Science, or any other piece of Good-breeding and fine Education that can be taught him, [which are no otherwise excellent than as][19] [61] they contribute to this, as this does above all things to the making him a wise, a vertuous and useful Man.

And it is not less necessary that a young Lady shou'd receive the like Instructions, whether or not her Temptations be fewer, her Reputation and Honour however are to be more nicely preserv'd;

obliged by their own Consent' *Cassandra. (But I Hope not) Telling What Will Come Of It: In Answer to the Occasional Letter. Num. I. Wherein The New-Associations, etc., Are Considered* (London and Westminster, 1704–5). The image of the wild ass as the epitome of freedom as licence was also invoked by Joseph Glanvill, in *The Zealous and Impartial Protestant* (London (1678), 1681, cited Goldie, 1991, 348), in an argument for coercion against Dissenters: 'while people run on without control in their own ways, they will not hearken, they will not consider . . . Like the wild ass, they snuff up the wind.'

18 Possibly Samuel Wesley (*q.v.*), *A Letter from a Country Divine to his Friend in London, Concerning the Education of Dissenters in their Private Academies . . .* (1703), second edition (London, 1704), mentioned by Astell in *A Fair Way with the Dissenters and their Patrons* (London, 1704), but more likely Locke.

19 The phrase in square brackets, present in the first edition (1700, p. 64) and the fourth appears to have been dropped in error from the foot of p. 60 of the third edition.

they may be ruin'd by a little Ignorance or Indiscretion, and then tho' she has kept her Innocence, and so is secur'd as to the next World, yet she is in a great measure lost to this. A Woman cannot be too watchful, too apprehensive of her danger, nor keep at too great a distance from it, since Man whose Wisdom and Ingenuity is so much Superior to hers! condescends for his Interest sometimes, and sometimes by way of Diversion, to lay Snares for her. For tho' all Men are *Virtuosi*, Philosophers and Politicians, in comparison of the Ignorant and Illiterate Women, yet they don't all pretend to be Saints, and 'tis no great Matter to them if Women who were born to be their Slaves, be now and then ruin'd for their Entertainment.

But according to the rate that young Women are Educated, according to the way their Time is spent, they are destin'd to Folly and Impertinence, to say no worse, and which is yet more inhuman, they are [62] blam'd for that ill Conduct they are not suffer'd to avoid, and reproach'd for those Faults they are in a manner forc'd into; so that if Heaven has bestowed any Sense on them, no other use is made of it, than to leave them without Excuse. So much and no more of the World is shewn them, as serves to weaken and corrupt their Minds, to give them wrong Notions, and busy them in mean Pursuits; to disturb, not to regulate their Passions; to make them timorous and dependant, and in a word, fit for nothing else but to act a Farce for the Diversion of their Governours.

Even Men themselves improve no otherwise than according to the Aim they take, and the End they propose; and he whose Designs are but little and mean, will be the same himself. Tho' Ambition, as 'tis usually understood, is a Foolish, not to say a Base and Pitiful Vice, yet the Aspirings of the Soul after true Glory are so much its Nature, that it seems to have forgot it self and to degenerate, if it can forbear; and perhaps the great Secret of Education lies in affecting the Soul with a lively Sense of what is truly its Perfection, and exciting the most ardent Desires after it.

But, alas! what poor Woman is ever taught that she should have a higher Design than to get her a Husband? Heaven [63] will fall in of course; and if she makes but an Obedient and Dutiful Wife, she cannot miss of it. A Husband indeed is thought by both Sexes so very valuable, that scarce a Man who can keep himself clean and make a Bow, but thinks he is good enough to pretend to any

Woman, no matter for the Difference of Birth or Fortune, a Husband is such a Wonder-working Name as to make an Equality, or something more, whenever it is pronounc'd.

And indeed were there no other Proof of Masculine Wisdom, and what a much greater portion of Ingenuity falls to the Men than to the Women's Share, the Address, the Artifice, and Management of an humble Servant were a sufficient Demonstration. What good Conduct does he shew! what Patience exercise! what Subtilty leave untry'd! what Concealment of his Faults! what Parade of his Vertues! what Government of his Passions! How deep is his Policy in laying his Designs at so great a distance, and working them up by such little Accidents! How indefatigable is his Industry, and how constant his Watchfulness, not to slip any Opportunity that may in the least contribute to his Design! What a handsome Set of Disguises and Pretences is he always furnish'd with! How conceal'd does he lie! how little pretend, till [64] he is sure that his Plot will take! And at the same time that he nourishes the Hope of being Lord and Master, appears with all the Modesty and Submission of an humble and unpretending Admirer.

Can a woman then be too much upon her Guard? Can her Prudence and Foresight, her early Caution, be reckon'd unnecessary Suspicion, or ill-bred Reserve, by any but those whose Designs they prevent, and whose Interest it is to declaim against them? it being a certain Maxim with the Men, tho' Policy or Good Breeding won't allow them to avow it always, that the Women were made for their Sakes and Services, and are in all respects their Inferiors, especially in Understanding; so that all the Compliments they make, all the Address and Complaisance they use, all the Kindness they profess, all the Service they pretend to pay, has no other Meaning, no other End, than to get the poor Woman into their Power, to govern her according to their Discretion. This is all pure Kindness indeed, and therefore no Woman has Reason to be offended with it; for considering how much she is expos'd in her own, and how safe in their Keeping, 'tis the wisest thing she can do to put her self under Protection! And then if they have a tolerable Opinion of her Sense, and [65] not their Vanity but some better Principle disposes them to be something out of the way, and to appear more generous than the rest of their Sex, they'll condescend to dictate to her, and impart some of their Prerogative Books and Learning! 'Tis fit indeed that she should entirely depend on their Choice, and walk with the Crutches they are pleas'd to lend her; and if she is furnished out with some Notions to set her a prating I should have said to make her entertaining and the Fiddle of the Company, her Tutor's Time was not ill bestowed: And it were a diverting Scene to see her stript like the *Jay* of her borrowed Feathers, but he, good Man, has not ill Nature enough to take Pleasure in it! You may accuse him perhaps for giving so much Encouragement to a Woman's Vanity, but your Accusation is groundless, Vanity being a Disease the Sex will always be guilty of; nor is it a Reproach to them, since Men of Learning and Sense are overrun with it.

But there are few Women whose Understandings are worth the Management, their Estates are much more capable of Improvement. No Woman, much less a Woman of Fortune, is ever fit to be her own Mistress, and he who has not the Vanity to think what much finer things [66] he could perform had he the Management of her Fortune; or so much Partiality and Self-love, as to fancy it can't be better bestow'd than in making his; will yet be so honest and humble as to think that 'tis fit she should take his Assistance, as Steward at least. For the Good Man aspires no further, he would only take the Trouble of her Affairs off her Hand; and the Sense of her Condescention and his great Obligations, will for ever secure him against acting like a Lord and Master!

The Steps to Folly as well as Sin are gradual, and almost imperceptible, and when we are once on the Decline, we go down without taking notice on't; were it not for this, one cou'd not account for those strange unequal Matches we too often see. For there was a time no doubt, when a Woman could not have bore the very thought of what she has been afterwards betray'd into, it would have appear'd as shocking to her as it always does to other People; and had a Man been so impolitic as to discover the least intimation of such a Design, he had given her a sufficient Antidote against it. This your Wise Men are well satisfy'd of, and understand their own Interest too well to let their Design go bare-fac'd, for that would effectually put a barr to their Success. So [67] innocent are they, that they had not the least Thought at first of what their Good Fortune afterwards leads them to! They would draw upon him, (if they wear a Sword) or fly in her Face who should let fall the least hint that they had such Intentions; and this very Eagerness to avoid the Suspicion, is a shrewd Sign that there is occasion for't.

But who shall dare to shew the Lady her Danger, when will it be seasonable to give her friendly Notice? If you do it e're she is resolv'd, tho' with all the Friendship and Tenderness imaginable, she will hardly forgive the Affront, or bear the Provocation; you offer her an Outrage, by entertaining such a Thought, and 'tis ten to one if you are not afterwards accus'd for putting in her Head what otherwise she could ne'er have dreamt of. And when no direct Proof can be offer'd, when matter of Prudence is the only thing in Question, every Body has so good an Opinion of their own Understanding as to think their own way the best. And when she has her Innocence and fair Intentions to oppose to your Fears and Surmises, and you cannot pretend to wish her better than she does her self, to be more disinteress'd and diligent in your Watchfulness, or to see farther in what so nearly concerns her, what can be done? [68] Her ruin is commonly too far advanc'd to be prevented, e're you can in Good-breeding reach out a hand to help her. For if the Train has took, if she is entangled in the Snare, if Love, or rather a Blind unreasonable Fondness, which usurps the Name of that noble Passion, has gain'd on her, Reason and Perswasion may as properly be urg'd to the Folks in *Bethlem* [Bedlam] as to her. Tell her of this World, she is got above it, and has no regard to its impertinent Censures; tell her of the next, she laughs at you, and will never be convinc'd that Actions which are not expressly forbid can be Criminal, tho' they proceed from, and must necessarily be reduc'd to ill Principles, tho' they give Offence, are of ill Example, injure our Reputation, which next to our Innocence we are obliged as Christians to take the greatest care of, and in a word do more mischief than we can readily imagine. Tell her of her own Good, you appear yet more ridiculous, for who can judge of her Happiness but her self? And whilst our Hearts are violently set upon any thing, there is no convincing us that we shall ever be of another Mind. Our Passions want no Advocates, they are always furnish'd with plausible Pretences, and those very Prejudices, which gave rise to this unreasonable Passion, will for [69] certain give her Obstinacy enough to justifie and continue in it. Besides, some are so ill advis'd as to think to support one Indiscretion with another, they wou'd not have it thought they have made a false Step, in once giving countenance to that which is not fit to be continued. Or perhaps the Lady might be willing enough to throw off the Intruder at first, but wanted Courage to get above the fear of his Calumnies, and the longer she suffers him to buz about her, she will find it the harder to get rid of his Importunities. By all which it appears that she who really intends to be secure, must keep at the greatest distance from Danger, she must not grant the *least* Indulgence, where such ill uses will be made of it.

And since the case is so, that Woman can never be in safety who allows a Man opportunity to betray her. Frequent Conversation does for certain produce either Aversion or Liking, and when 'tis once come to Liking, it depends on the Man's Generosity not to improve it farther, and where can one find an Instance that this is any security? There are very many indeed which shew it is none. How sensible soever a Woman may appear of another's Indiscretion, if she will tread in the same steps, tho' but for a little way, she gives us no assurance that she will not fall into [70] the same Folly, she may perhaps intend very well, but she puts it past her Power to fulfil her good Intentions. Even those who have forfeited their Discretion, the most valuable thing next to their vertue, and without which Vertue it self is but very weak and faint, 'tis like were once as well resolv'd as she, they had the very same Thoughts, they made the same Apologies, and their Resentment wou'd have been every whit as great against those who cou'd have imagin'd they shou'd so far forget themselves.

It were endless to reckon up the divers Stratagems Men use to catch their Prey, their different ways of insinuating which vary with Circumstances and the Ladies Temper. But how unfairly, how basely soever they proceed, when the Prey is once caught it passes for lawful Prize, and other Men having the same hopes and projects see nothing to find fault with, but that it was not their own Good Fortune. They may exclaim against it perhaps in a Lady's hearing, but it is only to keep themselves from being suspected, and to give the better Colour to their own Designs. Sometimes a Woman is cajol'd, and sometimes Hector'd, she is seduc'd to Love a Man, or aw'd into a Fear of him: He defends her Honour against another, or [71] assumes the Power of blasting it himself; was willing to pass for one of no Consequence till he cou'd make himself considerable at her Cost. He might be admitted at first to be *her jest*, but he carries on the humour so far till he makes her *his*; he will either entertain or serve her as occasion offers, and some way or other gets himself intrusted with her Fortune, her Fame, or her Soul. Allow him but a frequent and free Conversation, and there's no manner of Question but that his Ingenuity and Application will at one time or other get the Ascendant over her.

And generally the more humble and undesigning a Man appears, the more improbable it looks that he should dare to pretend, the greater Caution shou'd be us'd against him. A bold Address and good Assurance may sometimes, but does not always, take. To a Woman of Sense an artificial Modesty and Humility is a thousand times more dangerous, for he only draws back to receive the more Encouragement, and she regards not what Advances she makes towards him, who seems to understand himself and the World so well, as to be incapable of making an ill use of them. Wou'd it not be unreasonable and a piece of Ill-breeding to be shy of him who has no Pretentions, or only such as are [72] Just and Modest? What hurt in a Visit? or what if Visits grow a little more frequent? The Man has so much discernment, as to relish her Wit and Humour, and can she do less than be Partial to him who is so Just to her? He strives to please and to render himself agreeable, or necessary perhaps, and whoever will make it his Business may find ways enough to do it. For they know but little of Human Nature, they never consulted their own Hearts, who are not sensible what advances a well-manag'd Flattery makes, especially from a Person of whose Wit and Sense one has a good Opinion. His Wit at first recommends his Flatteries, and these in requital set off his Wit; and she who has been us'd to this high-season'd Diet, will scarce ever relish another Conversation.

Having got thus far to be sure he is not wanting to his good Fortune, but drives on to an Intimacy, or what they are pleas'd now a days, tho' very unjustly, to call a Friendship; all is safe under this sacred Character, which sets them above little Aims and mean Designs. A Character that must be conducted with the nicest Honour, allows the greatest Trusts, leads to the highest Improvements, is attended with the purest Pleasures and most rational Satisfaction. And what if the malicious [73] World, envious of his Happiness, shou'd take Offence at it, since he has taken all due Precautions, such unjust and ill-natur'd Censures are not to be regarded; for his part the distance that is between them checks all aspiring desires, but her Conversation is what he must not, cannot want, Life is insipid and not to be endur'd without it; and he is too much the Lady's Friend, has too just a Value for her to entertain a Thought to her disadvantages.

Now if once it is come to this, GOD help the poor Woman, for not much Service can be done her by any of her Friends on Earth. That Pretender to be sure will be the Darling, he will worm out every other Person, tho' ever so kind and disinterested. For tho' true Friends will endeavour to please in order to serve, their Complaisance never goes so far as to prove injurious; the beloved Fault is what they chiefly strike at, and this the Flatterer always sooths; so that at last he becomes the most acceptable Company, and they who are conscious of their own Integrity are not apt to bear such an unjust Distinction, nor is it by this time to any purpose to remonstrate the Danger of such an Intimacy. When a Man, and for certain much more when a Woman, is fallen into [74] this Toyl, that is, when either have been so unwary and indiscreet as to let another find out by what Artifices he may manage their Self-love, and draw it over to his Party, 'tis too late for anyone who is really their Friend, to break the Snare and disabuse them.

Neither Sex cares to deny themselves that which pleases, especially when they think they may innocently indulge it; and nothing pleases more than the being admir'd and humour'd. We may be told of the Danger, and shown the Fall of others, but tho' their Misfortunes are ever so often or so lively represented to us, we are all so well assur'd of our own good Conduct, as to believe it will bring us safe off those Rocks on which others have been Shipwrackt. We suppose it in our Power to shorten the Line of our Liberty when ever we think fit, not considering that the farther we run, we shall be the more unwilling to Retreat and unable to judge when a Retreat is necessary. A Woman does not know that she is more than half lost when she admits of these Suggestions; that those Arguments she brings for continuing a Man's Conversation, prove only that she ought to have quitted it sooner; that Liking insensibly converts to Love, and that when she admits a Man to be her Friend, [75] 'tis his Fault if he does not make himself her Husband.

And if Men even the Modestest and the best, are only in pursuit of their own Designs, when they pretend to do the Lady Service; if the Honour they wou'd seem to do her, tends only to lead her into an Imprudent and therefore a Dishonourable Action; and they have all that good Opinion of themselves as to take everything for Encouragement, so that she who goes beyond a bare Civility tho' she meant no more than Respect, will find it Interpreted a Favour and made ill Use of, (for Favours how Innocent soever, never turn to a Lady's advantage;) what shadow of a Pretence can a Woman have for admitting an intimacy with a Man whose Principles are known to be Loose and his Practices Licentious? can she expect to be safe with him who has ruin'd others, and by the very same Methods he takes with her? If an Intimacy with a Man of a fair Character gives Offence, with a Man of an ill One, 'tis doubly and trebly Scandalous. And suppose neither her Fortune nor Beauty can Tempt him, he has his ill-natur'd Pleasure in destroying that Vertue he will not Practise, or if that can't be done, in blasting the Reputation of it at least, and in making the World believe he has made a Conquest tho' he has found a Foil.

[76] If the Man be the Woman's Inferior, besides all the Dangers formerly mention'd, and those just now taken notice of, she gives such a Countenance to his Vices as renders her in great measure partaker in them, and it can scarce be thought in such Circumstances, a Woman cou'd Like the Man if she were not reconcil'd to his Faults. Is he her Equal and no unsuitable Match, if his Designs are fair, why don't they Marry, since they are so well pleas'd with each other's Conversation, which in this State only can be frequently and safely allow'd? Is he her Better, and she hopes by catching him to make her Fortune, alas! the poor Woman is neither acquainted with the World nor her self, she neither knows her own Weakness nor his Treachery, and tho' he gives ever so much Encouragement to this vain Hope, 'tis only in order to accomplish her ruin. To be sure the more Freedom she allows, the more she lessens his Esteem, and that's not likely to encrease a real, tho' it may a pretended kindness; she ought to fly, if she wou'd have him pursue, the strictest Vertue and Reserve being the only way to secure him.

Religion and Reputation are so sure a Guard, such a security to poor defenceless Woman, that whenever a Man has ill [77] Designs on her, he is sure to make a Breach in one or both of these, by endeavouring either to corrupt her Principles to make her less strict in Devotion, or to lessen her value of a fair Reputation, and wou'd perswade her that less than she imagines will secure her as to the next World, and that not much regard is to be given to the censures of this. Or if this be too bold at first, and will not pass with her, he has another way to make even her Love to Vertue contribute to its ruin, by perswading her it never Shines as it ought unless it be expos'd, and that she has no reason to Boast of her Vertue unless she has try'd it. An Opinion of the worst consequence that may be, and the most mischievous to a Woman, because it is calculated to feed her Vanity, and tends indeed to her utter Ruin. For can it be fit to rush into Temptations when we are taught every day to pray against them? If the Trials of our Vertue render it Illustrious, 'tis such Trials as Heaven is pleas'd to send us, not those of our own seeking. It holds true of both Sexes, that next to the Divine Grace, a Modest Distrust of themselves is their best Security, none being so often and so shamefully Foil'd, as those who depend most on their own Strength and Resolution.

[78] As to the Opinion of the World, tho' one cannot say it is always just, yet generally it has a Foundation; great regard is to be paid to it, and very good use to be made of it. Others *may* be in fault for passing their Censures, but we certainly *are* so if we give them any the least just occasion. And since Reputation is not only one of the Rewards of Vertue, that which always ought, and generally does attend it, but also a Guard against Evil, an Inducement to Good, and a great Instrument in the Hand of the Wise to promote the common cause of Vertue, the being Prodigal of the one, looks as if we set no great value on the other, and she who abandons her good Name is not like to preserve her Innocence.

A Woman therefore can never have too nice a Sense of Honour, provided she does not prefer it before her Duty; she can never be too careful to secure her Character, not only from the suspicion of a Crime, but even from the shadow of an Indiscretion. 'Tis well worth her while to renounce the most Entertaining, and what some perhaps will call the most Improving Company, rather than give the World a just occasion of Suspicion or Censure. For besides the Injury that is done Religion, which enjoyns us to avoid the [79] very Appearance of Evil, and to do nothing but what is of good Report, she puts her self too much in a Man's Power who will run such a risque for his Conversation, and expresses such a value for him, as cannot fail of being made use of to do her a mischief.

Preserve your distance then, keep out of the reach of Danger, fly if you wou'd be safe, be sure to be always on the Reserve, not such as is Morose and Affected, but Modest and Discreet, your Caution cannot be too great, nor your Foresight reach too far; there's nothing, or what is next to nothing, a little Amusement and entertaining Conversation lost by this, but all is hazarded by the other. A Man understands his own Merit too well to lose his time in a Woman's Company, were it not to divert himself at her cost, to turn her into a Jest or something worse. And wherever you see great Assiduities, when a Man insinuates into the Diversions and Humors of the Lady, Liking and Admiring whatever she does, tho' at the same time he seems to keep a due Distance, or rather exceeds in the profoundest Respect, Respect being all he dare at present pretend to; when a more than ordinary deference is paid; when something particular appears in the Look and Address, and [80] such an Obsequiousness in every Action, as nothing cou'd engage a Man to, who never forgets the Superiority of his Sex, but a hope to be Observ'd in his turn: Then, whatever the Inequality be, and how sensible soever he seems to be of it, the Man has for certain his Engines at work, the Mine is ready to spring on the first opportunity, and 'tis well if it be not too late to prevent the poor Lady's Ruin.

To wind up this matter, if a Woman were duly Principled and Taught to know the World, especially the true Sentiments that Men have of her, and the Traps they lay for her under so many gilded Compliments, and such a seemingly great Respect, that disgrace wou'd be prevented which is brought upon too many Families, Women would Marry more discreetly, and demean themselves better in a Married State than some People say they do. The foundation indeed ought to be laid deep and strong, she shou'd be made a good Christian and understand why she is so, and then she will be everything else that is Good. Men need keep no Spies on a Woman's Conduct, need have no fear of her Vertue, or so much as of her Prudence and Caution, were but a due sense of true Honour and Vertue awaken'd in her, were her Reason excited and prepar'd [83] to consider the Sophistry of those Temptations which wou'd perswade her from her Duty; and were she put in a way to know that it is both her Wisdom and Interest to observe it; She would then duly examine and weigh all the Circumstances, the

Good and Evil of a Married State, and not be surpriz'd with unforeseen Inconveniences, and either never consent to be a Wife, or make a good one when she does. This would shew her what Human Nature *is*, as well as what it *ought* to be, and teach her not only what she may justly expect, but what she must be Content with; would enable her to cure some Faults, and patiently to suffer what she cannot cure.

Indeed nothing can assure Obedience, and render it what it ought to be, but the Conscience of Duty, the paying it for GOD's sake. Superiors don't rightly understand their own interest when they attempt to put out their Subjects Eyes to keep them Obedient. A Blind Obedience is what a Rational Creature shou'd never Pay, nor wou'd such an one receive it did he rightly understand its Nature. For Human Actions are no otherwise valuable than as they are conformable to Reason, but a blind Obedience is an Obeying *without Reason*, for ought we know *against it*. GOD himself does not require our [84] Obedience at this rate, he lays before us the goodness and reasonableness of his Laws, and were there anything in them whose Equity we could not readily comprehend, yet we have this clear and sufficient Reason on which to found our Obedience, that nothing but what's Just and Fit, can be enjoyn'd by a Just, a Wise and Gracious GOD, but this is a Reason will never hold in respect of Men's Commands, unless they can prove themselves infallible, and consequently Impeccable too.

It is therefore very much a Man's Interest that Women should be good Christians, in this as in every other Instance, he who does his Duty finds his own account in it. Duty and true Interest are one and the same thing, and he who thinks otherwise is to be pitied for being so much in the Wrong; but what can be more the Duty of the Head, than to Instruct and Improve those who are under Government? She will freely leave him the quiet Dominion of this World, whose Thoughts and Expectations are plac'd on the next. A Prospect of Heaven, and that only, will cure that Ambition which all Generous Minds are fill'd with; not by taking it away, but by placing it on a right Object. She will [85] discern a time when her Sex shall be no bar to the best Employments, the highest Honour; a time when that distinction, now so much us'd to her Prejudice, shall be no more, but provided she is not wanting to her self, her Soul shall shine as bright as the greatest Heroes. This is a true, and indeed the only consolation, this makes her a sufficient compensation for all the neglect and contempt the ill-grounded Customs of the World throw on her, for all the Injuries brutal Power may do her, and is a sufficient Cordial to support her Spirits, be her Lot in this World what it may.

But some sage Persons may perhaps object, that were Women allow'd to Improve themselves, and not amongst other discouragements driven back by those wise Jests and Scoffs that are put upon a Woman of Sense or Learning, a Philosophical Lady as she is call'd by way of Ridicule, they would be too Wise and too Good for the Men; I grant it, for vicious and foolish Men. Nor is it to be wonder'd, that he is afraid he shou'd not be able to Govern them were their Understandings improv'd, who is resolv'd not to take too much Pains with his own. But these 'tis to be hop'd are no very considerable Number, the foolish at [86] least; and therefore this is so far from being an Argument against Women's Improvement, that it is a strong one for it, if we do but suppose the Men to be as capable of Improvement as the Women, but much more if according to Tradition we believe they have greater Capacities. This, if any thing, wou'd stir them up to be what they ought, and not permit them to wast their Time and abuse their Faculties, in the Service of their irregular Appetites and unreasonable Desires, and so let poor contemptible Women who have been their Slaves, excel them in all that is truly Excellent. This wou'd make them Blush at employing an immortal Mind no better than in making Provision for the Flesh to fulfil the Lusts thereof, since Women by a Wiser Conduct have brought themselves to such a reach of Thought, to such exactness of Judgment, such clearness and strength of Reasoning, such purity and elevation of Mind, such Command of their Passions, such regularity of Will and Affection, and in a word, to such a pitch of Perfection, as the Human Soul is capable of attaining in this Life by the Grace of GOD, such true Wisdom, such real Greatness, as tho, it does not qualifie them to make a Noise in this [87][20] World, to found or overturn Empires, yet it qualifies them for what is infinitely better, a Kingdom that cannot be mov'd, an incorruptible Crown of Glory.

---

[20] Incorrectly paginated as 78 in the third edition.

Besides, it were ridiculous to suppose that a Woman, were she ever so much improv'd, cou'd come near the topping Genius of the Men, and therefore why shou'd they envy or discourage her? Strength of Mind goes along with Strength of Body, and 'tis only for some odd Accidents which Philosophers have not yet thought worth while to enquire into, that the Sturdiest Porter is not the Wisest Man! As therefore the Men have the Power in their Hands, so there's no dispute of their having the Brains to manage it! Can we suppose there is such a thing as[21] good Judgment and Sense upon Earth, if it is not to be found among them? Do not they generally speaking do all the great Actions and considerable Business of this World, and leave that of the next to the Women? Their Subtilty in forming Cabals and laying deep Designs, their Courage and Conduct in breaking through all Tyes Sacred and Civil to effect them, not only advances them to the Post of Honour, and keeps them securely in it for twenty or thirty Years, but gets them a Name, and [88] conveys it down to Posterity for some Hundreds, and who wou'd look any further? Justice and Injustice are administred by their Hands, Courts and Schools are fill'd with these Sages; 'tis Men who dispute for Truth as well as Men who argue against it; Histories are writ by them, they recount each others great Exploits, and have always done so. All famous Arts have their Original from Men, even from the Invention of Guns to the Mystery of good Eating. And to shew that nothing is beneath their Care, any more than above their Reach, they have brought *Gaming* to an Art and Science, and a more Profitable and Honourable one too, than any of those that us'd to be call'd *Liberal*! Indeed what is it they can't perform, when they attempt it? The Strength of their Brains shall be every whit as Conspicuous at their Cups, as in a Senate-House, and when they please they can make it pass for as sure a Mark of Wisdom, to drink deep as to Reason profoundly; a greater proof of Courage and consequently of Understanding, to dare the Vengeance of Heaven it self, than to stand the Raillery of some of the worst of their fellow Creatures.

Again, it may be said, if a Wife's case be as it is here represented, it is not [89] good for a Woman to Marry, and so there's an end

---

[21] 'There is no such thing as good Judgment and Sense upon Earth', is the phraseology of the first edition (1700, p. 91).

of [the] Human Race. But this is no fair Consequence, for all that can justly be inferr'd from hence, is that a Woman has no mighty Obligations to the Man who makes Love to her, she has no reason to be fond of being a Wife, or to reckon it a piece of Preferment when she is taken to be a Man's Upper-Servant; it is no advantage to her in this World, if rightly manag'd it may prove one as to the next. For she who Marries purely to do Good, to Educate Souls for Heaven, who can be so truly mortify'd as to lay aside her own Will and Desires, to pay such an intire Submission for Life, to one whom she cannot be sure will always deserve it, does certainly perform a more Heroic Action than all the famous Masculine Heroes can boast of, she suffers a continual Martyrdom to bring Glory to GOD and Benefit to Mankind, which consideration indeed may carry her through all Difficulties, I know not what else can, and engage her to Love him who proves perhaps so much worse than a Brute, as to make this Condition yet more grievous than it needed to be. She has need of a strong Reason, of a truly Christian and well-temper'd Spirit, of all the Assistance the best Education can give her, and ought [90] to have some good assurance of her own Firmness and Vertue, who ventures on such a Trial; and for this Reason 'tis less to be wonder'd at that Women Marry off in hast, for perhaps if they took time to consider and reflect upon it, they seldom wou'd Marry.

To conclude, perhaps I've said more than most Men will thank me for, I cannot help it, for how much soever I may be their Friend and humble Servant, I am more a Friend to Truth. Truth is strong, and sometime or other will prevail, nor is it for their Honour, and therefore one wou'd think not for their Interest, to be Partial to themselves and Unjust to others. They may fancy I have made some discoveries which like *Arcana Imperii*, ought to be kept secret, but in good earnest, I do them more Honour than to suppose their lawful Prerogatives need any mean Arts to support them. If they have Usurpt, I love Justice too much to wish Success and continuance to Usurpations, which tho' submitted to out of Prudence, and for Quietness sake, yet leave every Body free to regain their lawful Right whenever they have Power and Opportunity. I don't say that Tyranny *ought*, but we find in *Fact*, that it provokes the [91] Oppress'd to throw off even a Lawful Yoke that sits too heavy: And if he who is freely Elected, after all his fair Promises and the fine

Hopes he rais'd, proves a Tyrant, the consideration that he was one's own Choice, will not render more Submissive and Patient, but I fear more Refractory. For tho' it is very unreasonable, yet we see 'tis the course of the World, not only to return Injury for Injury, but Crime for Crime; both Parties indeed are Guilty, but the Aggressors have a double Guilt, they have not only their own, but their Neighbours ruin to answer for.

As to the Female Reader, I hope she will allow I've endeavour'd to do her Justice, nor betray'd her Cause as her Advocates usually do, under pretence of defending it. A Practice too mean for any to be Guilty of who have the least Sense of Honour, and who do any more than meerly pretend to it. I think I have held the Ballance even, and not being conscious of Partiality I ask no Pardon for it. To plead for the Oppress'd and to defend the Weak seem'd to me a generous undertaking; for tho' it may be secure, 'tis not always Honourable to run over to the strongest party. And if she infers from what has been said that Marriage is a [92] very Happy State for Men, if they think fit to make it so; that they govern the World, they have Prescription on their side, Women are too weak to dispute it with them, therefore they, as all other Governours, are most, if not only accountable, for what's amiss, for whether other Governments in their Original, were or were not confer'd according to the Merit of the Person, yet certainly in this case, if Heaven has appointed the Man to Govern, it has qualify'd him for it: So far I agree with her.[22] But if she goes on to infer, that therefore if a Man has not these Qualifications where is his Right? That if he misemploys, he abuses it? And if he abuses, according to modern Deduction, he forfeits it, I must leave her there. A peaceable Woman indeed will not carry it so far, she will neither question her Husband's Right nor his Fitness to Govern; but how? Not as an absolute Lord and Master, with an Arbitrary and Tyrannical sway, but as Reason Governs and Conducts a Man, by proposing what is Just and Fit. And the Man who acts according to that Wisdom he assumes, who wou'd have that Superiority he pretends to, ack-

---

[22] Compare the phraseology of the first edition, where Astell seems to be referring to Locke or some other author on the 'Original' of government who uses the principle of merit: 'in this case Heaven wou'd not have allotted the Man to Govern, but because he was best Qualify'd for it. So far I agree with him' (1700, pp. 96–7). The fourth edition (1730, p. 126) follows the third.

nowledg'd Just, will receive no Injury by any thing that has been offer'd here. A Woman will value him the more who is [93] so Wise and Good, when she discerns how much he excels the rest of his noble Sex; the less he requires, the more will he Merit that Esteem and Deference, which those who are so forward to exact, seem conscious they don't deserve. So then the Man's Prerogative is not at all infring'd, whilst the Woman's Privileges are secur'd; and if any Woman think her self Injur'd, she has a Remedy in reserve which few Men will Envy or endeavour to Rob her of, the Exercise and Improvement of her Vertue here, and the Reward of it hereafter.

A
FAIR WAY
WITH THE
DISSENTERS
AND THEIR
PATRONS.

Not Writ by Mr. L---y, or any other *Furious Jacobite*, whether Clergyman or Layman; but by a very Moderate Person and Dutiful Subject to the QUEEN.

by Mrs Mary Astell

LONDON:

Printed by *E. P.* for *R. Wilkin*, at the *King's-Head*, in St. *Paul's* Church-yard, 1704.

Note on the Text

A Fair Way with the Dissenters and their Patrons of 1704[1] was Astell's answer to Daniel Defoe's anonymous *More Short-Ways with the Dissenters* of the same year. It belongs to the pamphlet skirmishing over the Occasional Conformity debate, initiated by the introduction of the parliamentary bill in 1702 to permit Dissenters who attended the Anglican Church at least once a year to enjoy the privileges of government office. Although the Corporation and Test Acts of 1673 had not been repealed, an entire class of occasional conformists had grown up, to whom no serious objections were made until the flagrant conduct of Sir Humphrey Edwin, a Presbyterian Lord Mayor of London, drew attention to the matter by attending in full regalia both Dissenting and Anglican services on the same Sunday. Opening shots were fired in what was to become a pamphlet war by Daniel Defoe, whose pamphlet, *An Enquiry into the Occasional Conformity of Dissenters*, of 1698, opposed any conformity on

---

[1] Astell's subtitle to this pamphlet is highly satirical, its reference being directly to the claims of Daniel Defoe (*The Shortest Way with the Dissenters: Or Proposals for the Establishment of the Church* (London, 1702), *More Short-Ways with the Dissenters* (London, 1704)) and James Owen (*Moderation a Vertue: Or the Occasional Conformist Justify'd from the Imputation of Hypocrisy* (London, 1703) and *Moderation still a Vertue: In Answer to Several Bitter Pamphlets* (London, 1704)) against Leslie (as a 'furious Jacobite'), and for themselves (as 'Men of Moderation'). But it is also designed to ensure that Leslie does not get credit for her pamphlet. In the Postscript it is clear that she is piqued Owen should have given her (anonymous) *Moderation truly Stated: Or a Review of a Late Pamphlet, Entitul'd, Moderation a Vertue* (London, 1704) only passing mention, classing it with Charles Leslie's *The Wolf Strip of his Shepherd's Cloathing: In Answer to a Late Celebrated Book Intituled Moderation a Vertue* (London, 1704) which he gave close scrutiny.

the Dissenters' part. In 1701 the new Lord Mayor of London, Sir Thomas Abney, repeated the performance of his predecessor, providing the occasion for republication of Defoe's tract; this time he replaced the Preface to the mayor with one to John Howe (*q.v.*), pastor of the Dissenting church to which Abney belonged, and a supporter of Occasional Conformity as a conciliatory measure. Defoe was no conciliator, and his anonymous *The Shortest Way with Dissenters* (1702), which followed, burlesqued the 'high flyers', Charles Leslie, the nonjuror, and the later to be impeached Henry Sacheverell (*q.v.*). Defoe's ironical ploy was to 'outHerod Herod' by advocating Draconian punishments for dissent, recommending 'Gallows instead of the Counter, and the Gallies instead of the Fines' (p. 21). Certain incautious 'high flyers' fell for it, chagrined when the authorship of these views was later revealed to them – Astell (p. 7) refers to Defoe's pamphlet having been taken for a work of Sacheverell, as he himself claimed (*More Short-Ways with the Dissenters*, 1704, p. 8). When Charles Leslie had fired back with *Reflections Upon Some Scandalous and Malicious Pamphlets viz. I The Shortest Way with the Dissenters*, and then issued an anthology of the exchange in the form of *The New Association, Part II*, Defoe's tone became more serious. What he had originally painted as a possible scenario, the persecution of Dissenters and closure of the Dissenting academies, he now presented as Tory policy. It was in defence of Tory policy that Astell responded with her *Fair Way with the Dissenters*, in which she defends the positions of Leslie and Sacheverell, arguing that one does not have to be an extremist to hold that obedience to the English constitution required conformity to the Anglican Church. Thus the point of her subtitle: *Not Writ by Mr L—y, or any other Furious Jacobite, whether Clergyman or Layman; but by a very Moderate Person and Dutiful Subject to the Queen.*

Astell may also have been guarding against another case of mistaken identity, complaining in the Postscript (p. 24) that the arguments of *Moderation truly Stated*, quoted anonymously by James Owen (*Moderation still a Virtue*, p. 3), had been largely overlooked, and to the extent that they had been treated, classed with those of Leslie. Leslie's work, *The New Association. Part II . . . An Answer to some Objections in the Pretended D. Foe's Explication in 'the Reflections upon the Shortest Way'* (1703), was after all a reply to Defoe's earlier pamphlet. And it was in the Supplement to this work that Leslie had introduced the arguments against Locke for which he was to become famous, but which Astell had anticipated in her *Reflections upon Marriage* (1700, pp. 29, 32, 38–41, 92–5).

A Fair Way was Astell's second essay into the Occasional Conformity debate. Her first had been the pamphlet, *Moderation truly Stated: Or a Review of a Late Pamphlet, Entitul'd Moderation a Virtue, or, The Occasional Conformist Justified from the Imputation of Hypocrisy* (1704); a response to James Owen's *Moderation a Vertue* (1703). Owen's pamphlet, in support of Occasional Conformity, had also drawn fire from the 'high flyer' Leslie, whose pamphlet, *The Wolf Stript of his Shepherd's Cloathing etc.* (1704), set the tone for the debate. Owen countered with another pamphlet, *Moderation still a Virtue: In Answer to Several Bitter Pamphlets: Especially Two, Entituled Occasional Conformity a most Unjustifiable Practice*, and *The Wolf Stripp'd of his Shepherd's Cloathing* (1704, Preface, p. ii). There he referred to Leslie 'the Wolf-stripper', one of those who '*harangue us with tedious Narratives of the late Civil Wars, and the Confusions that followed; and they impute all to the present Dissenter, who were most of them unborn*'. We have no evidence for the precise dating of Astell's third pamphlet of 1704, *An Impartial Enquiry*, written in response to White Kennett's memorial sermon of the same year, but it might be this to which Owen (*Moderation still a Virtue*, p. 3) refers, once again mistaking a work by Astell for that of Leslie.

In the Postscript to *A Fair Way with the Dissenters*, Astell responded to Owen's reply (*Moderation still a Virtue*). It was undoubtedly a matter of disappointment to her that Owen did not subject *Moderation truly Stated* to the scrutiny he gave Leslie's 'Wolf', as she refers to it (p. 24). The attention Owen pays Leslie's pamphlet, whose authorship he seems only to have discovered in time for the Preface and Postscript (see pp. iii, 3–4, 32, 59, 60 and 67–96), may well have been additional cause for the disclaimer in the subtitle of Astell's pamphlet, *Not Writ by Mr L—y, or any other Furious Jacobite* – to ensure that Leslie did not get the credit for her pamphlet.

Difficult to read out of context, this Postscript, when related to the relevant arguments of the earlier pamphlets, gives a very good indication of the mood and texture of pamphlet warfare, full of allusion, satire, invective and, at times, high style. Great care has been taken to track the references as far as possible in order to position Astell correctly in this debate, as an indication of the range of materials she consulted and of her more general *modus operandi* as a pamphleteer. Astell took the opportunity in this Postscript to restate the arguments of *Moderation truly*

Stated, despite the fact that Owen had paid them only cursory attention. Closely read, it provides an abstract of her earlier pamphlet, too long to reproduce here, as well as a digest of the literature to which she responds. The Occasional Conformity debate, conducted over the life of the three bills introduced between 1702–5, up to the passing of the Act in 1711, and its repeal in 1719, brought to light the full panoply of arguments for and against religious toleration.

The Folger copy of *A Fair Way with the Dissenters* (Folger Library, BX5202.A7.Cage), shows it to have been a hastily printed pamphlet. Not only are the marginal notes in some cases smudged, but pp. 21–8 are incorrectly paginated because the page numbers 19–20 are missing; and pp. 29–32 are paginated as pp. 21–4. Original pagination is indicated in bold type in square brackets: my notes refer to this pagination.

Punctuation and spelling are preserved, although s and double s, etc., are modernized. Astell uses italics to indicate quotations. Errors of transcription are noted, although the ubiquitous small variations of spelling and punctuation are generally not.

[1] A Fair Way with the Dissenters

WELL! If in Disputes in Print and Disputes at *Billingsgate*,[2] which, as they are manag'd, are equally scolding, he were to carry the day who rails loudest and longest; Wo be to the poor Church and its Friends, they could never shew their Faces or hold up their Heads against the everlasting Clamour of their Adversaries. For what Thunder may we expect from those *too violent Spirits*,[3] which these meek and good Christians *do not deny* they have *among them* (*More Short-Ways. p.* 21), when even your *Moderate Men*, your *Men of Temper*, those hearty Advocates for *Peace and Union*, who even *chal-*

---

[2] Billingsgate, one of the gates of London at which a fish market was established, became in the seventeenth century an epithet for the abusive rhetoric that characterized its commerce (*OED*).

[3] Defoe's reference on p. 21 of *More Short-Ways*, which Astell cites, is clearly to the 'high flyers', Charles Leslie and Henry Sacheverell, in particular Sacheverell, whose preaching he elsewhere describes as, '*a Fury* made up of a Complication of Malice, intollerable Pride, bigotted Zeal, and bloody Hellish Unchristian Principles' (p. 18). The passage at p. 21 is a skilful example of what pretends to be an Anglican confession to extremism. It reads in full (p. 21): 'When in King *James* the Second's Time his Majesty found, that in order to reduce the Church, it was his business to Caress the Dissenters, and accordingly publish'd an Immediate Indulgence, a great many of the Dissenters made warm by their former sufferings, clos'd eagerly with the Proposals, and would willingly have set their Hand to the work; but when the Men of Temper, *for we do not deny to have some too violent Spirits among us,* came to consider the Case, they found the design struck at the whole Body of the Church of *England,* they considered them as Protestants and Brethren, they considered the Methods useing with them as Destructive to the Laws, as to the Church, and a Plot as well on Liberty as Religion.'

The quotations which follow, given by Astell in italics, are in fact taken from pp. 20–24 of Defoe's work, and in this case her attribution seems to be slightly less exact than usual, something marked throughout the pamphlet.

87

lenge us to it, as much as to say, that we may have *Peace and Union* with them if we dare;[4] when these good Souls, not at all given to *Revenge themselves, against the Christian Principle* (p. 23), being only *forced to expose others for their own just Vindication, and who had much rather live in peace, and bury the Iniquities, the Rebellion, King-killing, Persecution Principles, Etc. of theirs and our Forefathers* (p. 24), than come to an *Account*; for which no doubt they have their Reasons. When even these meek Lambs, who never *Insult their Brethren* (p. 1),[5] are forced to make [2] use of *Rudeness, Ill-manners, Opprobrious Language* (p. 12), *Bitter Scurrilous Invectives* (p. 10), *Rallying and Bullying* (p. 2), *Barbarous Designs, Fools Coat, Knaves Coat and Traitors Coat* (p. 3), (tho when a Coat fits a Man, according to *Cyrus*[6] his Justice, he ought to wear it) *Lampooning, Insolent Behaviour* (p. 3), *Gallows and Galleys, Essence of Persecution* (p. 4),[7] *Gall not a little and Prejudice to Extremity* (p. 9), *Positive Untruths* (p. 10), and, but that the word sticks a little in their Throats, they'd almost said *Lies*, but *Falshood and Prevarication, Positive Falsities*, are what they make no scruple at all of uttering, *Envy, Pride, ungoverned Passion* (p. 11), *Black Notions, full of Malice and empty of Charity, Genuine Forgery* (p. 13). Are forced to call a Minister of Christ, *a Fury made up of a Complication of Malice, intolerable Pride, Bigotted Zeal, and Bloody, Hellish, Unchristian Principles* (p. 18); accuse him of *Debauching the Pulpit, and Scandalizing the Ministerial Function* (p. 10), and with an *Heart full of Malice, through a Mouth full of Cursing and Bitterness* (p. 14), to lay the *Trifles of Drunkenness and Lewdness*

---

[4] Astell refers to the opening sentence of Defoe's pamphlet, which reads (*More Short-Ways*, p. 1): 'It is not without just Ground, a Challenge of Peace was made to the Nation in the Name of the dissenters, that the World might know who were the Men, in spight of her Majesty's frequent Invitation to *Union*, and the pressing Exhortations she made from the Throne for *Peace*, are constantly the Aggressors, on every occason Insult their Brethren, and prompt the Nation to Unite in their Destruction.'

[5] Astell systematically satirizes Defoe and the Dissenters in the language he had reserved for the 'high flyers' in a pastiche of quotations taken from Defoe's attack on Sacheverell (*More Short-Ways*, 1704, pp. 7ff.) and Leslie (p. 3).

[6] The Cyrus in question may be the son of Cambyses and descendant of the founder of the Achaemenid Persian Empire, celebrated in Xenophon's *Cyropaedia*. But the association with treason makes it more likely to be his namesake, Cyrus, younger son of Darius II, accused on his father's death of treason against his brother, Artaxerxes II, and killed in battle against him in 401 BC.

[7] Defoe's language here refers to his own *The Shortest Way with the Dissenters* (p. 24), about which he has come clean (*More Short-Ways*, p. 4).

(*p.* 7) to the charge of two Famous Universities, besides those more substantial Crimes of *Unjust and Unfair Terms and Imposed Oaths*,[8] that is, Oaths to be true to the Government in Church and State, which if they were laid aside, the honest conscientious Dissenters, to get in two thousand of their Children, would *venture* the poor Babies *Morals*, in relation to the former *Trifles of Lewdness and Drunkenness*, nay even the Danger of being infected with *Farce in their Sermons and Buffoonery in their Preaching* (*p.* 9), which, for ought any one knows, may be suck'd in by them in a more natural Air. And to say all in a word, to accuse the whole Church of *Want of Justice*, (*p.* 4) of *Treachery* (*p.* 22), *Barbarities, Injustices*, (according to the *English* of these Correctors of our Stile and Manners) and *Ingratitude to Dissenters* (*p.* 23).

A heavy Charge! and what can be said to't? for were I ever so much disposed to bluster and make a noise, to treat these Folks with all that Contempt that is due to little Scriblers and Busiebodies, who, either for Bread, and to deserve their Wages of the Party, or out of an innate Love to Mischief, alarm the Mob, and impose upon the Ignorant and Careless Reeader [*sic*], by venting bold Slanders and notorious Untruths, in a plausible Stile and with some shews of Probability, with an Insolence peculiar to [3] themselves, and a matchless Effrontery;[9] yet alas for me! I go to Church every

---

[8] Defoe, *More Short-ways* (p. 7). The oaths in question were imposed by the Corporation and Test Acts of 1673.

[9] Astell is doubtless responding to Defoe's defence in *More Short-Ways* (p. 2) that his only crime in *The Shortest Way* was to take too seriously High Church polemic demanding the destruction of the Dissenters, for which he asks 'pardon of the Church of *England* . . . that he, like a too credulous Fool, gave any heed to such slight and cursory things as *Preaching*, and *Printing* of Books'. Tossing back Henry Sacheverell's slurs (*The Nature and Mischief of Prejudice and Partiality Stated in a Sermon Preached at St Mary's in Oxford at the Assizes held there, March 9, 1703/ 4*, second edition (London, 1708), p. 14) on the Dissenters as 'Double-dealing *Practical Atheists*, whose *Gain* is their *Godliness*, whose *Profit* is their *Religion*, and whose *Interest* is both their *God* and *Conscience*! Who can Betray and Sell their *Saviour* for *Money*', Defoe goes on to accuse the High Church party of cheap politicking (*More Short-Ways*, p. 2): 'What tho' the Author of whom we are now treating has declar'd from the Pulpit, that a Man can't be a true Son of the Church of *England*, but he must lift up the bloody Flag against the Dissenters; yet since Printing Books is but a Modern Contrivance *to get a Penny*, and ought to be prepar'd so as may best suit the Market, and Sermons are only long Speeches directed to, and made to please the Auditory, and consequently suited to their Circumstances and Humour, it does not therefore follow, that because they have Preach'd and Printed these things, they really Intended and Design'd the thing,

day, and of course hear the Scripture read in the Liturgy, and this has so dampt my Courage, that I dare not bring a *Railing tho a true Accusation* no not against the *Devil* himself, but can only say with Michael, the *Prince* of the Church, *The Lord rebuke thee.*

But Anger and Ill Language apart, and to deliver them from the fear of that which their Charity and good Nature would be so loth to find, that our *Discourses are Banter,* and our *Preaching Buffoonry;*[10] I shall frankly own with an Ingenuity they would do well to practise, that the *Total Destruction of Dissenters as a Party* (the Barbarous Usage that *More Short Ways* is so afraid of) is indeed our Design. 'Tis the Design of all honest Men and good Christians, even of the Dissenters themselves, if they may be believed, and if they are not notorious Hypocrites. And supposing the Bill against *Occasional Conformity*[11] aim'd at this, which is the very worst that Wit or Malice can charge it with; no violence was done in the least to the *Toleration Act,*[12] no *Ruin,* no Injury wou'd have followed to Dissenters; nothing indeed could have been more for their Interest and Real Good. For if I do not make it out before I have done, that to strike at *the Root of the Dissenting Interest* (p. 4), *to extirpate and destroy* Dissention (p. 3), and hinder its *Succession in the Nation,* neither hurts the Consciences, the Persons, nor the Estates of the Dissenters, *then I do nothing*; and promise to pull in my Horns and tamely be condemn'd, to hear only their Sermons and read all their

---

no, Good Men, it was far from their Thoughts. The Author therefore was most justly punish'd for his Folly, in believing any thing they said and pretending to Alarm the Dissenters for the little insignificant Performances of the Pulpit or the Press.'

Astell countered with the obvious response that it was Defoe who was the opportunistic party man and that the Tories were deadly serious in demanding the destruction of the Dissenting party. In *An Impartial Inquiry into the Causes of Rebellion and Civil War in this Kingdom* (London, 1704), she refers again to 'those Mercenary Scriblers whom all sober Men condemn, and who only write after the Fact, or in order to it, to make their own Fortunes, or to justifie their own Wickedness', probably with reference to Defoe who, along with John Tutchin (*q.v.*), was sued for libel in 1704.

[10] Here Astell has a scattershot approach to Defoe's text, picking epithets from here and there without textual acknowledgement, partly because Defoe repeats the epithets so much himself. The phraseology here is found in Defoe's *More Short-Ways,* p. 5.

[11] The Occasional Conformity Bills of 1702–5, introduced unsuccessfully by Tories into the House of Commons.

[12] The Toleration Act, allowing freedom of worship for Protestant dissenters, passed in 1689.

Pamphlets, and in fine, to be *Daniel Burgess*[13] and *Defoe's* Convert.

To the Business then: How often have we been told of the *fatal Consequences of our Divisions*, that *Disunion first weakens, and then destroys the Body Politick*; and that if we *are acted by the Spirit of Disunion, 'tis a sign the things of our Peace are hid from us, and that we are judicially devoted to Destruction*; and are therefore call'd upon *to heal the Breaches*, [4] by the great Advocates for what they term *Moderation*, being assur'd by them of the Dissenters willingness to come to *Terms of Accommodation*, that henceforth there may be no more Divisions among us, but that the Protestant Interest may be strengthened, and we may *all be Brethren?*[14] Where then is the harm of putting an end to the *Dissenting Party*, and removing all Marks of Distinction? Is not this what we really, and what they at least seemingly desire? Both sides agree in the end, tho' they cannot agree about the means of doing it.

Now suppose St. *Peter* and St. *Paul*, or Men who act by their Authority, are influenc'd by their Spirit, and preach nothing but their Doctrine, shou'd prevail upon our Dissenters to *mark such as cause Divisions and to avoid* them, and to maintain *the Unity of the Spirit in the Bond of Peace*; would not this be the *ruin of Dissenters as a Party*, and totally *destroy the Succession of them in this Nation?*[15] On the other hand, to make a supposition that may please them better; suppose Dissenters were agreed among themselves, and that they were able to tell us what will satisfie them; suppose *the Men of Moderation, who gave Peace to the Dissenters* (p. 19), shou'd open their Arms and the Doors of their Church as wide as Heart could wish, not leaving a Ceremony, or so much as the Creed and Lords Prayer, to offend a Conscientious Dissenting Brother; wou'd you be Coy? wou'd you still draw back, for fear of *Destroying the Succession of Dissenters?* no I warrant ye, Dissenters know their Interest a little better. So then I hope I have made good my Point, that Dissenters may be destroy'd as a *Party*, without any the least Damage, either to the Consciences or Interests of Dissenters. If I am in the wrong, pray tell me what your Writers mean by Moderate Episcopacy, by Comprehension and Union? are these only pretty

---

[13] Daniel Burgess (*q.v.*), Presbyterian preacher.
[14] This is the burden of Defoe's argument in *More Short-Ways*, but these are not his words.
[15] Defoe's *More Short-Ways*, p. 4.

words to draw us on to make our Court, that you may have the Honour of rejecting us; [5] and may shew the World what great Offers you refuse, only for the dear sake of the Dissenting Party and Interest? And that Division is so sweet a thing, so many Markets are to be made by't, that you wou'd not, scarce for Heaven it self for it's a place of Union, have Dissention extirpated; but had much rather part with Apostolical Succession, than with a Succession of Dissenters?

So then, Brother *Short-ways* has a little over-shot himself, in being so violently concern'd for the Destruction of Dissenters as a Party. The poor Man was to blame to discover the Mystery, it should have been kept among Friends, whilst the World had been amus'd with tender Consciences and grievous Persecutions; that is, in plain *English*, the keeping a Man out of a Place, who can't come into't but by violating his Conscience. For *some* there are who *have Charity* little enough to suggest, that this is *the very Essence of Persecution (p. 9)*: and truly one can't but think that *Short-ways* is of this mind, when he affirms it to be a *Positive Untruth*, that Episcopacy is Persecuted in *Scotland*: No says he, the *Church has fair Quarter* there *(p. 17)*; and how does he make it out? Why, they *may enjoy the Advantages of Places and Preferments*, as often as the Queen thinks fit to give them, *a thing we are denied here*, says he: We have Liberty of Conscience 'tis true, Indulged us by Law, whilst they are not allow'd to Worship GOD after their own Way, so much as in Private, so far as Presbyterians can hinder it, notwithstanding the Queens desire and Letter on their behalf; and therefore from these Premises it undeniably follows, that they have *fair Quarter*, and we are Persecuted for Conscience sake. Admirable Logick! only to be learn'd in Mr. *Morton's* Academy,[16] for *Oxford* and *Cambridge* are never

---

[16] Charles Morton (*q.v.*), Puritan divine, established a Dissenting Academy at Stoke Newington in the 1670s, of which Defoe was a proud pupil, as he admits in *More Short-Ways* (p. 5). Defoe is addressing the claims of Samuel Wesley, whose letter criticizing the Dissenting Academies as antimonarchical (Wesley, *A Letter from a Country Divine to his Friend in London, concerning the Education of Dissenters in their Private Academies*, second edition (London, 1704), had been published without his permission). Defoe comes strongly to the defence of the Academies here, noting correctly that Wesley like himself had been a pupil of Morton. Defoe was joined by Samuel Palmer, whose *A Defence of the Dissenters' Education in their Private Academies* (170?) attracted Wesley's rebuttal: *A Defence of a Letter on the Education of Dissenters* (1704), followed in turn by Palmer's *A Vindication of the Learning, Loyalty, Morals of the Dissenters. In Answer to Mr Wesley* (1705).

like to *match* it. Let this then pass for the Second Mistake, I would not for the World say *Positive Untruth* (*p.* 10), much less [6] that broad Ill-manner'd word *L—s*,[17] which our Friend *Short-ways* has happen'd to fall into.

A Third may be his talking for Peace and Union in one Page (*p.* 1), and in a little while being very angry at any thing that looks like *preventing Posterity*, from keeping up a *Succession of* Dissenters *in this Nation*. This is, says he, a *striking at the Root of the Dissenters Interest* (*p.* 4, 5); their Interest then, say I, is the main of their Religion; and Division is the Principal Article of their Faith. The Dissenters either believe our Communion Sinful and Damnable, or they do not believe it so; if the first, then they do that which so much provokes *Short-ways*, when he supposes it done by Mr. *S.*[18] towards Dissenters (*p.* 13), they exclude us from hopes of Salvation;[19] nay, they themselves do wilfully commit a Sin for *filthy Lucres sake*, as often as they become *Occasional Conformists* for Preferment. But if our Communion is not absolutely Sinful, but only would be so to them, because they doubt of it, and because their Consciences are tender, which is the only justifiable Reason for granting Liberty of Conscience; what necessity of Nursing up their Children in the same Doubts and Scruples? which, make the best of them, are but Weaknesses; must the Off-springs Consciences needs be of the same Cut and Fashion with their Fore-father? And were it not better both for their own Posterity, and for the Nation

---

[17] Defoe in *More Short-Ways* (p. 10) refers to Sacheverell's sermon of 9 March 1703/4, under discussion, namely, *Nature and Mischief.* There Sacheverell had enumerated five causes of the Dissenters' prejudice: '1. *Education* and *Custom.* 2. *Ignorance* and *Affectation.* 3. *Conversation* and *Company.* 4. *Authority* and *Example.* 5. *Interest* and *Party*' (pp. 9–15). Sacheverell had launched a vicious attack on the Dissenters, including the Dissenting Academies (pp. 23–4). Defoe (*More Short-Ways*, p. 10) countered by charging Sacheverell with 'positive Untruths, I am loath to say *L—s*, of which I'le prove, you have in this one Sermon debauch'd the Pulpit with about Fourteen', which he goes on to enumerate. Astell in turn structures her case against Defoe in terms of his fourteen points.

[18] Henry Sacheverell.

[19] Defoe, *More Short-Ways*, p. 13, denied the charges made by Sacheverell against the Dissenters of 'Phanaticism' and 'Diabolical Prejudices' (see especially Sacheverell, *Nature and Mischief*, pp. 14–15). He accuses Sacheverell of staking out an exclusivist position that none of the 'Eminent Persons' of his own Church would support: 'none of 'em would ever Advance a Notion so Black, so full of Malice, and so empty of Charity, that we are under *Diabolical Prejudices*, and consequently *cannot be sav'd out of your Church*, this is Popery in its Exalted Extreams'.

in general (to which certainly these great Pretenders to Publick Spiritedness ought to have some regard) to lay the Seeds of Dissention as much out of their Childrens way as possible, and not beat into their Heads such Fancies and Prejudices as would ne'er come there, were they not drove in by an aukward Education, or afterwards taken up upon Worldly and Unchristian Views, and for Temporal Advantage? *Short-ways* may call it *Nonsense* as long as he please (*p.* 5),[20] but surely could a Method be found out to prevent Posterity from falling into the Separation, it [7] would be one of the greatest Benefits could be done this Kingdom, and no manner of Prejudice to the Toleration Suppressing of their Schools would be a very good and necessary Work, were it like to destroy a Faction; which sure could do no manner of hurt to a truly Conscientious Dissenter. As for such as would keep up the Party and Separation to perpetuity, unless we're resolv'd to wink very hard and to take no warning of the Precipice, they plainly shew us, that the Ruin of the Church is the thing they are resolv'd on, and that their fear of being prevented in this Design is the only matter that Alarms them, how loudly soever they may Clamour, with their pretended Fears of their own Destruction.

Fourthly, It is not true that Mr. *Sacheverel* is the *Real Author of the Shortest-way*, or else your Friend *Defoe* is a Plagiary; that *Original* of Honesty, Truth and Ingenuity, being Printed among his *Handicrafts*, with his own *shining* Face in the front of them. As for Mr. *Sacheverel*, and those other Gentlemen whom *Short-ways* is so free with, they are of Age let them answer for themselves. Tho' if the *Revd. B—op*, the *Esq; M—*, the *Dr. H—* (*p.* 2), be any where but *in nubibus*, they ought to *be expos'd or the Slander silenc'd.*[21]

---

[20] Astell refers to one of the arguments against Dissent reported by Defoe (*More Short-Ways*, p. 5): 'That this design of suppressing their Schools does not Affect the Dissenters, they may serve God according to the Toleration their own Way, it only prevents Posterity following their Method.' To this Defoe responded 'this is such jesting with the dissenters, and such a civil way of telling them they are all Fools, that it can hardly be allow'd to pass without a little Satyr upon the Nonsense of it'. It is an argument that, undeterred, Astell repeats.

[21] Defoe, *More Short-Ways*, p. 2 reads: 'What tho' a Reverend B—op had frequently said we shou'd never be well in *England*, till all the Dissenters were serv'd as the *Huguenots* in *France*? What tho' Esq: *M—* has given it under his Hand, that he heartily prays God would give her Majesty the Grace to put all that was wrote there in the Book call'd *The Shortest Way* in Execution? What tho' Dr. H—

Short-ways wants no assurance that I can find, to speak out in Words at length, or if the modest Man's diffidence restrain him, there's a Mr. *Defoe*, who spares ne'er a Sovereign Prince in *Christendom*, will do it for him.[22] And since this exalted Person, and many of his rigid Dissenting Brethren, damn *Occasional Conformity*, and have writ against it, even in Contradiction to Patriarch *How*;[23] what harm I pray for a poor Church-man to *Banter* it a little, and to take a *loose* after the Mode of the Times, now Madness is so much in Fashion (*p.* 8)?[24] And it is not improbable, that *Short-ways* has discovered the true cause of the Politick Dissenters rigour against Brother *Occasional*; they would have the Government know, what they tell [8] you a Bishop has prov'd, was Queen *Elizabeth's*

frequently has Preach'd and Printed too, that the Dissenters were a Brood of Traytors, and the Spawn of the Rebels, and not fit to live?'. Defoe does not identify the Bishop here, or in *The Shortest Way* (pp. 5, 12–13) where he discusses the Huguenots; nor does he identify Dr H. or Esq. M. Henry Sacheverell might conceivably be Dr H. In *The Nature and Mischief*, p. 24, Sacheverell referred to the Dissenting Academies as 'These *Schools* and *Nurseries* of *Rebellion* [which] have *Spawn'd* That Multitude of *Factions*, *Hetherodoxs*, *Atheistical*, *Lewd* Books, and *Seditious* Libels, which are every day *Publish'd* against *Monarchy*, and the Establish'd *Hierarchy*, and *Religion*'. Criticism of Louis XIV's treatment of the Huguenots and its obvious parallels in the Church of England's treatment of Independents intensified after 1681. The debate begun in France between Jacques Benigne Bossuet, defending persecution, and Pierre Bayle, defending toleration, spread to England (Goldie, 1991, 338). Among the many divines who participated it is impossible to establish which bishop Defoe has in mind. Samuel Parker in *Ecclesiastical Polity* (1670) and *Religion and Loyalty: Or a Demonstration of the Power of the Christian Church within itself* (1684) compared John Owen (*q.v.*), leader of the Independents and known as 'Cromwell's Pope', with Donatus the schismatic whose persecution St Augustine condoned. He was an early advocate of intolerance, as was Edward Stillingfleet, Dean of St Paul's (1678–89) and Bishop of Worcester (1689–99), in his works *The Mischief of Separation* (1680) and the *Unreasonableness of Separation* (1681) (Goldie, 1991, 333, 342). Thomas Long, who refused the bishopric of Bristol and was never offered another, defended coercion against Dissenters, as did John Sharp, and Thomas Tenison (1636–1715), Archbishop of Canterbury.

[22] Astell's apparent riddle would seem to refer to the two Defoes, one author of *The Shortest Way with the Dissenters*, who made the case against Occasional Conformity; the other, author of *More Short-Ways*, who made the case for it.

[23] John Howe had argued for a radical separation of Church and state as promoted by Locke in his *Letter on Toleration*, which would leave religious doctrine to conscience and private belief and disempower the clergy (see Ashcraft, 1986, 482–4, 500–51; Schwoerer, 1990, 545).

[24] The italicized remarks are to Defoe's *More Short-Ways*, p. 9, not p. 8 as Astell indicates.

Practise, that *Persons of different Religions*, ought to be admitted, without Scruple or Caution, *into Places of Trust* (*p.* 9, 10);[25] the Laws notwithstanding, which can never be injur'd by being dispens'd with in Favour of Dissenters, and then *the Test would cease*, and *Occasional Conformity would die of course*;[26] and so no need of a Bill, the Business is done without it.

Fifthly, *Short-ways* manner of Proof, that his Tutor *Morton's*[27] Politicks *were not Antimonarchial*, nor *Destructive* to our *Constitution* (*p.* 5, 6), I know not whether to call a Falshood or a Flam. For tho' the antient *Manuscripts now above 25 Years old, are left at the Publishers for any one to peruse*; yet who this Publisher is, the Man in the Moon can tell; for my part I read no Direction to find him, either in Book or Title Page.[28] But one needs not thumb over and wear these choice

---

[25] Astell refers to Defoe's discussion in *More Short-Ways* (pp. 9–10) of *The Bishop of Salisbury's* [Gilbert Burnet's] *Speech in the House of Lords, upon the Bill against Occasional Conformity* (1704, p. 2), in which Burnet claimed Elizabeth I's precedent for religious toleration: 'It is certain she treated the Papists all along with a very particular Indulgence. She would have the Peers excused from the Obligation to take the Oath of Supremacy. She employed Papists in all Her Affairs: They were Privy-Councellors and Lords Lieutenants. Her Lord-Treasurer protested against all the Acts for the Reformation; and was known to be a Church-Papist, or an *Occasional Conformist*; and yet he continued in that great Post Fourteen Years, till he died. She encouraged the *Occasional Conformity* of Papists, and apprehended no Danger in that, even from them: And yet I hope, it will be acknowledged, that there was more reason to be afraid, considering both their Numbers, and the Hopes they had for many Years of a Popish Successor, than we have now to be afraid of the Dissenters.' (See *A Fair Way*, p. 16 and n.). This was an argument made not only with respect to England, but other nations. James Owen, for instance, in *Moderation a Vertue* (pp. 36–49), to which Astell responded with *Moderation truly Stated*, had presented 'a short View of the *four great Empires* of the World, the *Assyrian*, or *Babylonian*, that of the *Medes* and *Persians*, of the *Grecians* and *Romans*, in all which, *Dissenters* from the Publick Religion have been prefer'd' (p. 36).

[26] Defoe, *More Short-Ways*, p. 10. Defoe is referring to the various Test Acts directed at Roman Catholics and later Nonconformists; in particular, that of Elizabeth I of 1563, imposing the Oath of Allegiance and abjuration of the power of Rome on all officeholders but peers; and that of Charles II of 1673, which extended the provisions of the Corporation Act of 1661 to include all officeholders without exception, and which included a declaration against transubstantiation.

[27] Charles Morton.

[28] Defoe had owned in *More Short-Ways* (pp. 5–6) to being a pupil of '*Charles Morton of Newington Green*' and being able personally to testify: 'I must do that learned Gentleman's memory that Justice to affirm, that neither in his System of Politicks Government and Discipline, or in any other Exercises of that School, was there any thing Taught or Encourag'd, that was Antimonarchical, or Destructive to the Government, or Constitution of *England*; and particularly among the

Papers, *Short-ways* lets us know how well he profited under such Instructions, both in the Art of Reasoning and in Politicks. For 'Justice', says he, '*which is the end*, is superiour to the King that Executes, *who is the means*; therefore, Evil Administring Princes may be Depos'd!' (*p.* 8) Who but a Dissenter could ever have had Brains enough to pick this out of Mr. *Sacheverel's* Sermon![29] Tho' it follows most undeniably by a Chain of Mr. *Hobbes's* Consequences:[30] As thus, 'The Regular Administration of Justice, is the Grand End and Design, both of Government and Law' (says Mr. *Sacheverel.*);[31]

Now the End is always superior to the Means,

Therefore Justice is superior to the King, (says *Short-ways.*)

Therefore the People are so; for you know the People and Justice are Terms Synonymous.

Performances of that School, I find a Declamation relating to the benefit of a single Person in a Common-Wealth, wherein it is declar'd and prov'd from History and Reason, that Monarchy is the best Government, and the best suited to the Nature of Government, and the Defence of Property; which Discourse, together with the said Manuscripts, System of Politicks and Government, as Read in that School, and which are now above 25 Years old, are left at the Publishers of this Book for any one to peruse, as a Satisfaction of the truth of Fact.

    As Astell points out, however, Defoe's pamphlet does not give his publisher's name or address. Morton left behind important works that reflected the scientific and humanist curriculum of his academy and were textbooks at Harvard College, where he held tenure as Vice-President, for many years. See especially his *Compendium physicae* and *The Spirit of Man* (Boston, 1693).

[29] Astell paraphrases, rather than quotes, Defoe in *More Short-Ways* (p. 8), who analyzes Sacheverell's sermon, which he identifies only in the following terms 'Mr. *Sacheverell* of *Oxford* has blown his second Trumpet, to let us know he has not yet taken down his Bloody Flag, and that he was the Real Author of the *Shortest Way*, tho' another was Punish'd for it, and we see he has the face to let them know, he is still of the same mind.'

[30] This is probably a stock phrase for Thomas Hobbes' methodology. But the argument to which Astell sarcastically applies it is an Aristotelian syllogism, fabricated by Defoe (*More Short-Ways*, p. 8) out of Sacheverell's argument, which she here repeats, and no Hobbesian demonstration of Epicurean and Gassendist (*q.v.*) causality.

[31] Quoted by Astell from Defoe's *More Short-Ways* (p. 8), who quotes it in turn as 'the very first Lines' of Sacheverell's sermon under discussion, which begins, quoting 1 Timothy, 5:21, with the sort of charges against the Dissenters we find in Astell herself, of base and mercenary partiality (*Nature and Mischief*, p. 1): 'As all Government is Built upon Law, and all Law is Supported by the due Execution, and regular Administration of Justice, which is the Grand End and Design of Both: So there's Nothing that does more effectually Overturn Its Foundation, Countermine and Defeat Its good intention, and utterly Disappoint and Evacuate Its Force and Power, than a *Personal Prejudice*, or a Blind, Mercenary, and Base *Partiality*.'

Therefore they may Execute Justice when the King neglects it, for they always do it Impartially, they never *over-turn and destroy the end of Government*, nor Judge amiss in their own Cause!

[9] Therefore *Deposing Tyrannick Evil-Administrating Princes cannot be criminal*! and as to the *Learning* and *Honesty* of this *Performance*, let any *Oxonian match* it, and *out-do it if he can* (*p.* 8).[32] Especially taking in the *Design they own*, as *Short-ways* tells *p.* 14. 'of maintaining their Just Rights and Privileges as *English* men, and by all lawful Means to oppose and suppress all sorts of Tyranny and Oppression, as well Ecclesiastical as Civil.' *Other Designs* they have not, nor do we, or need we charge them with other, for this is sufficient to do the Business, if either their Writings or their Practices may be allowed to explain it. And because I do not love to make endless Repetitions, I shall refer my Reader for this Explanation to *Dissenters Sayings*,[33] or if this is out of Print, let him consult *Moderation truly Stated*, where he may find such *unanswerable Proofs, from such Just Authorities and Plain Matters of Fact* (*p.* 24),[34] (which, tho' *Short-ways* boasts of, yet is only produced by his Opposers, and which Dissenters have but little to say to,)[35] as make it out beyond a Contradiction, that Dissenters are by Principle and Practice irreconcileable Enemies to our Government in Church and

---

[32] The Oxonian in question is Sacheverell, to whom Defoe (*More Short-Ways*, p. 8) issues this challenge.

[33] *The Dissenters' Sayings Published in their Own Words* (1681), work of Roger L'Estrange (*q.v.*), in his capacity of first Surveyor of the Imprimery, a position he used to draw up a list of seditious pamphlets and propositions for the king (Schwoerer, 1993, 235). *The Shortest Way* (p. 1) begins with 'a story in his [L'Estrange's] Collection of Fables, of the Cock and the Horses'.

[34] Astell, *Moderation truly Stated*, p. 24, where Astell gives 'Precedents of Dissenters' from the New Testament, quoting John 4:20, 5:22 and Christ's opinion of the Samaritans, that '*they Worship'd they knew not what*'. On the basis of this internal evidence we can conclude *Moderation truly Stated* was produced earlier in the same year as *A Fair Way with the Dissenters and their Patrons* (London, 1704) (see Hill, 1986, 214 n.2).

[35] Astell implies that Defoe's claim in the closing sentence to *More Short-Ways* (p. 24) to expose calumnies against the Dissenters merely proves the Tory case. He had promised: 'And I design once a Month to give a particular of the Misrepresentations and base Treatment the Dissenters receive from this Party, till I have gone thro' the whole History, so I shall produce such unanswerable Proofs, such just Authorities and plain Matter of Fact, that I have no Apprehension of being disprov'd, having no need to help out our Cause with so weak and disadvantageous a shift as the refuge of Lyes.'

State, declar'd Opposers of Liberty of Conscience, when they themselves have the Power in their Hands, and the bitterest Persecutors. So justly might Mr. *Sacheverel* 'appeal to the Histories of our Kingdom, whether ever they gave the Church the least Favour or Quarter, when they had her under their Power.'[36]

In short, all Government in the Church, except their own Discipline is Tyranny. Let the worthy Mr. *Baxter* be my witness, who tells us, 'That *English* [10] Prelacy is the Product of Proud Ambition and Arrogancy, and contrary to the express Command of Christ' (*Disput. p.* 45); that it is a 'Government that gratifieth the Devil and Wicked Men' (*p.* 36); and that 'Bishops are Thorns and Thistles and the Military Instruments of the Devil' (*Concord. p.* 122).[37] And 'What is this Prelacy? (says Dr. *Owen*) a mere Antichristian Encroachment upon the Inheritance of Christ' (Thanksg. Serm. Oct. 14th 1651, *p.* 5).[38] And as for the State, every Government, and all even the mildest Administration is, in their Gibberish, Tyranny, if it does not pass through their hands, and is not managed according to their Humours. And their *Lawful Means of Suppressing Tyranny*[39] are just of the same piece with their Definitions of Tyranny. For if Seditious Pamphlets and Practices, Slanders and false Representations, speaking Evil of Dignities, Cabals and Conjurations, hounding on the Mob on the Crowns best Subjects, and

---

[36] Sacheverell, *Nature and Mischief* (p. 16), cited by Defoe in *More Short-Ways* (p. 23).

[37] Richard Baxter (*q.v.*), *Five Disputations of Church-Government, and Worship* (London, 1659), pp. 45, 36. There follows a marginal reference to 'Concord' and an indecipherable page number, possibly to Baxter's *Christian Concord* (London, 1653), where, like Bridget Hill (1986, 215, n.3), I was unable to find the letter of the text, although the spirit is to be found on pp. 96–7.

[38] Dr John Owen. Astell's reference is to the Thanksgiving Sermon he preached in fact on 24 October 1651, for the victory at Worcester over the invading Scottish army led by Charles: *The Advantage of the Kingdome of Christ in the Shaking of the Kingdoms of the World* (Oxford, 1651), p. 12. Note that Astell gets the date wrong.

[39] Defoe, *More Short-Ways* (p. 14), declared on behalf of the Dissenters: 'We own the design to enjoy our Liberty of Worshiping God according to our Consciences, which, to your great mortification, is now our Right by Law, and which her Majesty, to your yet greater Disappointement, has promis'd us to Maintain and Continue . . . We own also the Design of maintaining our just Rights and Privileges as English-men, and by all lawful Means to oppose and suppress all sorts of Tyranny and Oppression, as well Ecclesiastical as Civil.'

the like, be lawful Means, these they practise under Queen ANNE.[40] If *Rye-house* Conspiracies,[41] *Bothwell-Bridge*[42] and *West-Country* Rebellions[43] be so, these and more they have practised against Princes who frankly forgave them their Father's Murder, and their own twelve years Banishment.[44] If usurping all Royal Authority and maintaining a Bloody Civil War against their Sovereign, and at last, with an unheard of Impudence, arraigning him at their Bar, and beheading him at his own Palace-Gate; if these be *Lawful Means* we are sure they have made use of them. But then I pray what Means can be unlawful? These are the Dissenters gradual Steps in suppressing what they call Tyranny, and when we catch them upon the first Round of the Ladder, we may, without Breach of Charity, conclude, that they mean, as soon as they are able, to mount to the top of it.

Sixthly, *Short-Ways* will have it that my Lord *Clarendon's* History[45] tells us that K. *Charles I. brought all the Calamities of Civil War upon his own head.*[46] Bless me! what hideous Spectacles Prejudice and Prepossession are upon a Reader's nose! But when our Brother *Short Ways* has laid these aside, has wip'd his Eyes, and is willing to see clearly, I would then advise him to another Perusal of that excellent and useful History, which he will find to [11] be

---

[40] Anne, Queen of England and Great Britain.

[41] The Rye House Plot was revealed in 1683 and resulted in leading Whigs such as Lords Essex and Russell being executed for their alleged plot to kill Charles II. Others such as Shaftesbury, Locke and Burnet, who feared being implicated, thought it safest to go abroad.

[42] The battle in Scotland in 1679 at which the Covenanter rebels were defeated. The uprising followed the assassination of the leader of the Scottish Church, James Sharp, Bishop of St Andrews. Ironically, the Duke of Monmouth led the Royal troops at Bothwell Bridge.

[43] Monmouth's own rebellion, largely Dissenter, defeated at Sedgmoor in 1685 – the use of the plural may be hyperbolic, as Mark Goldie has suggested to me.

[44] Astell obliquely answers Defoe's challenge (*More Short-Ways*, p. 15) that the Dissenters did not 'do any thing to King *Charles* I. but what you [the Tories] did to his Son', referring to Charles II's indulgence towards Dissenters and the opposition he faced from the Tory party and particularly Clarendon (see Jones, 1987, Chapter 7).

[45] Edward Hyde, first Earl of Clarendon, *The History of the Rebellion and Civil Wars in England* (Oxford, 1702).

[46] Defoe, *More Short-Ways* (p. 15), refers to Clarendon, Tory doyen, whose fall and exile under Charles II in 1667 attested to already dubious loyalty in Defoe's view: 'has not a noble Lord vouchsafing to turn Author, and write the History of that Rebellion, has he not told us in the first part of his first Volume, that the ill Conduct of that Prince brought all the Calamities of Civil War upon his Head[?]'.

point blank against his Assertion, and particularly I recommend to him *p*. 52, 71, 166, 206, of Vol I. by which it appears, that the King had remov'd every Shadow of a Grievance, and that the like *Peace and Plenty and Universal Tranquillity was never enjoy'd by any Nation*, till miserably interrupted by these Enemies of Peace with their Unjust and Unreasonable Clamours.[47]

Seventhly, *Short-Ways* is under a great mistake when he tell us, in his Admirable English, That 'The Barbarisms and Bloudy Doings us'd with the Episcopal Party in *Scotland* amounted to few.' It seems then there were *some* Barbarous and Bloudy Doings, and if there were *any*, her Majesty has too much Wisdom and Goodness to think them *Trivial*. But whether they were few or many, the Accounts of their Sufferings, and several Books that were publish'd not long after the Revolution, besides many Living Witnesses, will

---

[47] Astell correctly cites Clarendon on the pacific moments of Charles I's reign. Clarendon notes sanguinely (*History*, I, p. 52) that, 'after some unquietness of the People, and unhappy assaults upon the Prerogative by the Parliament, which produced its Dissolution, and thereupon some froward and obstinate disturbances in Trade; there quickly follow'd so excellent a Composure throughout the whole Kingdom, that the like Peace and Plenty, and universal Tranquillity for ten years was never enjoy'd by any Nation'. Again, in a lengthier and more finely nuanced statement, he affirms (I, p. 71): 'It was now a time of great Ease, and Tranquillity; the King (as hath been said before) had made himself Superior to all those Difficulties, and Streights, he had to contend with the four first years he came to the Crown, at Home; and was now Reverenced by all his Neighbours, who needed his Friendship, and desired to have it; the Wealth of the Kingdom notorious to all the world, and the general Temper, and Humour of it, little inclined to the Papist, and less to the Puritan. There were some late Taxes, and Impositions introduced, which rather angred, than griev'd the People, who were more than repair'd by the Quiet, Peace, and Prosperity they enjoy'd; and the Murmur, and Discontent, that was, appear'd to be against the Excess of Power exercised by the Crown, and supported by the Judges in *Westminster*-Hall.' Clarendon (I, p. 166) cites the wording of the bill for a Triennial Parliament, where the Commons claimed 'to have sufficiently provided for the Security of the Common wealth; and that there remain'd nothing to be done, but such a return of Duty and Gratitude to the King, as might Testify their Devotions; and that their only End was to make Him glorious' – to which Clarendon makes the aside, 'those Fits of Zeal and Loyalty, never lasted long'. Astell's last citation to Clarendon here concerns the passing of the Bill of Attainder and the Act for the continuing of Parliament, upon which he comments (I, pp. 205–6): 'After the Passing these two Bills, the temper and spirit of the People, both within and without the walls of the two Houses, grew marvellous calm and composed; there being likewise about that time Pass'd [206] by the King, the two Bills, for the taking away the Star-chamber Court, and the High Commission: So that there was not a Grievance or Inconvenience, Real or Imaginary, to which there was not a through [*sic*] Remedy applied.'

inform the Reader. And convince him, that many Clergy-men were outed and ill-us'd, not for refusing the Oaths to the Government, for they took them as soon as they came into *England*, but merely because in their Consciences they approv'd of, and adher'd to Episcopacy. And as for Presbyterian Justice and Moderation, I refer him to Mr. *Kirkwood's* Case,[48] and to those Authorities and plain matters of Fact he so largely treats of.

Eighthly, Poor *Short-ways* was but little oblig'd to his Neighbours, when they suffer'd him to fall into so gross an Error, as to tell us that Dr. *Tennison*[49] was that *Incumbent at St. Giles's*, whom the Bishop of *London* refused to suspend for Preaching against Popery (*p.* 19). Why, every body can tell him that Dr. *Sharpe*,[50] the present most Reverend Archbishop of *York*, was the Man. But alas! this truly Pious and Learned Archbishop has *honestly appeared* for the *Bill against Occasional Conformity*.

[12] Ninthly, What does *Short-ways* mean by making those Bishops who were sent to the Tower, the only *Refuge, Deliverers and Restorers* of the *Church*, together with the Bishop of *London* (*p.* 18)?[51] Does not the good Man know that five of those seven were *Non-jurors*, and that the sixth, the now Bishop of *Exeter*,[52] as also

---

[48] James Kirkwood (fl. 1698), was a well-known Scottish grammarian and friend of Dr Gilbert Burnet who lost his teaching post at a school in Linlithgow for refusing to attend the Presbyterian kirk. Kirkwood sued his former employers for libel, earning substantial damages for his eviction and the action of his employers in throwing their books and fine Dutch furniture into 'the open and dirty street'. Kirkwood published an account of the litigation in *A Short Information of the Plea betwixt the Town of Lithgow and Mr James Kirkwood, Schoolmaster* (1690) (*DNB*).

[49] Thomas Tenison (1636–1715), Archbishop of Canterbury from 1694, was known for his moderation towards Dissenters. Hill (1986, 216, n.2) notes that Mary Astell rightly corrected Defoe at this point – it was John Sharp (1645–1714) and not Tenison who was the incumbent at St Giles. But Tenison was involved, apparently playing an active part in getting the suspension on Sharp removed.

[50] John Sharp was said to have been provoked 'by the tampering of Roman Catholics with his parishioners', and preached two sermons in 1686 that were said to reflect on the King. As a result his suspension was ordered (*DNB*).

[51] Henry Compton (1632–1713), Bishop of London (1675–1713), on 30 June 1688, one of seven, and the only bishop, who signed the invitation to William to accede to the British throne.

[52] Jonathan Trelawny (1650–1721), Bishop of Bristol (1685–9), Exeter (1689–1707), and Winchester (1707–21). Said by Burnet (*History of My Own Time*, 2 volumes: first volume edited by Gilbert Burnet, second son of the Bishop; second volume edited by Sir Thomas Burnet (*q.v.*) with a Life of the Author (London, 1724), II, p. 159) to have joined Henry Compton in signing the invitation to William of Orange, which he denied. He was one of the seven who took the oaths to William

the Bishop of *London*, are none of his *Men of Moderation*, who appear'd against the *Occasional Bill*? It is very true that the Church has great Obligations to those worthy Prelates and their Brethren, who vote with them, who are, under GOD and the Queen, her Support; and their Temper is moderate in a true and Christian Sense. But I deny that they are *Short-ways Men of Moderation* (*p.* 19), and therefore he's under a great mistake in supposing them to be so.

Tenthly, *Short-ways* is also under another mistake, when he tells us that Dissenters *chose War for our sakes, against King* James II (*p.* 23). The Man would say, if he has any Meaning, for these People seldom express themselves in the Common Dialect; but he should say, that they chose *our Offices and Employments in Corporations*, to which by Law we only are entitled, and every body knows upon what terms they were admitted to them. He should say, they at last began to smell a Rat,[53] and when they perceiv'd they were not like to be the Building, nor to rear up Presbytery upon the Ruines of the Episcopal Church, then they thought it time to shrink from under their Drudgery, and would be no longer the Scaffolding of Popery. So much for his Mistakes, for I will not at present screw them up to Fourteenthly.

Now give me leave to laugh a little, and 'tis at his telling us, That *The* Scots *have an undoubted Right to the Presbyterian Establishment*, because forsooth! *'tis the Original Protestant Settlement of that Nation* (*p.* 16). Dont ye think that the Papists furnished him with this Argument and pay him for venting it? For allowing Original Settlement [13] to be a Right, 'tis like they may have a better Claim than the most antient *Presbyterial Consistory*.[54] Unless Dominion is founded in Grace, and that no Rights or Settlements are of any

and Mary and yet remained a friend of Astell's interlocutor, Bishop Atterbury. See William Oldisworth, *A Vindication of the Right Reverend the Lord Bishop of Exeter* (1708).

53 William Sherlock (*q.v.*), opponent of, Henry Hickman, 'smelled a Socinian rat', *Speculum Sherlockianum* (London, 1674, p. 4, cited by Diamond, 1982, 113). Astell indulges in such allusions.

54 A consistory, from the Latin word for a 'standing place' or 'waiting room', originally applied to the meeting place of the Roman emperor's council or cabinet, and eventally to a council meeting, although 'as a translation of the corresponding French or L[atin] word ... [it was] never applied to anything English (*OED*). But in sixteenth- and seventeenth-century ecclesiastical debates it denoted a Presbyterian synod.

value, except those which some People more peculiarly call *Prot-estant! Episcopacy is an English Encroachment upon them*, says our mighty Reasoner, our Protestant Dissenter; so is the Reformation, say the Papists. And neither Poor Episcopacy nor Reformation it self, have any thing to offer in their own Defence, save certain Arguments taken out of the Bible, and from the Practise of the Primitive Church. Whereby they pretend to prove, that their Charter allows them to take footing wherever they can obtain it peaceably and Christianly, that is, by dint of Argument, and by patient and heroick Sufferings, or else by Authority of the Lawful Magistrate, and this without being guilty of any Encroachment, or any the least Injury to the Peoples Rights.

But if Episcopacy is not to be restored in *Scotland*, against the Constitution of the Nation, by the same Rule it is not to be destroyed in *England*, since it is our Constitution.[55] And then what becomes of that *Moderate Episcopacy*, those *Comprehensions* and *Uniting Projects*, which your *Moderation a Vertue*,[56] your *Calamys*[57] and other Dissenters are so full of? Certainly *English Men* have as good a Right to their Constitution as the *Scots* have to theirs, and, as we think, better Arguments to defend it, to be sure we have a longer Prescription. Nor know I what can be offer'd to the contrary, except that irresistible Argument, *Club-Law*, which pull'd down Episcopacy in 42, and unless the People, even the Scum of them, have a Native Right to set up what they please (how contrary soever to the Laws of the Land or to the Gospel) whenever they are but strong enough to execute their Projects.[58]

---

[55] One of the major lines of argument in Astell's *Moderation truly Stated* is that the Anglican episcopacy is constitutionally established and that to slander it is treasonous.

[56] Owen, *Moderation a Vertue* (1703).

[57] Edmund Calamy (1671–1732), historian of Nonconformity and biographer of Richard Baxter (1702).

[58] Astell is discussing the events in England and Scotland of 1642. In February 1642, several months before the outbreak of the Civil War, the King had reluctantly given his assent to the Bishops' Exclusion Bill, which prohibited not merely members of the episcopate but all clergymen in holy orders from occupying temporal offices in the state. It represented a triumph for the laity over the intrusion of clergymen into state positions, both at the centre of government and in the localities, which had been such a prominent feature of the 1630s under William Laud (*q.v.*). Shortly afterwards Parliament took even more drastic action by abolishing the episcopal office itself. In January 1643 both Houses of Parliament approved a bill which swept away any form of diocesan administration in England

[14] *Short ways* is grievously pinch'd when Mr. *S appeals to the History of our Kingdom, whether ever they gave the Church the least Favour or Quarter, when they had her under their Power (p. 23);*[59] and therefore no wonder that he winches and slings to some purpose in a senceless Exclamation; tho Mr. *S's* words are modest and cool, there being nothing, except the Truth of them, that can excite his Passion; for it is his own and not Mr. *S's* Conclusion, that *Because they never shewed us Quarter,* therefore *We will revenge our selves.* Nor is there, it seems, any great hurt in Retaliation, when from a *Presbyterian* hand; *Short-ways* himself can find a Reason for't in a neighbouring Kingdom, *p.* 17. But he may please to remember, that he and his Brethren have been told over and over, and I think our Practices in 1660 did shew we were in earnest, that the *Church of England* knows too well *what Spirit she is of* to *render Evil for Evil.* There can be no reason therefore why they are afraid of our Vengeance, but only because they are conscious that they justly deserve it.

Short ways helps us to an extraordinary piece of News, *viz.* that *the whole House of Peers, including the Lords Spiritual themselves,* have told us that *the Dissenters are no Schismaticks (p.* 62).[60] Suppose they had, which is more than he will be able to prove these two days, what then? it was never yet allow'd by any Christian Church, no nor by the *Presbyterian Consistory,* except when they got by't, that Lay men have a Right to determine such Points as these. As for Schism, to all those Authors he mentions, I'll oppose the single *Charge of Schism continued,*[61] which he and his Authors may answer if they can. But it is no new thing to hear Men cry out for new Proof, and to take no notice of the old, tho it be more than enough. This is the Ingenuity of the Church of *Rome,* and that dearest Spawn of hers our English Dissenters. But before they make new *Challenges,* and threaten us with what they [15] *will do,* it may become them to Answer, if not the Arguments which perhaps may be too tough, at least, the plain Matters of Fact that are produced

and Wales, while in October 1646 the offices of archbishop and bishop were formally abolished by parliamentary ordinance.
[59] Sacheverell, *Nature and Mischief* (p. 16) cited by Defoe in *More Short-Ways* (p. 23).
[60] Anon., *Dissenters no Schismaticks: A Second Letter to . . . Robert Burscough, about his Discourse of Schism* (1702).
[61] Edward Stillingfleet, *The Charge of Schism Renewed* (1680).

by Mr. *Wesley*,[62] the *New Association*,[63] the *Woolf*,[64] Etc. to say nothing of my Lord *Clarendon's* History, and the Accounts of their Antient Practises.

But these peaceable Men who would persuade the World that they are *only upon the Defensive*, that they only oppose our *own Attempts upon their just Freedom*, do it seems take this *just Freedom* to consist, in writing and spreading about among the People, *Abridgments*,[65] *New Tests*,[66] the *True-born English-man*,[67] *Shortest Ways*,[68] *Legions*[69] and a long *Etcaetera* of the like stuff; full of bitter Invectives, notorious Falshoods, and scurrilous Lampoons, on the Establish'd Church, the Government, and even the whole Nation, except a few Choice Men of their own Fraternity; and would have us believe that they have a Charter not to stand corrected, either by the Publick or Private Hands. 'Tis their *Just Freedom*, good Men! and what pity they should be depriv'd of it! to combine against the Constitution, to get into Offices by violating the Intention of the Laws, and so at last into Parliament, that they may be able to Repeal them; whilst no body ought to take notice of these Practices, or to give them any interruption! For one may safely appeal to every sober and considerate Person in the Kingdom, to every one who is not led away by Noise and Prejudice, whether any other Attempts have been made than a necessary provision against their Rude and Open, as well as their Clandestine Attempts upon others? I would

---

[62] Samuel Wesley, father of the Methodist leader, who although attending Morton's Dissenting Academy became strongly anti-Dissent, and in 1703 published *A Letter from a Country Divine*, attacking the Dissenting academies. Defoe, in *More Short-Ways* (p. 5), referred to 'The Reverend Mr. *Wesly* Author of two Pamphlets, Calculated to blacken our Education in the Accademies of the Dissenters'.

[63] A reference to two pamphlets by Charles Leslie: *The New Association of those called Moderate Church-Man [sic] with the Modern Whigs and Fanatics* (London, 1702), and *The New Association: Part II. With Farther Improvements* (London and Westminster, 1703), both attacking Dissenters. In the Supplement to *The New Association, Part II*, dated 25 March 1703 (pp. 6–7), Leslie gave what is believed to be one of the first systematic critiques of Locke's *Two Treatises* (Thompson, 1976, 187–9).

[64] Charles Leslie's *The Wolf Stripp'd of his Shepherd's Cloathing*.

[65] Calamy's *Abridgement of Baxter's Life* (1702).

[66] Defoe's *New Test of the Church of England's Loyalty* (London, 1702) and *A New Test of the Church of England's Honesty* (London, 1704).

[67] Defoe's *The True Born Englishman: A Satyr* (London, 1700/1).

[68] Defoe's *The Shortest Way with the Dissenters*, and *More Short-Ways*.

[69] See Defoe's *The Legion Memorial* (London, 1701), *The Legionites Plot* (London, 1702) and *The Legions Humble Address to the Lords* (London, 1704).

therefore desire them before they pretend to bring any Accusations against their Neighbours, to be pleas'd to Answer a few plain Queries. Not that they are the Tyth of what might be asked, but they are such as arise from the Pamphlet before me.

[16] 1. Whether the Ecclesiastical Commission issued out in 1689, the first year of *the Nations Deliverance*, was not intended *to Invite and Compliment the Dissenters* (*p.* 14)? and if not pray what was its meaning?

2. Whether one may not very innocently *beware of false Prophets*, who come in *Sheeps Cloathing*, since Truth itself has taught us, that *inwardly they are Ravening Wolves?*[70]

3. Whether *he who enters not in by the Door, but climbeth up some other way*, is any thing else but *a Thief and a Robber?*

4. Whether any Man can lawfully Preach, who is not lawfully sent? and consequently, let the *Doctrine* and *Faith* be what it may, there can be no true Ordinances, where there is no true Ministry, nor any true Ministry, but where the Succession and Authority is derived from Christ and his Apostles.

5. Whether a Causeless Separation from the Church be not Schism, and therefore whether *Occasional Conformists* at least, if not other Dissenters, are not Schismaticks (*p.* 20)?

---

[70] The text of Isaiah 65:25 had been given a famous gloss by Locke, attacking the Tory alternative to resistance, passive obedience, in Chapter 19 of the *Second Treatise*. In the conclusion to Astell's celebrated 1706 Preface to *Some Reflections upon Marriage, Occasion'd by the Duke & Dutchess of Mazarine's Case* (London, 1700; third edition, 1706), p. xxvi, and in the title of Leslie's pamphlet *The Wolf Stripp'd of his Shepherd's Cloathing* the words of Isaiah echo together with the old aphorism 'a wolf in sheep's clothing'. James Owen's pamphlet *Moderation still a Virtue: in Answer to Several Bitter Pamphlets: Especially Two, Entituled Occasional Conformity a Most Unjustifiable Practice*, and *The Wolf Stripp'd of his Shepherd's Cloathing* (p. ii), referred to Leslie as a 'Wolf-stripper' and it would be tempting to think that Astell's remarks referred to Owen, the subject of her Postscript, were it not that Owen's work seems to have been published too late for reference in the main body of her text. Sacheverell too, in *Nature and Mischief* (p. 15), in a passage singled out by Defoe in *More Short-Ways* (p. 10) had continued the idiom, with the rhetorical question: 'Are these the *Wolves in Sheep's Cloathing*, that are to be *Invited* and *Complemented*, even by Our *Superior Pastors*, into *Christ's Fold*, to Worry and Devour it?' Defoe in *More Short-Ways* (p. 3) is Astell's more likely source. There, with clear reference to the tracts of Lesie and Sacheverell, he declares: 'if your *Woolf Stript*, your *Associations*, your *Peace and Union*, be of any weight, then 'tis no Scandal to affirm that there is a barbarous Design on foot, in, and among some who call themselves the Members of the Church of *England*, to Extirpate and Destroy the Dissenters.'

6. Whether Dissenters who us'd to exclaim so loudly against Lord Bishops, and the whole Antichristian Hierarchy as they call'd it, are reconciled to the Order and Dignity of *my Lords the Bishops,* or only to the Person of *my Lord of Salisbury,*[71] Etc (*p.* 11)?

7. Whether it is consistent with that Piety and Strictness, to which Dissenters have all along pretended, to Burlesque the Holy Scripture, and an Expression particularly applied to our Saviour (*the Zeal of thy House has even eaten me up*) rather than lose an insipid Jest upon Mr. *Sacheverel?*

8. Whether it be Decent or Honest for those to accuse others of *foulness of Language* and *bitter Invectives,* Etc. (*p.* 12, Etc.) who are most notoriously guilty of the same themselves? and whether it were not fitter for them to take our Lord's [17] Advice, and to begin with the *Beam in their own Eyes,* e'er they attempt to give out the *Mote in their Brothers?*

9. Whether a Man does not want Common Sense as well as Logick, and is not fitter to Cry Pamphlets about the Streets than to write them, who is not able to distinguish the *Phanaticism of the Dissenters,* or even the Popery of the Papists (*p.* 12, 13), from that which is Christian and Good in either?

10. Whether Dissenters were only on the Defensive and not the Aggressors, shall I say, in 41 (*p.* 14)?[72] I need not go so far back, even within this two years? Now to *State this,* I hope I may as freely *have recourse* to a *New Test of the Church of* England's *Loyalty,* as *Short ways* has to the *Occasional-Bill.* And we find in that Temperate and Uniting Treatise, writ a few months after her Majesty's Accession to the Throne, and before there was a word of a Bill, or

---

[71] Gilbert Burnet. Defoe in *More Short-Ways* (p. 11) refers to 'my Lord of Salisbury ... in his Speech to the House of Peers', presumably the same he referred to earlier (p. 9) as 'the Reverend Bishop of *Salisbury*'s Speech in the House of Lords, where he proves 'twas the practice of Queen *Elizabeth* to admit of Persons of Different Religions into Places of Trust' (see Astell, *A Fair Way,* p. 8 and n.25 above). The speech understandably provoked controversy, evident from Charles Leslie's scurrilous reply, *The Bishop of Salisbury's Proper Defence from a Speech Cry'd about the Streets in his Name* (London and Westminster, 1704).

[72] Defoe argued (*More Short-Ways,* p. 14) 'We have always been upon the Defensive with you; we have ever been attack'd, and have only resisted your Violence', to which Astell replies by reminding him of the moves against the Crown of 1641: the passing of the Grand Remonstrance; the debating of the Root and Branch Bill (*q.v.*); resistance to the taxing powers of the Crown in the form of ship money (*q.v.*); abolition of the Star Chamber and High Commission and the Ulster insurrection.

any thing had been done or said against Dissenters; *that* 'tho' *Names* of Contempt have been often changed on either side; as Cavalier and Roundhead, Royalist and Rebels, Malignants and Phanaticks, Torys and Whigs, yet the Division has always been barely *the Church and the Dissenter*, and there it continues to this Day.'

11. Whether those Church-men who brought about the late Revolution did Well or Ill in't? If they did Well, why is it thrown in their Dish, why are they eternally reproach'd with it? If Ill, what's to be said but that they Repent, and for the future Detest and Abjure the Men and Principles that led them into it. But however it be, neither Papists nor Dissenters have any reason to reproach them, with that which was so conformable to the Principles and Practices, both of the one and of the other. And this leads me to the next Query;

12. Whether that same Revolution was founded upon Church, or upon Dissenting Principles? If the former, [18] why are Churchmen upbraided with forsaking their Principles, and breaking their Oaths, and so contemptuously used upon this Account, by the *New Test-maker*,[73] *Short-ways* and their Fellows? For upon that Supposition, their Accusations are all meer *Malice, Forgery and Slander!* But if the Managers of those Times did not act by their own, but by the Dissenters Principles; then pray is this the best Usage you can afford your Brethren for coming over to your Principles and Practices? Does not the *Injustice*, the *Treachery*, the *Insults* lie at your own Door? Certainly if this is your method (*p.* 22), and that you are firmly resolved against Joining or Uniting in any case, unless upon your own terms (*p.* 1); and that it is not enough to comply with you in some things, unless we come over in all; your Exhortations to Peace, Union and Moderation, are only meer Cant, and have no meaning but to persuade or wheedle, to fright or force us out of our *own* Principles, that when you have gain'd your Point, you may laugh at us as Knaves or Fools for quitting them.

13. Whether those who by breaking down the Fences, admit such into the Church as are firmly resolved never to unite with her, till they have fashioned her after their own Model, do not indeed and most effectually, whether or no they design to do so, betray and weaken, and by consequence destroy her?

---

[73] A reference to Defoe as author of the two pamphlets *New Test of the Church of England's Loyalty* and *New Test of the Church of England's Honesty.*

14. Whether, except we mean to wear the Bib and the Rattle[74] you design us, it can ever be fit to forget 41, unless you will first condescend to forget the fatal Principles and Practices of those unhappy days? And now I think *Short-ways* has his *Numbers* returned him in full tale, and let him make his best o' them.

As for his *French Parallel*,[75] p. 4. it is a mighty Compliment, and of the just size of the Men of his Party, towards the Queen and Church of *England*, whom he must think quite as well of as he does of the *French Monarch* and the [21] Church of *Rome*, or else he could never dream of such an odious Comparison. If he pleases I'll direct him to a more *parallel* Case, even the Practice of his great Forefathers in the *never to be forgotten* 41.[76] Never to be forgotten, because they will not suffer us to forget it, since they repeat its Methods every day. Hideous Outcries of Popery and Persecution, when there was no fear of either from any but themselves, who intrigu'd with Papists at the same time that they falsly accused the King of it (*See Lord* Clarendon's *Hist.*);[77] and had it in their Hearts

---

[74] 'The Bib and the Rattle' appears to be an elaborate play on the nursery metaphor used by Sacheverell in *Nature and Mischief* (p. 24), where he refers to the Dissenting Academies as 'These *Schools* and *Nurseries of Rebellion*'. Defoe in turn referred to Sacheverell as 'a Mercenary Renegado . . . hir'd to expose the private Accademies of the Dissenters, as Nurseries of Rebellious Principles' (*More Short-Ways*, p. 4).

[75] Defoe, referring to Sacheverell as a hired gun, claimed (*More Short-Ways* p. 4): 'I could easily run a parallel between these Gentlemen's Proceedings, and the present *French* King's, when he first went the *Shortest Way with the Protestants of* France, and could tell them that they seem exactly to follow his blessed Example, *viz.* First to deprive them of all Offices or Imployments in the State, then to take from them the Education of their Children, and then to the pulling down of their Churches, *Etc.* and so on to Gallows and Gallies.'

[76] Defoe, *More Short-Ways* (p. 15) accuses Sacheverell of falsehood no. 6: 'To fill up that one Page of Scandal, and make it pass for a true Libel, you go back to *the never to be forgotten* Year of 41.' Here he refers to Sacheverell's fifth charge against the Dissenters, promotion of '*Interest* and *Party*', in *Nature and Mischief*, pp. 9, 13. Sacheverell, speaking of the 'Malignant Virulence and Implacable Rancor of *Phanaticism*', at this point (p. 14) restates the argument that Dissenters have borrowed Jesuit theory and practice of resisting the king: 'For if We were to Consider its Progress, in all that *Series of Rebellions*, from its *Odious*, and *Never-to-be-forgotten Aera* of Transcendent Villainy, in the Year *Forty-One*, We shall find the same *Jesuitical Principles*, like a *Plotter in Masquerade*, only Changing the Name, but carrying on the same Machinations and Wicked practices in *Church* and *State*, to the Subversion of our Constitution in Both, down to this Present Day.'

[77] Hyde, *History*.

to persecute their Brethren, for we saw they did it with a vengeance when they got the Power. Scurrilous Libels and Lampoons spread throughout the Nation, neither better nor worse than our *Short-ways*, our *Legions*,[78] and a whole Swarm of Wasps from the same hive, which I will not lose time to mention.[79] They had their *Pryns*, *Burtons* and *Bastwicks*, as we have out *Tutchins*, *Stevens's* and *Defoes*,[80] to corrupt the People and fire the Mob. With an unprecedented Insolence they arraign'd the Proceedings and invaded the Privileges of Parliament, Bully'd the House by posting up the *Straffordians*,[81] which their Successors have imitated in their *Black-Lists*, to expose all who were not as mad as themselves, to the Fury of the Rabble; they had their Petitioners[82] and Tumults, as we have

[78] In 1701 a petition was presented to Parliament by Kentish men in favour of supporting William in a war against France. When the petitioners were imprisoned by the Tory majority in the House of Commons, Defoe responded with the *Legion Memorial* – so-called because of the signature: 'Our name is Legion, and we are many', which he presented to the House. The petitioners were released and much debate ensued.

[79] Astell's metaphor is uncannily close to that of Charles Leslie's famous Supplement (p. 3) to *The New Association, Part II*, in which, referring to the republicans and Locke, he speaks of 'Their Books and Pamphlets (with which the Nation has of late so much Swarm'd)' (cited Goldie, 1978, 231 n.8). The main body of the *New Association, Part II* was specifically addressed to the refutation of Defoe's *The Shortest Way with the Dissenters*.

[80] William Prynne (*q.v.*), the Rev. Henry Burton (1578–1648) and Dr John Bastwick (1593–1654) were Puritans who opposed the episcopacy, for which in 1637 they were jointly tried, convicted and pilloried. John Tutchin, to whom Edward Ward's (*q.v.*) notorious *Secret History of the Calves-head Club* (London and Westminster, 1703) was dedicated, had attacked the monarchy and defended Defoe over *The Shortest Way with the Dissenters*. William Stephens (*q.v.*) had recommended discontinuing the observance of the anniversary of the execution of Charles I, putting him in the same camp in Astell's eyes.

[81] Thomas Wentworth, first Earl of Strafford (1593–1641), influential statesman under Charles I, defender of the royal prerogative and friend of William Laud. Created Lord Lieutenant of Ireland in 1640, he was designated commmander over Irish and English troops to invade Scotland on behalf of the King, for which, under the Long Parliament, and at the instigation of John Pym (*q.v.*), he was convicted of treason, impeached and executed. Machinations of the King and Queen, which suggested the imminence of a French invasion, and the discovery of a court plot to release him and introduce Irish and Dutch troops into England, had produced a climate in which it was difficult for the King to pardon Strafford and he stood firm.

[82] Astell draws a parallel between the anti-Straffordians and the Kentish Petitioners, whose similar appeal to the free-born rights of Englishmen had been a catalyst for the fall of the Stuarts. Lord Somers (1651–1716) and Daniel Defoe had leapt

had our Petitioners and Legions;[83] they garbled the *House of Lords*, as others would now the *House of Commons*, till they got one after their hearts desire. There being no Difference, that I can find, between *those* Times and *these*, but that their Fathers had the Nation's Purse in their Hand, which, GOD be thanked, their Sons are not like to finger, so long as such an *Honest and Loyal House of Commons*, as the Nation is at present blest with, fills St. *Stephen's* Chapel; and this is the true Reason of all their Rage against this House, a House that us'd to be so much their Darling. But when their Forefathers [22] had got the Purse and Power into their hands, which is all that is wanted by their Successors, what followed? I tremble to think! a bloody Civil War, the Destruction of all Laws and Rights, and of the whole Constitution Ecclesiastical and Civil; Anarchy and Confusion, Tyranny and Oppression alternately; the most detestable Murder of the best of Kings, and, as far as their Power would reach, the Extirpation of the whole Royal Family. And if this is not Truth, or if it is not a very just and sufficient Reason, tho not to retaliate, yet to secure our selves and the Constitution by all lawful and probable Methods, against the like Violence for the time to come, I desire *Short-ways* will be pleased to inform me. For that this was not the *readiest Method*, the *Shortest Way* with the Church and the Government (*p.* 4), I hope even *Defoe* himself has not the Face to deny. And I must always be of opinion that this is the only effectual way to that *Peace and Union* they so heartily desire, this is what in truth they aim at, and mean by't, even the bringing all Opposers to truckle under them. 'But that these Gentlemen should pretend to (nay really tread in) those very Steps, and yet at the same time be angry to be told they design the rest, is imposing Things upon the World, too gross to go down' (*p.* 4, 5).

And now, after all that has been said, I leave my Reader to infer, and I think the Premises will warrant the Conclusion, that to lay open the Secret Designs of the Dissenters, which are conceal'd under the Colour of Conscience, and a world of other plausible

to the defence of the right of subjects to petition. Somers, citing Locke's *Two Treatises*, argued precisely that government was a pact between property-owners and that people's consent to government as a protection agency entailed that they might also submit grievances where their liberties seemed to be jeopardized.

[83] Further references to the Kentish Petitioners and their defence by Defoe. See *The Legionites Plot* and *The Legions Humble Address to the Lords*, as well as numerous pamphlets written in response to *The Legion Memorial*.

Pretences; to pull off these Disguises, and to make all the good Laws we can, to defend us from their Treachery, as well as from their more open Attempts; as it is a necessary Duty which we ow to our Sovereign, our Church, and our Country, and even to our own Preservation, so it is in [23] reality the greatest Service can be done Dissenters. For besides, that it preserves the Publick Peace, in which they also have a share, it restrains them, if not from a *Malicious Inclination* towards that detestable Sin of Persecution, at least from being actually Guilty of it. A Sin which the good Men so much exclaim against, and which therefore no doubt the Devil is most apt to tempt them to. And consequently by some seasonable Laws, we may prevent that Destruction which this Crime will Infallibly bring on them, in this World perhaps, but to be sure in the next.

Postscript

Concerning Moderation still a Vertue[84]

Whilst this Sheet was in the Press, *Moderation still a Vertue* came to my hands, which is not so properly an *Answer* to the *Pamphlets* it pretends to reply to, as a second Edition of *Moderation a Vertue* with some Enlargements, neither answering the Arguments nor disproving the Matters of Fact, but waving the one and recriminating upon the other; and therefore all that needs be said to't may be dispatch'd in the few remaining Pages, leaving the Enlargements to those whom they may concern.

The *Moderate Author* tells us pretty often, he *has prov'd* that which his *Answerers* demonstrate he has *not prov'd*, and the Reader needs only compare them to be satisfied I do him no Injury. But most Readers care not for this Trouble, so the last Word commonly carries it, tho the Force of the Argument lies only in the good Assurance. This is the Secret of Writing, and the true Reason why Writers, tho they are ever so solidly answered, will never be silenced.

[24] Our Author has an admirable way of dispatching his Opposers; those who take no notice of what is not to the purpose, he says *do not answer him*; those who reply to every shadow of an Argument that is offered for his Cause by himself or others, he tells

---

[84] To the original text Mary Astell added a Postscript in reply to *Moderation still a Vertue*, the second contribution of the Rev. James Owen to the debate on Occasional Conformity. Among works Owen addresses in this response to critics of his earlier *Moderation a Vertue* is Mary Astell's *Moderation truly Stated*.

you are verbose (*Pref. p.* 2, 3).[85] But he did wisely in over-looking *Moderation truly stated*, for to have consider'd it would have lost him one half of his Book.[86] And it is very true that several Pages of it are *Verbose and Virulent*, for they are taken up in answering the Dissenters Arguments against Schism and Toleration in their own Words ([*Moderation truly Stated*] *p.* 53 *to* 60),[87] and their Virulency against the Government in Church and State as by Law established ([*Moderation truly Stated*, pp.] 70 *to* 78, 79, 80. 95).[88] There you may find that those Expressions about Schism, which our Author is so offended at *p.* 21. are the very words of Mr. *Edwards* the Presbyterian (*p.* 54).[89]

---

[85] Here the author to whom Owen refers is none other than Mary Astell herself, whom Owen in *Moderation still a Virtue* (p. ii), refers to as '*the verbose and virulent Author* of Moderation truly stated'.

[86] It was undoubtedly a matter of disappointment to Astell that Owen (*Moderation still a Virtue*) did not subject her own pamphlet to the scrutiny he gave Leslie's *The Wolf Stript of his Shepherd's Cloathing*. Astell's work is referred to anonymously and is clearly classed by Owen with that of Leslie, referred to as 'the Wolf-stripper'. This fact and the attention Owen pays Leslie's pamphlet, the authorship of which he seems only to have discovered in time for the Preface and Postscript (see Owen, *Moderation still a Virtue*, pp. iii, 3–4, 32, 59, 60 and 67–96), was probably cause for the disclaimer in the subtitle of Astell's pamphlet, *Not Writ by Mr L—y, or any other Furious Jacobite*, to ensure that Leslie did not get the credit for this pamphlet of hers.

[87] Astell is referring to *Moderation truly Stated*, pp. 53–60 and following, where she takes up the 'Dissenters Arguments against Schism and Toleration', deferring to 'what has been writ upon this Subject by much better Pens'. The texts to which she refers, as indicated in the marginal notes, include Edward Stillingfleet's *The Mischief of Separation* (1680) and the *Unreasonableness of Separation* (1681); 'Pryn's *Full Answer to J.* Goodwin' (William Prynne, *A Full Reply to Certaine Briefe Observations and anti-Queries ... Together with Certaine Briefe Animadversions on Mr John Goodwins Theomachia* (London, 1644); Samuel Rutherford (*q.v.*), *Free Disputation [against Pretended Liberty of Conscience]* (1649); and Cawdry [Daniel Cawdrey's] *Independency a Great Schism* (1630). Could [Thomas] Edwards' *Epistle Dedicated to the Lords and Commons before his Gangraena* (1646) be actually the Preface (which talks about the Lords and Commons) to *The Third Part of Gangraena: Or a New and Higher Discovery of the Errours ... of the Sectaries of these Times*, in response, *inter alia*, to William Dell's *Right Reformation ... In a Sermon ... Preached to the Honourable House of Commons, November 25, 1646* (London, 1646)?

[88] In these pages of *Moderation truly Stated* referred to, Mary Astell reviews some forty items from the parliamentary debates and pamphlet literature over Occasional Conformity.

[89] Owen (*Moderation Still a Virtue*, p. 21), refers to one of his adversaries (unnamed) as 'rank[ing] Schism *in the same degree of Guilt with* Adultery *and* Murder, *and think[ing] the* Blood of Martyrdom *can't wash away its Guilt*'. Astell gives the impression that it is she to whom Owen refers, but this is not the case; she goes

I should be too verbose, did I reckon up all our Author's Mistakes and Disingenuities; he tells us that the *Stater opposes all Moderation, and confounds it with Lukewarmness in the Essentials of Religion (Pref. p.* 2).[90] The next Page to that he quotes will shew him his Error, for there *Moderation* is made to consist in the *Proportioning our Esteem and Value of every thing to its real Worth ([Moderation truly Stated] p.* 6).[91] Nay, he himself subscribes to the *Stater's* true Notion, in that very place where he misrepresents it, so that *Moderation* is still *truly stated.* But is not true that his Answerers allow no Moderation to Protestant Dissenters; I have not the *Wolf* by me,[92] and will not trust to my Memory; but one of the other *addresses the Occasional Conformists with all the Good-will one Christian bears another.* And the *Stater*[93] earnestly invites them to Union (*p.* 39), and has a *true Compassion for Dissenters in Conscience (p.* 49, 50), believing the greatest number of the Separation to be of this sort (*p.* 92, 93). But for *Dissenters in Faction,* such as mislead Well-meaning Men, and disturb the Publick Peace, what Moderation can they lay claim to? our Author himself will at least *seem* to be against them. All Disputes amongst Christians ought to be managed with Charity, Temper and decent Language, and it does not appear to

on to point Owen to p. [53–]54 of her text, *Moderation truly Stated,* where she had demonstrated, precisely to the author of *Moderation a Vertue* (p. 27), these to be the views of the Presbyterian divine Thomas Edwards, in his *Further Discovery* (p. 197). The same Edwards, in his *Epistle Dedicated to the Lords and Commons before his Gangraena,* confesses himself to being a Schismatic. These works of Edwards' are discussed in Astell's *Moderation truly Stated.*

[90] Astell is quoting, almost verbatim, the charge Owen (*Moderation still a Virtue,* p. ii) is levelling against her: 'Some of them *violently oppose all* Moderation, *and confound it with* Lukewarmness *in the* Essentials *and* Vitals *of Religion; so the verbose and virulent Author of* Moderation truly stated (p. 5, 24)'. Owen correctly references his source, which is *Moderation truly Stated* (p. 5).

[91] Astell quotes directly from her own work (*Moderation truly Stated,* pp. 5–6).

[92] The 'stater' is Mary Astell in *Moderation truly Stated,* and Astell is punning. She goes on to refer to Leslie's *The Wolf Stript of His Shepherd's Cloathing,* a response to James Owen's *Moderation a Vertue,* which comes in for his particular condemnation as typical of 'the little insignificant Adversaries to *Moderation,* who add a greater *Lustre* to it by their impotent Attempts to *sully* it' (p. 3). It is interesting that, in the case of 'the *Wolf',* at least, Astell is not willing to paraphrase from memory, although this was quite acceptable by seventeenth and eighteenth century conventions of citation, and was practised by her on occasion.

[93] The 'stater' once again would appear to be Mary Astell herself, although the page references she gives to *Moderation truly Stated* (pp. 39, 49, 50, 92, 93) relate in only a general way to the rather liberal paraphrase of her argument she gives here, most clearly stated in the earlier work at pp. 92–3.

me that the Author of *Occasional Conformity an unjustifiable Practice* [*Occasional Conformity a most Unjustifiable Practice*, as cited by Owen, *Moderation still a Virtue*, p. 3], or the *Stater* offend against this Rule. 'Tis confess'd some Expressions are bitter, but it is only because they are true (*See* Mod. truly Stated, *p.* 81); and our great Pretenders to Moderation can't justly complain of *disingenuous Reflections on the Dissenters* (Mod. still a Ver. *p.* 4),[94] till they have struck out those **[25]** many Pages of their own which are full of such Reflections upon the Church, and those they think fit to call *High-Churchmen* (Mod a Ver. *p.* 19, *etc.*).[95]

Our Author tells us, that *Moderation a Vertue remains unanswer'd*, and that his Answerers *over-look the Principal Design, and some of the Principal Parts of it* (Mod. still *p.* 4. 22. 24. 32. 39, 40. 46. 56, 57. 62. 75. 94. 101. 104).[96] I make no doubt that those who have read the Answerers are of another Mind; for to say nothing of the two that he Replies to, the *Stater*[97] has fully consider'd the *two main things* he says he *had in his Eye* ([*Moderation still a Virtue*], *Pref. p.* 3 [p. ii]); for to what purpose was *Moderation* rescu'd from those False Glosses which he and his Brethren had put upon it? Why was it *truly Stated*, but in order to *Recommend it* ([*Moderation truly Stated*], *p.* 32, Etc.)? And as

---

[94] This appears to be a reference to the title of Charles Leslie's *Reflections upon some Scandalous and Malicious Pamphlets* (London, 1703). On p. 4 of *Moderation still a Virtue*, which Astell accurately cites, Owen seems not to be referring to *Moderation truly Stated*, but rather the anonymous author of *Occasional Conformity a most Unjustifiable Practice*, who along with Leslie, bears the burden of his critique in this pamphlet. However, Astell takes the opportunity to vindicate herself by referring the reader to p. 81 of *Moderation truly Stated*, a particularly virulent and witty passage (including a poem 'in the manner of the *French* Satyrist') which 'justly', she claims, charges the Dissenters with responsibility for the regicide.

[95] Astell refers to Owen's reflections on the differences between ministers in the 'Episcopal Church' and the Dissenting churches in *Moderation a Virtue*, pp. 18–21, which at p. 19 seem harmless enough. She probably has more serious objections to what he has to say at pp. 20–1, where he singles out the nonjurors and Jacobites (among whom she numbered friends).

[96] The italicized words are in this instance quotations from Owen's Preface to *Moderation still a Virtue*, p. iii. The page references which follow relate only generally to the purported points Owen is making.

[97] The 'two [Answerers] that he Replies to' are the authors of *The Wolf Stript of His Cloathing* (Leslie) and *Occasional Conformity a most Unjustifiable Practice*; 'the stater' is once again Mary Astell (to whom he does not, in her view, adequately respond) and to whose *Moderation truly Stated*, the references to 'pp. 32, etc., and 60 etc.', apply.

for *Hypocrisie*, the *Stater* professedly Charges it on the *Occasional-Conformist*, endeavouring to make good the Charge from the beginning to the end of the Book ([*Moderation truly Stated*] *p.* 60, Etc.); and the Reader it's like may think it is made good, whatever the *Moderate Author* may say to the contrary. For if a Pharisaical Profession of greater Purity, Moderation, *etc.* than our Neighbours attain to, and not coming up to these Professions, but being guilty of the very same Violence, Persecution, *etc.* which we unjustly impute to others; if pretending to do that on a Religious Account, which proceeds only from a Secular Motive; if crying out *Conscience*, when 'tis Party and Sinister Designs that move us; if this is Hypocrisie, the *Stater* has produc'd *incontestable Precedents*, that it lies at the Dissenters Door, and our Author has not yet clear'd them from the *Imputation*. And as for such as are *Occasional-Conformists*, but not to qualifie themselves for a Place, tho' they may be free from Hypocrisie, our Author would do well to justifie them from that Unreasonable Separation, that Scandal, that Weakening of the Prostestant Interest, which is imputed to them.

He owns that a *formal Answer* is made to *his First and Second Chapters* (*p.* 35 [?]) ([*Moderation still a Virtue*] *Pref. p.* 3), so that I shall say no more to them but only this, that the Case of our Lord and his Apostles in relation to the Jewish-Church being clearly *Stated* [*Moderation still a Virtue, p.* 35], and in a few Words, the *Stater* proves to him in return to his first Proposition, that his Precedents are not to the Purpose, which he himself as good as owns by allowing them not *Parallel* (Mod. truly Stated, *p.* 17, 18, 19); for, (*as he has been told*) *how Sacred and Incontestable* soever they are, they can be [**26**] no *Warrant* but in a *Parallel* Case.[98] And as for this and the other Arguments, whoever will be at the Pains to compare them, will find that they are not at all weakened by his late pretended Answer.

Nor are his other Propositions[99] *over-look'd* or *unanswered*, so far as a Modest Respect to our Law-givers, in not determining of what was under their immediate Consideration, would allow. As for the

---

[98] The italicized words are quoted by Astell from *Moderation truly Stated*, p. 19, the rather obscure argument about parallel cases being raised by the author of *Occasional Conformity a most Unjustifiable Practice*, at p. 3, according to Owen, *Moderation still a Virtue*, p. 5.

[99] The propositions in question, seven in number, constitute the chapters of Owen's *Moderation a Vertue*. As restated in his *Moderation still a Virtue* (pp. 2–3, italicized in the original), it is to these propositions that Astell systematically refers.

Third, how *formidable* a *Creature* his *Occasional-Conformist* is, [*Moderation still a Virtue*, p. 2] has been fully consider'd (O.C.[Occasional Conformity] unjustifiable, *p.* 51. *and* Mod. truly Stated, *p.* 37),[100] and the Estimation made from Men of his Principles when they were in Power* (*Ib. p.* 62. 65 *to* 79) nay even from the Dissenters own Opinion of one another, (*p.* 51, 52. 80):[101] and from their present Declarations (*p.* 88, 89, 90, 95. *and elsewhere.*), and Practices compar'd with their former. And since he affirmed, that *the Difference between the Church and the Dissenters is inconsiderable*, the proper Inference was drawn from it, they were intreated for their Countries sake, for GOD's sake, and even for their own, to heal our Breaches, and not to keep up a Separation and stand out against their Lawful Superiors, since they allow our Communion is not Sinful, and that Union at this time is so very necessary ([*Moderation truly Stated*] *p.* 49, 50. 60).

In answer to his Fourth, he was told that a Government can never be well served, when those are employed on Publick Trusts, who do not approve, or heartily assent to the Constitution; that the

---

[100] Astell is here referring to Owen's argument from *raison d'état*, that 'Princes *who understood their own Interest* [*know*] *better than to exclude Persons from publick Places, for their being Dissenters from the Religion of the State*; And that there is danger too in excluding Dissenters' (*Moderation truly Stated*, p. 36). Astell's response in *Moderation truly Stated* (pp. 62–79), was to reformulate the argument as two questions: 'First, *In fact*, whether the Dissenters have either been Friends to the *Church of England*, or good Subjects to their Prince, when it was in their power to be otherwise? ... And, Secondly, Whether by their Principles they can be so?' To these (rhetorical) questions she gave an extended reply in the form of a history of Puritanism and Parliament in the Civil War period.

[101] The placement of these sets of references is indicated in the text as shown and with the closest approximation to the symbol Astell uses (*, †, | |). Astell refers to the comparison of conflicting views among Independents, in *Moderation truly Stated*, at pp. 51, 52 and 80, which she documents with quotations from Edward's *Gangraena*, p. 87 and the *Second Part of Gangraena: Or Further Discovery* (London, 1646), p. 240; the Preface to Coleman-Street's *Conclave Visited* (1648); an *Extract of the Act*, 26 December 1644 (establishing A Committee of Both Kingdoms); [Peter] Sterry's *England's Deliverance* (London, 1651), p. 7; [John] Saltmarsh's [*The Smoke in the Temple ...*] *Answer to* [*Master*] *Ley* (London, 1646), p. 7; [John Goodwin's] *Thirty Queries Modestly Propounded* (1646), p. 7; [John] Bastwick's *The Several Humble Petitions of John Bastwick* (1641); [John Price's] *Pulpit Incendiary* (1648), p. 45; *Truth Triumphing over Falsehood* (London, 1645); William Prynne, John Goodwin, *Innocencies Triumph* (London, 1644); and Milton's *Iconoclastes in Answer to a Book Intitl'd Eikon Basilike* (London, 1649), p. 237. Of Milton she says, p. 80, that he was 'a better Poet than Divine or Politician'. The page references which follow are also to *Moderation truly Stated*.

Ecclesiastical Government is a part of our Constitution, and that Men who approve it but *Occasionally*, and *Statedly* dislike it, will Serve it accordingly ([*Moderation truly Stated*] *p.* 31).

To the Fifth it has been said, that if *Non-Conformity* were only a Matter of Conscience, Dissenters might be brought off it by coming *Occasionally* to our Churches, and observing how much more edifying our Worship is than their own ([*Moderation truly Stated*] *p.* 95): But *Occasional-Conformity* is made an Engine to promote Secular Interests; and for the Reasons above, it Weakens and Undermines the Church, and keeps up our Divisions ([*Moderation truly Stated*] *p.* 95, 96).

How our *Moderate Author* can allow himself to be so Peremptory in condemning a Bill that had pass'd a House of Commons by a great Majority; and whose Subject Matter the Lords approv'd so far forth ([*Moderation truly Stated*] *p.* 34. 98 (*see also their Proceedings* [October, p. 31])), as to condemn *Occasional-Conformity* merely for a Place, and to consent to exclude *Occasional-Conformists* from the Government, tho' they cou'd not agree to other [27] Circumstances, I leave him to consider. And it is very strange, that he a *Stated Dissenter*, shou'd be better acquainted with the Church's Interest, and more concern'd for it, than her Constant Members and Dutiful Sons ([*Moderation truly Stated*] *p.* 37 *to* 40. 82); This is a Paradox too gross to pass upon us.

His seventh Proposition, wherein he gives Examples of Dissenters employ'd in most Governments ([*Moderation truly Stated*] *p.* 99), the *Stater* thought might be let alone, till he had accounted for the Precedents brought him of the Tricks that the Dissenters have play'd us in our own Country, whenever they got into Office, and were strong enough to shew their skill. But another Answerer has more particularly shew'd him, that the Precedents he concludes with are no more to the purpose than those he began with, for there are no *Occasional Conformists* among them (O.C. unjust. *p.* 52, *to the end.*), to the *Point* I should have said, for they may serve the purpose of amusing the simple and inconsiderate.

In sum, the Cause our *Moderate Author* undertook, has been fully examined, First as to the Religion of it (Mod. truly Stated, *p.* 1 *to* 26).[102] Mistaken Moderation has been exposed (*p.* 5. 10, Etc.). The

---

[102] From here to the end, page references are to *Moderation truly Stated*, and can be assumed to be correct, unless otherwise noted.

Artifice for pleading so mightily for Moderation has been detected, and of producing our Author's pretended Precedents for it ([p.] 81); as also how its pretended Advocates treat those whom they cajole under this pretence (*p.* 2). Moderation has been defined and truly stated, with relation to Zeal, Order and Decency (*p.* 17, *p.* 81). It has been shewn how far Scripture-Moderation is concerned in our present Controversie (*p.* 6 *to* 10). Our Author's Precedents have been examined (*p.* 10 *to* 14), and no Resemblance found between them and our Occasional Conformists (*p.* 14 *to* 20). Examples of a nearer Likeness have been brought him from Scripture, such as *Korah's* and his Separatists, the Worshippers in high Places, *etc* (*p.* 20 *to* 25). And an eminent Example in *Nehemiah*, of an honest and couragious, a regular and steady concern for the Church of GOD, has been recommended (*p.* 21 *to* 24). Our Author has been directed to St. *Paul's Laws for Uniformity* (*p.* 25): has been told the difference between the Apostles Compliances, who were Governours and might determine such indifferent things as they saw fit, and the unnecessary and unauthorized Separation of a number of People, from such as have the Rule over them (*p.* 19). It has been shewn that the Separation is groundless, even upon their own Principles (*p.* 59, 60), and by the declared Opinions [28] of their own Authors (*p.* 43. 55, Etc.). And the *Moderate Author* is now desird, since he thinks his Answerers Arguments defective, to reply to what Mr. *Calvin*, Mr. *Baxter*, the *Presbyterian Ministers*, Mr. *Edwards* and others have writ against Schism (*p.* 61. *p.* 57 *p.* 53, Etc.).[103] And let him tell us, if he can, and if he thinks fit to discover the Secret, why they still keep up a *Division*, since by their Practices they allow that they can lawfully communicate, and by their Principles are therefore *bound in conscience to submit* (*p.* 55. *and* 60); and since they themselves confess that *Divisions are so pernicious*, at this time especially (*p.* 33)?[104]

Their Reasons for Separation, such as Human Mixtures, sinful Impositions, greater Edification, have been fully answer'd (*p.* 40,

---

[103] In fact Calamy's *Abridgement of Baxter's Life* (1702, pp. 95, 96) is cited at p. 61; Baxter's own works are cited at p. 71 of *Moderation truly Stated*; Edwards at pp. 56 and 58; and Calvin not at all; which suggests that Astell did not check her own text. (Owen, *Moderation still a Virtue* discusses Baxter at p. 61, but nothing related at pp. 57 or 53.)

[104] Astell both quotes *Moderation truly Stated* at p. 60 and paraphrases it at p. 33.

Etc.). The evil Effects of these Pretences have been shewn from Mr. *Baxter* and others of their own Writers (*p.* 61). The true Reason of them has been laid open (*p.* 51 *to* 60). Their Objections against the Liturgy have been answer'd (*p.* 44, Etc. 60); their *Call* examined (*p.* 44);[105] their *Gift of Prayer* shewn to be either a meer Humane Art, or else a Blasphemous Pretension (*p.* 46, 47); it has been made appear, that the Want of Discipline, which they so loudly complain of (*p.* 45, 46), is to be imputed to themselves, who weaken the Authority of the Church, and hinder the Effect of her Censures, by their unreasonable Separation (*p.* 47). It has been shewn what Conscience is; and how they quit their pretensions to Conscience to threaten us (*p.* 48, 49). They have been told of the Church's Charity and Readiness to receive them into her Bosom, in the Spirit of Meekness (*p.* 36); but that, how willing soever she may be to condescend to their Weakness (*p.* 37), 'tis impossible for her to reconcile Contradictions, or to give them Satisfaction, till they agree among themselves what will please them (*p.* 50 *to* 54): for, except in opposing the Church, they are as oposite to one another as they are to us (*p.* 51). They accuse one another of Impositions and Persecutions (*p.* 43. 51, 52. 80). When they themselves are in power they violently exclaim against Toleration, and will by no means allow it, exposing the great Evil of Schism (*p.* 55 *to* 59. 64). They are therefore earnestly exhorted to Unity and render'd inexcusable if they neglect it (*p.* 53 *to* 59). And as the Toleration does not excuse the Schism (*p.* 49 *to* 51), but only takes off the Penalty that the Laws inflicted upon Nonconformity (*p.* 50); so it is made appear that Faction (*p.* 91, 92), not Conscience, keeps up our *Divisions* (*p.* 95. 116).[106]

[21] Secondly, the question concerning Occasional Conformity has also been examined, with relation to Policy and the Civil Government (*p.* 26, Etc.), and since the Welfare of the Nation depends upon the choice of the Hands through which the Administration passes (*p.* 29), it has been made appear, that those only who are satisfied with the Constitution and heartily approve it, will serve the Government faithfully and support it (*p.* 31, 32). And that since

---

[105] In fact Astell discussed the Dissenter's 'Call' and 'Gift of Prayer' at pp. 45–7 of *Moderation truly Stated.*

[106] Once again, Astell gives a quite liberal overview of her earlier text, to which some of these citations relate in only a general way.

Occasional Conformists are not well-affected to the Ecclesiastical Government, which is a part of the Constitution, they are not fit to be trusted by it (*p.* 31). Nor are they better Men than their Neighbours, as our Author would insinuate (*p.* 32).[107] Hypocrisy, which is prov'd upon them, being a great Immorality. Their sinister Intentions towards the Constitution (*p.* 32. *and throughout the Book.*), is also prov'd from their former and present Actions (*p.* 62. 70); whereby is shewn that the Constitution is that which they really fall foul on (*p.* 78), whatever their Pretences may be, and that nothing but its Ruine will content them (*p.* 88. 95. 116): that, in order to this they began to cry out of Persecution in Queen *Elizabeth's* Reign (*p.* 78), by which, as an *Independant* tells us, the *Presbyterians* mean the being *not suffer'd to oppress their Brethren* (*p.* 80).[108] Their evil Behaviour towards that Queen and her Royal Successors, even to her Present Majesty is shewn (p. 82. 88. 67).[109] As also that they never wanted the Will, when they had the Power to hurt (*p.* 69. 103); For they declare against Neuters ([p. 63] *p.* 80), and persecute all who will not comply with them (*p.* 63).[110]

[107] These arguments are made, at the pages indicated, in *Moderation truly Stated*, to rebut Owen's fourth proposition, 'That the employing of [Dissenters] in Public Trusts, strengthens the Church' (p. 2 of *Moderation still a Virtue*, pp. 24–7 of *Moderation a Vertue*). Astell is at her best in this argument, maintaining that Occasional Conformity in religion correlates with Occasional Conformity in government, and is by any account unconstitutional, given that allegiance to the Church of England is legally established.

[108] The citation in *Moderation truly Stated*, from p. 80 of which this is quoted, reads, 'So says the Independent to the Presbyterian in the *Pulpit Incendiary*, p. 45, (1648). He who would be further Inform'd in their Apothegms may consult Different Sayings, 1683.'

[109] Astell's analysis of the conduct of the Dissenters in the reigns of Elizabeth and Anne produces some of her finest political analysis, including disquisitions on the maxims that 'the *Little Finger* of an Usurp'd Power, is heavier than the *Loins* of a Lawful Prince' (*Moderation truly Stated*, pp. 66–7); and that 'a Wise Prince ought to put himself in no bodys hands, nor should he put it in any Man's Power to Ruin him' (*Moderation truly Stated*, pp. 82–3).

[110] Here Astell is quoting from the *Declaration of England and Scotland Jan. 30. 1643*, as cited in *Moderation truly Stated* (p. 63), where they took care 'to give publick Warning to all *Neuters*, to rest no longer upon their Neutrality, but that they address themselves speedily to take the *Covenant*, and joyn with all their Power in defence of this Cause against the* Common Enemy, (*The Term by which they were pleased to denote their Sovereign King*, Charles Ist), *etc.* Otherwise (say they) we do declare them to be Publick Enemies to their Religion and Country; and that they are to be Sentenc'd and punish'd as profess'd Adversaries

Nor are their Principles better than their Practices, as has been prov'd at large in their own Words (*p.* 70. 91. 112).[111] You have a Specimen of their ill Language and Spite to the Church, to the State, nay even to Parliaments (*p.* 72), as well as to K. *Charles* I., whose Murder they justifie even to the last (*p.* 73).[112] Our Author indeed, in this his second Edition (*p.* 77), gives us an Abhorrence of this Wicked Action (or, in his moderate Language, the *Tragical End of that unhappy Prince*) subscribed by about sixty Ministers in their *Vindication* (*p.* 74. 77).[113] But is it not this very same *Vindication* that tells us, *p.* 6, 7. *That it was the woful Miscarriages of the King himself (which we cannot but acknowledge to be many and great) in his Government, that have cost the three Kingdoms so dear and cast him down?* So that it seems all they dislik'd was only the *present way of Tryal.* For those godly Ministers threw the King's pretended Miscarriages in his dish, even in his greatest Affliction: and that they may not be for [22] got, our Author gives an invidious List of them, *p.* 80, 81. But if he had any Ingenuity or Respect for an Injur'd Prince, her Majesty's Royal Predecessor, from who she derives her Blood and Crown; nay, if he had but any regard to Truth, he would also have told us, from the same noble Historian he mentions (*Vol.* 1. *p.* 166. 206, 207. *also p.* 52. 53. p. 71. 90. 103),[114] that the King had redress'd all their Grievances, and

and Malignants. In *Scotland*† (†*See* Sir Henry Vane's *Speech at a Common Hall,* Oct. 27, 1643) he who should not take, or who deferr'd taking the *Covenant,* was to have all his Rents and Profits confiscated, was not to enjoy any Office or Benefit, and to be cited before the next Parliament, *Etc.*"'

[111] In *Moderation truly Stated* (p. 70) Astell had given a sample from Archbishop Richard Bancroft's *Dangerous Positions* (1641), Book II, Chapters 12 and 13; Case's *Sermon Etc.,* 30 September 1543, p. 45, comprising 'such as *false, bastardly Governours of the Church, Incarnate Devils, Cogging, Confining Knaves, Impudents, Shameless Dolts, Hogs, Wolves, a Troop of bloudy Soul Murderers, Idle Shepherds, Dumb Dogs, Greedy Dogs, Vile Wretches,* and what not.'

[112] At pp. 72–3 of *Moderation truly Stated* Astell gives an impressive list of examples of refusal to extend toleration to their enemies, and determination to subordinate the monarchy to the yoke of their confession, by some of the staunchest advocates of Toleration and Dissent.

[113] 'Our Author' in the previous paragraph refers to Owen, as author of *Moderation a Vertue* and *Moderation still a Virtue.* At p. 82 of the latter Owen refers to 'the Tragical End of that Unhappy Prince', but 'his Second Edition', unavailable to me, clearly includes an elaboration. The list of 'the King's pretended Miscarriages' appears at pp. 80–1 of the 1704 edition, as Astell goes on to state.

[114] Owen, in *Moderation still a Virtue* (p. 82) cites the Earl of Clarendon's *History,* Book III, 184, not the passages which Astell cites.

granted all they could ask; that the things so much complain'd of (as Tonnage and Poundage), were no more than had been done by the King's Predecessors without any exception; and that the like Peace and Tranquillity was never enjoy'd by any Nation, till these Peaceable and Moderate Men, as they would be thought, put all into a flame. But supposing that excellent Prince had been as bad as the worst of his Revilers would represent him. What then? Neither the Laws of GOD nor of the Land, gave his Subjects any Authority to use him as they did. Supposing then that the Presbyterians had no Design upon the Life of the King, when they despoil'd him of his Sovereignty, will this excuse them? It would not excuse them in an ordinary Case; for he who being about an Unlawful Action, shall happen to kill a Man tho' undesignedly, is reckon'd Guilty of the Murder before GOD and Man. And truly I think there could not have been said a more severe and spiteful thing against the Revolution in 88, than the supposing as our Author does *p.* 82, that it can't be justified but by justifying the Parliament in 42.[115]

Our Author then approves those Principles and Practices that brought a Royal-Head to the Block, and that is granting all that his Answerers desire: for certainly her Majesty and all her Faithful Subjects ought to be upon their Guard against such a Moderation as this. These Moderate Men once gave us a fatal Example of their *Short-way* with the Church (*See* Mod. truly Stated, *p.* 79); they have not quitted their Designs against her (*p.* 89, 116); her Destruction is their Fundamental Principle (*Ib. p.* 88); 'tis to own their Adherence to this, that they keep *Stated Communion* with Dissenting Congregations, as Mr. *Calamy* lately own'd (*p.* 89);[116] all which have been prov'd upon them. The Artifices they formerly us'd, and have of late renew'd, have been display'd, their way of making Tools (*p.* 84. 90. 96. 101. 105. 112);[117] Aspersing those who

---

[115] Owen, *Moderation still a Virtue*, p. 82, made in fact a rather telling point against Divine Right and hereditary monarchy, when he claimed: 'I cannot see how those Gentlemen that so fiercely condemn the *Parliament* in 1642, can approve the Revolution in 1688, which was founded in the Invitation of the Pr. of O. by a certain Number of *Lords*, and *Gentlemen, out of Parliament*. And they that disapprove of the Dethroning of K. *J*. II. cannot be true to the Present Government, which is Establish'd on the same Foundation with that of K. WILLIAM'.

[116] Calamy, in his *Abridgment of Baxter's Life*, p. 559.

[117] Astell's source for the claims documented in *Moderation truly Stated*, at the pages cited here and following, is overwhelmingly Clarendon's *History*.

hinder their ill Designs (*p.* 96, 97); their Encroachments (*p.* 101); Clandestine Arts to bring about Alterations (*p.* 90, 91. 96. 98); [23] their Methods and restless Industry in Ruining King and Kingdom in 41, which are but too plainly repeated (*p.* 90. 96). So ill Use do they make of the Church's Moderation (*p.* 84. 88.); so little are they to be won by Condescensions, which cost the Martyr his Crown and Life (*p.* 94, 95 96); whereas Queen *Elizabeth* preserv'd hers by Resolution (*p.* 112, Etc. 103), in keeping up Establishments (*p.* 91), by Firmness and steady Conduct (*p.* 82. 94). It is shewn therefore how necessary it is to be upon our guard, since we had a dismal instance that the worst Consequences have proceeded from inconsiderable Beginnings (*p.* 84). That no ill Usage of theirs shall tempt us to use them ill (*p.* 95. 99); but it ought to make us so wise as to secure our selves against them, without any Design upon their Toleration (*p.* 92). The granting of which was certainly a great Instance of the Church-mens Temper and Charity, how ungratefully soever it is received, and what should provoke them to recal what they granted so freely? The Church, as our Author has been told, abounds in Charity and Moderation, even in his Sense, towards *Conscientious* Dissenters; but what should hinder her from restraining the *Factious* Dissenter from doing mischief, since even our Moderate Author will not undertake his Vindication (*p.* 92, 93)? Which Distinction is as old as Queen *Elizabeth*'s days, and was first made by her Ministry (*p.* 93, 94). All Contentions and the Struggles of Parties being indeed only kept up by a few leading and self-ended Men, who have no other Aim, whatever they may pretend, but their own Interest, as has been prov'd (*p.* 93, 106, Etc.).[118] Tho nothing can be more ridiculous than this Practice of Lewd and Self-interested Mens pretending to be Patriots (*p.* 106. 110). And if there appears any Bitterness in this, it arises only from the Plainness and Force of Truth, which ill Men cannot bear, tho it be the greatest Charity (*p.* 81).

They have also been told what may be fit for them to do, if they would have their former Practices forgotten (*p.* 110, 111); and that eagerness after Offices is no good Sign of deserving them (*p.* 112).

---

[118] The disquisitions on self-interest and its perils, which Astell delivers in *Moderation truly Stated* (pp. 93, 106) against the Whigs, perhaps with specific reference to Locke and the Shaftesbury circle, are among her most passionately expressed political views.

The Opinion of the Lords and Commons concerning *Occasional-Conformity* (*p.* 34), and the Bill that was brought in against it (*p.* 98), has been collected. And it has been made appear, that if the Church's best Friends may be Judges (*p.* 37), this Bill was not against, as our Author would suggest (*p.* 37, Etc.), but very much for her Interest (*p.* 38, 39. 82. 90 Etc. 116, Etc.); it has been shewn why Reasons for the Bill, and for maintaining [24] the Establishment, have been produc'd (*p.* 116); and such as may weigh with Men of Estate and Interest, tho' they have not that Sense of Religion which all of us ought to have (*p.* 110); the Common Objections are answer'd, and shewn to be Sophisms; nor would this Bill have brought any new Incapacity upon Dissenters, it would only have declar'd that Incapacity they have brought upon themselves (*p.* 99). And the Reader has no doubt by this time collected from the Premises, that the Reason why Pagan Princes might safely employ Jews and Christians, does by no means hold with respect to our Dissenters (*p.* 99, 100).

To conclude, the Author ought either to disprove the Authorities cited out of their own Writers, or else to prove to us that the Modern Dissenters have deserted the Principles, and do not approve the Practices of their Fore-fathers, who began with the same Pretences, that our Moderate Author uses, Reformation and Gospel Purity; tho, notwithstanding all these Pretences, it was Secular Interest that abolish'd Episcopacy and set up Presbytery, as he fairly owns, *p.* 82. But till this is done, he must allow us to make all the Provisions we can, that they may never any more Triumph in the Ruin of GOD's Church among us; and this is truly the State of the Question, which I leave to the consideration of all Impartial Readers.

An Impartial

ENQUIRY

INTO THE

CAUSES

OF

𝕽𝖊𝖇𝖊𝖑𝖑𝖎𝖔𝖓 𝖆𝖓𝖉 𝕮𝖎𝖛𝖎𝖑 𝖂𝖆𝖗

IN THIS

KINGDOM:

In an EXAMINATION of

Dr. *Kennett's* SERMON, *Jan.* 31. 170¾.

And Vindication of the

ROYAL MARTYR.

by mrs mary astell

LONDON:

Printed by *E. P.* for *R. Wilkin* at the *King's Head*
in St. *Paul's* Church-Yard, 1704.

Note on the Text

Astell's pamphlet is a reply to Bishop White Kennett's sermon, *A Compassionate Enquiry into the Causes of the Civil War*, preached on the anniversary of the death of Charles I, 31 January 1704. Kennett's sermon earned him notoriety for Whig tepidness on the merits of Charles, while Astell's reply is one of the famous set pieces of the Tory canon lamenting the death of the Royal Martyr, appealing to standard authorities, the Bible, the Earl of Clarendon and Henry Foulis, with broadsides in all directions.

Kennett is referred to by Astell as a writer in the Convocation Controversy who had assisted Archbishop Thomas Tenison to assert William's prerogative forbidding the convocation of the lower clergy in Parliament. Archbishop of Canterbury from 1694 to 1714, Tennison was William III's appointee and replacement for Archbishop William Sancroft, Astell's nonjuring friend. Sancroft and Edward Hyde, first Earl of Clarendon, the former Mary Astell's patron, the latter her intellectual mentor and much-cited source, were representative of the Anglican hierarchy of the 1680s, Laudian descendants uncompromising on the status and independence of Anglicanism. Astell, a firm supporter of the autonomy of the Anglican hierarchy, like her High Church authorities, represented what Goldie (1978, 64) has suggested to be the real roots of Tory constitutionalism in the revolt against James: the choice of church over king.

Astell's analysis, which patterns the problems of 1688 on those of 1641, is not merely an elaborately crafted ruse to bypass the censor. It reflects the perceptions of contemporaries, who could overlook the hiatus between the Civil War and Restoration and see real parallels in the two successful attempts in one century to unseat Stuart Kings. Astell thus vindicates the trend of recent historiography (see Scott, 1988, 460–1) to take seriously the claims of contemporary critics of the Restoration who analysed the Revolution of 1688 against the benchmark of 1641. Excuses for resistance were the same ('Popery' and 'Arbitrary Government'), so were the fears – civil war without cease, on the one hand, or capitulation to the forces of Continental counter-revolution, spearheaded by the French, on the other. Astell attacks Kennett for inflating fears of Popery and the French threat – classic scare tactics of the Shaftesbury circle, to which Locke belonged – when it was Pym and the Presbyterians who had wreaked havoc with the polity.

Astell's references are to the published, somewhat toned-down, as he tells us (*Compassionate Enquiry*, prefatory Advertisement, p. 1), second edition of White Kennett's sermon, a slim pamphlet of twenty-eight pages, which attracts a rebuttal of more than double the length. Astell creates a sort of pastiche out of his pamphlet, in which hardly a word he wrote goes unquoted, but not necessarily in context, and succeeds in making him sound more Whiggish than the text would allow. Astell renders him a surrogate for Locke, making much of his passing reference to motives of self-preservation (p. 19) and fears of citizens for their liberties and estates, when in fact, the most sustained passages of his political theory suggest a rather old-fashioned view of the well-ordered polity, that relies on the metaphor of the body (p. 16). What is most remarkable about Astell's work is not only its perspicacity in analysing the basic tenets of Whig political theory, and specifically Locke's, but also its representativeness of arguments that came to characterize the Augustan Tory position. It is sometimes forgotten that Sir Robert Filmer's *Patriarcha* was first and foremost a refutation of Scholastic arguments for popular sovereignty as they were, in the 1630s, already infecting Protestant political thought (Sommerville, 1982, 1991). The great debates that had raged under James I between Cardinal Bellarmine and perceived counter-reformation defenders of the right to depose unlawful kings against supporters of the English Protestant Kingdom had their efflux in the later debates between Hobbes and Filmer, Filmer and Locke. Filmer was republished between 1679 and 1680 during the Exclusion Crisis to support the Tory cause. It was highly desirable for Locke, like Hobbes, to be able to establish distance between their theories and those of the patriarchalist, whose very fundamentalism posed a problem in times of dynastic uncertainty. Locke, needless to say, was not keen to be classed with the Scholastics. It was up to him to give the lie to Filmer, and later exponents of his views such as Foulis, that popular sovereignty had roots independent of Popery. Most notable in Astell's *An Impartial Enquiry* is the genealogy of theories of popular sovereignty that it records, taken from Henry Foulis, where Jesuits and defenders of Papal power are thrown together with Calvinists and Whigs. Thus once again the Jesuits Mariana (*q.v.*), Suarez, Molina and Bellarmine, were declared to be in unholy alliance with the radical Protestant sects, the Diggers, the Levellers (*q.v.*), Milton and Locke (see *An Impartial Enquiry*, p. 26).

Two years later White Kennett once again preached a commemorative sermon on the occasion of Charles I's death, 30 January, this time to both Houses of Parliament. He was one of only four Whig bishops ever to do so (Goldie, 1978, 51). On that day he delivered a very mild set piece, and finally seemed to capitulate to the Tory cause in 1715 with a sermon on resistance to the King as a species of witchcraft, citing the Articles, Canons and Homilies against rebellion which constituted the Tory litany, and on which Astell also draws, concluding with an exalted argument for divine right: 'Kings and Princes do in a more especial Manner represent the Majesty of God himself; are his Viceregents and Deputies here on Earth' (White Kennett, *The Witchcraft of the Present Rebellion*, 1715, p. 5, cited Goldie, 1978, 325). Whether this is testimony to Astell's persuasive powers, or evidence for the inconstancy of a bishop whose affiliations until 1700 had been Tory (Goldie, 1980a, 499), is debatable. As a moderate Tory herself, the distance between Astell and Kennett was less great than the tone of her pamphlet would suggest.

Astell's textual references are reliable unless otherwise noted. It is clear that Astell, or her printer, if it was he who inserted the marginal notes, is working directly from the published second edition of Kennett's sermon, as she claims (p. 3), and not quoting or paraphrasing from memory. It is likely, given that the placement of the marginal notes is not always accurate, that they were organized by Astell but placed by the printer. Wherever possible the note has now been checked and inserted in round brackets where it belongs in the text. Errors of transcription are noted, except in the cases where the page number is given for the beginning but not for the conclusion of the passage, because the full passage is easy enough to locate. Similarly, small variations of spelling and punctuation, and the use of quotation to create a misleading impression, are not usually noted, because they are ubiquitous. Astell uses italics to indicate quotation; major variations from the texts she cites are noted. The original pagination of Astell's pamphlet is indicated in square brackets in bold type and it is to this pagination that my notes refer.

[3] An Impartial Enquiry into the Causes of Rebellion and Civil War

It was not till *Feb.* 27 that I met with Dr *Kennet's* Sermon. Having heard it much commended, and finding it in a second Edition, I was inclined to Read, and for the same reasons to make some Remarks upon it.[1] To his Person and Character I am utterly a Stranger, any farther than that I have been told he was a Writer in the Convocation Controversy; but whether he was in the Right, or in the Wrong, neither my Leisure nor Abilities allow me to judge: nor had I so much as known that his Sermon occasion'd any *Noise*, or *Stories*, or *unreasonable Scandal*, had not he himself been pleas'd to *Advertise* the World of it.

St. *Botolph's* being a Parochial Church, since he stiles himself *Minister* of it, I suppose he officiates there, either as Rector, Vicar, Lecturer or Curate,[2] 'tis all one to me; for be it which it may, it obliges me to shew him that Respect which is due to a Clergy-man of the *Church of England*; who, by his Office of *Archdeacon*, is yet more particularly bound to an exact Observation of her Doctrine, Rubricks, and Canons, because it is his Duty to require this Obedience from others.

---

[1] White Kennett, *A Compassionate Enquiry into the Causes of the Civil War. In a Sermon Preached in the Church of St Botolph Aldgate, On January 31, 1704. the Day of the Fast of the Martyrdom of King Charles the First* (London, 1704).

[2] Astell cannot pretend not to know that White Kennett, DD was 'Archdeacon of *Huntington* and Minister of St *Botolph* without *Aldgate*', since this is boldly stated on the title page of the pamphlet she is addressing.

Now one of her Canons (founded upon an Apostolical Injunction deliver'd to Bishop *Titus*, *Put them in* [4] mind to be subject to Principalities and Powers, *and to obey Magistrates*) enjoining, 'That all Ecclesiastical Persons shall, to the utmost of their Wit, Knowledge and Learning, purely and sincerely (without any colour of Dissimulation) teach, manifest, open and declare, four times every Year (at the least) in their Sermons, That the Queen's Power within her Realms of *England, Scotland* and *Ireland*, etc. is the highest Power under GOD, to whom all Men do, by GOD's Laws, owe most Loyalty and Obedience afore and above all other Powers or Potents in the Earth;'[3] and no time being so fit to inculcate Obedience as that wherein we deplore the most villanous and unparallel'd Breach of it: I make no question but that, as the Doctor's *uncorrupt Blood and Principles* (*Page* 8.),[4] engage him to pay that Loyalty and Obedience in his own Person which the Laws Ecclesiastical and Civil command, even tho' he has no *Jewish Fondness* in him, but partakes of *the Spirit of a Free People* (*Pag.* 20.);[5] so he likewise took care to lay hold of this very proper opportunity to teach that same Loyalty and Obedience to his Hearers. Especially since he professes to enquire, *as he is satisfied in his own Conscience, without Partiality or any other By-respect*, p. 6. (which Period is a little perplex'd, but we will not be over-critical;) and also reminds us, that *the Ministers of the Gospel are to know no other Politicks but Simplicity and godly Sincerity.*[6]

---

[3] This is a fairly accurate transcription of the first of fifty-three *Injunctions Given by the Queens Majesty, As well to the Clergy as to the Laity of this Realm*, published in 1559, the first year of Elizabeth's reign. See the 1675 edition (first edition, 1604) of the Church of England's, *A Collection of Articles Injunctions, Canons, Orders, Ordinances and Constitutions Ecclesiastical* (London), p. 67.

[4] Astell applies Kennett's remarks on the 'Natural Distast to a *French* Power', inherited from '*English* Fore-fathers' by those 'whose Principles and Blood are not corrupted' (*Compassionate Enquiry*, p. 8), for her own purposes. Such uses of the text are customary with her, and other examples are discussed below. Where no annotation is made it can be assumed that Astell is faithful to Kennett's text, with minor variations of syntax, spelling and punctuation.

[5] Kennett discusses 1 Samuel 8:10–18, where Samuel told 'the *Israelites*, that the *manner of their King* should be (as in other Nations) *to take their Sons and Daughters* to his own arbitrary Use and Service; and *to take their Fields and Cattle* at his private Will and Pleasure' (*Compassionate Enquiry*, p. 20). Kennett takes this to be an instance of 'Tyranny and Oppression [that] were a Grievance *Here* [i.e. in England] in the remotest times', inimical to 'the Spirit of a Free People'. This Astell interprets as showing 'no *Jewish Fondness* in him'.

[6] Kennett, *Compassionate Enquiry*, p. 5.

It will follow then, that the Design of his Sermon and Enquiry, is, as it ought to be, to remove the *cursed Causes* of our Civil War, whatever they were, *and to prevent the like fatal Effects for the future*; which is the best [5] way we know of *to attone for the past Iniquities* (*Pag.* 2.). The *leading Causes of this days Evil, improv'd by wicked Arts and Designs, were five*, according to the Doctor's Computation (*Pag.* 6.), tho' in reality all may be reduc'd to the *French Interest* and *Alliance*, especially if you join to it *the Apprehensions and Fears of Popery thence arising*; for these *led on the Jealousies of Oppression and Illegal Power, which tended more and more to*, and *help'd to* produce the other two.[7] So that upon the matter, the *French Alliance*, at least with the Fears of Popery attending it, was, in his account, the main Cause of the Civil Wars: and so the Dr. makes it expresly *p.* 13, 15. the rest being only a chain of Effects proceeding from it.[8]

---

[7] Fear of the French alliance or the 'French Threat' was diffuse in the seventeenth century. It was given salience by the marriage of Charles I to Henrietta Maria, sister of Louis XIII, King of France in the year of James I's death, 1625. Further evidence was adduced in the form of the sanctuary given at the French court to the Duchess of Portsmouth, Charles' favourite mistress, and later to James II, his wife and infant son. The French threat, like the Spanish alliance, provided the international focus for Protestant forces rallying against the Papacy. So, Frederick, Elector Palatine, and the Electress, Elizabeth, Charles' favourite sister, eldest daughter of James I, raised hopes of a continental Protestant Alliance, which foundered in Prague, where they proved no match for the Habsburgs. In the 1670s William of Orange took up the gauntlet, using the propagandist Peter Du Moulin to turn the British Parliament against the French alliance. (See Schwoerer, 1977, esp. 846–8, for an excellent analysis of the Revolution of 1688–9 as the outcome of a carefully staged propaganda coup by William.) William III thus became the rallying point for a new Protestant effort to address the French threat, central to the concerns of the first Earl of Shaftesbury and his circle. We have evidence in the recently published minute of Locke to Edward Clarke (Bodleian MS Locke e.18, fo. 4v, in Farr and Roberts (1985)), where Locke declares: 'let us owne King William to be our King by right. Who ever refuse this, what doe they in effect but plainly call him Usurper! For what is an Usurper but a King actually in a throne to which he has noe right. I wonder not to hear that the French King cals him soe, as the most pernicious opinion can be fixed on him, and I should as little wonder that those who will not owne his right to the crown should joyn with the French King or any body else to dispossess him they judg an Usurper.'

[8] Ashcraft (1986, 185ff.) and McNally (1989) have noted 'no slavery, no popery!' as catch cries of Shaftesbury and his party. Scott (1988, 460–1) has made an important contribution to the historiography of the period, in noting the degree to which contemporaries drew parallels between these twin demons in the reigns of Charles I and II. Astell's analysis follows this pattern.

As for those *wicked Arts and Designs* by which this *Cause was improv'd*, (*Ibid.*)[9] and who they were that improv'd it, we hear of them all at once towards the End of the Sermon (*Pag.* 24.): There we are told, that the *Prime Engines* were *Men of Craft, dreadful Dissemblers with* GOD (what is meant by adding *and Heaven*, I know not, for the Dr. is too zealous against Popery, to suffer us to imagine that he takes in Angels and Saints.) *What artificial Fasts! what procuring Prayers!* (a new Epithet) *what deluding Speeches! what Abuse of Holy Scripture! what a stretch in Hypocrisy!* in order to the *Fatal Blow* (*Pag.* 25.).

These are all popular Arts, and such as Factious Men do not fail to make use of in all Ages: But one wou'd think that the *Body of English People* were *Good-natur'd in* the worst Sense, to be impos'd on by them, or to receive any Suspicions, or to believe any Fears or Calumnies they cou'd raise, to the Prejudice of a *good* and [6] merciful Prince (*Pag.* 18, 19.), who had *too much Honour and Conscience for ill Designs*, who never *propos'd to injure his Subjects, or to alter the Constitution* (*Pag.* 18.); who was *an Orthodox and most Regular Prince, stedfast in the Faith and Communion of our Church*, to whole *Memory* we in *Justice* own, no *Prince* had *his Heart more fix'd on the Improvement of the Church* (*Pag.* 14.), and *Support and Honour of the Clergy*, as the Dr. confesses; who besides that Impartiality and Sincerity of which he makes profession, gives us no reason, from the Beginning to the End of his Sermon, to think that he wou'd say any more in favour of the *Martyr* than Truth extorted from him.

But sure we of this Age, who have this dismal Tragedy so fresh in our Memories, must be the greatest Fools in nature, if we suffer our selves to be bubbled any more by Men of the same Principles, and by the same Artifices so often detected, and so justly abhorr'd. Have we not had Warnings enough to beware of those Miscreants, who set whole Nations on fire, only that their own despicable selves may be talk'd of, and that they may warm them at the Flame? Men who are equally ruinous to Prince and People, who effectually destroy the Liberties of the Subject under pretence of defending them; who bring in Popery, for they act by some of the very worst Popish Principles, whilst they rail against it!

---

[9] Kennett, *Compassionate Enquiry*, p. 6, in fact.

Far be it from us to think that the Body of the Nation ever concur'd in that Villany we deplore, or even the Majority, any further than by a Supine Neglect of opposing it vigorously and in time. Wicked Men are active and unwearied, they stick at no Methods, use the vilest Means to carry their Point. They become [7] the Flatterers of Mens Follies, and the Panders of their Vices, to gain them to their Party. They Bribe, they Threaten, they Solicit, they Fawn, they Dissemble, they Lye, they break through all the Duties of Society, violate all the Laws of GOD and of Man, where they can do it with present Impunity. They fright the Timorous, and tire out the Impatient; if they meet with any of an invincible Spirit and Prudence to countermine them; all the hard Words, all the scandalous Stories that may be are thrown upon these Men, they are Malignants, High-flyers, and what not: No Stratagems are omitted to make them weary of Well doing. No wonder then that by such ways as these they get what passes for a Majority, and draw in thoughtless Men, who are so far from approving their Villanies, that they do not so much as suspect them. For one of their Arts is to lay their own Designs of overturning the Government, at the Door of those very Men, who are it's most faithful Supporters.

But as it will ever become a wise Government to be watchful over every little Cloud of Faction, and to suppress it in its Rise, so there is no Artifice us'd by Factious Men that Governours ought to be more upon their Guard against, than those suspicious Fears and Jealousies, that are artfully instill'd into the Minds of the People, by Cunning Men and their Instruments. I do not only mean that Governours shou'd provide against this, by taking care that their *Good be not Evil-spoken of,* and by *cutting off occasion* as much as in them lies, *from those that desire* and seek *occasion;* for after all this caution, [8] Factious Men will still find something to misrepresent. A sad instance of which, we have in their Usage of our Royal Martyr; whose very best Actions, as well as those Mistakes and Infirmities that are incident to Humane Nature, they took occasion to Calumniate. But Governours must vigorously exert that lawful Authority GOD has given them, to *be a Terror to Evil-doers, as well as a Praise and Encouragement to those who do well.* They shou'd not suffer Men to infect the Peoples Minds with evil Principles and Representations, with Speeches that have double Meanings and equivocal Expressions, *Innuendo's* and secret Hints and Insinuations.

An honest Man dares always *speak out;* he who means well, needs no Softnings, no cautious Periphrases; no aimings at something he wou'd have you *think,* but which he does not care to *say,* laying in Provision to bring himself off, if you shou'd charge him with it. This, how well soever it may suit the Politicks of the Age, how much soever it may be the Practice of the *Wise Men, as the World calls them (Page 5.),* is not at all consistent with the *Simplicity of the Gospel,* or the Courage and Spirit of a Free-man, an *English-man.*[10] Governours therefore may very justly animadvert upon, and suppress it. For it is as much their Duty, and as necessary a Service to the Public, to restrain the Turbulent and Seditious, as it is to protect the Innocent, and to reward the Deserving. This, no doubt, the Doctor was very well aware of; and therefore takes care to inform us very particularly, how *Doubts* and *Fears* contributed to our deplorable Civil Wars. And he thought us wise enough [9] of our selves to infer, that we ought above all things to detest and banish them, otherwise, it's like, we should have heard somewhat of it in his Second Inference, *p.* 26.

For till those Men have done pretending to Doubts and Fears, and I know not what Apprehensions, who have formerly destroy'd their innocent Neighbours, and overturn'd the Government by such Pretences, our Affairs can hardly be well manag'd Abroad, because we can never be united at Home. That supine Indifferency for excellent Establishments, which some are pleas'd to miscal *Charity;* that Faint Heart and Double Mind, that Want of Regular Zeal, which they would put upon us instead of *Meekness,* may hasten our

---

[10] Astell's language mocks the language of the country Whig, exemplified by John Tutchin, who combined reverence for the ancient constitution, Parliament and 'Native Right' with xenophobia, declaring of the constitution 'she's as well beloved now by all true *Englishmen,* as she was by our Forefathers a Thousand Years ago' (*Observator,* 7–10 April 1703). His views were set out in the *Observator* from 29 September to 7 November 1703, focusing on resistance and targeted at Charles Leslie (see Phillipson, 1993, 217). They were bound for this reason to have come to the attention of Astell, who gives the impression that Kennett held the same views. Tutchin admired 'those two great men, Mr. Sidney and Mr. Lock', defenders of ancient liberty, 'the one against Sir Robert Filmer, and the other against a whole Company of Slaves', but the only occasion on which he names Locke (*Observator,* 14–18 September 1706, cited Phillipson, 1993, 218), is too late for Astell's pamphlet.

Ruin, but can never *heal our Breaches*. For we have the sad Experience of our Civil Wars to inform us, that all the Concessions the King and his Loyal Subjects cou'd make to the Factious and Rebellious, cou'd not satisfie; no, not tho' they were at first, all that they had the confidence to desire, and their Confidence never fail'd them: They were ever stiff in their own way, still contending to bring over others to themselves, whilst they wou'd concede to nothing.

And, what was the thing they aim'd at, and at last unhappily effected? What but the Ruin of the Government in Church and State? The bringing *the Necks* of their Fellow Subjects, *Englishmen*, who *had the Spirit of a Free People!* under their own infamous *Yoke*, and *their Feet into* the most reproachful *Chains (Page* 20.); becoming themselves the Actors of those Arbitrary and Illegal Actions, which they had so loudly, and in great measure, [10] falsly imputed to their Lawful Superiors. And the *Freeborn* People of *England*, for all their *Spirit of Honour and Genius to Liberty (Page* 20.), even those great *Fore-Fathers*, whose *Off-spring we are (Page* 17.), had the *disdain of serving* in the most slavish manner, and of wearing the heavy and shameful *Yoke* of some of the vilest of their Fellow Subjects (*Page* 20.): Till GOD was pleas'd to restore our Monarch, and with him the Exercise of our Religion, and the Liberties of the *English* Nation. But this is a common Story, which every body knows, and therefore the Doctor wou'd not lose his time upon't; only in my mind, and whatever might be in his, methinks the whole course of his Sermon inculcates this necessary Lesson, Beware of every one who wou'd draw you into *a necessity* of *believing*, that your *Liberties and Estates are in some danger*, who wou'd give you such a *Prospect*, and work you into such a *Persuasion*, and so draw you in by the old Cant of *Self-Preservation*, tho' they seem to demonstrate ever so great a *necessity (Page* 18.):[11] Much more ought you

---

[11] Here Astell introduces her attack on the principle of self-preservation, a trope to which she frequently returns. In *The Christian Religion as Profess'd by a Daughter of the Church of England* (London, 1705, pp. 305–6), Astell explicitly references the argument in Locke's *Two Treatises* (Book II, Chapter 149, 1988, p. 367), claiming: '312. What then is *Self-Preservation*, that Fundamental Law of Nature, as some call it, to which all other laws, Divine as well as Human, are made to do Homage? and how shall it be provided for? Very well; for it does not consist in the Preservation of the Person or Composite, but in preserving the Mind from Evil, the Mind which is truly the Self, and which ought to be secur'd at all hazards. It is this *Self-Preservation* and no other, that is a *Fundamental Sacred and*

to abhor being *drawn in* by the bare *meaning* of it, at least if you have any regard to real Self-Preservation, and think your Souls of greater moment than your Lives or Estates. Nay, even for the very Preservation of these Dear Lives of yours, since, if you dare believe our Lord himself, the surest way to save your Lives is to be ready to part with them; and the most likely way to lose them, is this unchristian Desire of saving them (St. *Matth.*, 8. 35.).[12] For such Arts as those, the putting such *Thoughts* into the Heads of the *Good-natur'd English People*, was that which *seduc'd them* [11] *into that Unnatural Rebellion,*[13] which has had so many dismal Effects upon this Nation.

The Doctor having thus secur'd the Prince against the unreasonable Fears and Jealousies of the People; for sure, a Man of good and sincere Intentions, must *mean* to do this, whether or no he is happy in expressing this his *meaning*: The next thing to be done, is to make some Provision for the *True English Hearts*, the *Good-natur'd People (Page* 7.), against *the Thought and Dread of Oppression and Illegal Power (Page* 16.). 'Tis a hard thing indeed, to fence against Peoples *Thoughts* and *Apprehensions*! For, tho' *Wisdom* will be *justify'd of her Children,* yet *there is a Generation who curse their Father, and do not bless their Mother,* who *are pure in their own Eyes, and yet are not washed from their Filthiness: A Generation, O how lofty are their Eyes! and their Eye-lids are lifted up; whose Teeth are as Swords, and their Jaw-teeth as Knives to devour (Prov.* 30. 11, *etc.).*[14] Such a Generation as this will say of *John Baptist,* who *came neither Eating nor Drinking,* that he *hath a Devil;* and of the *Son of Man,* who *came Eating and Drinking, behold a Gluttonous Man, and a Wine-bibber, a Friend of Publicans and Sinners (St.* Matth. 11, 16, *etc.).*[15] They will even ascribe the Miracles of the Son of GOD to

---

unalterable Law, as might easily be prov'd were this a proper place; which Law he obeys, and he only, who will do or suffer any thing rather than Sin.'

[12] Matthew 8:25, in fact; possibly a typographical error, given that chapter 8 has only thirty-four verses. The passage refers to Christ's response to the disciples' call 'Lord, save us: We perish', calming the waves and admonishing them, 'Why are yee fearefull O yee of little faith' (1611, Authorized Version).

[13] Astell's frequent unreferenced remarks to 'the good natur'd *English* People . . . seduced into that Unnatural Rebellion', are to Kennett, *Compassionate Enquiry,* p. 18. See also Astell, *Impartial Enquiry,* pp. 11, 54.

[14] Astell's quotations from Proverbs 30:11–14, are quite faithful to the text.

[15] Matthew 11:16–19, in fact.

the Power of the Devil, tho' Satan is wiser than to be divided against himself.

But can we fancy, that the *Body of a Good-natur'd English People* (*Page* 18.), are of that Generation? Tho' *the least Attempts towards Slavery and Exorbitant Power,* has always *rais'd up the Appearance of a Yoke, that our Fore-fathers were not able to bear,* and Princes ought to remember *that we are their Off-spring* (*Page* 17.): Tho' the People [12] of *England* are *Free,* and we are like to hear no such *fond* Answers from them, as the *Israelites* gave *Samuel,* when he told them the manner of the Kingdom, 1 *Sam.* 8.[16] Yet surely, the *uncorrupted English Blood and Principles,* will never allow them to *use their Liberty for a Cloak of Maliciousness,* but to use it *as the Servants of* GOD (1 St. *Peter* 2. 16, *etc.*); who has been pleas'd to declare his Will in this matter very particularly, and very frequently to enjoin us to render to *Caesar the things that are Caesar's, and unto* GOD the things that are GODS;[17 to] *Fear* GOD, and to Honour the King; to pay to all our Superiours what is any way their *due, not only to the Good and Gentle, but also to the Froward.* For to be *patient* when we *suffer* for our *Faults* is no great matter; but to do *well,* and patiently to *suffer* Evil for *doing so,* is an Heroic Action, it is the Christian's Business, that to which he is *call'd,* in imitation of his Great Master: See 1 S. *Pet.* 2.[18]

It is not to be suppos'd therefore, that now we are Reform'd from Popery, one of whose worst Doctrines and Practices is Disobedience to the Civil Magistrate; it is not to be imagin'd, I say, that we shou'd have a *Thought* or *Strength of Fear* (*Page* 14.), upon an *unjust Occasion* (*Page* 10.), especially we our selves being Judges![19] or that we shou'd be *drawn* into any necessary Revolutions; much less, any *Unnatural Rebellions,* but *for the meaning at least of Self-Preservation* (*Page* 18, 19.)! A Great High Priest at the Head of a *Sanhedrim,* and upon a very great *Occasion,* having laid it down for a Maxim to all Posterity (S. *John* 11. 49, 50.), 'That they know

---

[16] Kennett, *Compassionate Enquiry*, p. 20.
[17] Matthew 22:21; Mark 12:17; Luke 20:25; Romans 13:7.
[18] 1 Peter 2:17–20.
[19] Astell's cryptic remarks refer to the justifications for the Great Rebellion that White Kennett gives in public fears of a return to Popery because of the Catholicism of Charles' wife, Queen Henrietta Maria, who surrounded herself with 'Swarms of Jesuits and other Emissaries from *Rome*' (*Compassionate Enquiry*, pp. 13–14); this Astell takes to be insufficient reason.

nothing at all, nor consider, who do not find it [13] expedient, that one Man shou'd die for a People, rather than that a whole Nation shou'd perish'. For doubtless it was but a Compliment of the *fond Israelites*, when they told *David* that he was *worth ten thousand of them; Caiaphas*, one of their *Off-spring*, cou'd have taught them better things.[20]

And, Oh! how happy had it been for the Peace of the Martyr's Reign, if even Doubts and Suspicions had been wanting (Page 18.)! If Hardships (the softest Name we can call them by) had not serv'd to exasperate the Minds of the People, and prepar'd them by degrees to be led out first in Riots and Tumults, and then in Troops and Armies, against their Lawful Sovereign (Page 19.)! Poor *good-natur'd People*, to be forc'd to this upon *Thoughts, Suspicions*, and *Hardships!* Doubtless, they never meant such *ill Effects*, any more than the King did those, which the Dr. tells us were *beyond* his *Intentions*, but which rais'd *such a Jealousy, and spread such a damp upon the English Subjects, that it was unhappily turn'd into one of the unjust Occasions of the Civil War (Page 9.).* But who cou'd help this Civil War? Since the *People* THOUGHT *themselves too much under* French *Counsels and a* French *Ministry? (See Lord* Clarend. v. 1. p. 100, 101, 103, 220.)[21] The *Scots* and Mr. *Pym*[22] told them so; and well they might, for they corresponded with *Richlieu*, and receiv'd his Pension, and Arms and Ammunition from him. But without this *Thought*, the good People, alas! *cou'd never have been drawn into this Great Rebellion!* How we come to call it a Rebellion, is another Question: which *Harrington*[23] shall answer.

> *Treason does never prosper; what's the Reason?*
> *For if it prosper none dares call it Treason?*

[14] The People were *not secure* in their *Legal Rights and Tenures*, at least they *thought* so *(Page* 18.).[24] There was *Ship-mony, Loans*, and *Benevolences* exacted, which they, good Souls! had no Notion

---

[20] Astell's references here are to the gospel according to John 11:49–50.
[21] Edward Hyde, first Earl of Clarendon, *The History of the Rebellion and Civil Wars in England, begun in the Year 1641* (Oxford, 1702).
[22] John Pym, parliamentary statesman.
[23] Sir John Harington (1561–1612), *Epigrams* (1618), Book IV, no. 5, 'Of Treason', listed in the *Oxford Dictionary of Quotations*, third edition (Oxford, 1979), 242.
[24] Astell returns to commentary on Kennett's sermon, to which the marginal notes from pp. 14 to 22 of her text refer.

of (*Page* 19.). The King, 'tis true, had set this Right; but why shou'd you trust him who once has Injur'd you? or to whom you have been Injurious? There was *an unhappy Suspicion of an Arbitrary Executive Power* (*Page* 21.), and the *Spirit of a Free People* will always shake off the *Yoke. For Tyranny and Oppression were a Grievance Here in the remotest Times of Old* (*Page* 20.). *And for the Future* (hear, and take Warning O ye English Princes!) *it shall never be attempted,* or which is the same thing, *thought* to be attempted, *without bringing down Ruin and Confusion upon those who shall attempt it* (*Page* 21.), or whom Crafty Men, I shou'd say Good Patriots, shall tell the People, and make them *think* that they design to attempt it. *Protector Dick*[25] indeed was not so politic, nor so lucky as his Father; but had he and his Off-Spring kept the Saddle, to be sure our 30th of *January* Fast had been turn'd into a 3rd of *September* Thanksgiving: and Dr. *Harrison's England's Lamentation for her Good Josiah,*[26] had not been the only Sermon wherein we shou'd have celebrated the Glorious Memory of the Pious and Blessed *Oliver,* that Deliverer and Saviour of the Nation from Popery and Arbitrary Power!

I hope then *our Rights,* and the Rights of Englishmen, *tender Lovers of their Faith and Country* (*Page* 11.), *have been retrieved, and committed down to Posterity, beyond a Capacity of their being ever depriv'd of them* (*Page* 27.); for the Dr. has very wisely, and very industriously establish'd that Supreme Law, the Safety of the People: it being evident from [15] him, that it is not enough that a Prince be *Orthodox, Regular* (*Page* 14.), free from *Ambition* and *Sinister Ends;* that he have ever so much *Clemency* and *Justice, Honour* and *Conscience* (*Page* 18.); that he be *one of the most Vertuous and most Religious of our English Princes* (*Page* 1.); the Royal Martyr was all this: yet this notwithstanding, if he manages so as to give occasion for Fears and Jealousies, if there be the *least Attempts towards Exorbitant Power,* (and this Exorbitancy is not yet defin'd) the *Appearance of a Yoke* (*Page* 17.), or so much as *the Remoter Fears and Apprehensions of one* (*Page* 18.); nay, if THOUGHTS do but

[25] Oliver Cromwell (*q.v.*).

[26] The sermon of Thomas Harrison (*q.v.*), close associate of the Cromwell family, preached on the death of Oliver Cromwell, *Threni Hibernici: Or Ireland Sympathising with England and Scotland in a Sad Lamentation for the Loss of their Josiah* (Dublin, 1659).

rise in the Peoples Hearts, and they are pleas'd to have certain MEANINGS *(Page* 19.); or if the *Influence of others (Page* 19.), and the Contrivance of his *Ministers beyond his Intention (Page* 9.); or the *Intrigues* of a *Mazarine,* a Foreign Minister *(Page* 10.*)*; or the *Designs* and *Sham Pretences* of a *Cromwell (Page* 25.*),* a home-bred Traytor, shall *bring a Suspicion upon him,* tho' *he himself* be ever so *innocent (Page* 18.); yet the *Good Prince,* we find by experience, must *answer* for all, and *pay down his Royalty and his Life (Page* 19.*)*! It must be confess'd, that *this is a Subject towards the dubious and dangerous side,* and *may be liable to be censur'd sooner than to be rightly understood (Page* 5.*).* But a *Minister of the Gospel,* one who is *sure of the sincerity of his Heart (Page* 24.*),* and who *thinks Truth, Justice, and Charity to be nearly concern'd in this matter (Page* 5.*),* will not baulk it. And when we have consider'd a little the necessity of this freedom of Speech, it is not to be doubted but the Reader will be as well *satisfied in his own Conscience (Page* 6.*),* as the Dr. is in his.

Now to speak out plainly, and without Disguise; since there is an Act of Parliament, as yet unrepeal'd, for [16] the Observation of the Martyrdom of King *Charles* I. and that neither the *Calveshead Club*[27] can revel and sing, nor Mr. *Stephens*[28] Preach it down; since a Dr. *Binks,*[29] a Mr. *Sherlock,*[30] a Bishop of St. *Asaph,*[31] and some few more, take occasion to Preach upon this Day such antiquated Truths as might have past upon the Nation in the Reign of K.

---

[27] The Calves' Head Club *(q.v.)* was founded shortly after Charles I's death to commemorate the regicide and celebrated every 30 January to 1734.

[28] William Stephens, Whig divine.

[29] William Binckes *(q.v.).*

[30] William Sherlock, Dean of St Paul's.

[31] My research suggests that Astell is referring to a sermon preached before the two Houses of Parliament the same day as Kennett's sermon, by George Hooper *(q.v.) A Sermon preach'd before the Lords Spiritual and Temporal in Parliament Assembled, in the Abbey-Church of Westminister, on Monday Jan. 31st 1703/4, the Fast-Day for the Martyrdom of King Charles the 1st. By George Lord Bishop of St Asaph* (London 1704). The fly leaf indicates 1 February 1703 as the date of publication, the title page date of 1703/4 reflecting the difference between the old and new calendars. Rev. D. R. Thomas, in his *History of the Diocese of St Asaph* (London, 1874, pp. 219–35), lists the bishops of the diocese from the legendary 'St Mungo the Amiable' c. AD 560 to his own day. Thomas' brief biography of Hooper, like the entry in the *DNB,* does not mention this sermon, which I was fortunate to find in the Folger Shakespeare Library's excellent collection. But Thomas (pp. 219–35) does not indicate that any other bishops of St Asaph preached commemorative sermons on Charles I's anniversary either.

Charles II. or in *Monmouth's* Rebellion,[32] but since that time have been quite out of Fashion; since no Revolutions (unless by Foreign Conquest) can be compass'd, tho' ever so necessary, but upon those Principles by which the Martyr lost his Head; since a good-natur'd People are prone to Compassion, and the Beheading of a King at his own Palace Gate, is so shocking an Action that Men can't but detest all the ways and means that tended thereunto; since the Memory of this is reviv'd every Year by a Solemnity; and which is yet worse, since my Lord *Clarendon* has so unluckily display'd the whole Contrivance, so that Men can't renew those Methods without being observ'd and countermin'd; and yet it may often happen to be necessary for a Man's Affairs to bring about a Revolution, either to piece his broken Fortunes, or to gratify his Ambition or Revenge, or to restore himself to the Posts he formerly enjoy'd, or for which he thinks himself best qualified; and tho' when a Prince does any irregular or disobliging Action this may be a good Pretence, yet a *Civil War* may be *indeed begun more out of Hatred to a Party,* who are, or who we fear may be uppermost, than out of *any Dissatisfaction* to the Prince: for these, and no doubt for other Reasons, 'tis highly necessary, the *Truth* which we have taught of late, the *Justice* we have practis'd, and [17] *Charity*, which always begins at home, taking care in the first place to make our own Fortunes, are all of them nearly concern'd to keep this Fundamental Right in the Peoples view, *viz.* 'That Power is originally from the People, and that Princes are responsible to them for the exercise thereof.' The People must ever and anon be reminded as plainly as we dare, and as Prudence, the Humour of the Times, and the Service of the Cause will permit; that this Right has often been exercis'd; that there are many Precedents, or that the Suspicion, the very *Thought and Dread of Popery, Oppression, and Illegal Power* (*Pag.* 16.), the very *Prospect* that *their Liberties and Estates were in some Danger* (*Pag.* 19.), have drawn in their great Forefathers to stand upon their Guard, *meaning Self-preservation* (*Pag.* 19.); and that Princes, how sacred soever they be, must not think to *attempt* upon the Liberties of a Free People, without *bringing down Ruin and Confusion upon themselves* (*Pag. 21.*).

---

[32] James Scott, Duke of Monmouth (1649–85), son of Charles II's mistress, Lucy Walters, and possibly Robert Sidney, but recognized by Charles II as his son, led an abortive insurrection against James II in 1685.

For if a Busie Man, or Party of Men, have Policy and Courage enough, and some lucky Opportunities to persuade the People into Jealousies and Fears, and to Head them against their Sovereign, 'tis all a case whether the *Dangers* are Real or Imaginary; if they happen to succeed, they shall find Advocates enough to Justify them, Success will Crown the Work.

Is it not an Inconsistency to deplore the Fate of *Char.*I. and to justify that of other Princes? If we think their Fall to be Just, and his to be Unjust and Deplorable, we may in time come to abhor those Principles that brought him to the Block, and the Practices that flow from them, as being equally destructive of [18] the Best, as well as of the worst Princes; and then what will become of the Peoples Right to shake off an Oppressor? Must we take that dull way which *David* took, and which the old-fashion'd Homilies talk of, Wait God's time, and let him go down to the Grave in Peace?[33] Why at this rate we may tamely have our Throats cut; and sure it is better to be beforehand with him! If you deny us the Lawfulness of this Self-defence, we have done twenty Actions that we can't justifie. But who cares to lay his hand upon his heart, and say, I have sinn'd? or to condemn himself for what he us'd to boast of as Meritorious? How difficult is it for a Man to unravel the Actions of 15 or 20 Years! to unsay that which he has so long Practis'd and Preach'd, and Got by! St. *Paul*, 'tis true, brought himself to preach that Faith which once he destroy'd; but he had an uncommon Vertue; and besides, he Persecuted the Truth ignorantly in Unbelief, which may not be every Man's Case. Will God be extreme to mark what we have done amiss, and call us to a rigorous Repentance? Is it not enough to plead good Intentions, humane Frailties, and great Example? To have probable Doctors, plausible Opinions, and a great Number on our side, and among these, some who, by all that appears to us, are Men of Sense and Integrity; who make use of those Reasonings, and venture their Souls upon them? And why shou'd we be more scrupulous than our Neighbours? He shall

---

[33] Astell's reference to the homilies is to the second part of the Sermon on Obedience, citing 1 Kings 18–20, where David silently suffers the indignities forced on him by Saul, and the lesson drawn from it in the Second Part of the Sermon against Wilful Rebellion. See Church of England, *Certain Sermons or Homilies Appointed to be Read in Churches in the Time of Queen Elizabeth* (London, 1687), pp. 110–11, 600–1.

never Rise in the World, nay, he is in a fair way towards Starving, whose Conscience is overnice. 'Tis true, the first Christians were enjoin'd to forsake all, and follow Christ; but sure this was a [19] temporary Command; it ought to be accommodated to our present Circumstances, or else it is a hard Saying, who can hear it! But tho' we cou'd be persuaded to sacrifice our selves, we must not give up the Interest of GOD's True Religion, and the Rights of Posterity. 'Tis true, GOD does not need the sinful Man, and we are told that we must not do Evil that Good may come, and are assur'd that the Gates of Hell shall not prevail against the Church of GOD; but Miracles are ceas'd, and the Question is whether our Attempts are evil, and we resolve it shall always be a Question. This is the best way to keep our Minds quiet, and we may make it a Question so long, till at last we persuade our selves that it is out of question, and that it ought not so much as to be suppos'd an Evil.

Is it not best therefore, when these 30th of *Januarys* come about, to persuade our selves and the People, with as much respect to King *Charles's* Memory as the matter will bear, that this *Good Prince*, tho' he meant no hurt, was over-persuaded by a Popish Queen, and high Church men, such as the *Laudean* Faction, and Arbitrary Ministers, to do things worthy of blame. That tho' matters were afterwards carry'd too far, farther than the Honest Presbyterians, and the *Tender* and *Loyal* moderate Men intended (*Page* 25.), yet the King may thank himself for it; for he gave the Occasion by the *French Alliance*, and the Consequences of it. See the Dr. *p.* 9, 10. *He might justly impute many of his Troubles to those Fears and Jealousies of Popery which really began with that Alliance*, see *p.* 13. And these were so strong and plausible, that they *lost him the* [20] *Hearts* of his *People*, and *almost* his *Good Name*, see *p.* 14. And *happy had it been*, if he had not some way or other given Occasion to those *Suspicions*, which produc'd the Civil War; if he had not by several Acts, *Hardships (to call them by that Name only) exasperated* the *Minds* of the *People*; see *p.* 18, 19, 21.[34] If even *Prophaneness* had not been too much countenanc'd, and the Reprover of it *stigmatiz'd* with *a Severity that was thought cruel*; see *p.* 23.

Such an Indictment as this, drawn up against this unfortunate Prince, with *Plainness of Truth* and *Sincerity of Heart* (*Pag.* 25.),

---

[34] Astell's quotation is in fact from Kennett, *Compassionate Enquiry*, p. 19.

even when it is said to be *dangerous*, and an *invidious Subject*, but yet entred upon with *Simplicity and godly Sincerity for the sake of Truth, and Justice, and Charity* (*Pag.* 5.); may, it's like, open Peoples eyes, and convince them that a Friend to Popery, and an Invader of our Liberties, a Prince in whose Reign *the People*, the *good-natur'd* People, *thought themselves too much under* French *Counsels and a* French *Ministry* (*Page* 10.), ought not to stand as a Martyr in our *English* Calendars; the Example is dangerous, and the Consequences pernicious. 'Tis a lasting Reproach to Honest Men, who are *tender Lovers of their Faith and Country* (*Page* 11.), and who are ready upon all Occasions not only to Deplore the very *Thoughts* and *Suspicions* of Popery and Arbitrary Power, but to exert themselves in *Troops and Armies against their Lawful Sovereign* (*Page* 19.), whenever this *Thought* takes them; if so be their *strength of Fear* is but duely supported with a strength of Arms (*Page* 14.).

What greater Service then can be done our Country, and those Noble Assertors of its Rights and Liberties, than to let Princes know, that they must, from the very [21] beginning, avoid every thing that may raise a *Suspicion; a Thought*, in the Peoples Minds, of their Inclinations to *France*, to Popery, or Arbitrary Power? Since it is not enough to retract past Mistakes, King *Charles* did this, but to no manner of purpose. Or rather, to prevent all Misunderstanding, 'tis best for them at first *To part with their Power, and Trust it to them*, as Mr. *Hambden*[35] answered one of his Fellow Members,

---

[35] John Hampden (*q.v.*), statesman, famous for his opposition to ship money. Clarendon (*History of the Rebellion*, II, p. 205) says of him that 'he was rather of Reputation in his own Country, than of publick discourse, or fame in the Kingdom, before the business of Ship-money: but Then he grew the Argument of all Tongues, every Man enquiring who, and what He was, that durst, at his own charge, support the Liberty and Property of the Kingdom, and rescue his Country, as he thought, from being made a Prey to the Court'. These remarks, taken from Clarendon's extended eulogy to Hampden written in 1647, are echoed in a character sketch of Hampden inserted by Clarendon in 1669 into his *History*, I, p. 147, which Astell cites. Hampden was not however opposed to monarchy, attributing the importunities of Charles to his evil ministers. He is famous for his admonition to colleagues, to which Astell appears to be referring (*An Impartial Enquiry into the Causes of Rebellion and Civil War in this Kingdom* (London, 1704), p. 21): 'Perish may that man and his posterity that will not deny himself in the greatest part of his fortune (rather than the king shall want) to make him both potent and beloved at home, and terrible to his enemies abroad, if he will be pleased to leave those evil counsells about him, and take the wholesome advice of his great counsell the parliament' (*Weekly Intelligencer*, 27 June–4 July 1643 as cited in *DNB*). Astell appears to rely heavily on the account given by Clarendon

who ask'd him, What they cou'd desire more of the King, seeing he had granted them so much?

Further, If it can be prov'd or insinuated, that King *Charles* I. deserv'd what he suffer'd, or at least that he gave too *just Occasion* for it, (for when one treats of Causes and Effects, it's usual to trace them up to the last Link, and fix there) this will make Princes cautious what *Counsels* they fall into, or what Ministers they use. Since *it is possible* (we have had more than one fatal Experiment) *that the Influence of others may bring a Suspicion upon Princes, when they themselves are Innocent; and in many Cases, a Suspicion artfully improv'd, shall work up as much Mischief as the real Guilt wou'd do* (*Page* 18.). 'Tis best therefore for Princes to be always Gracious to that Party which is apt to suspect, to imploy these, if they mean to fit quiet in their Thrones, so long at least, as till these Suspectors found greater Interest in removing them. For the other dull Souls, who are not apt to suspect, who are fitter for a *Yoke*, and not so uneasie under it, will rest contented.

Perhaps some *Few*, who want a *better Mind*, may *misapprehend* all This, improve it to *unreasonable Scandal, and* [22] *industriously spread their Calumnies thro' all the Town*,[36] as if this Doctrine were destructive of Government, and wou'd make the best Princes uneasie in it. But the Doctor has sufficiently provided against this, he has done Justice to the Martyr's Memory, in giving a fair Character of his Personal Vertues, *p.* 14, 15 and letting us know, that he meant well, *p.* 9, 18, 19. He calls the *Civil War the Great Rebellion*; and the Murther of the King, *that Horrid Fact committed on the Lord's Anointed* (*Page* 4.);[37] and we must not think so ill of the Reader's

of Hampden's role in the Ship Money debate, who summed him up thus: 'In a word, what was said of *Cinna*, might well be applied to Him; "he had a Head to contrive, and a Tongue to perswade, and a Hand to execute, any mischief." His death therefore seem'd to be a great deliverance to the Nation' (*History*, II, p. 206).

[36] Here Astell is quoting from the Advertisement to the second edition of Kennett's sermon, *Compassionate Enquiry*, where he is referring, in fact, to the calumnies committed against him 'by the Misapprehension of some Few who heard [his sermon], and by the confident Report of a far greater Number who did not hear it', which caused him to have it printed.

[37] Kennett, whom Astell is quoting, uses typical Tory language. So Sacheverell, in his famous sermon preached at Oxford, 9 March 1703/4, *The Nature and Mischief of Prejudice and Partiality Stated in a Sermon Preach'd at St Mary's in Oxford at the Assizes held there, 9 March 1703/4* (second edition) (London, p. 24), to which Defoe responded in *More Short-Ways with the Dissenters* (London, 1704), coun-

Understanding, as not to suppose him able to reconcile all this. But besides, the Doctor has laid in a sufficient Antidote against the Poison of Rebellious Principles, by the great Zeal he expresses *against Popery, that irreconcilable Enemy, not only to our Reform'd Faith and Worship, but to our Civil Rights, and Liberties, and Properties, to our Establish'd Laws, and to all our settled Constitution (Page* 11.): And by his Prayers, and earnest Endeavours, to keep it at a distance from us (*Page* 26.).

Now they who are curious to know what Popery is, and who do not rail at it at a venture, know very well, that every Doctrine which is profess'd by the Church of *Rome*, is not Popish; GOD forbid it shou'd, for they receive the Holy Scriptures, and teach the Creeds. But that Superstructure of Hay and Stubble, those Doctrines of Men or Devils, which they have built upon this good Foundation, this is Popery; and it is upon account of our rejecting those Corruptions, that we stile our selves Reform'd. It is not necessary to enumerate those Errors here; the Learned Writers of the *Church of England* having sufficiently expos'd them in those excellent [23] Tracts, whereby they most Gloriously defended the Truth with their Pens, in a Primitive manner, in the late Reign. I shall only take notice of one Error, which is proper to my present purpose, and that is the *Deposing Doctrine*, which is as rank Popery as Transubstantiation, and has ever been so accounted by *Church of England* Writers.

The Learned Reader knows where to satisfie himself of the Truth of this, much better than my Want of Learning can direct him. And for the *English Reader*, I need only refer him to an admirable Book, which will sufficiently confirm and satisfie his Aversion to Popery, and convince him of the Pernicious Practices of that Church; it is *Foulis's History of Popish Treasons and Usurpations.*[38]

---

tered in turn by Astell in *A Fair Way with the Dissenters and their Patrons* (London 1704), also referred to the English Civil War of the 1640s as 'That *Horrid Rebellion*'.

[38] Henry Foulis, *The History of the Romish Treasons and Usurpations: Together with a Particular Account of Many Gross Corruptions and Impostures in the Church of Rome, Highly dishonourable and injurious to Christian Religion* (London, 1681). The Preface, interestingly, is addressed to 'Gentlemen', and not to the customary patron. Foulis explains his purpose in general, and the addressees in particular, by pointing out that in the mud-slinging between Catholics and Anglicans the word 'traitor' carries a heavy freight. The 'Gentry (who in this and other matters are apt to be Priest-rid) now use it as the onely Argument to bespatter the Church

The First Edition of which, was bought up and suppress'd by the Papists; but there is a Second Edition, printed for *Chiswel*, and others, in 1681. To which, if the Reader adds another Book by the same Author, Entituled, *The History of the Wicked Plots and Conspiracies of our pretended Saints*, Second Edition, printed at *Oxford*, for *Davis*, 1674.[39] he will be able to judge who among us are most in the *French* Interest, and most inclin'd to Popery, notwithstanding their Clamours against both: And who they are who copy to the Life, after the Original that the Papists have set them.

'Tis pity indeed, that both these Books are *Folio's*; so that the common Reader, who stands in most need of them, may want Money to purchase them, and Time to read them.[40] I shall therefore, for his Satisfaction, transcribe a few Passages out of the former, Book 2. Ch. 3 The Title of which Chapter is, *That Subjects*

[39] of *England*; and I fancie, have got some Proselytes by the Strength of these Reproaches' (p. ii).

[39] Henry Foulis, *The History of the Wicked Plots and Conspiracies of Our Pretended Saints: Representing the Beginning, Constitution and Designs of the Jesuite*, second edition (Oxford, 1674). In the Dedication of this book, dated 1662, to his brother Sir David Foulis, Baronet, 'and his virtuous consort', the Lady Catherine Foulis, Foulis makes a point of rejecting the customary patronage of powerful figures. He claims not to understand 'the craving and desiring *Protection*: since a Good Book is its own Patronage'. The Preface is dedicated to the Reader, with a clear purpose: 'Some three years ago, *viz.*, 1659. through the dissention and obstinacy of two wicked Parties, the *Rump* and the *Army*, the Nation was almost ruin'd; sometimes this, and sometimes that, and other times God knows what, being chief Lords of mis-Rule.' Astell pays Foulis an accolade in *Moderation truly Stated: Or A Review of a Late Pamphlet, Entitul'd, Moderation a Vertue* (London, 1704, p. 63) as: 'A Man who had his Education among the Dissenters and consequently knew them the better for that reason, and who is so far from having any good-will to Popery, that he has Writ one of the smartest Books against it. You will not indeed have so many Examples of the Treasons and Usurpations of our Pretended Saints as you have of those of the *Church* of *Rome*, but considering the Time that these Histories take in, you will find that the Dissenters have made pretty good use of their Time and Opportunities.'

[40] Astell's remark is an interesting reflection upon print culture in her day when affordable pamphlets were published in a volume that, at its peak, reached 2,000 items a year in print runs of around 1,000, sometimes going through several editions (see Goldie, 1980a, 517). Folio editions, by contrast were less affordable and, if we read her right, less frequently read. From this point on Astell embarks on the citation of a list (numbered alphabetically) of twenty-six Catholic authorities supporting popular sovereignty and the right to depose heretical kings. For this she draws on Foulis (*The History of the Romish Treasons*, pp. 75ff.), although not always following his order. In the cases where she departs from him, her improvements are not always entirely accurate, as noted below.

of themselves, [24] *may depose their Kings and Governours.* 'The Right of Deposing and Abdicating Kings and Princes, is not only in the Church, but Example and Reason shew us that sometimes it falls to the People', says (a) *Benzonius,*[41] a Bishop of *Loretto* ((a) *In Canticum Magnif. l.* 3. *c.* 27. *dub.* 6. *p.* 134.). *Coquaeus*[42] tells us, (b) nay, tells King *James* I. against whose *Monitory Preface* he wrote, 'That without the Pope, the Subjects themselves may pull their Kings from their Thrones' ((b) *Exam. Praef. Monit. p.* 49.). *Coquaeus* was a *French-man* 'tis true, but *Becanus*[43] the *Flanderkin* is no better, in a Book he writ concerning our Affairs; for, after *a great deal of clutter,* (says my Author) about *a mutual Compact between King and People,*

[41] Astell gives Foulis' (*The History of the Romish Treasons*, p. 75) citation to 'Rutilius Benzonius, Bishop of the Miraculous Loretto', accurately. Except that Foulis' citation, indicated as from Benzonius' work, *Jus deponendi & abdicandi* (e folio *Rut. Benz.*), is given in Latin: 'Reges ac Principes no solum Ecclesiae sed interdum populis competere ratione & exemplis ostenditur. Comment in Conticul Mognificat, l.3. c.27. dub.6. p. 134.' Did Astell translate it? Or was this one of Foulis' sources she checked out for herself, as indicated on p. 48? Benzonius is not listed in any of the usual general or religious encyclopaedias, nor are his works listed in the *National Union Catalog*.

[42] Astell quotes Foulis (*The History of the Romish Treasons*, p. 75) directly, who says, '*Leonardus Coquaeus*, endeavouring to prove that the *Pope* hath power to depose Kings, in one place brings his Argument by way of comparison, that if Parliaments do sometimes depose Kings, why may not the Pope much more do it? And in another place speaks more plain, that[g] *without the Pope the subjects themselves may pull their Kings from their Thrones* (*[g]* Imo judicarem, [quod] non expectata sententia Summi Pontificis posse[t] talem Principem à subdictis deponi. Id. p. 49)'. He adds: 'But I warrant you that King *James*, against whom he wrote, would never be converted by this *French-man*'. Foulis has amended Coquaeus' Latin, inserting the material indicated in square brackets. See F. Leonardus Coquaeus Aurelius, *Eremita Augustinianus* (Léonard Cocqueau, d. 1615), *Examen praefationis monitoriae, Iacobi I, magnae Britanniae … in quo examine resellitur & apologia ipsa regis, & summi pontificis brevia ad Catholicos Anglos defenduntur.* (1610).

[43] Martinus Becanus (*q.v.*), author of *Controversia anglicana de potestate pontificis et regis*, (1613). Astell seems to know little about Becanus and when he wrote beyond what she finds in Foulis. She appears to be paraphrasing Foulis' (*The History of the Romish Treasons*, p. 75) translation of Becanus' Latin aphorism, which he renders thus:

   Don *breaks his Troth, burns my poor house, what then?*
   May I his slave, go and burn his agen?

Foulis, referring to Becanus as 'the Brabantine Jesuite' observes of 'the old Rime': 'but this in this case is a false rule with us, being no compact, nor the parties equals; so that, do but translate his Riming Proverb to agree with the cause in hand, and we shall see the consequence to be false.' And again, 'This used to be the common Logick to the borderers or Moss-troopers; but we see ours, if held affirmatively, cannot prosper in a setled Kingdom.'

which if Kings *do not keep, the People may slip their Necks out of Collar*. For which he brings an Old Rhime:

Frangenti fidem, fides frangatur eidem.

As much as to say, Take heed of playing the Knave with me; for if you dare venture on't, you shall find to your cost, that I can be as great a Knave as you can be for the Heart of you. *He goes on to extol the Power of the People*, affirming, (c) 'That when a King is depos'd, tho' there remaineth a lawful Heir, to whom the Kingdom of Right doth belong, and this too apparently known to all; yet, if the People do chuse another, and throw his Heir aside, the other so chosen is true King' ((c) *Controv. Angl. p.* 120).[44] I know not in what Age *Becanus* liv'd; but can one help fancying, that he held the Chair, and presided at some certain Consults? An *English-man*, who calls himself *John Rastel*,[45] (d) writing in behalf of Dr. *Harding*, (against Bishop *Jewel's* incomparable [25] Defence of the Reformation, in opposition to Popery) tells us, 'That whereas every Commonwealth is greater than the Prince which governeth it, and may depose the same upon lawful Cause; and whereas Riot and Doltishness are Causes sufficient so to do, (as making the Prince unable to Govern well) it follows consequently, that if the whole Estate of *France* deposed *Chilperick*, and erected *Pipine*, there was *no Fault* committed in so doing' ((d) *A brief shew of the false Wares pack'd together in the named Apology of the Church of* England. *p.* 93.).[46]

---

[44] Astell accurately reproduces Foulis' (*The History of the Romish Treasons*, p. 75) translation of Becanus, for which he also gives the Latin.

[45] John Rastell (*q.v.*), author of *A Briefe Shew of the False Wares Packt Together in the Named, Apology of the Churche of England* (Louvain, 1567).

[46] Foulis (*The History of the Romish Treasons*, p. 75) is once again Astell's source for John Rastell, whom he refers to as 'Master of Arts and Student of Divinity, then living at *Lovan*'. Foulis (p. 76) professes to being unsure whether there even was 'such an Englishman or no as this John Rastell', and produces a source for a William Rastell 'who wrote several Books against Bishop Jewell'. Rastell's true identity does not concern him much, as he confesses, but what does concern him is that Rastell, 'whosoever is the man', 'wrote against Dr. *Jewel* in behalf of Dr. *Harding*'. The way Foulis (p. 75) words it, what Rastell knew about Jewell he took from Harding, so in treating the opinions of one, he is at the same time treating those of the other. John Jewell (1522–71), Bishop of Salisbury, had entered a long controversy with Thomas Harding (1516–72), an Oxford contemporary, and prebendary of Salisbury, who had refused to take the Oath of Supremacy and fled to Louvain. It is altogether likely, then, that Harding was Rastell's mentor, and that his works, which covered most aspects of the English Reformation, were for the latter authoritative texts.

155

But *Chilperick*, says my Author, from *Paulo Morigi*,[47] *was Godly and Peaceable*, and when put in a Monastery, led an *Angelical Life*. 'If the King turns Tyrant, the People may depose him, and chuse another', says (e) *Bellarmine*[48] ((e) *De Concil. l.* 2.). And again, (f) ''Tis the Consent of the People, that constitutes Kings or other Governours over them; and so, if Cause be given, they may turn the Kingdom into an *Aristocracy* or *Democracy*, or the contrary' ((f) *De Laicis. l.* 3. *c.* 6.). And he also tells us, (g) that *Martinus ab Azpilcueta*,[49] the Famous *Spanish* Lawyer, was of Opinion, 'That the People never transferr'd their Power so much upon, and into the Prince, but that in some Cases they might resume it again from him'. ((g) *Recognit. l. de Laicis. c.* 6.) *Suarez*[50] in this Case, defends *Bellarmine* and *Navarre*,[51] (h) ((h) *Defens. fid. Cath. l.* 3. *c.* 3. § 3.] and himself affirms, (i) 'That if a King of a Lawful Title and Pos-

---

[47] The event to which Rastell's defence of the right of the people to depose incompetent kings refers is the deposition of Childeric III (d. c. 751), King of the Franks and the last of the Merovingian dynasty, by Pippin III (d. 769), the Short, son of Charles Martel, in 751 (*Enclyclopaedia Britannica*). Pippin, convenor of the councils which formed the Frankish Church, and virtual creator of the Papal states, made his move after conferring with Pope Zacharias, and was made 'Patrician of the Romans' and recrowned by Pope Stephen II for his services. This particular royal deposition seemed the worse for the fact that Childeric was a saintly man, as attested by Paolo Morigi, whose *Hist. de personaggi illustri religiosi*, I.3.c.18. – *Essenda di natura pia egli menò vita Angelica* (Bergamo, 1593), Foulis (*The History of the Romish Treasons*, p. 76) cites. Pope Zacharias seems to have betrayed unusual pragmatism in the case, advising Pippin that 'it were better to name king him who possessed the power than him who possessed it not' (*Enclyclopaedia Britannica*). Surprisingly, Foulis seems to have confused Childeric for Chilperic, the name of two other Frankish kings.

[48] Astell reproduces the citations given by Foulis (*The History of the Romish Treasons*, p. 76) also in the Latin, to the works of Robert Bellarmine. 'De laicis sive secularibus' is an important section of Bellarmine's *Disputationes de controversiis Christianae fidei, adversus hujus temporis haereticos* (3 volumes, 1581, 1582, 1593), which had gone through some twenty Latin editions by Astell's day.

[49] Martin de Azpilcueta (1492?–1586), Spanish lawyer, whom Astell follows Foulis (*The History of the Romish Treasons*, p. 76) in quoting secondhand from Bellarmine.

[50] Francisco Suarez, SJ (1548–1617), *Defensio fidei catholicae et apostolicae aduersus anglicanae sectae errores*, first edition (Coimbra, 1613). The text asserts Papal supremacy, attacks the divine right of kings and the Oath of Allegiance instituted by James I in 1606. Foulis (*The History of the Romish Treasons*, p. 76) has no more to say about him than Astell repeats, except that, as usual, he gives the Latin texts as well.

[51] Martin de Azpilcueta was also known as Dr Navarrus, the name by which he is identified at this point in Astell's source, Foulis (*The History of the Romish Treasons*, p. 76).

session govern tyrannously, then that the People, by their Parliament, may depose him': ((i) *Defen. fid. l.* 6 *c.* 4. § 15.] *Yet he wou'd have the People do this in their own Defence.* Estius,[52] a Hollander, *of a great Name both for Learning and Moderation*, tells us, (k) 'That the Nobles and People, by the Authority residing in them, may defend themselves from Tyranny, and not only chuse [26] themselves a Lawful Prince, but also, Cause being given, may throw him from the Throne again' ((k) *Com. in* 4 *lib. Sentent. l.* 2. *p.* 444.). The Voluminous *Tostatus*[53] asserts, (l) 'That a King may be depos'd, not only by the Pope, but the People too' (l) *Com. in III.Reg. Cap.* 2. *Quest.* 35.), *being* (m) 'plac'd in that Greatness for the good of the People, not his own; and if he do otherwise, he is not a King but a Tyrant, and so may be depos'd' ((m) *Ib. Cap.* 12. *Quest.* 4.]. In like manner, *Bannes*,[54] another Famous *Spaniard*, (n) ((n) *In* 2. 2. *D. Tho. Ques.* 12. *Art.* 2. *Col.* 480. *Ib. Col.* 481.] allows the People

---

[52] Guilelmus Estius (1542–1613). The doubtful accolade paid him by Foulis (*The History of the Romish Treasons*, p. 76), which Astell excerpts, goes on: 'an honour to both his Country *Holland*, and his University *Douay*, though in one place' ('Annotat. in *Machab.* 1.1.c.2.v.22) he speaks so much between the teeth, that he seems onely to hint his Opinion to the case in hand: Yet in another of his Books he speaks boldly and to the purpose, confident enough of the truth of his cause, since he thinks that he hath the Scripture, and St *Augustine* to back him'. Here Foulis quotes the Latin and his translation, which Astell repeats, from Estius' *In quator libros sententiarum Petrus Lombardus commentaria, quibus pariter S. Thomae summae theologicae* (Duaci, 1615–16, Sent. l.2. p. 444), which existed in several Latin editions by his day.

[53] That Alonzo Tostado (d.1455), Bishop of Avila, was 'voluminous' is attested in Astell's source, Foulis (*The History of the Romish Treasons*, p. 76), who says ''tis thought that he wrot a sheet for every day he lived', as stated in his epitaph. Tostado authored various works of biblical commentary, theology and teachings on Church–state relations. Each volume in the twenty-eight volumes of his collected works of the Venice 1615 edition is titled separately. It is difficult to establish which of these, or of the thirteen volumes of the Cologne 1613 edition, Astell's references, clearly to two separate volumes, might refer to. Nor is it any clearer in Foulis (p. 77), her source, except that he gives the Latin text as well as the English translation.

[54] Domingo Banes (1528–1604), Spanish Dominican, theologian, confessor and friend to St Theresa of Avila, and author of a four-volume commentary on the *Summa theologiae* of St Thomas Aquinas, apparently the work cited here (*The New Schaff-Herzog Encyclopedia*, p. 434). Foulis (*The History of the Romish Treasons*, p. 77), Astell's source, gives a fuller account, which discloses not only that '*Dominican Bannes* gives the people sole authority over their Kings to depose them', whether or not the Pope approve; but that 'if the Pope should declare the King to be an Heretick, then the Subjects are obliged to quit themselves from their obedience to him, and fight against him', if they think they can win – an important proviso, as Foulis notes.

to depose their King without the Pope, nay tho' the Pope tolerate him. *Andreas Philopater*,[55] (o) ((o)*Responsio ad Edictum Reginae Angliae*. 158, 160, 221, 162.) our Country-man, who is thought to be *Joseph Creswell*, or *Robert Parsons*, or both these Jesuits in Club, told the World, in Answer to Queen *Elizabeth's* Laws, That this Proposition about Subjects deposing Kings, is 'the certain, determined, and undoubted Opinion of all Learned Men, and plainly agreeable and consonant to the Apostolical Doctrine; and that it is not only lawful, but that they are oblig'd to't upon their Consciences, and Pain of their Souls'. And they had their Reasons for all this fine Doctrine; for at that time, the *Spaniards* had as great a mind to *England*, as the *French* may have now: (p) *Tannerus*,[56] no

---

[55] See Robert Parsons' (*q.v.*) anonymous *Elizabethae, Angliae reginae haeresin Calvinianam propvgnantis, saevissimvm in Catholicos sui regni edictum* (London, 1592). Astell's settling for either or both of the identifications of Andreas Philopater (*q.v.*) – as Creswell and or Parsons – appears to be what she makes of the prevarication in Foulis (*The History of the Romish Treasons*, p. 77), who after consulting Alegambe's *Bibliotheca*, which also prevaricates, concludes that 'he leaves us in the Suds'. The case of Philopater appears to be another instance where Astell checked out the source for herself, and in this case made an error. Foulis' reference is to Section 157, for which he gives the Latin also: 'Atq; haec certa, definita & indubitata virorum doctissimorum sententia, doctrinae Apostolicae conformis plane & consona est'. This accurately translates in the form Astell repeats from Foulis. But Section 158 which begins similarly, with the words 'Atque haec certa, definita et dubitata virorum doctissimorum sententia, doctrinae Aspostolicae conformis planem . . .', goes on to treat a different subject, that of marital fidelity according to Paul, Corinthians 1:7. Section 160 (p. 108) is where Parsons sets out the conditions for the legitimate overthrow of heretical princes in words which Astell paraphrases: 'Est igitur certissima, et indubitata haec communis Doctorum omnium Catholicorum sententia, de subditorum obligatione, ad Principes Haereticos repellendos, si fidei Catholicae iniuriosi sunt'. In Section 162 (p. 110) he claims it to be a precept of divine law and the first duty of conscience for Catholics to rid themselves of heretical princes, discussing in Section 221 (p. 151) the issue of sedition and its sanctions.

[56] Astell, on Foulis' (*The History of the Romish Treasons*, p. 79) authority is referring to a work by the Jesuit, Adam Tanner (1571–1632), renowned for disputation, undertaken with Jacob Gretser (1560–1625), against the Protestant theologians Philipp and Jacob Heilbronner (1548–1618) and Egidius Hunnius (1550–1603), at the Colloquy of Ratisbon, 1601, in the presence of Maximilian of Pfaltzgraven on the Rhine and Philip Ludwig, Prince of Bavaria (*National Union Catalog*). Foulis observes that '*Adamus Tannerus*, a German Jesuit of great repute in his Country, both with the Emperour and other Princes; yet for all the many favours received from them, he must not contradict the Principles of his Order and Church; and therefore he positively maintains that Kings may lawfully sometimes be deposed: and because he would not seem to do any thing without Reason, he thus tells you upon what goodly foundation this bad Principle stands.'

mean Man in his Country *Germany*, notwithstanding the Favours of the Emperor and Princes, tells us, 'That as the People do deliver their Power up to the King, so, upon just account, they can take it from him again'. And further, 'Every Commonwealth hath the Authority to see, that they have a Lawful Head; and he, who from the Pastor of the People turns to the Wolf, is no lawful Governour'. ((p) *Theol. Schol. Tom. 3. Disp. 4. Ques. 8. dub. 3. Num. 32, 33.*] According to *John Major*[57] (q) a *Scotch-man*, and [27] *Buchanan's*[58] Master, but who got his Divinity from the *Sorbonne*, 'The People are above their King, and in some Cases may depose him' ((q) *In Quarz. Sent. Dist.* 11. *Quest.* 10.]. *Emanual Sa*,[59] a Famous *Portuguese* Jesuit, in his Aphorisms, says expresly, (r) 'That if the King Tyranizes, and do not execute his Office, and when there is any other just Reason for so doing, (any *Meaning* it's like, any *Thoughts, Apprehensions, Fears or Suspicions*) then the People may dethrone Him, and elect Another' ((r) *Aphorism. v. Princeps.* §. 2 and again under the Head Tyrant §. 2]. But *Peter de Ledesma*,[60] the *Spaniard*, tho' he wou'd have the Pope or Emperor consulted, yet if this can't be done conveniently, (s) 'the People may then, says he, *call a Parliament, and depose their King*; nay, *and Kill* him too'. ((s) *Theol. Moral. Tract. 8. c. 18. p. 512.*) *Feuardentius*[61] (t) will have it, 'That the Parliament, compos'd of the Clergy, Nobility and Commons, representing the Majesty and Power of the Whole Kingdom, as a General Council of Bishops does the whole Church, may depose their King, being a Tyrant, and hateful to Religion and the People, and

---

[57] John Major (*q.v.*), historian and Scholastic divine.

[58] George Buchanan (*q.v.*), historian and scholar. The characterization of Major and Buchanan, for whom Foulis (*The History of the Romish Treasons*, p. 79) has mild words, is cribbed by Astell.

[59] Manuel de Sa (1530–96), whose *Aphorisimi confessariorum, ex doctorum sententiis collecti* (15?) existed in various Dutch, German and English imprints by Astell's time. Astell follows Foulis (*The History of the Romish Treasons*, p. 78) in citing from Sa's *Aphorism V, Princeps*, Section 2, and *V Tyrannus*, Section 2, both of which he gives in Latin. The aside in parentheses is her own.

[60] Buitrago Alonso de Ledesma (fl. 1600), whose spiritual reflections have survived in several Spanish editions, but no work of this title, which Astell copies directly from Foulis (*The History of the Romish Treasons*, p. 78). I can find no reference to Ledesma in any of the usual general or religious encyclopaedias.

[61] François Feuardent (1539–1610), 'one of the most furious of all *Franciscan* Orders', according to Foulis (*The History of the Romish Treasons*, p. 79), whom Astell follows in citing from *In librvm Esther commentarii, concionibus Christianis accommodat* (Cologne, 1695), p. 87.

then may chuse another in his Place' ((t) In his Comment on *Ester.*
p. 7.). *Lessius*[62] the *Dutch-man*, goes a step further; for, says he, (u)
'If the Prince grows so much a Tyrant, that he *seems* Intolerable,
and no other Remedy appearing, the People, or Parliament, or *any*
other in Authority, may depose him, and declare him an Enemy;
nay, and act against his *very Person* too, he then ceasing to be
Prince'. ((u) *De Justitie et Jure. 1 2. c.* 9. *Disp.* 4. §. 12.) *Heisius*[63]
and *Keller,*[64] two *German* Jesuits; *Cenalis,*[65] a *French-man; Molina,*[66]

---

[62] Leonard Lessius (*q.v.*) is referred to by Foulis (*The History of the Romish Treasons*,
p. 65) as 'a Jesuite of great repute' who wrote 'under the false name of *Guilielmus*
Singletonus'; and again as 'a *Belgick* Jesuit, of as great repute as most of that Order'
(p. 83). His tone does not seem to be satirical. In general he seems to hold Jesuits
in greater esteem than Franciscans, but in this case there may be a special reason
for his mild words. Lessius became professor of theology at the Jesuit College at
Louvain in 1585, a post he held until his death. In 1587 he was censured by his
faculty, known for its Augustinianism, because he did not uphold the efficacy of
salvation by grace alone. Lessius was a theological liberal in other respects too,
although not so liberal as to tolerate other confessions (*The New Schaff-Herzog*
Encyclopedia). Astell may have checked out Lessius for herself, because she cites
only '*Disp.* 4, Section 12', whereas Foulis (*The History of the Romish Treasons*, p.
83) gives Section 10 and Section 12, in Latin and English, as usual. But Foulis
gets his nationality right whereas Astell has him a '*Dutch-man*'.

[63] Sebastianus Heissius, referred to by Foulis (*The History of the Romish Treasons*,
p. 81) as 'the *Germane* Jesuit' who supported '*the view that Kings may be deposed*
by their Subjects (Refutatio Aphorismorum, c.3 ad Aphor. 1. p. 158. Section 94).
I could find no reference to Heissius in any of the usual encyclopaedias.

[64] Referred to by Foulis (*The History of the Romish Treasons*, p. 81) as '*Jacobus Kell-*
erus, the *German* Jesuit', citing his *Tyrannicidium seu scitum Catholicorum de tyranni*
internecione, Questions 2, 3.

[65] Robert Ceneau (1483–1560) otherwise known, and referred to by Foulis (*The*
History of the Romish Treasons, p. 81), as '*Robertus Cenalis*, who shews himself a
lusty Champion for this cause against Kings, whom, he saith, may be brought to
a *tryal and deposed*'. Foulis follows with the Latin, citing *Rob. Cenalis Arboricensis*,
de utriusq; gladii facultate, Tom. 2, p. 119. Presumably this is a further commentary on Aquinas. The epithet 'Arboricensis' in the title refers to Ceneau's own
title 'Diuina clementia Episcopo Arboricensi'. The Folger Library holds two different works by Ceneau, who does not appear in any of the usual encyclopaedias.

[66] Luis Molina (1535–1600), a Spanish Jesuit most famous for his contribution to
the debate over the relation of divine grace to free will, *Liberi arbitrii cum gratiae*
donis (1588) (*The New Schaff-Herzog Encyclopedia*). Among his many works are
a commentary on the first part of Thomas Aquinas' *Summa theologica*, and the
De justitia et jure, 6 volumes (Mainz and Antwerp, 1593–1609), from which Foulis
is quoting on the right of subjects to resist the king. Foulis (*The History of the*
Romish Treasons, p. 83) says of '*Ludovicus Molina*, another *Spanish* Jesuite, and
of as great repute as any, [that] he speaks a little more plainly; first, he saith that
any body may kill a King in his own defence'. Second, '*The people*, saith he, *may*
depose their King, and punish him when he is deposed.' And finally, elaborating, "*Tis*
not lawful for private men to kill the King, before he be declared deposed'. Once again

Salon[67] and *Sota*,[68] *Spaniards; Filliucius*,[69] *an Italian*; (w) *Sayer*[70] ((w) *Clavis Regia. l.* 7. *c.* 10, §. 3.], and (x) *White*,[71] ((x) Grounds of Obedience and Government. *p.* 122, *etc.* 133, *etc.* 151, *etc.*] *English-men*, are all of the same mind. It were indeed endless to rake into this Channel; nor shall I [28] repeat any of those abominable Tenets whereby they allow the Murther of Kings, a Doctrine for which *Mariana*,[72] the *Spanish* Jesuit, is so Infamous. My Author Mr. *Foulis*, has a whole Chapter under this Title, *That Kings may law-fully be kill'd by their own Subjects*;[73] and his Book sufficiently shews, how often, and how effectually they practis'd this cursed Theory. I shall therefore conclude this Stuff with the words of our Country-man *Parsons* the Jesuit, under the Name of *R. Doleman*,[74] in his

Foulis gives the Latin, quoting from *Molina* de justitia, Tom. 4. Tract. 5. disp. 6. Section 2.

[67] Referred to by Foulis (*The History of the Romish Treasons*, p. 81) as 'the *Spanish Fryar Mendicant, Michael Salon*', citing In D. *Tho.* Tom. 1. col. 1157.

[68] Domingo de Soto (1494–1560), Spanish Dominican, an important figure at the Council of Trent, where he defended Aquinas' teachings on original sin, grace, predestination, good works, etc. Among his many works is the *De justitia et jure libri septem* (1556) (*The New Schaff-Herzog Encyclopedia of Religious Knowledge*). He is referred to by Foulis (*The History of the Romish Treasons*, p. 81) as 'the learned *Dominican* of the same Nation, *Dominicus Soto*', citing *De justitia*, l. 5. Question 1. Art. 3.

[69] Foulis refers to him as 'the *Italian* Jesuit, *Vincentius Filliucius*, citing Moral Ques-tion Tom. 2. Tract. 29. c.1. Section 12.

[70] Gregory Sayer (1560–1602), author of *Cvis regis sacerdotum casuum conscientiae* (Antwerp, 1619). Astell later cites Foulis' (*The History of the Romish Trea-sons*, p. 81) reference to 'the *Benedictan* of our own Country ... *viz. Gregory Sayer*', who agrees with the Dominican Soto on the lawful deposition of kings.

[71] Thomas White (*q.v.*), author of *The Grounds of Obedience and Government* (London, 1655). Foulis (*The History of the Romish Treasons*, p. 81) refers to 'Mr. *Thomas White* an *English* Priest, well known amongst us for his odd stile and opinions with several others'. Foulis' references to White's *Grounds of Obedience and Government*, are more extensive than Astell's: viz., to 'pag. 120, 123, 124, 133, 135, 136, 151, 154, 157, *Etc.*'

[72] Juan de Mariana, Spanish Jesuit. Foulis (*The History of the Romish Treasons*, pp. 80–1) speaks of '*Johannes Mariana* the *Spanish* Jesuite, sufficiently known for his variety of Learning and the smooth stroke of his Pen, and no less for his pernicious Principles spread over the world to encourage Treason and Murther, amongst his other Impieties, he perswades Subjects to War against their Kings, telling them that in some cases they may also *depose them*, nay, *Murther them* too'. Foulis cites *Jo. Mar.* de Regi & Regis Institutione, lib. 1. cap. 6. pag. 57.

[73] Henry Foulis, *The History of the Romish Treasons*, pp. 82–9. This is the (second) edition which Astell earlier specifies.

[74] Alias Robert Parsons, author of *A Conference abovt the Next Svccession to the Crowne of Ingland* (London, 1594). Although Foulis (*The History of the Romish Treasons*, p. 86) discusses Parsons too, whom he presents as one who debated

Conference about the next Succession of the Crown of England, (z) ((z) Printed 1594. Part I. *c.* 5. *p.*120.) where he wou'd have us believe, that it is *most absurd, base and impious, to hold, that only Succession of Blood is the thing without further Approbation, which makes a King; and that the Peoples Consent, and the Coronation, is not needful.* (a) He tells us, That the *Commonwealth* may *not only put back the next Inheritors upon lawful Considerations; but also dispossess them that have been lawfully put in possession, if they fulfil not the Laws and Conditions, by which, and for which, their Dignity was given them* ((a) *Ib.* Part r. *c.* 2. *p.* 32. and again, *p.* 36.*).* He is a mighty Man for the *Original Contract,* and labours to prove, (b) That *if one side go from his Promise, the other stands not oblig'd to perform his* ((b) *Ib. c.* 4. *p.* 73.); nay, That (c) *the Commonwealth is not only free from all Oaths made by Her of Obedience and Allegiance to such unworthy Princes, but is bounden moreover, for saving the whole Body, to* Resist, Chasten, *and* Remove *such Evil Heads, if She be able* ((c) *Ib. p.* 77, 78.).

It is very observable, that this Book of *Parsons* the Jesuit was Reprinted by the Ruling Party in 1648, with an *Imprimatur.* The Garb indeed was somewhat alter'd, *Parsons* writing by way of Dialogue, and this other [29] Edition being by way of Speeches. The Dialogue was also Reprinted a little before the Restoration: and again, when the Bill of Exclusion was afoot (as I remember) there was *An History of the Succession* out of the same Forge. And if any one will read that Book of *Parsons,* and compare it with the *Debates, Enquiries, Measures,* etc. which upon several occasions have appear'd among us, 'tis like he may be apt to forgive the honest Jesuit for all his Inveteracy against *Q. Elizabeth,* and the Mischief he wou'd then have done his Country, considering the good Service his admirable Principles have since perform'd! But why may not Protestants make lawful Prize of Popish Doctrines, as well as of Popish Altar-pieces? When the *Israelites* had no Swords of their own, the Text tells us

Morton, later the Bishop of Durham, it is not to the same work that he refers, but rather *A Quiet and Sober Reckonning with M. Thomas Morton,* (1609) Chapter 5, Section 44, p. 321. Here Astell seems to have found her own source, in what was surely Parsons' most famous work on popular sovereignty. Her quotations are less than accurate, combining paraphrase with quotation as was conventional in her time, but in a highly interpretive way. Parsons (*Conference,* p. 120) does not mention 'People's Consent', or that 'Coronation is not needful', just as he does not mention 'Original Contract', but only coronation oaths and the fact of the Prince's power being 'subdelegat' (p. 73).

that *they went down to the Philistines, to sharpen every man his Share and his Coulter, and his Axe and his Mattock.*

We see then, that this is the declar'd Doctrine of the *Roman* Doctors, of all Orders, and of all Nations; the Good-natur'd *English*, the Loyal *Spaniard*, the Well-bred *French*, the Trusty *Dutch-man*, and Stout *German*, as well as of the *Scotch* and the *Italian*. And I shall only at present make a small Request to those good Protestants who profess it, (*viz.*) that if it is not Popish, but true Orthodox Protestant Doctrine, they wou'd be pleas'd to prove it to us from Authentick Protestant Authors; for I make no reckoning of a *Buchanan*,[75] a *Milton*,[76] or any of those Mercenary Scriblers whom all sober Men condemn, and who only write after the Fact, or in order to it, to make their own Fortunes, or to justifie their own Wickedness. Or rather, and which is much **[30]** better, let it be prov'd to us from Holy Scripture, and those best Expositors, as well as Practisers of Holy Writ, the Primitive Church.[77]

But if they will not, or cannot give us this Proof, then I wou'd beg them, for their own Credit sake, to talk no more against Popery, much less to affix this odious Name, either openly or indirectly, upon Men who are the greatest and truest Enemies to Popery, since they themselves espouse some of the vilest Popish Doctrines.[78] Let them not upbraid any one, and much less the best Patriots, and Her Majesty's most Dutiful and Loyal Subjects, with a Design of bringing in the *French* and Arbitrary Power; since they themselves are

---

[75] George Buchanan, historian and scholar.

[76] John Milton, poet, pamphleteer and republican.

[77] Once again Astell reveals her sophistication. The *topos* of the Primitive Church flags Arminians (*q.v.*), Erastians and all those who protested against the doctrine and ritual of the Laudian Church. The sheer number of political polemicists who undertook to examine Primitive Christianity in order to show the pagan deviations of the Catholic Church, to which Anglicanism of this type was deemed to have fallen heir, is very large. It included Thomas Hobbes, in his *Historia ecclesiastica* (London, 1688), John Locke's *The Reasonableness of Christianity as Delivered in the Scriptures* (1695) and its imitators, works by James Owen, Astell's protagonist in *A Fair Way with the Dissenters*, and William Whiston's five volume *Primitive Christianity Reviv'd* (1711–12).

[78] By this sentence, difficult to parse, Astell accuses the Presbyterians of being more Popish than the very Catholics they rail against. Popery, 'this odious Name', signifies ecclesiastical dominion and interference in sovereign affairs, Astell implies. Those very Protestant protestors who play up the French Threat most – Milton, already mentioned, and Locke, unmentioned – are most guilty of Popery in this sense, while loyal friends of the King who might, incidentally, be Catholic, are their victims.

zealous Advocates, industrious and indefatigable Bustlers for Principles that will bring in any body: a *Philip of Spain,*[79] or a *Lewis of France,*[80] or the *Great Turk* himself,[81] if he were near enough: Principles upon which we know that Offers and Addresses were once made to *Richlieu*[82] and the *French* King, from the good Protestant *Scotch* and *English* who began our Civil Wars; and by which, when this Foreign Assistance fail'd them, a *Rump,*[83] an *Oliver,*[84] an Anybody was set up, against their Lawful and too Merciful Sovereign: Principles that Justifie the Rebellion in *Hungary,*[85] which is like to

[79] Astell is referring to Philip III of Spain (1578–1621), son of Philip II and his fourth wife Anne, daughter of Emperor Maximilian II. Philip II, ruler of a despotic monarchy, was himself ruled by his ministers. His relations with Charles I underwent many vicissitudes. From 1614 to 1618, Charles, then Prince of Wales, negotiated for the hand of Philip's daughter, the Infanta Maria. But Philip's role in the ouster in 1620 of Charles' sister Elizabeth, Princess Royal and Electress of Palatine, and her husband Frederick, the Elector, from the Bohemian throne predisposed Charles to war with Spain. The ramifications of these opening shots in the Thirty Years War consumed the early years of Charles' reign and all of Philip's.

[80] Astell's reference must be to Louis XIII (1601–43), King of France and brother of Henrietta Maria, Queen consort of Charles I. Son of Henry IV of France and Queen Marie de' Medici, Louis was married to Anne of Austria, daughter of Philip III of Spain. Planned by his mother, who hoped by this marriage, and that of her husband's sister, Princess Elizabeth, to the future King Philip IV of Spain, to cement the Catholic Alliance between France and Spain, this web of dynastic marriages constituted the basis of the French Threat, as Protestant England saw it. A threat Astell, for complicated reasons, was bent on defusing.

[81] Astell's reference to the Ottoman Empire, by the familiar English epithet, is generic, perhaps a common scare tactic. There is no evidence of Turkish interference in the European dynastic struggles she is detailing.

[82] Cardinal Richlieu was reported by Clarendon (*History*, vol. 1, pp. 100, 101, 103; cited by Astell, *An Impartial Enquiry*, below, p. 41) as sending agents, arms and supplies to Scotland to foment war: '*Pym* himself being a *French* Pensioner; and the *Scots*, who were the first Incendiaries, keeping a Correspondence with *France*, and receiving Directions and Assistance from *Richelieu*.'

[83] The remnant of the Long Parliament (restored in May 1659) which was dissolved by Monk in February 1660. Later the term Rump was extended to refer to the earlier remnant of the same Parliament from the time of Pride's Purge (December 1648) to its dissolution by Cromwell in April 1653 (*OED*). It is in the wider sense that Astell is most probably using it.

[84] Oliver Cromwell.

[85] On 26 August 1619, upon the death of the Emperor Matthias, the Bohemian estates deposed the Habsburg Archduke Ferdinand of Styria (1578–1632) from the Bohemian throne to which he had been previously accepted. They chose in his place the Elector Palatine, Frederick V and his wife, Electress Elizabeth (1596–1662), eldest daughter of James I. Crowned later that year, the Calvinist Elector, whose religion had previously recommended him to the Protestant citizens of Bohemia over the Catholic Habsburgs, with or without the approval of his wife

prove the greatest Thorn in the sides of the *Confederates*; the Deposition of the King of *Poland*,[86] and any thing, indeed, that a Company of Traitors are strong enough to execute. For if these Principles are good, how easie is it to renew the Measures of *Forty One*[87]

(who had been raised in the Church of England), embarked on an insensitive policy of iconoclasm which provoked open rebellion. Ferdinand of Styria, now crowned Holy Roman Emperor, was able to muster the resources that Frederick lacked, the money promised from the Evangelical Union which he headed, and from England not being forthcoming. The battle of Prague of 8 November 1620 saw the ouster of the Palatines as a result. Clarendon, Astell's usual source for Charles' reign, has nothing to say on this episode, which lies outside the boundaries of his *History*, and mentions Frederick, the Elector of Palatine, and his wife the Electress Elizabeth only late, in Book XIV (*History*, III, pp. 409–25), giving a retrospective preparatory to his account of the Restoration. It is not clear, therefore, what source Astell used at this point, or, since her terminology is rather vague, whether she used any, and was not simply conveying in common knowledge. Her reference to the rebellion in Hungary 'prov[ing] the greatest Thorn in the sides of the *Confederates*', concerns the desires of the Parliament to come to the aid of the Protestant Frederick and Elizabeth against the Catholic Habsburg alliance.

86 Astell may be referring to the deposition of John II Casimir, King of Poland 1648–68, against whom the devastating Thirteen Years War had been waged by Russia. Upon its heels, invasion by Charles X of Sweden in 1655 forced the ouster of the King. The formation of a general league against Sweden, initiated by the alliance between Emperor Leopold and John Casimir, in 1657, turned the Russian might against the Swedes, leading to the reinstatement of the Polish King. If this is indeed the incident to which Astell refers, it is noteworthy, but quite consistent, that she comes to the defence of monarchy, even in the case of a Catholic king being deposed by Protestants. There are frequent references in Charles Leslie, for instance, to Poland as a lesson to advocates of popular government (Leslie, *Rehearsals*, I, no. 51, 21 July 1705). It is also possible that Astell's reference is to the Hungarian rebellion of 1704–5, which John Tutchin applauded as an instance of the right of resistance, but which Defoe deplored in *The Review* (also known as *A Review of the Affairs of France*, 2 September 1704; cited Phillipson, 1993, 218). Astell may have written her piece, the last in the series of three written in 1704, after having read Defoe's critique. Tutchin's journalistic treatment of the rebellion (*Observator*, 12–15 December 1705) is too late for Astell's piece, however.

87 Astell refers to the events of 1641, in the phraseology of Clarendon, Charles Leslie, Henry Sacheverell, her probable sources, and others as 'the *Rebellion in Forty One*', the '*Usurpation of Forty-One*'. See Sacheverell's sermon of 9 March 1703–4 (*Nature and Mischief*, p. 14), the subject of Defoe's critique in *More Short-Ways* (p. 24), critiqued by Astell in *A Fair Way with the Dissenters*. See also Charles Leslie's, *The New Association of those called Moderate-Church-man, with the Modern-Whigs and Fanaticks to Under-mine and Blow-up the Present Church and Government*, third corrected edition (London, 1702, pp. 3, 9, etc.) and Leslie's *Cassandra: (But I Hope not) Telling What Will Come of It. In Answer to the Occasional Letter ... Num I. Wherein the New-Associations, etc., Are Considered* (London, 1702, p. 10). Parallels drawn between '41 and the exclusion crisis of 1679–83 by contemporary writers, including Astell, have only recently received

even under the best of Princes! It is but setting up (a) Cunning and Popular Men (*See Lord* Clarend. *Vol.* 1. (a) P. 145, 146.), and good [31] Speakers, such as a Lord *Say*[88] and Lord *Kimbolton*[89] in the House of Lords, and persuading such Tools as a Lord

a satisfactory explanation by historians. Jonathan Scott (1988, 460), gives a clue in the perception of continuity between Revolutionary and Restoration politics. The propensity of the two Charles for repetition gave rise in particular to 'the rebirth, in the reign of Charles II, of those ugly sisters Popery and Arbitrary Government', which had bedevilled the reign of Charles I (c.f. Miller, 1973, 89, who dismisses the parallels drawn by contemporaries as anachronistic).

[88] First Viscount Saye, William Fiennes, 1582–1662. Astell's reference is to Clarendon (*History* I, p. 145), who says of 'Lord Viscount Say [that he was] a man of close and reserv'd nature, of a mean and a narrow fortune, of great parts, and of the highest Ambition: but whose Ambition would not be satisfied with Offices and Preferments, without some condescensions and alterations in Ecclesiastical matters. He had for many years been the Oracle of those who were call'd Puritans in the worst sense, and steer'd all Their counsels and designs. He was a notorious Enemy to the Church, and to most of the eminent Church-men, with some of whom he had particular contests. He had allways opposed and contradicted all acts of State, and all Taxes and Impositions which were not exactly Legal, and so had as eminently and as obstinately refused the payment of Ship-money as Mr *Hambden* had done.'

[89] Lord Kimbolton, alias Lord Mandeville, is not listed in the *DNB* or the *Encyclopaedia Britannica*. Clarendon's sketch of him (*History*, I, pp. 145–6), to which Astell refers, is as follows: 'The Lord *Mandevile*, eldest Son to the Lord Privy-Seal, was a person of great civility, and very well bred, and had been early in the Court under the favour of the Duke of *Buckingham*, a Lady of whose Family he had married: he had attended upon the Prince when he was in *Spain*, and had been call'd to the House of Peers in the life time of his Father, by the name of the Lord *Kimbolton*, which was a very extraordinary favour. Upon the death of the Duke of *Buckingham*, his Wife being likewise dead, he married the Daughter of the Earl of *Warwick*. A man in no grace at Court, and look'd upon as the greatest Patron of the Puritans, because of much the greatest Estate of all who favour'd them, and so was esteem'd by them with great application and veneration: though he was of a life very licentious, and uncomfortable to Their profess'd Rigour, which they rather dispensed with, than they would withdraw from a House where they receiv'd so eminent a Protection and such notable Bounty. Upon this latter Marriage the Lord *Mandevile* totally estranged himself from the Court, and upon all occasions appear'd enough to dislike what was done there, and engaged himself wholly in the conversation of those who were most notoriously of that Party, whereof there was a kind of Fraternity of many persons of good condition, who chose to live together in one Family, at a Gentleman's House of a fair fortune, near the place where the Lord *Mandevile* liv'd, whither others of that *Classis* likewise resorted, and maintain'd a joint and mutual correspondence and conversation together with much familiarity and friendship ... by which generous way of living, and by his natural civility, good manners, and good nature, which flow'd towards all men, he was universally acceptable and belov'd; and no man more in the confidence of the Discontented and Factious party than He, and

Essex,[90] etc. to follow them; (b) a *Pym and Hambden,*[91] etc. among the Commons; and getting a Covetous and Cowardly *Lenthal*[92] into the Speaker's Chair ((b) P. 147, 136.); (c) having a Ld. *Holland*[93], etc. in credit with the Prince ((c) P. 122. *etc.*), and a Duke of (d) *Hamilton*[94] in the height of Confidence with him, to betray him even in his Bed-chamber ((d) P. 120, 166.): It is but putting an (e) *Oliver St. Johns,*[95] etc. into Places of Trust, ((e) P. 167, 200.) bringing an

none to whom the whole mass of Their designs, as well what remain'd in Chaos, as what was Form'd, was more entirely communicated, and no man more consulted with.' Clarendon (I, p. 146) lists Mandeville, along with the Earl of Bedford and the Lord Saye, as 'the three Lords . . . nominated as the Principal Agents in the House of Peers' of the Popular party.

[90] Robert Devereux (*q.v.*), Third Earl of Essex and parliamentary general. Clarendon (*History*, I, p. 146) said of him 'though he was no good Speaker in Publick, yet, by having sate long in Parliament, was so well acquainted with the order of it in very active times, that he was a better speaker There than any where else, and being allways heard with attention and respect, had much Authority in the debates'.

[91] John Hampden, statesman.

[92] William Lenthall (1591–1662), elected by the Long Parliament Speaker of the House of Commons on 3 November 1640. Clarendon (*History*, I, p. 136) records: 'Mr *Lenthall*, a Bencher of *Lincolns*-Inn (a Lawyer of competent practice, and no ill reputation for his affection to the Government both of Church and State) was pitch'd upon by the King, and with very great difficulty rather prevail'd with than perswaded to accept the charge. And no doubt a Worse could not have been deputed of all that Profession who were then return'd; for he was a man of a very narrow, timorous nature, and of no experience or conversation in the affairs of the Kindgom, beyond what the very drudgery in his Profession (in which all his design was to make himself rich) engaged him in. In a word, he was in all respects very unequal to the Work, and not knowing how to preserve his Own dignity, or to restrain the licence and exorbitance of Others, his Weakness contributed as much to the growing Mischiefs, as the Malice of the principal contrivers.'

[93] Henry Rich (*q.v.*), first Earl of Holland.

[94] James Hamilton (*q.v.*), third Marquis and first Duke of Hamilton. Astell here refers to the infamous charge made by Lord Reay and reported by Clarendon (*History*, I, p. 120) that Hamilton intended to make good his family claim to the throne of Scotland, a charge to which Charles refused to listen, taking Hamilton into his bedchamber as proof of his trust in him (*DNB*).

[95] Oliver St John (*q.v.*), Chief Justice. Astell refers here to Charles I's elevation of St John to the office of Solicitor-General, on which Clarendon comments on the page cited (*History*, I, p. 167): 'he became immediately possess'd of that Office of great trust; and was so well qualified for it, at that time, by his fast and rooted malignity against the Government, that he lost no credit with his Party, out of any apprehension or jealousy that we would change his Side: and he made good their confidence; not in the least degree abating his malignant Spirit, or dissembling it; but with the same obstinacy, opposed every thing which might advance the King's Service, when he was his Sollicitor, as ever he had done before'.

(f) *Essex, Warwick*,[96] and the rest, into the Privy Council, ((f) P. 155.) in hopes to take them off, and to appease the Party, but in truth to obstruct the King's Business, and to weaken his Authority: And then, tho' the Royal and English Heart be continually labouring for the Good of the People, these evil Ministers may easily pervert and misrepresent the best Intentions and most noble Designs. For Princes, how good soever, are neither infallible in their Judgments, whether of Things or Persons, nor exempt from the Passions of Humane Nature. And if the Principles and Measures that brought the Royal Head to the Block be so tenderly handled, and so carefully pursu'd woe unto us! for how much soever we make shew of detesting the Consequences, whilst the Premises please, we are in the high Road towards drawing the fatal Conclusion! We may harangue as much as we please against Popery and Arbitrary Power, so did our *Forefathers* whose *Off-spring we are*, and all the World knows to what End and Purpose; these being only the Baits that cover the Hook of home-bred Cabals and Rebellious Projects. Strange! that such Principles shou'd be suffer'd in a [**32**] Christian Nation, a Nation that has smarted so severely by them! But stranger yet, that any Prince shou'd Employ and Trust Men of these Principles! 'Tis certain he can have no hold of them; for whenever they get Power, and *Think* that a Change will be for their Interest, they will never want Pretences to throw him out of the Saddle. Nor will they be long in persuading themselves that it will turn to their own Account, even tho' the Prince may have heap'd the utmost Favours on them. For in all Changes there's something to be got, by the Mercenary and Rebellious Hands that effect them. Forbid it Heaven! that they shou'd ever any more be able to give us a Tryal of their Skill.

But as Mr. *Foulis* (f) (*History of the Popish Treasons and Usurpations*, B. 2. C. 3. p. 74.)[97] very honestly tells us, 'If we allow that

---

[96] Robert Rich (*q.v.*), second Earl of Warwick and older brother of Henry Rich, Earl of Holland.

[97] Astell's quotation is faithful to the original, one of Foulis' most magnificent rhetorical exhortations, except for small variations of punctuation, and the omission of a few words. Not content with the general, Foulis goes on to the specific, a scathing denunciation for which the passage Astell quotes is merely a preface: 'When the Sacrilegious *Presbyterians*, prompted by their Master the Devil, were resolved to Murder that famous Arch-bishop of *Canterbury* (Dr. *Laud*) for fashion-sake, they would have something to say.' And then he offers the rather amusing

People may lawfully Rebel against Princes, and at the same time be Judges of the justness of the Reason; to be in Authority will be a Slavery, the Word Monarch absolute Nonsense, the King oblig'd to obey every man's Passion and Folly; nor Peace nor Justice can be expected, the Nation being in a perpetual Hurly-burly every other day, as of late times, new Magistrates starting up by Strength of Policy: and he that's still uppermost of this *Leap-frog* Government, will extort Obedience, confirm'd by Oaths, from his suppos'd Subjects, which will ruin the Honest, and damn the rest with Perjury. Change, as a Novelty, at first is rather a Pleasure than Gain to the People, and at last a Burden and Ruin; and what a Factious People once resolve on, they will never want pretence of Reason, themselves being Judges.' – Certain I am, that Christian Religion does no where [33] allow Rebellion; and if a Heathen and a Christian (*a Papist or a Protestant*) do the same Fault, it is not the Unbelief (*or Errors*) of the former, that makes him more wicked in the Act than the Religion of the latter; and he that bawls out the Liberty of Conscience and Loss of Religion to vindicate his Rebellion, has too much of Atheism in him, to be a true Christian. He is not indeed a Christian, and least of all the most Reform'd and Perfect Christian, who makes 'that which shou'd have no Arms but Prayers and Tears, a Pretence to prove the Devil a Saint, and Treason an Article of Faith'.

Our Excellent Church instructs us better, which is the Reason perhaps that many are her open Enemies, and that some, who wou'd be call'd her Sons, do secretly undermine her. She teaches us to acknowledge in our daily Prayers, That GOD is *the only Ruler of Princes*; that the Parliament is *assembled under our most Religious and Gracious Queen* (*Liturgy. Prayer for the Queens Majesty. Prayer for the Parliament*); and therefore can have no Coercive Power over their Princes. In the Communion Service we are taught to own in our very Prayers, That the *Queen* is GOD's *Chosen Servant*, GOD's

analogue: 'I warrant you the ancient *Swedes* thought themselves as pretty Religious blades as any, when they slew their good King *Eric Stenchil*, because he intended to bring in Christianity among them. Our late *Puritans* made it one of their main pleas in Print and Pulpit for their fighting against the King, because forsooth, he intended to bring in Popery.' Foulis (*The History of the Romish Treasons*, p. 74) concludes his argument by maintaining that 'he that bauls out the liberty of Conscience, and loss of Religion to vindicate his Rebellion hath too much of Atheism in him, to be a true Christian'.

Minister, but *our Queen and Governour;* that she has GOD's Authority; that it is GOD's Word and Ordinance that we *should faithfully serve, honour, and humbly obey Her, in* GOD, and *for* GOD, that is, in the Apostle's Words, *not only for Wrath, but for Conscience sake.* Where then is the Original and Supreme Authority of the People? Besides, this is the Law of the Land, as well as the Doctrine of the Church, for the Liturgy is Established by Act of Parliament: [34] which may be one Reason why some are so willing to have it Review'd. It is a lasting and daily Reproach to their Disloyalty, reminding them how far they have gone towards the breach of that excellent Constitution, about the Preservation of which they make so great and so Hypocritical a Clamour: For, allowing that the People have a Right to Design the Person of their Governour; it does by no means follow that they Give him his Authority, or that they may when they please resume it. None can give what they have not: The People have no Authority over their own Lives, consequently they can't invest such an Authority in their Governours.[98] And tho' we shou'd grant that People, when they first enter into Society, may frame their Laws as they think fit; yet these Laws being once Establish'd, they can't Legally and Honestly be chang'd, but by that Authority in which the Founders of the Society thought fit to place the Legislature. Otherwise we have been miserably impos'd upon by all those Arguments that were urg'd against a Dispensing Power.

And since our Constitution lodges the Legislative Power in the Prince and the Three Estates assembled in Parliament; as it is not

---

[98] This is the classic Lockian argument against enslavement taken from the *Second Treatise* (Book II, Chapter 4, Section 23, 1988, p. 284): 'This *Freedom* from Absolute, Arbitrary Power, is so necessary to, and closely joyned with a Man's Preservation, that he cannot part with it, but by what forfeits his Preservation and Life together. For a Man, not having the Power of his own Life, *cannot* by Compact, or his own Consent *enslave himself* to any one nor put himself under the Absolute, Arbitrary Power of another, to take away his Life, when he pleases. No body can give more power than he has himself; and he that cannot take away his own life cannot give another power over it.'

Astell in *The Christian Religion* (pp. 305–6), scrupulously proved the references for the argument in Locke's *Two Treatises*: '*No Man having a power to deliver up this Preservation, or consequently the means of it, to the absolute Will and arbitrary Dominion* [306] *of another,* but *has always a Right to Preserve what he has not a Power to part with* (*Two Treatises of Government*, B.2, S.149.), as a certain Author says in another Case where it will not hold.'

in the Power of the Prince and one of the Houses, to Make or Abrogate any Law, without the Concurrence of the other House, so neither can it be Lawfully done by the Prince alone, or by the two Houses without the Prince.[99] All such pretended Acts, and all the Consequences of them, being illegal and Void in themselves, without the Formality of a Repeal, as is evident to every honest Man, if he will but attend [35] to common Sense, plain *English*, and the unalterable Reason of things. I hope then we shall hear no more of the People's Supremacy till these Good Men have got *the Act of Uniformity* Repeal'd.[100] But, alas, what do Laws signifie to Rebels, who have Power to Break or Cunning to Evade them! For all sides must allow, that there are even yet many other Good Laws in force, which sufficiently condemn those Principles and Practices in which they glorys.

To dismiss this Point, and to give the Reader a due Antidote against those pernicious *Popish Principles*, and Rebellious Practices; I desire him to Read the Homily of our Church *against Disobedience and wilful Rebellion*. He may meet with the Book in a Country Church; or, if he pleases, may purchase it at an easie rate in *Twelves*, printed 1687.[101] Let no Man dispise this true Reform'd Doctrine, because it is not set off with the false Rhetorick and plausible Expressions of Late Writers: for, if he pleases, he may in that Grave and Scriptural Stile be much better inform'd in the Duties of a Christian Life, and Arm'd against Popery, than by most of our

---

[99] Astell in this remarkable statement makes reference to the official theory of the 'balanced' or 'mixed' constitution of 'three estates', king, lords and commons, set out in the *Answer to the XIX Propositions*, issued in June 1642 on behalf of Charles I and against his parliamentary opponents. Recent scholars have debated to what degree this is an expression of classical republican theory. At the time the statement was read less as empowering king or commons than as empowering bishops, the lords spiritual, and counterpart to the lords temporal, of the second estate, under attack in the Parliament of 1640–1. Clarendon, Astell's mentor, supported the independent authority of the Anglican Church and was the principal advocate of 'mixarchy'. He was the unnamed target of Hobbes' attacks on the doctrine, and its role in the fall of Charles I, in *Behemoth: Or the Long Parliament* (ed. Ferdinand Tönnies, reissued with an Introduction by Stephen Holmes (Chicago University Press). See Mendle, 1985; and the review of Mendle by Tuck (1987; 570–20).

[100] The Act of Uniformity (*q.v.*) in question is that passed in 1662 by the Cavalier Parliament.

[101] Church of England, *Certain Sermons or Homilies Appointed to be Read in Churches.*

Modern Sermons. It was that Glorious Reformer Q. *Elizabeth, of famous Memory*, who *appointed Homilies to be Read in Churches*.[102] They have the stamp of Lawful Authority on them, and are the Authentic Doctrin of the *Church of England*, as appears by her Canons made in a Synod 1603, and confirm'd by Royal Authority. See Canons 46. and 49.[103]

It were too long to repeat all that the Homilies teach us in opposition to the above-mention'd Popish Errors: as, that *Lucifer* was the *first Author and Founder of Rebellion* (*Pag.* 584, 585.);[104] that *it is the first, the greatest, and the very root of* [36] *all other Sins*; that *Kings and Princes, as well the Evil as the Good, do Reign by* GOD's *Ordinance*, and that *Subjects are bounden to obey them* (*Pag.* 586.);[105] that it were *a perilous thing, to commit unto the Subjects the Judgment which Prince is Wise and Godly, and his Government Good, and which is otherwise* (*Page* 589.);[106] that *indeed a Rebel is worse than the worst Prince, and Rebellion worse than the worst Government of the worst Prince that hath hitherto been* (*Pag.* 590.); that allowing *it is evident to all Mens eyes, that the Prince be indiscreet and evil indeed,* (*Pag.* 591.)[107] what then? *Shall the subjects both by their Wickedness provoke* GOD, for their deserv'd Punishment, to give them an indiscreet or

---

[102] The *Book of Homilies* (*q.v.*), first promulgated by the Church of England in 1547. According to the 1562 Preface for the 1563 edition '[the Queen] hath . . . caused a Book of Homilies, which was heretofore set forth by her most loving brother . . . to be printed anew' (*OED*).

[103] Church of England, *A Collection of Articles, Injunctions, Canons, Orders, Ordinances and Constitutions Ecclesiastical* (London (1604) 1675). Canons 46 and 49, promulgated by the Church of England in 1603 in Latin, both concern the power to preach, and both commend the Homilies as sanctioned by public authority in true faith for public instruction (Church of England, *Collection of Articles*, pp. 291–2).

[104] Astell's citations refer to the 'First Part of the Sermon Against Disobedience and Wilful Rebellion' in the 1687 edition of the *Book of Homilies*, the page numbers she indicates having been transferred from the margin. Once again italicization indicates quotation from the Homilies.

[105] The 'First Part of the Sermon Against Disobedience and Wilful Rebellion' (*Book of Homilies*, 1687 p. 586), citing Romans 13: 'Let every Soul be subject unto the higher Powers, for there is no Power but of God, and the Powers that be, are ordained of God.'

[106] The 'First Part of the Sermon Against Disobedience and Wilful Rebellion' (*Book of Homilies*, 1687, p. 589), citing Ecclesiastes, 10:16, and Proverbs, 28, 29 'of undiscreet and evil Princes'.

[107] The 'First Part of the Sermon Against Disobedience and Wilful Rebellion' (*Book of Homilies*, 1687, p. 591): '*God* (say the Holy Scriptures.) *maketh a wicked Man to Reign for the sins of the People* (Job.34.10, Hos. 13.6).'

evil Prince, and also Rebel against him, and withal against GOD, who, for the Punishment of their Sins, did give them such a Prince? This *were double and treble evil, by provoking GOD* more to plague them (*Pag.* 592.). That no Goodness in the Men who Rise and Rebel, no Unkindness and mortal Enmity in the Prince towards them, tho' he be hated of GOD, and hurtful to the Commonwealth, no Concern for our Country, no Courage and height of Spirit, can authorize an Insurrection. *David* had all these Pleas and more, *he was, by GOD's appointment, Heir Apparent to the Crown and Kingdom,* and yet he wou'd by no means lift up his hand against the Lord's Anointed, but faith, *Let him live until GOD* appoint and work his end, either by natural Death, or in War by Lawful Enemies, not by traiterous Subjects (*Pag.* 600, 601.).[108] *For GOD,* says the Church in her Homily, *does shew, that he allows neither the Dignity of any Person, nor the multitude of any People, nor the Weight of* ANY CAUSE, as sufficient for the which the Subjects may move Rebellion against their Princes (*Pag.* 620.).

[37] Having said thus much in justification of the Doctor's Sermon, who, if he be a Clergy-man of the Church of *England*, and so zealous an Enemy to Popery, as he professes to be, must needs (to be sure *ought* to) teach Obedience, according to the Doctrine of the Church of *England*, even to Evil, and much more to Good Princes, in opposition to those vile Deposing Doctrines taught by the Church of *Rome*. We come now, as Charity obliges us, to consider what may be offer'd for those his Auditors, who were offended at his Sermon; and of this as briefly as I can. The Doctor says, 'That he hopes with Plainness of Truth, and he is sure with Sincerity of Heart, he has with due Compassion enquir'd into the most visible Causes of the Civil War' (*Sermon. Pag.* 25.).[109] And he thinks, 'Truth, Justice, and Charity, to be nearly concern'd in this Enquiry' (*Pag.* 5.). Now some who have read this Sermon with all imaginable Candor, who have no Personal Dislike to the Doctor, or are so much as acquainted with him or his Principles, further than what his Sermon expresses, are however of Opinion, that his Account of the *main Causes* of the *Civil War*, is neither True, nor Sincere and Ingenuous, nor Seasonable.

---

[108] The 'Second Part of the Sermon Against Disobedience and Wilful Rebellion' (*Book of Homilies*, pp. 601–2).
[109] This paraphrase of White Kennett (*Compassionate Enquiry*, p. 25) is close.

First, It is not true: As any Man may be satisfied, who will give himself the Pleasure and Profit of reading my Lord *Clarendon's* incomparable History; or by consulting Mr. *Foulis's History of our pretended Saints, Sir William Dugdale's Short View,*[110] *Dr. Nalson,*[111] or the Declarations and Papers that pass'd on both sides; or even their own partial Writers, in some of which, even in *Will. Lilly's Monarchy or no Monarchy,*[112] and in *John Cook's Appeal,*[113] the [38] same *Cook* that was their Solicitor against their Sovereign, he may find as great, or a greater Character of this excellent Prince, than the Doctor gives him. Tonnage and Poundage,[114] as much as is made of it, had been taken by his Majesty's Predecessors, before an Act of Parliament, without exception (*See Lord* Clarend. V. 1. *p.* 207.): And those other pretended Grievances were only the reviving *Obsolete Laws*, when the Parliament had refus'd to supply the King's pressing Necessities, whereby (in the Noble Historian's words) 'the Subject might be taught how unthrifty a thing it was, by too strict a detaining of what was his, to put the King as strictly to enquire what was his own' (*Ib. p.* 53.).[115]

'Tis true, there was a Match with *France*, from whence the *Queen was joyfully receiv'd*, as the same Noble Person tells us (*Ib. p.* 32.

---

[110] Sir William Dugdale (*q.v.*), whose *A Short View of the late Troubles in England* Oxford (published anonymously in 1681), attacked anti-Royalists.

[111] The Dr Nalson in question is probably J. Nalson (*q.v.*), author of *The True Liberty and Dominion of Conscience*, second edition (London, 1678), who argued, p. 13, that religion was 'the only bond of union, the only maintainer and preserver of those respective duties which are owing from one to another, in those little primitive societies of mankind' that constitute the family. Without it 'neither the obligations of nature, education, or reason, are powerful enough to keep men within the limits of their duty'.

[112] In 1651 William Lilly (*q.v.*) published his *Monarchy and no Monarchy*, in which he asserted that 'England should no more be governed by a king.'

[113] John Cook (*q.v.*), Solicitor-General and Prosecutor in the case against Charles I. Numerous editions were published of his brief, to which Astell refers, *King Charles His Case: Or, An Appeal to All Rational Men, Concerning His Tryal at the High Court of Justice: Being, for the Most Part, That Which Was Intended to Have Been Delivered at the Bar, if the King had Pleaded to the Charge* (1649).

[114] On Tonnage and Poundage see Clarendon's account (*History*, 1, pp. 53, 100), cited by Astell, of how Charles tried to regularize imposts which had an ancient provenance. Those opposed to this particular use of the royal prerogative saw his fiscal measures as forced loans. Much of the debate in Charles' first Parliaments turned on these matters.

[115] The striking accuracy of Astell's quotations from the Earl of Clarendon, here as elsewhere, suggest that she must have had his volumes beside her as she wrote.

and *p.* 22.).[116] But what Service will this do the Doctor? There was also a Treaty for a *Spanish* Match; and there was a Match between the King's Daughter and the Prince of *Orange*, before the Civil War broke out.[117] But were any of these, or was one of them more than the other, the cause of that War? By all that appears, the Doctor has not yet prov'd it. For tho' he lays down definitively, *I say*, 'those Clouds and gathering Signs of Popery did all arise from the Interests and Intrigues of a *French* Court', *p.* 15. and that '*Fears and Jealousies really began with the* French *Alliance*', *p.* 13. Yet he had told us no further off than in the former Page, That the *Spanish* Match *gave Universal Jealousie and Discontent*; so much, that if it had not broke off, *we know not what might have been in the end thereof*, p. 12, 13.

The Doctor is very minute in his account of the *Evils* [39] and *Mischiefs* brought over by *a Royal Consort from the* Bourbon *Family*; (*viz.*) The *French Servants* grew *Insolent*, the King humbled them; *this created a Diffidence between their Majesties*, and a War between *England* and *France*.[118] Well! one wou'd think that all goes Right thus far. But the falling out of Lovers, is, it seems, the renewing of Love; The King and Queen are Reconcil'd; there follows a Rebellion in *Scotland*, a Massacre in *Ireland*, and a Civil War in *England*, by a wonderful Chain of Consequences![119] And to carry them a

---

[116] Astell refers here to Clarendon's report (*History*, I, pp. 32, 22), of the success of the French match which concluded with the marriage of Princess Henrietta Maria to Charles I.

[117] Astell refers to the negotiations conducted between James I and Philip III of Spain for a marriage settlement between Charles, Prince of Wales, and the Infanta Maria, begun in 1616 but suspended in 1618 and finally abandoned in 1624. The marriage between Mary, the daughter of Charles I and Henrietta Maria, and Prince William of Orange, took place in 1641.

[118] Kennett (*Compassionate Enquiry*, p. 9), gives this unfavourable account of the consequences of the marriage in 1625 of Charles I to Henrietta Maria (1609–69), youngest daughter of Henry IV of France and his wife Marie de' Medici. The marriage agreement between the Catholic Princess and the Protestant Prince of Wales had stipulated both that some relief be given English Catholics from the Penal Laws, and that Henrietta Maria be permitted to retain her French attendants at court, both sources of tension between the King and his consort as early as 1626.

[119] Charles I and Henrietta Maria resolved their differences in 1628. The rebellion in Scotland in 1637 over Charles' introduction of Laudian religious practices, in particular a new prayerbook, and the appointment of bishops to prominent positions in Scotland, occasioned the Scottish National Covenant in 1638, binding its signatories to defend Presbyterianism to the death. The war with Scotland

little further, This Civil War drove the King's Family into Foreign Kingdoms; this produc'd a Popish Successor, this new Fears and Jealousies, this a Protestant Invader, this a Glorious Deliverance, this a new Settlement, this new Oaths, new Fears, and so forth, to the end of the Chapter![120] And, I pray, let the Doctor say, if there was not something Good, as well as something Bad, produc'd by this *French* Alliance!

As for the other Causes assign'd by the Doctor, it is but too true, that the People were wrought up into *Apprehensions and Fears of Popery, to Jealousies of Oppression and Illegal Power;* there was too much *Prophaneness and Immorality* on all sides, and the very height of *Hypocrisie and Perfidiousness* flam'd among the Rebels *(Pag.)*.[121] But I deny, that the King and his Faithful Subjects were the cause of this; and will never grant it, till I find better Proofs than have yet been offer'd. Neither the Doctor's *Apparently*, nor the People's *Thought* p.10. will ever convince an Honest Man, even tho' he had some biass and inclination, to believe, or rather to wish, he might find **[40]** by way of Excuse for his Country-men, that the *People* had any just cause, to *think themselves under* French *Counsels and a* French *Ministry.* If They or the Doctor will *think* so right or wrong, who can help it! Only let me recommend to all such Thinkers, Mr.

was a major contributing cause of the English Civil War. The massacre in Ireland of 1641, to which Astell refers, was a further case of Charles' incompetence. Having promised certain concessions to the Irish in return for a large grant from the Irish Parliament, Charles characteristically reneged, supporting a policy of extortion under his Lord-Deputy Strafford. In 1641 Catholic insurgents liberated much of the country, just failing to seize Dublin, and numbers of Protestant Irish were massacred. The English retaliated, landing a Scottish army in Ulster in 1642, marking the beginning of a war in Ireland that was not concluded for fifty years.

[120] Astell refers here to the dispersal of the English royal family to Europe and the marriage of the children of Charles I and Henrietta Maria into European royal houses: Mary to William of Orange, presumably the 'Protestant Invader' to whom Astell here refers; Henrietta to the Duke of Orleans, brother of Louis XIV; Charles II (1630–85) to Catherine of Portugal. James II (1633–1701), here referred to by Astell as the 'Popish Successor', married Anne Hyde, daughter of the Earl of Clarendon. Upon his wife's death as a professed Catholic in 1671, James converted. This particular set of alliances gives some idea of the considerable commitment to Catholicism in Royalist circles, and the greater leniency of High Church Tories, Clarendon and Astell included, towards Papists compared with Presbyterians.

[121] The marginal note gives no page number, in fact, but Kennett's list of the five causes of the Civil War which Astell paraphrases is at p. 6.

Lock's Chapter *of the Association of Ideas*; they need not be afraid to read it, for that ingenious Author is on the right side, and by no means in a *French* Interest![122] And indeed, till People will observe the excellent Precepts of our Holy Religion, and that in particular, of calling no Man Master upon Earth, of following no Popular Speaker and Leader of a Party, they will easily be persuaded to *think*, as every Cunning and Factious Man will have them.[123]

[122] Astell's reference to John Locke for a Whiggish theory of the relation between ideas and evidence is an indication that Astell was familiar with the chapter, 'Of the Association of Ideas', added to the fourth edition of Locke's *Essay Concerning Human Understanding* published in 1700 (Locke, *Works*, London, 1823, II, pp. 148–57). The implications for her argument are profound. Locke is politically correct for Kennett, she suggests, and could not be in league with the French, being already politically implicated in Shaftesbury's machinations against Charles II and the French Threat – Whig language for Charles' attempt to make common cause with Louis XIV to shore up absolute monarchy and French extract subsidies in exchange for the prorogation of the English Parliament (Jones, 1987, 150–1). See Locke's minute to Edward Clarke, Bodleian MS Locke e. 18 (published in Farr and Roberts, 1985, 397; Goldie, 1991). Too frequently modern commentators, misreading this passage, assume Astell, like Wollstonecraft, Macaulay and later feminists, to be drawing conclusions about the neutrality of the mind as a computer of sense data based on Locke's epistemology. See for instance, Kinnaird (1979), Squadrito (1987, 60), and Scaltsas (1990, 141). In *Moderation truly Stated* (pp. 10–11), Astell had demonstrated a technical understanding of Locke's theory of the 'association of ideas', with her pointed remark: 'then Lukewarmness and Indifferency in our Profession, is the only sense in which *Moderation* can be taken in the present context; if with the *Great* Mr. *Locke*, it be our constant care to annex to the word a determinate Idea'.

[123] The passage must be read as an elaborate satire of Locke's views. Locke, while professing to 'observe the excellent Precepts of our Holy Religion', was a latitudinarian, if not a Deist; while claiming to call 'no Man Master upon Earth' and follow 'no Popular Speaker and Leader of a Party', he was of course the follower of Shaftesbury, who exactly fitted that description. This kind of double talk is facilitated, she seems to be suggesting, by Locke's sensationalist psychology, which easily allows people 'to *think*, as every Cunning and Factious Man [i.e. Locke] will have them'. Earlier observations of a consistent type seem also to be aimed at Locke, classed among 'those Mercenary Scriblers whom all sober Men condemn, and who only write after the Fact, or in order to it, to make their own Fortunes, or to justifie their own Wickedness' (Astell *An Impartial Enquiry*, p. 29). Portentous remarks in *Moderation truly Stated* (pp. 93–4, 106) extend the theme, once again, one suspects, addressed to Locke: 'And for what End and Purpose is all this ado? for what do they Rent the Church of Christ, and tear the Bowels of their Country by intestine Broils? for what but to advance themselves, to gratify their Passions and their Vices! The People never get by Divisions and Revolutions, they lose their Peace and Quiet, their Money is exhausted in Taxes, and their Blood in War, only to raise a few *New Men*, and that the cunning Folks who manage all, may make their Markets. So that all their goodly Pretences of Redress of Grievances, and their bustle about Liberty and Property, have no other meaning, no other Conclusion, but their Own Advancement.'

The Doctor tells us, *p.*7. That there was continually a secret Aversion between the *French* and the *English*; I will not dispute with him for the Times of Yore; and let there be as great an Antipathy as he can wish at present, and as *fix'd and rooted*, the more so the better. But I shou'd be glad to know, from what Secret History he learnt, that there was such an Antipathy in the 16th and part of the 17th Centuries. For, by all that I can find, from the Days of Queen *Elizabeth* to the Restoration, or thereabouts, the Aversion was to the *Spanish* Nation; the People of *England* rejoicing extremely at the breaking off the Match with *Spain*, and the entring into the *French* Alliance. *The Queen*, as my Lord *Clarendon* tells us (Vol. 1. *p.* 22.), being *brought home triumphantly, to the Joy of the Nation.* Wou'd it either be true or fair to infer, that because the *English* and *Dutch* are Rivals in Trade, and because a Leading Peer among the *Whiggs*, and who [41] consequently wou'd be thought a Great Patriot and Friend to Liberty, and very much in the Interest of his Country, took the freedom to say in the House of Lords, *Delenda est Carthago*,[124] that therefore all Alliances with the *Dutch* must needs be fatal to us! But enough of this, which has no *meaning* but to shew, That King *Charles* I. did not Match with *France* against the Genius and Inclinations of his People: Neither did the King receive any Aid or Assistance from the *French* Interest, as the Doctor wou'd have us believe, *p.* 10. but it is evident, that his Rebellious Subjects did; (*See* Lord Clarend. Vol. 1. *Page* 220.] *Pym* himself being a *French* Pensioner; and the *Scots*, who were the first

---

[124] Astell most likely refers to the famous speech of 5 February 1673, given by Anthony Ashley Cooper, Earl of Shaftesbury, referred to by Thomas Burnet as 'a base complying Speech' (*DNB*), urging prosecution of the Dutch War, the Dutch being common enemies in trade. Shaftesbury was Locke's patron and the *DNB* reports, on the basis of the Shaftesbury papers, that 'when Shaftesbury delivered his famous "Delenda est Carthago" speech against Holland, Locke, as the third Lord Shaftesbury states, had to stand at his elbow with the written copy as prompter'. Like the reference to Locke on the association of ideas, this is another of Astell's flash-forwards to secure the analogue between the 1640s and later crises of the monarchy. Once again Locke is in the picture. Scipio's speech, perhaps because of Shaftesbury's speech, was on the mind of Defoe too, who in *The Shortest Way with the Dissenters: Or Proposals for the Establishment of the Church* (London, 1702, p. 19), put these words into the mouths of the Tory high flyers on the subject of the Dissenters: 'I do not prescribe Fire and Fagot, but a[s] *Scipio* said of *Carthage, Dilenda est Carthago*; they are to be rooted out of this Nation, if ever we will live in Peace, serve God, or enjoy our own.'

Incendiaries, keeping a Correspondence with *France*, and receiving Directions and Assistance from *Richelieu*. (*Ib. p.* 100, 101, 103.]

Popery was the Cry 'tis true, but the Establish'd Church was the thing aim'd at; 'twas this they covenanted to destroy Root and Branch: (*Lord Clar.* v. 1. *p.* 266.] The Tumults began with *No Bishops, No Bishops*, then no *Common Prayer*; and when they had the King at their Mercy, nothing wou'd satisfie them but *a course for attaining the just Ends*, (as they call'd them) *express'd in the solemn League and Covenant* (Foulis's *Hist. of our Protest. Saints. p.* 90, etc. and *p.* 209.);[125] that is, the pulling down the Church, and the depriving the King of all his just and legal Rights. Nor wou'd even this have satisfy'd them, without the Destruction of his Person: And for what Reason? but because *they consider'd what themselves might suffer, if he shou'd come to Reign again*, as their own Historian *May* himself confesseth, saith my Author (*Ib. p.* 133.]. Their Guilt indeed, was a strong and well-grounded *Apprehension*: But who might they thank for it? It was this that wou'd not [42] suffer them to be quiet, when the King had redress'd all their pretended Grievances, mov'd every Shadow of Oppression, and granted them all that they had the confidence to ask. (*Lord* Clar. Vol. 1. *p.* 166, and 206.]

The short is; The true and the principal Cause of that Great Rebellion, and that Horrid Fact which compleated it, and which we can never enough deplore, was this: Some Cunning and Self-ended Men, whose Wickedness was equal to their Craft, and their Craft sufficient to carry them thro' their Wickedness; these had *Thoughts* and *Meanings* to destroy the Government in Church and State, and to set up a Model of their own Invention, agreeable to their own private Interests and Designs, under the specious Pretences of the Peoples Rights and Liberties. They did not indeed speak out, and declare this at first, for that wou'd have spoil'd the Intrigue, every body wou'd have abhorr'd them; but a little Discernment might have found what they drove at. For to lessen and

---

[125] Solemn League and Covenant (*q.v.*) Astell's error in the title of Foulis' *History of the Wicked Plots* may mean that she is quoting from memory. While the exclamatory 'No Bishops, No Bishops' appears on p. 90 of this edition, the material at pp. 209 and 133 does not appear to be related, and I could find no references to 'their own Historian May' in Foulis' text.

incroach upon the Royal Authority, is the only way to null it by degrees, as an ingenious Person observes upon this Occasion.

Our Governours, it's certain, were of this Opinion, ascribing the Civil Wars to those Traiterous Positions which at that time obtain'd. And therefore, we find the two Houses in Parliament lawfully Assembled by their Sovereign's Writs, and he at the Head of them; we find them *declaring the sole Right of the Militia to be in the King*: And that both, or either Houses of Parliament, 'cannot nor ought to pretend the same, nor can, or lawfully may arise or levy any War, Offensive or Defensive, [43] against his Majesty, his Heirs, or lawful Successors'. (13 *Car.* 2. *Chap.* 6.] Pursuant hereunto, in another Act, they enjoin an Oath to be taken by all Members of Corporations, whereby they declare, that they believe, 'That it is not lawful upon *any Pretence whatsoever*, to take Arms against the King, and that they do abhor that Traiterous Position of taking Arms by his Authority against his Person, or against those that are commissioned by him'. (13 *Car.* 2. *Chap.* 1.] And by the *Act of Uniformity*, all Clergy-men are enjoin'd to subscribe the same Words, by way of Declaration. (14 *Car.* 2.]

Secondly, The Doctor's Enquiry *is not fair and ingenuous*; for to be thus, it ought to be impartial. Even his account of the Prophet *Jeremiah's* Reproof of the Wicked *Israelites*,[126] is, to say the best, very short and imperfect: *Idolatry*, 'tis true, was the great and crying Sin of the *Jews*; it was that to them, which I wish I cou'd not say, *Rebellion* has been to *England*. God had *laid the Cities of Judah waste and desolate* for this Sin; yet this, notwithstanding, their Posterity *forgot the Wickedness of their Fathers*, and return'd to the same Abomination (*Page* 3.). What is the natural Inference from hence, but that we shou'd be *admonish'd by their Example*. Our Rebellious Principles, *that Sin against the Publick Peace, overturn'd the best Constitution in the World, made our whole Island a Field of Blood* (*Page* 1.), *etc.* as we every Year deplore. And if we will still do wickedly, that very Wickedness which cost us once so dear, if we will still continue those Traiterous Principles and Seditious Practices, what can we expect, but the utter Destruction of our Name and Nation!

[44] But Idolatry was not the only Sin of which the *Jews* were guilty, and for which the Prophet reproves them. As wicked as they

---

[126] Kennett, *Compassionate Enquiry*, pp. 2–4, citing Jeremiah 44:2, 6, 8, 9, 10, 21, 22.

were, they had the face to say, *I am Innocent, I have not Sinned*, Jer.
2. 35. They made great Pretences to Religion, crying out, *The Temple
of the Lord, the Temple of the Lord*, ch. 7. 4. At the same time, that
there was not a *Man* among them that *executed Judgment*, or that
fought the Truth: Not only the *Poor* and *Foolish*, but even the *Great
Men*, who ought to *have known the Way of the Lord, and the Judgment
of their GOD*, even these had altogether broken the Yoke and burst
the Bonds, ch. 5. 1, 4, 5. They were all *Adulterers, an Assembly of
treacherous Men*; they *bent their Tongues, like their Bow, for Lies, but
they were not valiant for the Truth; supplanting their Neighbours,
Deceiving, walking with Slanders, proceeding from Evil to Evil*, ch. 9.
2, *etc*. They were cunning Politicians, *Wise to Evil, but to do Good
they had no Knowledge*, ch. 4. 22. *Violence and Spoil was heard in
Jerusalem*, ch. 6. 7. *And because of swearing, the Land mourned*: There
was *Wickedness even in the House of God*, ch. 23. 10, 11. *They belied
the Lord*, ch. 5. 12. *trusted in lying words, that cannot profit*; ascrib'd
their Wickedness even to Providence itself, with the vilest Hypocrisie, *We are deliver'd*, said they, *to do all these Abominations*, ch. 7. 8,
10. They profess'd *to be Wise*, and that *the Law of the Lord was with
them*: But *every one from the least even to the greatest, was given to
Covetousness; from the Prophet, even to the Priest, every one dealt falsly,
saying, Peace, Peace, when there was no Peace*. Neither were *they asham'd of their Abominations*, ch. 8. 8, 10, *etc*. *They held fast Deceit,
they refus'd to return*, [45] ch. 8. 5. *trusting in man, and making flesh
their Arm, their heart departed wickedly from the Lord*, ch. 17. 5. *they
strengthened the hands of evil doers, perverting the words of the living
GOD*, saying *to every one that walked after the Imagination of his own
heart, no evil shall come upon you*, ch. 23. 14, 17, 36. The very *Pastors
destroy'd and scatter'd the sheep*, ch. 23. 1. *Among the people were found
wicked men, who laid wait, who set a trap, whose Houses were full of
deceit; therefore they are become great, and waxen rich; they are waxen
fat, they shine, they surpass the deeds of the wicked* – and yet *they
prosper* – 5 26, *etc*. for why shou'd they be *smitten?* since *they receiv'd
no correction?* ch. 2. 30. *They made their faces harder than a rock, they
refus'd to return*, ch. 5. 3. A most deplorable Account of a profligate
Nation ripe for Destruction! since neither God's Mercies nor his
Judgments wrought any Repentance in them.

The Dr. Leaves the *Example* and the *Admonition* against Idolatry
upon our Minds (*Page* 4.); but one wou'd be glad to know, whether

or no he really thinks that there are any among us in danger of *Apostatizing from their own Faith and Communion to Idolatry? (Page 3.)* If our People had been in this Mind, no doubt they wou'd have declar'd themselves in a late Reign, when they had Opportunity and Encouragement. I do not think that Popery is since that time furnish'd with better Arguments; and I dare say it has had no Encouragement these two Years, whatever it might have had till that time. To what purpose then is an Admonition and Guard, where there is no Danger? But we know there is a flaming and inveterate Schism within our Walls, tearing out the Bowels of the Church [46] and of all true Religion; and the Danger lies in falling off to this: tho' by some Mens way of talking, one would be apt to think that they reckon it no great matter whether we do or no.

As for the Causes of the Civil War, I desire to ask, with all due Respect, whether a Man who enquired *without Partiality, or any other By-respect (Page 6.)*, wou'd not have found more than those assign'd by the Dr.? And whether a faithful Relator wou'd not have given an Account of all he found? 'Tis certain other Men who liv'd in those Times, who had the best Opportunities of Information, and took them, give other Reasons for our Distempers. Thus we learn from my Lord *Clarendon (Vol.* 1. *p.* 253.), That this deplorable Calamity proceeded from the Ill Arts of Factious Men, their *absurd Lying, bold Scandals, boundless Promises, abject Flatteries, and Applications to the Vulgar-spirited.* Their Fetches and Art in drawing Consequences, and other Tricks and Ways to draw Men in, and make Tools of them (*Ib.* 164, 165, 198, *etc. Vol.* 2. *p.* 170, 146, 150.). Their *Factious Preachers, and the Licence of the Press (*Vol.* 1. *p.* 151, 157, 160.); the Remisness of (a) A. B. *Abbot*,[127] under the

---

[127] George Abbot (1562–1633), created Archbishop of Canterbury, following the death of Archbishop Richard Bancroft in 1610. Abbot was an enemy of William Laud and of Popery more generally, rating only the Protestant reformers, Waldo, Wycliffe, Huss and Luther 'the noble worthies of the Christian world'. As Archbishop he was perceived to favour the parliamentary cause, was hostile to the Spanish marriage negotiations, was not on good terms with Sir Edward Coke, and his relation with James soured also. He crowned Charles I, but opposed the forced loan, for which he was punished in 1627, by being stripped of his power and effectively replaced by a commission of five bishops, which included Laud. Not surprisingly he incurred the wrath of Clarendon who (*History*, I, p. 68), in his character sketch of Abbot, which Astell cites here, noted: 'He had been Head, or Master of one of the poorest Colledges in *Oxford*, and had Learning sufficient for that Province. He was a man of very morose manners, and a very sowr aspect,

specious name of Moderation ((a) *Ib.* 68, 69.); (b) the Fear and Jealousies that were artfully and unreasonably infus'd ((b) *Ib.* 195, *etc.* 203, 205.); (c) the Cabals of disaffected Men ((c) *Ibid.* 127.); (d) Activity of the Factious, and Remisness of the Loyal Subjects, who were too easily outwitted by them ((d) *V.* 2. *p.* 112, 127. *V.* 1. *p.* 209, 253.); (e) the Animosity that was among the King's faithful Servants ((e) *V.* 1. *p.* 126.); (f) the teizing and worrying his Friends till they were quite dispirited ((f) *Ib. p.* 166.); (g) their ways to remove faithful Counsellors, and to fill the Board with a number of such as only weakened and betray'd the Royal Authority ((g) *Ib.* 139, *etc. Ib.* 155, *etc. See also p.* 319, *etc.*); [47] (h) getting their own Creatures into Employments upon pretence to take them off, but indeed to obstruct and ruin the King's affairs ((h) *Ib.* 167, 187, 217, 253, 257, 261.): and in short, two things, says that noble Author, were of *most fatal Consequence* to the King's Service, and to the Safety and Integrity of all honest Men (*V.* 1. *p.* 153.); one was, the *Committee* for *Preparatory Examinations*; 'For such an Inquisition (besides that the same was contrary to the Practice of former times) wou'd easily prepare a Charge against the most innocent Man alive;' where liberty should be taken to torture, pervert, and apply all private Discourse, 'according to the Conscience and Craft of a diligent and malicious Prosecution:' the other was, 'Examining upon Oath Privy Counsellors, upon such matters as had pass'd at the Council Table'.[128] Add to this, that the *Vigilant* and *Active* Mr. *Pym* knew very well how to raise and keep up the Peoples *Fears* and *Jealousies* (*Ibid p.* 196, 197.), by alarming them with *Desperate Designs and Conspiracies*, to deprive the People of *their Property* and *Birth-right* (*Page* 137.). And well he might be acquainted with such Designs, since they were forg'd among his own Party (*Page* 209.). But this was a Secret, and there were other Plots to be talk'd of to amuse the People, which Mr. *Pym* was pleas'd to keep *in petto*, lest he

---

which, in that time, was call'd Gravity; and under the opinion of that Virtue, and by the recommendation of the Earl of *Dunbar*, the King's first *Scots* Favourite, he was prefer'd by King *James* to the Bishopric of *Coventry* and *Litchfield*, and presently after to *London*, before he had been Parson, Vicar, or Curate of any Parish-Church in *England*, or Dean, or Prebend of any Cathedral-Church; and in truth totally ignorant of the true Constitution of the Church of *England*, and the State and Interest of the Clergy; as sufficiently appear'd throughout the whole course of his life afterward.'

[128] These are verbatim quotations from Clarendon, *History*, I, p. 153.

shou'd *hinder their farther Discovery* (*Page* 196.). I wish the Reader
wou'd be so just and kind to himself and his Country, as to Read
and consider that useful and valuable History my Lord *Clarendon*
has left us, and then he will be able to satisfie himself what were
the true Causes of our Civil War, and by what Methods it was
brought about, and who they are that tread in the same steps.

[48] And that out of the Mouth of two Witnesses every word
may be establish'd, another Author, who by his Books appears to
have taken nothing upon trust, but to have given himself the trouble
of reading all their Writers, some of whose Quotations I have exam-
in'd, and can affirm (which is more than can be said of all
Authors)[129] that he is very just and punctual; this Gentleman freely,
and without scruple, assures us,'That the *Long Parliament* were the
King's greatest Enemies, the *only Cause* of his Ruin, and the Murderers of many Loyal Gentlemen' – And he further tells us, That
they were 'the first Contrivers of these Wars, they consulted the
Rebellion, they broach'd it, and gave it life by their Votes and Declarations' (*Hist. of our Pretend. Saints, p.* 204, 205.). And again, 'The
Blood of many thousand Christians, shed in these Wars and before,
crieth aloud against Presbytery, as the People only guilty of the first
occasion of Quarrel' (*Ibid.* 105.). Of whom *Grotius* says, 'That he
looks upon them as factious, turbulent, and Rebellious Spirits'.[130]

---

[129] Astell vouches for the credentials of Foulis, her source second only to Clarendon,
giving us an insight into her own scholarship. It would be very interesting to
know in whose library this checking went on. In the first line of *The Christian
Religion* (p. 1) Astell thanks the dedicatee, Lady Catherine Jones, for lending her
the anonymous *The Ladies Religion* (1697), indicating perhaps the source for those
works, among the many cited in *An Impartial Enquiry* (pp. 24–8), that she personally checked out. Suggestions on those works Astell checked in this way are made
in the notes where apposite.

[130] Astell is misleading on this point. The quotation is not from Grotius, but a
comment Foulis (*History of the Wicked Plots*, pp. 105–6) makes on 'the ever great
Grotius', as 'one born and bred amongst [the Presbyterians], yet so farr satisfied,
or rather nauseated with their manners, that he looks upon them as factious,
turbulent, and rebellious spirits, and so not fit for Subjects'. The work of Grotius,
to which Foulis refers as *De Antichristo in append. post annotat. in evangel.* p. 65,
is the *Appendix ad interpretationem Locorum Novi Testamenti quae de Antichristo
agunt aut agere putantur* (Amsterdam) but clearly not the 1641 edition, where the
statement cannot be found at p. 65.

It is worth noting that the authority of Grotius was invoked by the country
Whigs, rather than Sidney or Locke, in support of resistance – as for instance
by John Tutchin, *Observator*, 15–18 September 1703 and 13–16 October 1703
(cited Phillipson, 1993, 218). But Grotius, while supplying a taxonomy of con-

Was not one of the Causes of the Civil War, 'That small or rather no Authority or Power, that is allow'd the King (as the same worthy Gentleman notes) by the *Presbyterians*,' or *Whiggs*, or whatever you will call them? For they are all of the same Original, they act upon the same Principles and Motives, and tend to the same End, who place the Supreme Power originally in the People, giving them a Right, or at least an Allowance to resume it, whenever they believe they have a sufficient Cause; that is, in plain *English*, whenever they think fit, and are strong enough to put their *Thoughts* [49] and *Fancies* in execution. Hence comes their looking upon themselves as 'but *Conditional Subjects*, who are to acknowledge their King no longer than he serves their turn, and is subservient to their Fancies'. And when the Fancy takes them, they will find occasion, and do not want 'Wickedness, to throw Aspersions upon their Sovereign, and to instigate the People to Rebellion, by assuring them of the Lawfulness of Subjects fighting against their King.' Thus have we found another Train of Causes, *leading Causes*, besides those assign'd by the Doctor; which if he knew nothing of before, 'tis hop'd he will now be pleas'd to reflect on a little.

The Dr. takes Notice of our Princes Matches with *France*, and of the Anger and Aversion our People had to that Nation; but was it always so? I have a good old *English* Homily by me, (*Hom against Rebel.*] which shews that upon Occasion, the *Good-natur'd People of England*, have *thought* themselves free from this Aversion. Otherwise, 'a great many Nobles, and other *English-men*, Natural Subjects, wou'd never have taken part against the King of *England*, with the *French* and *French-men*,' as they did in the Reign of King *John*. 'They wou'd not have sent for the *Dauphin* of *France*, receiv'd him and his Army, swore fealty to him; expell'd their Sovereign Lord the King of *England* out of *London* and *Lincoln*, which they deliver'd to the *Dauphin*, and at last forc'd their Sovereign to submit himself to that foreign false Usurper the Bp. of *Rome*, and to surrender his Crown to the *Pope's* Legat'. (Part 6.] So near were the *English* People, with all their *Natural Distaste*, to the delivering themselves [50] up to a *French* Power, if the Providence of GOD, and the Endeavours of their Injur'd King, had not preserv'd them from this Shameful Conquest.

ditions for legitimate conquest, was nevertheless a strenuous opponent of theories of resistance (see Goldie, 1978, 579).

When the Dr. told us, that the People *thought* themselves too much *under French Counsels, and a French Ministry*, p.10. he shou'd have also inform'd us, whether they had any just Reason for these Suspicions; otherwise, these *Thoughts* prove nothing but the Thinkers folly, and how easily they become the Tools of Evil and Seditious Men, even of the very *French*. For it may be gather'd from the Dr's. Words, which are capable of various Constructions, that the *French* Intrigues rais'd these Suspicions in the People, on purpose to ruin the King. And are they not *Good-natur'd People, Free-born* English-men, who will give ear to such Intrigues! Had they only *deplor'd the unhappiness* of their fond Suspicions, they might have pass'd with me for good well-meaning Christians, *tender Lovers of their Faith and Country (Page* 11.). But supposing their Jealousies had been ever so true and just, I do not find, either in my *Bible* or in the *Statute Book*, that they had any Authority to *begin a Civil War; for to War against the Supreme Authority, the King was Treason, according to the Laws of the Land, and Damnable according to the Word of* GOD. (*Hist. of our Pret. Sts. p.* 104.)[131]

As no Good Christian wou'd punish a Man for Matters of mere Opinion, nor restrain him from Worshiping of GOD in his own Way, according to the best of his Understanding; so the Dr. I suppose is not Ignorant, at least, he may easily inform himself, that in the Penal Laws against the Papists (*Page* 11.), they are not consider'd as Men [51] of an Erroneous Faith, but as Factious and Rebellious Subjects. And if none were to be Tolerated, but those who are free from Treasonable Principles and Seditious Practices, I doubt, the Act of Toleration wou'd extend to very few: such a Test as this, wou'd effectually provide that Security, which was design'd by the Government in the Bill against *Occasional-Conformity*. There were many Causes that contributed to the Felicity of Q. *Elizabeth's* Reign, but her magnanimous Resolution, and stout Exertion of her just Authority, were none of the least. And it is very observable, that she wou'd never endure to have a Successor

---

[131] It is worth noting that Foulis appends to this passage, accurately cited by Astell, the aside in parentheses: 'Let *Buchanan* and such as he, by supposing the Apostles and the Spirit, to deal with us, like Hypocrites, evince to the contrary.' Foulis is Astell's likely source for the extended list of twenty-six 'pretended saints', enumerated from a to z, which Astell gives between pp. 24 and 28, and in which Buchanan figures as an *éminence grise*.

declar'd, but left it to the Decision of the Laws, thereby preserving her People within the due Bounds of their Duty, and restraining them from making Court to the Rising Sun, which is the Mischief of all Governments, the Nurse of Faction and Disorder, especially when the Prospect lies out of the Nation.

When the Dr. was wishing, *Oh how happy had it been* (*Pag.* 18.*)*, *etc.* one would think that for the sake of *this happy Nation,* and *best Constitution* (*Page* 16.), he shou'd have added a Wish or two more, *viz.* that the *good-natur'd English People* had not been *seduc'd into an unnatural Rebellion* by mere *Thoughts* and *Suspicions* (*Page* 18.); or have fancy'd themselves into a *necessity* of *believing,* or rather Imagining without any manner of necessity, scarce any colour for it, that they might be *led out first in Riots and Tumults, and then in Troops and Armies against their Lawful Sovereign* (*Page* 19.)*!* Or had consider'd what *hardships* they made him suffer, by engaging him in a War with *France,* and granting no Supplies to support it, nor even to defray the necessary Expence of his [52] Houshold, whereby he was under a real *necessity* to provide for himself, by ways his Predecessors had not us'd, because they had been otherwise supply'd! Or had been contented and quiet, after the King had redress'd all their *Real,* and even their *Imaginary Grievances!* For he who wou'd give a true and sincere Account of Things, ought as well to take notice of what was done to allay their Fears, as of what was pretended to raise them.

Whereas, if the Causes of the War (*Page* 9, 10, 19, 21, 22, 23.) are represented thus by halves, and all the Calumnies that the Martyr's greatest Enemies cou'd throw upon him, are either industriously reckon'd up, or cautiously intimated; what cou'd plain and honest Hearers, who understood only down-right Sense, being Strangers to nice Turns and fine Expressions, Sofenings and Meanings, which they had been taught to call Jesuitical; what cou'd these Honest Men think, but that the true *meaning* was, to throw all the Odium of this Reproachful Rebellion upon the King, as if he suffer'd nothing but what he brought upon himself? And consequently, how cou'd they help being Scandaliz'd at it? Especially, since if he did not give a just Cause; yet he gave *an unhappy suspicion* (*Page* 21.) of that Tyranny and Oppression, which *Free-men* cou'd never bear (*Page* 10.). It is insinuated at least, if not somewhat more; *p.* 10. that he had *Aid and Assistance* from the *French,* and was in their *Interest.*

Whatever his *Intentions* were (*Page* 9.), yet the *Opportunity* he gave, his *Compliances with his entirely belov'd Royal Consort*, the *Interest the leading Roman Catholicks gain'd at Court* (some way or other) lost him the *Peoples Hearts, and almost robb'd him of his* [53] *Good-Name* (*Page* 13, 14.). The Peoples Minds were *exasperated by Hardships, to call them by that Name only,* says the Doctor, who does not entirely acquit the King, but only tells us in an emphatical Expression, 'that he himself did not *hastily* contrive or command any of those hard Measures' (*Page* 19.). He did it then, but not hastily: 'HE HAD his Ministers to propose them, and his very Judges to approve them.' So had the Martyr's Son, and yet we justifie the Abdication of the one, why not then upon the same Principles, the Beheading of the other? The Difference between them is but small; the Doctor hints the Parallel, *p.*21. who does not say, that an *Arbitrary Executive Power* was not set up in K. *Charles* the *First's* Reign, but only that it 'was *much more effectually* set up in a later Reign': Upon which words, they who understand *English* need no Comment. If it be either plainly shewn, or secretly insinuated, that 48 is so like 88,[132] and that what the *Forefathers* acted, proceeded from much the same Causes, by which their *Off-Spring* were influenc'd; what can plain Men think, but that since we are taught to justifie and thank GOD for what *we of yesterday remember* (*Page* 21.); by a parity of Reason, there can be no great harm in the Actions of our Forefathers, which might well enough be forgot, or remember'd to other Purposes than the Act of Parliament enjoins.

Besides, might not well-meaning Men, unus'd to Distinctions, and Salvo's for Conscience, which they have been taught, is one of the worst Corruptions of the Church of *Rome,* and of the worst Members of that Church, the [54] *Jesuits*; Men, who have learn'd from the Pure Doctrine of the Reformation, drawn from that uncorrupt Fountain the Holy Scripture, that the Goodness of the End or Intention, can by no means attone for the Evil of the Action, but that such as dare do *Evil that Good may come,* draw upon their Heads *a just Damnation.* Might not such honest Hearers as those, be offended at the extenuations that were offer'd for their good-natur'd

---

[132] The parallels between the Engagement Controversy of 1647–8 and the events, beginning with the Exclusion Crisis of 1679, leading up to 1688, are a topos in the genre to which Mary Astell's *Impartial Enquiry* belongs. On the subject of the Exclusion Crisis more generally, see Skinner, 1972.

Country Men's Rebellion, believing they struck at the very Roots of Morality? Nor is the matter mended in Print, for *Suspicions, Thoughts and Meanings, p.*18, 19. being in a different Character, the Doctor intends we shou'd take notice, that he lays an Emphasis on them. But now, if *Doubts* and *Suspicions,* a *Thought,* a *necessity of Believing* (Page 18.), a *Prospect* and *Persuasion,* a *Meaning of Self-Preservation* (*Page* 19.), or even Self-Preservation, when Life is really in Danger, can lessen the Guilt of this *Unnatural Rebellion,* and all the *Horrid Facts* it produc'd; what will they not excuse! He who robs upon the High-Way, has his *Prospects,* and *Persuasions,* and *Necessities*; and when he resists the Officers of Justice, he only means *Self-Preservation.* Even *Caiaphas* and the *Jews,* had their *Meanings* and *Apprehensions, If we let this Man alone,* say they, *the Romans will come and take away both our Place and Nation*; which Words the Doctor has very appositely apply'd, *p.* 14.

Further, The Doctor intimates in his Advertisement, that tho' *nothing is omitted,* yet something is *added,* tho' not *material.* Now, if it shou'd happen that those Passages, [55] *p.* 4, 14, *15, (*In which 15th *Page, there seems to be an Addition, unless the Doctor had the Spirit of Prophesie, (which he lays claim to, p.* 21. And for the future, etc.) *For the Queen did not declare her Royal Bounty to the Parliament, in relation to small Vicarages, till* Feb. 7.)[133] and 18, where something is said in the Martyr's Favour; and *p.* 24, 25, where the Vileness of his Enemies is touch'd upon, shou'd be that no *Material* Addition, an honest Hearer wou'd have yet more reason to be offended. This is observable, That those Periods wherein the Royal Martyr is well spoke of, may be omitted without disturbing the connexion of the Discourse. And that that Paragraph in which is one of the best Passages in the whole Sermon, (*p.* 24. *But the prime Engines, etc.*) is of a length disproportionable to all the rest. But I lay no stress on this; the Doctor may clear it when he pleases, by shewing (as he offers in his Advertisement) the Original to the Bookseller who Prints this.

---

[133] In fact it is the King's inclination to restore Impropriations (which placed the profits of ecclesiastical property in the hands of laymen) and augment small vicarages, on which Kennett (*Compassionate Enquiry,* p. 15) focuses, as an indication of Charles' sincere desire to protect the Church of England. He says nothing about the dating of the Queen's action in this matter, one of the many instances of Astell's distortion of the text.

Once more; An Impartial Enquirer wou'd have taken notice of the *Dissoluteness* in the Parliament's Army, as well as of that in the *King's*. If he never heard of any Complaints of the former (*Page* 20.),[134] I will shew him, when he pleases to command it, the *University's Complaint*, and *the Country's Complaint of the barbarous Outrages committed by the Sectaries*: Or, he may please to consult Mr. *Foulis* (*Hist. of our Pretended Saints. p.* 139.). And I believe, he will hardly find in any Nation, no not in a Popish Country, an Instance of Dissoluteness and Prophaneness equal to that of those zealous Reformers, as they wou'd be thought, who ridicul'd the Holy Sacrament of Baptism, by carrying their Horses to the Font, doing the same to Pigs, *etc.* and not only making *Westminster* Abby, (and indeed prophaning all or most of the Cathedrals in *England*) but even the very Altar their Brothel!

[56] As for the stigmatizing of *Pryn*, whose Name the Doctor does not think fit to give us, *p.* 23.[135] for that wou'd have spoil'd the Reflection thrown upon the Martyr: my Lord *Clarendon* will tell you, for what good Reasons he was *punish'd; (viz.)* 'for a most Pestilent Seditious Libel, in which, the Honour of the King, Queen, Counsellors and Bishops, was with equal License blasted and traduc'd' (*See* Lord Clarend. Vol. 1. *p.* 158, 159.). And if I forget not, (for I have not the Book by me) this very *Histrio-Mastix* is fill'd with Invectives against the Queen. What sort of *Truth, Justice* and *Charity* then, what *Sincerity of Heart* must that needs be, which leads a Man to affirm, or even to insinuate, that *Pryn* was *stigmatiz'd* for *reproving Impiety!*

The Doctor, I suppose, does not mean to infer, that the *Scandal* of the *Stage*[136] is a just Cause of Civil War (*Serm p.* 5, 25.); were

---

[134] Astell seems to be referring here to Kennett's claim concerning the docile nature of the English people: 'the *Romans* found our *British* Ancestors inclin'd rather to Obedience than to Subjection, Quiet and Helpful', for which he cites Tacitus' *Agricola* (*Compassionate Enquiry*, p. 20).

[135] But Kennett does give the title of William Prynne's tract, the *Histrio-Mastix* (The Player's Scourge), in a marginal note. The work was construed as an attack on court society in general, and Queen Henrietta Maria's associates and women actors in particular. Its publication, late in 1632, coincided with rehearsals of Walter Montague's *The Shepherd's Pastoral*, a masque in which the Queen was acting to celebrate Charles' birthday. Prynne's critical work cost him his ears. Interestingly, Astell claims not to have the book to hand as she writes, implying that she does have the other works to which she refers, which the high level of accuracy of her quotations would confirm.

[136] Astell here refers to the subtitle to Prynne's *Histrio-Mastix*: *Against the Intolerable Mischief and Abuses of Common Plays and Play-Houses*, given by Kennett (*Compassionate Enquiry*, p. 23).

this allow'd, there has been more cause of late than ever. Nor can he be ignorant, that a very *Learned* and Ingenious *Tract* has been *writ against this growing Evil (Page 23.).* 'Tis true, the Author has not been *prosecuted* for it, *with a Severity that was thought to be Cruel;*[137] but he has suffer'd very much upon other Consciencious Accounts, which it is believ'd he does not think less Meritorious. And this leads me in the last place to observe,

Thirdly, That supposing the Doctor's Enquiry were both true and candid, yet it is *not seasonable.* I hope he will give me leave to ask him, Whether, if he had liv'd in the Martyr's Days, and had really thought, that an Alliance with *France* wou'd have produc'd so much Mischief as, he says, it did; or, if upon that Match he had observ'd, that People were enflam'd at the Queen's [57] Exercise of her own Religion; whether he cou'd then, as an honest Man and a Christian, have urg'd all those plausible Arguments to incline the King to that Alliance, or have offer'd, what yet in Reason may be said for a Royal Consort's being allow'd to serve GOD publickly in her own way? Wou'd not a good Man rather have taken the other side of the Argument, and dissuaded the King, as much as in Duty he cou'd, from that Alliance? and when it was made, have advis'd the most private Exercise of a Religion that gave so great Offence?

The Application is obvious; Are *we under any such Calamity* as a *French Alliance? (Pag. 25.)* Nay, in his own words, we are *hardly under any prospect of it.* What *Meaning* then, in a Harangue about the Mischiefs of such an Alliance? *The Dangers of Popery now stand at the safest Distance from us; and our Guides and Governours have oppos'd and vanquish'd Popery, even in the Times of greatest Danger. We have not so much as the Apprehension of Illegal Power and Oppression, under this Auspicious Reign (Page 26.). Our Rights are transmitted to Posterity, one wou'd think, beyond a Capacity of their being depriv'd of them (Page 27.).* I wish I cou'd say, that the Life and Spirit of Religion, is as secure as the outward Profession of it; but alas! too much *Prophaneness* and *Hypocrisie* still remains among us; and therefore, that part of the Doctor's Sermon which relates to these, so far as it barely relates to them,[138] is very proper and

---

[137] Here Astell misrepresents Kennett, who named the tract in question, the *Histrio-Mastix*, and claimed the contrary, that the author was in fact prosecuted for it, 'with a Severity that was thought to be *Cruel' (Compassionate Enquiry,* p. 23).

[138] Kennett, *Compassionate Enquiry,* p. 28.

very necessary. But for the rest, the Doctor might have known, had he pleas'd, that the Dangers lie the other way. For there are but too many among us, who are very dextrous at playing the Old Engines of Confusion and Rebellion, *Fears* and *Jealousies*, loud but unreasonable Out-cries of *Popery* and [58] *Arbitrary Power*.[139] 'It was not only Printing which they made use of to vindicate Rebellion, (against K. *Charles* I. says my Author, it may be a little warmly; but who can be cool when they reflect on such Outragious Practices?) but also, and that a main one too, Pulpit-Prating, for I dare not call such Babbling Preaching; where nothing was yell'd out, but *Persecution! Persecution!* O the Cruelty and Knavery of the King! O the Idolatry of the Queen! O the Wickedness of the Malignant, Antichristian Army!' (*Hist. of the wicked Plots and Conspiracies of our pretended Saints. p.* 182.)

There is still a Party, and that a restless and busie one, who act by those very Principles that brought the Royal Martyr to the Block; and there are yet too many, for be they ever so few, they are too many, who, instead of deploring that Crying and National Sin, justifie and rejoice in it. How then can it become a Minister of the *Church of England* to do that which *Hugh Peters*[140] and his Fellows us'd to be set about, 'the vilifying his Majesty in Print, running thro' all the Misfortunes of his Reign', (*Ib. p.* 114.) still implying that his own 'Sins (or Mistakes, the *Influence* of others over him, or the *Opportunities* he gave them, *etc.* (*Serm. p.* 9, 10. *p.* 13, 18.)) were the occasion of them all?' How can an Episcopal Divine imply anything tending to what was once said by the *Scotch* Professor *Rutherford*,[141] speaking of the Reasons of GOD's Judgments on the

---

[139] Astell's percipient remarks on events of the 1640s look forward to a future, in which she is located, where the effort to displace universal monarchy (that of the Pope) and arbitrary government (that of Louis XIV) produces a Protestant alliance (that which brought William III to England) which threatens to bring back the very phenomena under attack, but in the name of a different cause. Astell quotes the angry piece from Foulis with emphases added.

[140] Hugh Peters (1598–1660), an Independent divine whose sermons during and after the trial of Charles I justified regicide, despite his personal disclaimer. Foulis (*History of the Wicked Plots*, p. 114) says of him: 'Several of the Sectaries like *Hugh Peters* were set up, to prattle out the necessity of a Reformation in Goverment, so that people might take the change more peaceably'. Foulis' somewhat heated remarks on the influence of the print media follow, from which Astell excerpts a couple of lines, interpolating her own observation in parentheses.

[141] Samuel Rutherford, principal of St Mary's College, St Andrews University, and participant as a commissioner of the Church of Scotland in the Westminster

Nation, 'Others say, Rebellion against the King is the Cause, but (says he) rather the not timous rising to help the Lord and his Oppress'd People against the Mighty, is the Cause. The Defection of both Kingdoms to Altar-Worship, Imagery, Idolatry, Popish and Arminian Doctrines?' (*Hist. of our pret. Saints p.* 186.) *etc.* And pray, what was the *Altar-Worship? etc.* what but the Regular Worship of the Church as by Law [**59**] establish'd? Or, in a word, can a Man who makes a *compassionate Enquiry into the Causes of the Civil War*,[142] and upon such a Solemnity as the deploring of *that Horrid Fact committed on one of the most Virtuous and most Religious of our* English *Princes? (p.* 1, 2.) Can he allow himself to speak almost in the words of 59 *Presbyterian Londoners*, whose undutiful and unchristian Pulpit-Talk, help'd to lay the Royal Head upon the Block, and who tell us in their Vindication, 'That it was the woful Miscarriages of the King himself (which we can't but acknowledge to be many, and very great) in his Government, that have cost the three Kingdoms so dear, and cast him down?' (*Vindic. of* London Ministers. *p.* 6, 7. 1648.] *etc.*

In the Name of Wonder, what do these People mean, who are at present so loud against Popery and Arbitrary Power! Tho' 'tis indeed no Wonder, for their Meaning is too plain and evident! When their Prince was not only in a League with some of the most rigid and persecuting Popish Princes, but even with the Pope himself: When Mass was as public, and as much frequented, as in any King's Reign since the Reformation, scarce excepting King *James* the Second's; when there were more perverted to the Romish Religion, and more considerable Persons, than were even in the Reign of a declar'd Papist, excepting those Worthy Patriots, who Apostatiz'd from GOD, to qualifie themselves to betray their King

---

Assembly from 1643, was renowned for his anti-Arminian views. The passage in Foulis' *History of the Wicked Plots* (p. 186), referring to an incident in the Westminster Assembly on 25 June 1645, is prefaced by the question: 'What do you think of another of these Champions, *viz.* Mr. *Samuel Rutherford?* No lesse man then Professor of Divinity at St *Andrews*, who thus yell'd out his malice against the Kings friends'. Foulis (p. 204) discusses at length how 'seditious Predecessors [of the 'Saints' – i.e. Presbyterians and Parliamentarians] in the University of St *Andrews*, insteed of Divinity, had thrust up these Politick Questions' – about the extent and limits of royal power.

[142] The title of Kennett's sermon, to which the note refers. Astell goes on to deplore the Presbyterians, Whigs and the plight of the nonjurors under William III, relieved only under Queen Anne.

the more effectually; When our Protestant Religion and *English* Liberties were defended by Popish Hands, with Protestant Swords in them! then not a Fear, not a word of the Danger of Popery!

As little did we hear of *Illegal Acts* and *Arbitrary Power*, of *Oppression* and *Persecution,* in a Reign that tugg'd hard for a [60] Standing Army in time of Peace; that had Interest to suspend the *Habeas Corpus* Act several times, tho' it be the great Security of the *English* Liberties; that outed 7 or 8 Reverend Prelates, the Ornament and Glory of the *English* Church, besides several of the inferiour Clergy, and Members of the Universities, and that only for *Conscience sake,* and because they cou'd not swallow such new Oaths, as they believ'd to be contrary to the old ones: And tho' 12 of them were thought so deserving, that there was a Provision made in their Favour, even by that Act that depriv'd them of their Freeholds and Subsistance, of their Rights as *English-men* and Ministers of GOD's Church, yet not one of them enjoy'd, in that Human, Charitable and Religious Reign! the Advantages which the *Body of the Good-natur'd* English *People* design'd them. Who cry'd out Persecution? or put in a word for a Sister Church, when Episcopacy was destroy'd Root and Branch in a Neighbouring Kingdom, that us'd to interest it self mightily in our Affairs, and still believes it is under Covenant Engagements, to work the same Blessed Reformation here? And tho' all of the Clergy, who were but suspected to be favourers of Episcopacy, were treated in the most outragious and cruel manner; 'tho a whole Clan of defenceless Men were barbarously Massacred in cold Blood, after promises of Security; which Action, if not done by Authority, was done at least by connivance, the Actors being protected and kept from Punishment. When – *etc.* more might be said, but let this suffice; nor are these bare *Suspicions, Doubts, etc.* no, they are true and notorious Facts; which will be remembred, and call'd by their proper Names, whatever a Set of Men may endeavour to the contrary.

[61] But no sooner was her Majesty happily plac'd in the Throne of her Fathers, thro' GOD's great and most seasonable Mercy to an unworthy People, but all the old Clamours are reviv'd, tho' she has done nothing to Provoke, but every thing to Oblige them! Tho' her only fault, if Duty and Respect will allow that Expression, consists in too much of the Royal Martyr's Clemency and Goodness; Her Majesty's Reign having left us nothing to wish, but that she had

less of K. *Charles* and more of the Spirit of Q. *Elizabeth*, since a Factious People can no way be kept in bounds, but by a sprightly and vigorous Exertion of just Authority. And what's the Reason of the present Clamours? What but that the Faction know that the Queen has an *English Heart*; that she was not only Educated in our Episcopal Church, but that her Judgment confirms her in it; she is the Royal Martyr's Grand-daughter, the Lineal Heir of his Crowns and Vertues, and they have no hopes that she will betray the Church, under pretence of Defending it; which are Causes enow to alarm the Party! But sad Experience has taught us to decypher their Gibberish! we know too well, that in their Dialect *Popery* stands for the *Church of England*; the *Just* and *Legal Rights* of an English Monarch are call'd *Arbitrary Power*; by the *Privileges* of either *House*, they mean such exorbitant Power as may enable them to *Tyrannize* over their Fellow Subjects, nay over their very Sovereign; *Liberty of the People*, in their Language, signifies an unbounded Licentiousness, whereby they take upon them, whenever they think fit, to Oppose, or even to Remove their Governours, provided they are strong enough to compass their wicked purpose; and to be reproach'd by [62] them for being in a *French Interest*, signifies neither more nor less, than to be a faithful Subject, able to smell out their Plots, and to counterwork their pernicious Designs.

To come then to account for the Causes of our deplorable Civil Wars, we may be allow'd to do it in this manner: Tho' Government is absolutely necessary for the Good of Mankind, yet no Government, no not that of GOD himself, can suit with their deprav'd and boundless Appetites. Few govern themselves by Reason, and they who transgress its Laws, will always find somewhat or other to be uneasie at, and consequently will ever desire, and as far as they can endeavour, to change their Circumstances. But since there are more Fools in the World than Wise Men, and even among those who pass for Wise, that is, who have Abilities to be truly so, too many abuse and warp their Understandings to petty and evil Designs, and to such Tricks and Artifices as appear the readiest way to attain them. Since Riches and Power are what Men covet, supposing these can procure them all they wish; Hopes to gain more, or at least to secure what one has, will always be a handle by which Humane Nature may be mov'd, and carry'd about as the cunning Manager pleases. And therefore of *Necessity* in all Civil Wars and Commotions, there must be some Knaves at the Head of a great many Fools, whom the other wheedle and cajole with many plausible Pretences, according to the Opportunity, and the Humour of those they manage. These are made to believe strange things of their Governours and their Arbitrary Designs, which wou'd surely take effect, did not the Prudence and Industry of those vigilant Patriots disappoint them. They discover Plots which themselves have [63] made; they give up Liberties upon a valuable consideration, and when time shall serve, know how to procure to themselves the Honour of Retrieving them. And what do they ask of the People for all this Care and Trouble, and Public Spirit? only to stand by and assist them; to follow where they lead, and to depend upon their Wisdom and Honesty with an implicit Confidence? For they, good Men, are incapable of ill Intentions or selfish Designs! no, the Liberty of the People, and Good of the Nation, is all they contend for! Now under this *Prospect* and *Persuasion*, must not the People of *necessity* be drawn in, for *Self-Preservation*, and to support these fair Speakers!

There's not much to be done at first, Men are not call'd upon to take measures that choque and startle: all that is requir'd of them, is only to oppose the Designs of a Party (that is, in truth, of the Friends of the Government) against whom our cunning Men have rais'd dreadful Apprehensions. These seem to desire no more but to keep what they have, for the Encroachments are small at first, and industriously conceal'd. So Advances are made by degrees, and the unwary People are trap'd by them, without perceiving the Snare, till they are entangled in the greatest Crimes. For the Sword being drawn, the Scabbard must be thrown away; the Devil and his Instruments, Seditious Men, being always ready to persuade those who have yielded to their Temptations, that it is too late to Repent; and that when our Reverence for Superiours is once broke through, the only way to be safe, is to harden our selves in Wickedness.

I will not pretend to justifie all the Actions of our Princes, but it is much more Difficult; nay, it is impossible to [64] justifie, or honestly excuse the Behaviour of our People towards them. Tyranny and Oppression are no doubt a grievance; they are so to the Prince, as well as to the Subject. Nor shou'd I think a Prince wou'd fall into them, unless seduc'd by some of his Flattering Courtiers and Ambitious Ministers; and therefore our Law very Reasonably provides, that these, and these only, shou'd suffer for it. But are Sedition and Rebellion no Grievances? they are not less, perhaps more Grievous than Tyranny, even to the People; for they expose us to the Oppression of a multitude of Tyrants. And as *we here in this Nation* may have suffer'd by the former, so have we oftner and much more grievously by the latter. The accursed Roots of which are I fear still left among us, and there are but too many wicked ones who cultivate these Tares with the utmost Arts and Industry. May GOD inspire the Heart of his Vicegerent with the Spirit of Courage and Understanding, to restrain and keep under *all such workers of Iniquity, as turn Religion into Rebellion, and Faith into Faction.* That so She may never leave it in their power to prevail either against her Royal Person or her Good and Faithful Subjects, *or to triumph in the Ruin of* GOD's Church among us; seeing they have not fail'd upon occasion to give us too too evident Proof, that when they have the Power to hurt, they never want the Inclination.

Biographical Notes

Act of Uniformity In 1662 the Cavalier Parliament, which established a rigid Anglican orthodoxy, passed the Act of Uniformity. This Act demanded the reordination of many pastors, gave unconditional consent to *The Book of Common Prayer*, advocated the taking of the oath of canonical obedience, and renounced the Solemn League and Covenant. It forced the clergy to take oaths of allegiance and nonresistance to the Crown and an oath recognizing the King's supremacy in the Church. Nearly one-fifth of all clergymen were denied their livings for failing to do so. As a result of the Act of Uniformity, English Puritanism entered the period of the 'Great Persecution', wherein Puritanism became a form of Nonconformist Protestantism. (*New Encyclopaedia Britannica*)

Anabaptists A term used to describe various groups throughout sixteenth-century Europe who refused to allow their children to be baptized, reinstituting instead the baptism of believers. They were present in England from the sixteenth century, although Anabaptist views seem to have been confined to refugees from the Low Countries. Luther and Calvin vigorously denounced the Anabaptists who were severely persecuted by both Roman Catholics and Protestants. (*The Oxford Dictionary of the Christian Church*)

Anne, Queen of England and Great Britain (1665–1714). Anne was the second daughter of James, Duke of York, who was to become King James II in 1685. Despite her father's Roman Catholic religion, Anne was raised a Protestant at the insistence of her uncle, King Charles II. In 1683 Anne married Prince George of Denmark, although it was

Anne's friend, Sarah Churchill, who proved to be more influential in her early life. It was Sarah who persuaded Anne to support the Protestant William III of Orange, who was married to Anne's elder sister, Mary, when William overthrew their own father in 1688. The death of Anne's only child in 1700 meant there were no Protestant successors to the Stuart line. Anne thus agreed to the 1701 Act of Settlement, which designated the Hanoverian descendants of King James I of England her successors, rather than her own exiled Catholic brother James, the Old Pretender. On the death of William the following year, Anne became Queen. She had long been considered a patron of women's causes, was the dedicatee of various works by women both as Princess Anne of Denmark and Queen. It was in this capacity that Mary Astell applied to her for support for her *Serious Proposal* (1694–7) for the education of women. Anne was devoted to the Anglican Church and detested both Catholics and Dissenters. Although she sympathized with the High Church Tories, she tried to remain independent of their political influence, and disagreed with their strategy in England's war against France and Spain. Her poor health forced her to rely increasingly on her ministers, however, and the Whig junta came to prevail. Anne died in 1714 and was succeeded by King George I. (*New Encyclopaedia Britannica*)

Arminianism This is the name given to a doctrine, first advocated by the Dutch theologian Jacobus Arminius (1560–1609), which spread to the English Church in the seventeenth century. It challenged the doctrines of predestination and justification by faith alone which had formed the core of beliefs in the traditional English Church. Instead, it stressed free will and the importance of works along with faith. In 1618 an international synod was called in Dort, Holland, to rule on the Arminian doctrines which the orthodox Calvinism believed to be Roman heresies. The five doctrines were declared inadmissible or heretical, and the Arminians were given the choice of recantation or exile. Although Arminians were viewed as radical reformers, their English leaders, such as Archbishop William Laud, were also the leaders of the established church government. However, this did not prevent them from being accused of Popery. Laud, who stressed the importance of church ceremony, was thought to be a Roman sympathizer. (*New Encyclopaedia Britannica* and *Encyclopaedia of Philosophy*)

Atterbury, Francis (1662–1732). Tory Bishop of Rochester. Born in Buckinghamshire, he was educated at Christ Church, Oxford. When James II attempted to force his Catholic creed upon the unwilling University, Atterbury, as a Protestant, wrote in defence of the Church of England. Atterbury received holy orders around 1687 and soon gained a reputation as a preacher. He was made chaplain to King William and Queen Mary even though he was regarded as a controversialist for his opposition to Erastianism, the ascendancy of the state over the Church. In 1701 he received the degree of DD and despite his bold advocacy of the rights of the clergy, Atterbury remained a favourite at court. Queen Anne made him her chaplain in ordinary, and in 1704, Dean of Carlisle. Since the time when convocation, largely due to Atterbury's work, had resumed its functions, Atterbury had been an active participant in the lower House assemblies, and he soon became almost as prominent a figure in the House of Lords. In 1713 he was made Bishop of Rochester and Dean of Westminster. Atterbury, who had Jacobite leanings, refused to sign the 1715 Declaration of Confidence in the government of King George I, and increasingly alienated himself from the King. Around 1717 he began to hold direct communications with the Jacobites, and was imprisoned in the Tower in 1722 for his alleged role in the attempt to restore the Stuart line. He was found guilty, stripped of all his ecclesiastical offices, and 'banished for ever from the realm'. He entered the service of James II's son, the Old Pretender, in Paris. However, James did not treat him well and in 1728 Atterbury retired to the south of France, where he later died. His body was returned to England and privately buried in Westminster Abbey. (*DNB*)

Baxter, Richard (1615–1691). Presbyterian divine. Born in Shropshire, he was ordained in 1638, but took neither a clearly conformist nor Nonconformist stance. In 1641 he was made lecturer (preacher) in Kidderminster, Worcestershire. When the Civil War erupted in 1642, the people of Worcester sided with the King, while Baxter sided with the Parliament, and he was driven out of Worcester. In Coventry he officiated as chaplain to both the townspeople and soldiers. He said of the Civil War that 'both sides were to blame ... and I will not be he that will justify either of them'. In 1647 he retired from duties as army chaplain due to ill health. He returned to Kidderminster and resumed his prolific writings. In 1660 he went to London as one of the King's chaplains, but retired from the Church of England on the passing of the Act of Uniformity, and suffered much ill treatment under Charles II and James II. When the tumult of the Restoration was past, he left London and continued to write and preach until he was jailed along with other Nonconformists. He was released in 1686, after serving around eighteen months, and in 1688 pursued his lifelong principles by entering enthusiastically into the coalition of Protestant Dissenters and the clergy of the Church of England against the Catholic James II. Mary Astell, in *Moderation truly Stated* (p. 71) referred to the 'godly Mr. *Baxter*' as an Occasional Conformist: 'one of those *Moderate Dissenters*, that . . . *sometimes receiv'd the Lord's Supper in the Communion of the Church of England*'. (*DNB*)

Becanus, Martinus (1563–1624). Author of numerous Latin works defending the Roman Church, five of which were translated into English, Becanus made an intervention into the controversy over the English royal supremacy in ecclesiastical affairs. *De dissidio Anglicano*, was translated into English as *The English Jarre: Or Disagreement Amongst the Ministers of Great Brittaine, Concerning the Kinges Supremacy*, Translated J. W[ilson] P[riest] (1612). It attracted the response of Richard Harris, *Concordia Anglicana de primatu ecclesiae regio: adversus Becanum De dissidio Anglicano*, G. Hall imp. R. Redmer (1612); translated and published as *The English Concord, in Answer to Becane's English Jarre [1702]: Together with a Reply to Becan's Examen of the English Concord*, H. L[ownes] f. M. Lownes (1614). The work to which Astell refers in *An Impartial Enquiry* (p. 24) is Becanus' *Controversia Anglicana de potestate pontificis et regius* (1613). (*Encyclopaedia Britannica*)

Bellarmine, Robert (1542–1621). Italian cardinal and theologian. Born in Tuscany and educated by the Jesuits in Rome, Piedmont and at Padua, he excelled in Thomist philosophy and the study of classical Greek. He joined the Order and was sent in 1569 to lecture on theology at the University of Louvain, where he became acquainted with the Calvinist doctrines flourishing in the Low Countries. In 1576 he was recalled to Rome by Pope Gregory XIII to teach theology at the newly founded Roman College. During this period he produced the famous *Disputationes de controversiis Christianae fidei adversus hujus temporis haereticos* (3 volumes, 1581, 1582, 1593), generally taken to be a definitive defence of Papal power, which called forth many Protestant rebuttals, including that of Thomas Hobbes. In 1589 he was required by Sextus V to accompany a Papal delegation to France, following the murder of Henry III. Created a cardinal by Clement VIII in 1599, he was, after 1605, retained by Pope Paul V to defend the Church in its battle with schismatic civil powers in Venice, France and England. In the case of England his interventions were signal, involving him in public criticism of James I for his severity on Catholics in the aftermath of the Gunpowder Plot, and a posthumous rebuttal of the work of William Barclay denying the temporal power of the Pope, published in 1610 as *De potestate summi pontificis in rebus temporalibus*. Although Bellarmine gave the Pope an indirect right to depose heretical rulers, he was a moderate on Papal power, invoking the displeasure of Paul V for not making a stronger statement, on the one side, and the condemnation of French theologians, including Bossuet, for his defence of ultramontanism against claims for autonomy of a Gallician Church, on the other. Bellarmine had a much misunderstood friendship with Galileo, whose work he approved, subject to scientific demonstration. (*Encyclopaedia Britannica*)

Binckes, William (d. 1712). Dean of Lichfield. Educated at St John's College, Cambridge, he graduated with an MA in 1678. He was made prebendary of Lincoln in 1683, and of Lichfield in 1697 and took the degree of DD in 1699. He is most known for his sermon, preached to the lower House of convocation on 30 January 1701, on the martyrdom of Charles I, to which Mary Astell makes reference in *An Impartial Enquiry* (p. 16). In this sermon he argued that the execution of Charles I was an act of even greater enormity than that of the crucifixion of Jesus Christ, because Charles I was in actual possession of his crown whereas Jesus Christ was merely an uncrowned king of the Jews. He suffered no reprisals for publishing this sermon, and in 1703 was made Dean of Lichfield. In 1705 he was appointed as prolocutor to convocation. (*DNB*)

Book of Homilies The Convocation of January 1542 agreed to the plan of issuing prescribed homilies for the use of 'disaffected and unlearned' clergy. The first collection was produced twelve months later but, probably due to Henry VIII's refusal to authorize it, was not released until early in Edward VI's reign in 1547. A second book of homilies, although probably completed in 1563, was not published until

1571, during Elizabeth I's reign. It contained twenty-one homilies, with the twenty-first homily, *Against Rebellion*, being added in 1571 in response to the Northern Rebellion of 1569. From Elizabethan times, the *Homilies* formed a considerable component of Anglican preaching, and became as important as *The Book of Common Prayer* and the *Thirty-Nine Articles* as a repository of Anglican doctrine. They were revived at the Restoration in 1660 and were frequently cited by the later non-jurors. (*The Oxford Dictionary of the Christian Church*)

Buchanan, George (1506–1582). Historian and scholar. Born in Stirlingshire, Scotland, he studied at St Andrews under John Major, as Astell tells us (*An Impartial Enquiry*, pp. 26–7) and in Paris. In 1536 Buchanan returned to Scotland and worked as a tutor to Lord James, one of James V's natural sons. King James urged Buchanan to satirize the morals of the clergy, which he reluctantly did. This earned him the ire of Cardinal Beaton, and James, interested only in the political ends, did not defend Buchanan when Beaton demanded to prosecute him and other Scottish reformers. Buchanan fled to France, teaching Latin in Bordeaux for three years, before teaching in the college of Cardinal le Moine, Paris, in 1544. In 1547 he was invited to teach at the college at Coimbra in Portugal where he was accused, in 1548, of writing against the Franciscans. He was imprisoned by the Inquisition until 1551. While working as a tutor in France and Italy, Buchanan studied the Bible so that he might form an opinion on religious controversies. Around 1562 he returned to Scotland and openly declared himself a Protestant. He immediately took part in the government of the Church, sitting in the assemblies of 1563–8, and was employed as a tutor to Queen Mary. In 1570 Buchanan was appointed as tutor to the young King James at Stirling, and was made Keeper of the Privy Seal, which entitled him to sit in both the Privy Council and the Parliament. In 1579 he published the most important of his political tracts, *De jure regni*, in which he defended legitimate or limited monarchy. He argued that monarchs have a duty to their subjects to be good kings, and even suggested the popular election of kings. Despite its popularity, *De jure regni* was suppressed by an Act of Parliament in 1584. In 1582, after his death, Buchanan's last work, a history of Scotland entitled *Rerum Scoticarum historia* was published. (*DNB*)

Burgess, Daniel (1645–1713). Nonconformist Presbyterian minister. Born in Middlesex, he studied at Oxford University before being taken to Ireland by Roger Boyle, first Earl of Orrery, in 1667, where he acted as a domestic chaplain to Nonconformist gentry. He was ordained in Dublin, but returned to England in 1674 because of his father's ill health, and was imprisoned at Marlborough for preaching. In 1685 he came to London where he gained fame as an exuberant preacher, for which he is mentioned by Astell in *A Fair Way with the Dissenters* (p. 8). However, differences amongst his congregation led to a large secession from his ministry and in 1710 the Sacheverell rioters set fire to his meeting-house. (*DNB*)

Burnet, Gilbert (1643–1715). Bishop of Salisbury. Born in Edinburgh, he was educated at Marischal College, Aberdeen. An industrious scholar, he was made probationer of the Scottish Church in 1661, visiting England in 1663, where he became acquainted with the Cambridge Platonist Ralph Cudworth, the orientalist Pococke, the mathematician Wallis, and the scientist Robert Boyle. Burnet practised extemporary preaching and in 1666 wrote against the oppressive policy of the Scottish bishops. In 1669 Burnet was appointed professor of divinity at Glasgow University and was intimately involved in the scheme of conciliation which required a great diminution of the power of the bishops. During this period he wrote his *Modest and Free Conference between a Conformist and a Nonconformist* which expressed his liberal views regarding Church government. In 1673 Burnet wrote *Vindication of the Authority, Constitution, and Laws of the Church and State of Scotland*, which supported the cause of episcopacy and the illegality of resistance purely on religious grounds. In the same year he and Stillingfleet, in James, Duke of York's presence, briefed the Catholic hierarchy, a bold measure, which together with his remonstrances against Charles II's evil life, earned him banishment from the court. Burnet's favour with James, initially due to Burnet's altercation with Lauderdale, the Scottish High Commissioner, ended abruptly when Burnet was forced to testify against his royal patron during an investigation by the Commons of Lauderdale's regime. During the Popish Plot of 1678–80, Burnet protested against the persecution of the Roman Catholics, so incurring the ire of both the court and the extreme anti-Popery party, the circle of the first Earl of Shaftesbury. Meanwhile the first volume of his *History of the Reformation in England* was published in 1679, followed by the second volume in 1681. The Rye House Plot of 1683 resulted in the execution of Burnet's two best friends, Essex and Russell, and

Burnet thought it safest to go abroad. He went to France where his extremely warm reception angered James. Returning to England, Burnet was dismissed in 1684 from his posts as chaplain at the Rolls and lecturer at St Clements for preaching a vehemently anti-Popish sermon. He then travelled extensively through Europe, including Rome, where he was warmly received by Pope Innocent XI, and Geneva, where he played his anti-Popery card. In 1686 he accepted an invitation to reside with the Prince of Orange at The Hague. Burnet urged William to have his fleet ready to invade England and obtained from Mary, consort of the Prince, a promise to place all power in William's hands should they succeed in attaining the throne. Burnet drafted William's declaration and accompanied him to England in 1688. He was rewarded for his services with the bishopric of Salisbury, and took his seat in the House of Lords where he zealously advocated toleration. He preached the coronation sermon, and in 1689 worked in an official capacity to further an accommodation between the Anglican and Presbyterian Churches. In 1698 Burnet was appointed to attend Peter the Great, and his laborious work, *Exposition of the Thirty-Nine Articles of the Church of England*, was published. Burnet attended William on his death-bed in 1702 and in 1703 strongly opposed the bill against Occasional Conformity, publishing his speeches on this and the Sacheverell impeachment. It is in this context that he is mentioned by Mary Astell in *A Fair Way with the Dissenters* (p. 16). He spent his later years living in Clerkenwell, and his most important work, the *History of My Own Time*, was not published until after his death. Due no doubt to the intolerance of the Scottish Church and Scottish law, which permitted the torture of prisoners, witnessed by Burnet in the case of his uncle, the Covenanter Lord Warriston, and threatened in his own case by the agents of James II, Burnet was steadfast in his support of liberty of conscience. His 1689 tract, *An Enquiry into the Measures of Submission to the Supream Authority*, the most liberal of all his writings, published before Locke's *Two Treatises* (1690), takes as its first precept the principle that 'men are born free'. Mary Astell's observation, 'If *all Men are born free*, how is it that all Women are born slaves?' (*Reflections upon Marriage*, 1706, p. xi), could as well refer to Burnet as to Locke. (*DNB*)

Burnet, Thomas (1635?–1715?). Master of the Charterhouse. Thomas Burnet was Yorkshire born. He was admitted to Clare Hall, Cambridge, as a pupil of Tillotson and, when Ralph Cudworth vacated his mastership of Clare Hall in 1654 to become a Fellow of Christ's College, Burnet followed him, becoming Proctor of Christ's in 1667. Through the influence of the first Duke of Ormonde, his patron, he was appointed to the mastership of the Charterhouse in 1685, despite complaints that, though in orders, 'he wore a lay habit'. The same sort of reasoning stood in the way of his later appointment to a bishopric even though, after the Revolution, he had served William as chaplain in ordinary and clerk of the closet. Burnet lived quietly on in the Charterhouse and devoted himself to writing, for which he earned the reputation of an elegant stylist in Latin as well as English and was eulogized by Addison. The two-volume *Telluris theoria sacra* appeared in Latin in 1681 and in an English version, dedicated to the King, in 1684, which Charles is said to have admired. Burnet's theory of creation, according to which the world, like a gigantic egg, was crushed at the deluge and flooded from within, its shell forming mountain ranges, attracted great controversy, and the admiration of Steele, who addressed it in *Spectator* no. 146. In 1692 Burnet went on to publish his *Archaelogoiae philosohicae sive doctrina antiqua de rerum originibus* in Latin and English, attempting to reconcile his theory with Genesis – unsatisfactorily from the point of view of his many critics. As a consequence he was forced to resign his clerkship of the closet. In 1697 Burnet published anonymous *Remarks* upon Locke's *Essay*, to which Locke responded in his answer to Stillingfleet, attracting *Second Remarks* (1697) and *Third Remarks* (1699) from Burnet, who argued against Lockian sensationalist psychology. Burnet also acted as Leibniz's informant on Locke, in exchanges of letters in 1695–6, 1698 and 1700 presenting him as a radical and subversive figure in a way that may have substantially influenced Leibniz's own politically conservative views (Jolley, 1975, 23–4, 30–1). Burnet's own Deist works, *De fide et officiis Christianorum* and *De statu mortuorum et resurgentium*, in which he rejects original sin and the 'magical' theory of the sacraments, were not published in his lifetime, perhaps for fear of further heresy charges. His works were republished several times after his death. Thomas Burnet is reported to have held a favourable opinion of Astell (Norton, 1961, 59–60) and may well have been among her sources on Locke and Shaftesbury. (*DNB*)

Calves' Head Club A club established shortly after the death of Charles I to mock his death. Its meetings were held on his anniversary, 30 January, and the dishes served were a cod's head, to represent

Charles the man, a pike to represent tyranny, a boar's head to represent the King preying on his subjects, and calves' heads representing Charles and his followers. An axe and a toast celebrated the regicides and a copy of *Ikon Basilike* was burned. After the Restoration the club met secretly, its first mention in print being *The Secret History of the Calves' Head Clubb* by Edward Ward, reprinted in the *Harleian Miscellany*. In 1734 the diners were mobbed, which put an end to further meetings. Astell refers to its irreverant revels in *An Impartial Enquiry* (p. 16). (*Enclyclopaedia Britannica*)

Calvinism Calvinism refers to the theological system of John Calvin, a French reformer and theologian, who added some of his own doctrines to those characteristic of Lutheranism. Lutheranism taught that Scripture was the only rule of faith, that human free will no longer existed after the fall of Adam, and that justification by faith was possible without works. Calvin's additions included the doctrines of the inadmissibility of grace, the certitude of salvation and absolute predestination. However, Calvin differed from Luther in his view of church–state relations, as Calvin believed the state should be subjected to the church. In Britain, despite Calvinist doctrines infiltrating into the *Thirty-Nine Articles*, the spirit of the Episcopalian system generally opposed it. Calvinism did gain a firm footing however, in the Nonconformist Churches, especially in Scotland. (*The Oxford Dictionary of the Christian Church*)

Cambridge Platonists The Cambridge Platonists were a group of influential philosophical divines who flourished at Cambridge between 1633 and 1688. Led by Benjamin Whichcote, principal disciples included Ralph Cudworth and John Norris. The Cambridge Platonists were educated as Puritans, but reacted against the Calvinist emphasis on the arbitrariness of divine sovereignty. They argued that ritual, church government or detailed dogmas are not essentials of Christianity, but rather that a Christian could choose whatever forms of religious organization were helpful. Because of their toleration of religious diversity, they were referred to as 'latitude men', but were often condemned as Unitarians (*q.v.*) or atheists because they stressed morality above dogma. (*New Encyclopaedia Britannica; The Oxford Dictionary of the Christian Church*)

Charles I, King of England (1600–49). Second son of James VI of Scotland and Anne of Denmark, Charles became heir apparent on the death of his brother Prince Henry in 1612. In 1614 James' quarrel with his second Parliament induced him to enter marriage negotiations with Philip III of Spain for his daughter the Infanta Maria; negotiations were broken off in 1618 and finally abandoned in 1624. His marriage was given urgency after the death of James I on 27 March 1625, and on 1 May of that year, following negotiations conducted by the Earl of Holland, Charles was married by proxy to Henrietta Maria, sister of Louis XIII, King of France. On 18 May of the same year Charles' first Parliament met in an atmosphere of war fever. Charles was prepared to promote the war with Spain, which the two Houses of Parliament so ardently desired, as revenge for the alliance's role in the deposition of Frederick, Elector Palatine, and the Electress, Elizabeth, Charles' favourite sister, eldest daughter of James I, from the Bohemian throne following the Battle of Prague of 8 November 1620. Foreign policy setbacks, including military disasters at Cadiz (1625) and the Isle of Rhé near La Rochelle, bedevilled his first three Parliaments (1625, 1626 and 1628–9). The Dissolution Parliament in March 1629 marked the beginning of eleven years' personal rule, during which he used forced loans and other unpalatable practices for revenue raising. These years saw a rapprochement with Spain abroad and the ascendancy of Archbishop Laud at home. Discontent culminated with the armed revolt of the Scots against Laud's ecclesiastical programme in the Bishops' War. Recalling Parliament, first the Short and then the Long Parliament in 1640, Charles forced through a series of bills for constitutional change. Civil War broke out in 1642, Charles surrendered to the Scots in 1646 and began parleying with various groups for his reinstatement. The Army intervened in 1648 and the Rump appointed a high court which found Charles guilty of treason. He was executed on 30 January 1649, a day that was commemorated by the anniversary ceremonies, to which White Kennett's sermon, Astell's subject in *An Impartial Enquiry*, belongs. (*DNB*)

Clarendon, Earl of, see **Hyde, Edward**.

Congregationalism The fundamental principles of Congregationalism rest on the belief in the independence and autonomy of each local church. It professes to represent the principle of democracy in Church government, as all members of the Church, being Christians, are 'priests unto God'. From the late sixteenth century in England,

Separatism began merging into Congregationalism, but the movement was driven underground by fear of persecution. However, the movement reemerged, with the Independents, as they were now being called, becoming leaders in the struggle against Charles I and William Laud. It was the Independents who ultimately formed the backbone of Oliver Cromwell's army. (*The Oxford Dictionary of the Christian Church*)

Cook, John (d. 1660). Regicide. Trained as a lawyer at Gray's Inn, he was appointed Solicitor-General by Parliament in 1649, to act as Prosecuter at the trial of King Charles I. As a reward for his services, he was made Chief Justice of Munster, in Ireland, and granted Irish lands. He was appointed a justice of the court of the upper bench of Ireland. However, following the Restoration, Cook was recalled to England to face his own trial and was executed in 1660. Cook's brief, *King Charles His Case: Or, An Appeal to All Rational Men, Concerning his Tryal at the High Court of Justice*, to which Astell refers in *An Impartial Enquiry* (p. 37), was published in several editions. (Dzelzainis, 1991; *DNB*; *British Biographical Archive*)

Cooper, Anthony Ashley (1621–83). Baron Ashley and first Earl of Shaftesbury. Born into a Dorsetshire gentry family, Cooper, following his education at Exeter College, Oxford, joined Lincoln's Inn in 1638, and in 1639 married Margaret Coventry, daughter of the Lord Keeper, which was to connect him to George Savile, Lord Halifax. By 1643, Cooper had become an avowed supporter of the Royalist cause and led horse and troop regiments in defence of Charles I in Weymouth and Dorchester. Cooper underwent a sudden change in allegiance however, and in January 1644 resigned all his commissions under the King and went over to the side of the Parliament, commanding parliamentary forces in Dorsetshire. In 1653 he was made MP for Wiltshire under Oliver Cromwell's Parliament, and served on the Council of State. Cooper initially supported Parliament's decision to hand over power to Cromwell, but when he realized that the Protector was disposed to rule alone, Cooper led the coalition of Presbyterians and republicans opposed to Cromwell in the 1656 Parliament. In December 1659 Cooper, now in command of the London forces, seized the Tower and persuaded the fleet to declare for Parliament. The Parliament was restored by the military and Cooper took his seat as MP for Downton, playing a leading role in obtaining the restitution of the excluded members, and planning the restoration of Prince Charles. Despite having fought against the King, Cooper was admitted to the Privy Council and received a formal pardon in 1660. He urged leniency for the regicides. In 1661, Cooper was raised to the peerage as Baron Ashley of Wimborne St Giles, and was appointed Chancellor of the Exchequer and Under-Treasurer. He took a liberal line against Clarendon's repressive measures, opposing the Act of Uniformity and the Militia Act. He also advised and supported Charles II in his first Declaration of Indulgence in 1662–3. With the fall of Clarendon, Cooper supported the more tolerant Buckingham and became a strong partisan of the scheme to legitimize Monmouth as the successor to the throne in 1670. In 1672 he approved Charles II's Declaration of Indulgence for Protestant Dissenters, and also in that year was made Earl of Shaftesbury and Baron Cooper of Pawlet, as well as Lord Chancellor. In 1673, Shaftesbury warmly supported the Test Act, which made it impossible for a Catholic to hold office. This Act led to the forced dismissal of several of the King's favourite ministers, a move which angered Charles. Shaftesbury then went even further and began his own course of anti-Catholic agitation. At the same time he urged prosecution of war against the Dutch, as rivals in trade and enemies of monarchy, in the famous *Delenda est Cathargo* speech, for which Locke 'had to stand at his elbow with the written copy as prompter' (*DNB*), and to which Astell refers contemptuously (*An Impartial Enquiry*, p. 41). In November 1673 Shaftesbury was dismissed and ordered to leave London. However, shortly afterwards Charles offered him large sums of money and honours to return. Shaftesbury refused these offers and instead placed himself at the head of the parliamentary opposition to the court. He began to excite popular feeling by loudly expressing fears of a Catholic rising. In 1674 he was dismissed from the Privy Council and ordered to leave London, but he continued to lead the agitation for the dissolution of Parliament. After refusing to leave London he was imprisoned in the Tower in 1677, and was only released after begging pardon in February 1678. In 1679 Shaftesbury supported the Exclusion Bill, to exclude James from the throne, and introduced the Habeas Corpus Act. He continued to support Monmouth's bid for the throne over that of James, and in 1681 was committed to the Tower on a charge of high treason. He was released the following year with the charge being dismissed by the Whig Grand Jury. However, he continued to plot against the King, and, hearing of further warrants for his arrest, fled to Holland in 1682, where he died the following year. (*DNB*)

Cooper, Anthony Ashley (1671–1713). Third Earl of Shaftesbury and moral philosopher. Grandson of the first Earl of Shaftesbury, he was elected member for Poole in King William's second Parliament in 1695. He became Earl of Shaftesbury in 1699 on his father's death, and attended the House of Lords regularly until William's death. Although his health limited his participation in political struggles, he was an ardent Whig. He did his best to influence elections and to support the war party. It was rumoured that William wanted to make him Secretary of State. His *Characteristics of Men, Manners, Opinions, and Times*, which first appeared in 1711 and was reprinted four times by 1773, indicates his religious scepticism. In this respect he revolted against the teachings of John Locke (see his contemptuous remarks in *Advice to an Author*, Part. III, Section 1) who had superintended his education. His most systematic work, *Inquiry concerning Virtue*, which was first published surreptitiously by the Deist John Toland, shows affinities to Cambridge Platonism, the work of Ralph Cudworth and Cumberland, and became the inspiration for the 'moral sense theories' of Francis Hutcheson, his follower. His work is marked by the cosmopolitanism, classical education and code of honour of his class. It attracted the criticism of Leland, Warburton, Bishop Berkeley and Mary Astell, whose *Bart'lemy Fair* is a virulent attack on Shaftesbury's *Letter concerning Enthusiasm* (1708), addressed to Lord Somers (whose name is not given), and occasioned by the 'French prophets' (1708). (*DNB*)

Cromwell, Oliver (1599–1658). English soldier, statesmen and Lord Protector of the Commonwealth. Born at Huntingdon, he was educated by enthusiastic and strongly anti-Catholic Calvinists at Sidney Sussex College, Cambridge. In 1628 he was elected as MP for Huntingdon to the Short Parliament, and gained a reputation in that brief three weeks by attacking Charles I's bishops for the importance they placed on rituals and episcopal authority. Around 1638, after a long period of religious depression, Cromwell 'was given to see light' (*DNB*) and became a religious enthusiast. In 1640 he gained a seat in the Long Parliament as MP for Cambridge. The following year he was one of the parliamentarians to present to Charles I a 'Grand Remonstrance', consisting of over 200 clauses, ranging from grievances over taxes and monopolies to pleas to censure the corrupt clergy. In 1642 when the King started to raise an army, Cromwell began to organize his own constituency to defend Cambridge. During 1643 he gained a reputation as a soldier and a military organizer and was able to convince the Commons to create a new army which would not only defend eastern England, but which would attack the enemy. In 1644, after an alliance had been concluded with the Scots, Cromwell was appointed to the Committee of Both Kingdoms, which assumed responsibility for the overall strategy of the Civil War. Once the war was over, however, the House of Commons wanted to disband the army as quickly as possible, and Cromwell tried, unsuccessfully, to reconcile the two sides. In the second round of the Civil War, launched by the Royalists now in league with the Scots in 1648, Cromwell led his men in successful battles in Wales, Northern England and Scotland. Following the execution of Charles I, Cromwell served as the first chairman of the Council of State, the executive body of a one-chamber Parliament. The first few years, however, were chiefly occupied by campaigns against the Royalists in Ireland and Scotland, and in the suppression of a rebellion by the extremist Puritan party, the Levellers, within the Commonwealth army. In 1649, as Commander-in-Chief and Lord Lieutenant of Ireland, Cromwell waged a ruthless military campaign against the Irish, in revenge for the massacre of English settlers eight years earlier. On his return to England in 1650 Cromwell led an army into Scotland where Charles II had been acknowledged as the new King. After a difficult battle the Scots were beaten, and the defeat, the following year, of Charles' army which had advanced into England, signalled the end of the Civil Wars. The army was once again unhappy with Parliament, arguing that it was corrupt, so Cromwell dissolved the Long Parliament in 1652 and nominated an assembly to take its place. However this 'Little Parliament' proved too hasty and radical and failed to consult Cromwell. In 1653 a *coup d'état* led by Major-General John Lambert forced the remaining members to surrender power into Cromwell's hands. Cromwell reluctantly accepted the title of Lord Protector, as he believed there was no other legally constituted authority left. Prior to his first Protectorate Parliament in 1654, Cromwell and his Council of State had passed over eighty ordinances, aimed at law reform, the establishment of a puritan church which would tolerate other religions, better education and decentralized administration. As a result, good judges were appointed both in England and Ireland and Cromwell recommended that murder, treason and rebellion be the only crimes punishable by death; committees known as Triers and Ejectors were established to oversee the conduct of the clergy and schoolmasters; Jews were readmitted; and grammar schools flourished. Also in 1654, Cromwell negotiated a successful end to the Anglo-Dutch War. Cromwell failed, however, to get unanimous recognition by the parliamentarians of the authority which had been conferred on him by the army, and was troubled by vociferous republicans. Around ninety of them refused to sign an engagement to be faithful to him and to Parliament, and even those who did sign continued to impose restrictions on provisions which Cromwell felt could not be compromised, such as his authority over the army, his veto over legislation and the amount of religious toleration guaranteed by the constitution. When in 1655, they delayed the vote of supplies for the army and navy, Cromwell quickly dissolved the Parliament. In response to the evidence of plots by the Levellers and Fifth Monarchy Men which emerged at this time, Cromwell divided the country into twelve divisions, each under the leadership of a major-general. A legal challenge to his authority led to the lawyers involved being sent to the Tower. In 1655 a proclamation was issued prohibiting the use of the prayerbook. Many hardships were inflicted on the ejected Anglican clergy, and several Anabaptist preachers were jailed. Despite this, religious toleration for those who were not antagonistic to Cromwell was greater than it had been before his reign. In 1655 Cromwell joined France in an alliance against the aggressively Catholic Spain. In order to raise money to continue the war with Spain Cromwell reluctantly convened his second Parliament in 1656. In 1657 a proposal for the revision of the constitution and the restoration of the monarchy was introduced. Parliament voted in favour of Cromwell taking the title of King, but as the army was deeply against the restoration of the monarchy, he refused. The title Lord Protector was then simply substituted for King, and Cromwell was a second time installed as Protector in 1657. However, the new constitution increased his powers extensively, and he was able to nominate his own successor as well as nominate members to the newly formed second chamber. More importantly, a fixed sum was allocated to the maintenance of the army and navy which made him largely independent of parliamentary subsidies. When Parliament met in 1658 however, the republican leaders refused to recognize the new House of Lords. With Charles II preparing to launch an attack on England, Cromwell was able to muster support against the external threat, and so overcome the domestic one, by dissolving his last Parliament. He died of fever later that year. After the Restoration Cromwell's embalmed remains were dug out of their tomb at Westminster Abbey. His head was impaled on a pole on top of Westminster Hall and his body was buried beneath the gallows at Tyburn. (*DNB; New Encyclopaedia Britannica*)

Cudworth, Ralph (1617–1688). Divine. Born in Somerset, he graduated from Emmanuel College, Cambridge, with an MA in 1639 and became a popular tutor. In 1645 he was appointed, by parliamentary authority, as head of Clare Hall and was unanimously elected to the regius professorship of Hebrew. In 1646 he graduated as BD, and became a leader of the Cambridge Platonists, noted for their open-mindedness on political questions. In 1647 Cudworth preached a sermon before the House of Commons protesting against the exaggerated importance the Puritans attributed to dogmatic differences. In 1650 Cudworth was presented to the college living of North Cadbury in Somerset, and was created DD in 1651. In 1654 he was elected master of Christ's College, Cambridge, and was one of the advisors on Walton's Polyglot Bible. In 1662 Cudworth was presented to the rectory of Ashwell in Hertfordshire, and was installed as the prebendary of Gloucester in 1678. He is known for originating the controversial theory of a 'plastic nature' to combat doctrines of chance and constant divine interference. His major works included *The True Intellectual System of the Universe* (1678), which refutes atheism, and a *Treatise concerning Eternal and Immutable Morality*, published posthumously in 1731, which is partly derived from Plato's work and which argues for the independence of the intellect upon sense. (*DNB*)

Davenant, Charles (1656–1714). Political economist. Obtained the degree of LLD by 'favour and money', and sat as an MP in the first Parliament of James II, and the 1698 and 1700 Parliaments of King William. He was also Commissioner of the Excise between 1678 and 1689. He wrote a large number of political tracts in which he attacked with some bitterness various ministerial abuses, and also the clergy. When on the accession of Queen Anne commissioners were appointed to treat for a union with Scotland in 1702, Davenant successfully applied to be their secretary. He continued to write political and economic tracts during Anne's reign, although with a different tone. In

1705 he was appointed Inspector-General of the Exports and Imports. His work, *Essays upon Peace at Home and War Abroad*, written in 1704, to which Mary Astell responded in her lengthy prefatory remarks to *Moderation truly Stated*, urged the necessity of all parties in the state uniting to carry on the great continental war. (*DNB*)

Defoe, Daniel (1661?–1731). Dissenter, journalist and novelist. Although he had undergone the theological and philosophical courses necessary to qualify him as a minister, he felt a career as a Dissenting minister was 'precarious and often degrading'. Defoe imbibed the political principles of his teachers and friends, joining in meetings to protect witnesses from intimidation during the Popish Plot, and joining William's army in 1688. He became prominent in the last years of William's reign as a writer in defence of the King's character and policy. Like the early Dissenters in general, he did not object to the Church establishment on principle. Rather, he steadily maintained the Church to be a necessary barrier against Popery and infidelity. He attacked the Jacobites in his writings, and was prosecuted for libel several times. Defoe wrote his 'An Academy for Women' in *An Essay upon Projects* (1697) in response to Astell's *A Serious Proposal*, and joins her in defending education for women, although charging her with promoting the cause of nunneries. As a central figure in the pamphlet warfare over Occasional Conformity, Defoe fired the opening shots with a series of pamphlets, among them *The Shortest Way with the Dissenters*, in which he had parodied the Tory 'high flyers' Charles Leslie and Henry Sacheverell. Their responses, that of Leslie in particular, suggested that he had not been wide of the mark, as he pointed out in *More Short-Ways with the Dissenters*, to which Astell herself responded with *A Fair Way with the Dissenters* (1704). Many of Astell's references to libellous 'scriblers' and party men would appear to be to Defoe. While serving a jail sentence for libelling the Church, Defoe started the *Review*, a regular periodical devoted to politics, which attracted vigorous debate from Charles Leslie in the *Rehearsal*, which commenced publication in 1704, and which provided the forum for a critique of John Locke, in many respects Defoe's mentor. From around 1718 he took less interest in political matters, but continued to write on many diverse topics. He published over 250 works including *Robinson Crusoe*. (*DNB*)

Descartes, René (1596–1650). French philosopher and mathematician. From the age of ten he spent eight years at a Jesuit College, where his outstanding aptitude for mathematics became evident. He remained a devout Catholic all his life. He served in the Dutch army until 1619, and then joined the army of Maximillian, Duke of Bavaria, for a further two years. After some European touring he settled in Holland for twenty years, and it was here he produced all his writings. Descartes is regarded as the father of modern philosophy, as he formulated basic philosophical concepts such as the relationships between mind and matter and between mathematical ideas and reality. Descartes, despite the boldness and originality of his thinking, was still a conformist. His *Discourse on Method*, while acclaimed intellectually, incurred the displeasure of both Catholic and Calvinistic ecclesiastical authorities. To allay suspicions of heterodoxy he published two editions of *Meditations on the First Philosophy*, apparently as a genuine attempt to provide a *modus vivendi* for science and religion. (*European Authors, 1000–1900*)

Devereux, Robert, third Earl of Essex (1591–1646). Parliamentary general and son of Robert, the second Earl and Frances Walsingham, widow of Sir Philip Sidney. His early and disastrous marriage to Frances Howard was arranged by the King, whose cause he did not completely desert until late in the piece, despite his disapproval of Charles' political and ecclesiastical proceedings. In August 1640 he had been one of the twelve peers to sign the petition drawn up by Pym and St John urging Charles to summon Parliament. When the Long Parliament met he numbered among the leaders of the opposition who were created Privy Councillors by Charles to win them over. On 4 July 1642, Essex became a member of the Parliamentary Committee of Safety and on 12 July was appointed General of the parliamentary army and declared a traitor by the King. He proved a lacklustre general, resigning his command in 1645. With his death without issue in 1646 the earldom became extinct. Clarendon's (*History*, I, p. 146) character sketch of Essex is disparaging, and Astell (*An Impartial Enquiry*, p. 31) follows him. (*DNB*; Clarendon's *History*, I)

Dissenters, see Nonconformists.

Dodwell, Henry (1641–1711). Scholar and theologian. Born in Dublin, he was educated at Trinity College, where he was elected scholar and later fellow of the college. However, in 1666 he was obliged to resign his fellowship when he refused to take holy orders. In 1688

Dodwell was appointed Camden professor of history at Oxford University, but was deprived of this position also in 1691 when he refused to take the Oath of Allegiance to William and Mary. In 1710, Dodwell decided to return to the established Church from which, as a nonjuror, he had been excluded. He died the following year. Dodwell was regarded as an excellent scholar and wrote on many diverse topics. His works included *Two Discourses against the Papists* (1676); the *Book of Schism*, a controversial piece which provoked opposing publications from Richard Baxter; and a treatise entitled *Against Occasional Communion* (1705). *(DNB)*

Doleman, R., see **Parsons, Robert**.

Dugdale, Sir William (1605–86). Historical author and state messenger. Born in Warwickshire, he was appointed a pursuivant (messenger of the state) in 1638. He accompanied Charles I to Oxford when it became the Royalist headquarters in October 1642, and received from the University the degree of MA. He was created Chester herald in 1644. In 1655 the first volume of his monumental work *Monasticon*, which contained a mass of information about the history and biography of English monarchism and of cathedrals and collegiate churches, was published. This was followed in 1656 by another major work entitled *Antiquities of Warwickshire*, and in 1658 by *The History of St Paul's Cathedral in London*. With the Restoration, Dugdale immediately resumed his heraldic functions with the blessing of the Crown. Yet another major work was published in 1675–6, *The Baronage of England: Or an Historical Account of the Lives and most Memorable Actions of our English Nobility*. He was made Garter king-of-arms and knighted in 1677. His *A Short View of the late Troubles in England*, published anonymously in 1681, was highly critical of anti-Royalists. *(DNB)*

Edwards, Thomas (1599–1647). Puritan divine and author of *Gangraena*. Educated at Cambridge University, he was referred to as the 'Young Luther', imprisoned for his outspoken views, recanted, but nevertheless found himself among those 'suppressed or suspended' by Laud. Permitted to preach again, he campaigned against 'popish innovations and Arminian tenets' and was prosecuted in the high commission court. Under parliamentary rule Edwards proved a zealous supporter, who also contributed money to the cause. He achieved real prominence in his crusade against the Independents, with the publication, in 1644, of *Antapologia: or a Full Answer to the Apologeticall Narration of Mr Goodwin, Mr Nye, Mr Sympson, Mr Burroughes, Mr Bridge, Members of the Assembly of Divines*; and the yet more virulent *Gangraena*, of 1646. The sheer venom of Edwards' attack produced a host of replies, among them tracts from John Lilburne, John Goodwin (author of the anonymous *Cretensis: Or A Briefe Answer to an Ulcerous Treatise ... intituled 'Gangraena'*) and Jeremiah Burroughes (*Vindication*, 1646). These prompted *The Second Part of Gangraena: Or a Fresh and Further Discovery of the Errours, Heresies, Blasphemies*, and another round of replies. To this Edwards responded with *The Third Part of Gangraena: Or a New and Higher Discovery of Errours*. Resentment by Independents, now the dominant party, was at this point so great that Edwards wisely retired to Holland where he promptly died from an ague. Edwards' *Gangraena* is frequently cited by Astell, who makes reference to his *Antapologia* as well. (*DNB*)

Engagement Controversy Controversy that raged around the secret treaty, or 'engagement', negotiated at Carisbrooke in 1647 between Charles I and commissioners representing the Scottish government. (*OED*)

Enthusiasm Dating at least from Spenser's *Shepherd's Calendar* (1579), the term retained its Greek meaning of possession by a God, supernatural inspiration, prophetic or poetic frenzy. In the seventeenth century it was applied more generally to the followers of Descartes and Cambridge Platonists and, by the eighteenth century, stood for what was deemed ill-regulated or misdirected religious emotion, extravagance of religious speculation or confidence in divine inspiration. So, Henry More, author of *Enthusiasmus triumphatus: or a Discourse* (1656), in *An Explanation of the Grand Mystery of Godliness* (1660) prophesied, 'If ever Christianity be exterminated, it will be by Enthusiasme', while Shaftesbury (1671–1713), in his *Characteristics* (1711), definitively declared (Section 7, 1.53) 'Inspiration is a real feeling of the Divine Presence, and Enthusiasm a false one.' Shaftesbury's earlier *Letter concerning Enthusiasm*, occasioned by the 'French Prophets' of 1708, clearly provoked Mary Astell, whose *Letters Concerning the Love of God* came under the broad rubric of Enthusiasm. Her *Bart'lemy Fair* (1709) is a stinging reply to what was a dangerous charge in London in this decade, inflamed and embarrassed by the appearance of French Protestant zealots it could not accommodate. (*OED*)

Essex, third Earl of, see **Devereux, Robert.**

Exclusion Crisis In 1679, when rumours of a Popish Plot were rife and anti-Catholic hysteria was at its height, a bill was introduced into Parliament to exclude Charles II's Catholic brother James, Duke of York, from the throne. Charles responded by co-opting the leading exclusionists, including the Earls of Shaftesbury, Halifax and Essex into his government and offering to safeguard the Church during his brother's reign. However, the House of Commons passed the Exclusion Bill, and Charles promptly dissolved Parliament. In the second Exclusion Parliament of 1679 the Commons again voted to bypass the Duke of York in favour of his daughter Mary and William of Orange, but this was rejected by the House of Lords. Parliament was again dissolved, as was the next Parliament, at Oxford in 1681, when the Exclusion Bill was reintroduced. However Charles II, whose finances had since improved due to a subsidy from his cousin Louis XIV and increasing trade revenues, was able to get by without calling another Parliament. He proceeded to remove his Whig opposition from their places of power, so that the Tories came to dominate London. In 1683 the Rye House Plot was revealed and resulted in leading Whigs being executed for their alleged plot to kill Charles. When Charles died unexpectedly in 1685, James acceded to the throne with no major protests. (*New Encyclopaedia Britannica*)

Filmer, Sir Robert (c.1595–1653). Political writer. Born in Kent, he was educated at Trinity College, Cambridge, and knighted by Charles I. Being a strong Royalist he suffered much during the Civil War, with his house being plundered several times, and being imprisoned in Leeds Castle in Kent in 1644. His major work *Patriarcha: Or The Natural Power of Kings Asserted* was not published until 1680. His political treatises defended patriarchal theory and attacked the social compact doctrine of Hobbes and others. Criticized by Locke, Filmer became noteworthy as a political philosopher because of his unusual efforts to preserve traditional values, especially the doctrine of the 'divine right of kings'. He argued that the notion of the divine right of kings was merely a modern manifestation of the biblical notion of the right of inheritance, as reflected in the Old Testament. (*DNB*; Kiernan, 1966)

Foulis, Henry (1638–69). Author. Graduated from Oxford University with a BA in 1656, and an MA in 1659. He took the degree of BD at Cambridge in 1667, becoming sub-rector of his college and attacked with equal venom the Presbyterians and Papists in his writings which included *The History of the Wicked Plots and Conspiracies of our Pretended Saints* and *The History of Romish Treasons*. Astell, citing the latter work in *Moderation truly Stated* (p. 63), gives her own biographical sketch of him: 'A Man who had his Education among Dissenters and consequently knew them better for that reason, and who is so far from having any good-will to Popery, that he has Writ one of the smartest Books against it.' Foulis is one of Astell's major sources for *An Impartial Enquiry*, pursuing a line of argument to which she was most sympathetic. In his *History of . . . our Pretended Saints* (p. 204), he observes, 'Thus of one hand, I find the great *Gustavus Adolphus*, highly applauded, but that he was a *Protestant*; and on the other, our Queen *Elizabeth*'s sister, Queen *Mary*, as greatly commended, but that she was a *Roman*-Catholick; yet, for either of these simply, aspersions are not to be cast upon Magistrates, or others, more inferiour.' (*DNB*)

Gassendi, Pierre (1592–1655). French philosopher. Born at Provence, France, he was educated at Digne and at Aix. At the age of twenty-one he was appointed professor of rhetoric at Digne. In 1614 he received a doctorate in theology at Avignon and was ordained as a Catholic priest in 1616. From 1617 to 1623 he was professor of philosophy at Aix. In 1634 he was elected provost of the Cathedral of Digne. In 1645 he was appointed professor of mathematics at the Royal College of Paris. Gassendi 'was a leading opponent of Descartes' and although his theological views were orthodox, he revived and championed the *materialist atomism* of Epicurus as a semi-scientific explanation of the working of the natural world'. Gassendi, by reintroducing to Europe the Epicurean doctrine that the highest moral good was to be sought in 'tranquillity of soul', also exerted a considerable influence on moral and political theory. (*The Encyclopedia of Philosophy*; Kiernan, 1966; *The Concise Encyclopedia of Western Philosophy and Philosophers*)

Grotius, Hugo (1583–1645). Dutch jurist, statesman, poet, theologian and historian. Grotius was an infant prodigy, mastering Latin and Greek by the age of twelve and graduating with a Doctor of Law degree from the University of Leyden at sixteen. He was appointed Historiographer of the States of Holland in 1599, and specialised in international law. From 1612 he was involved in an Erasmian project aimed at reuniting the Christian churches, and in 1613 visited England seeking support for this project. However, following the Synod of Dort (see Arminianism) in 1618, Grotius was arrested for his association with the Arminian delegates, whose views were antagonistic to the Calvinist theory of predestination. He was sentenced to life imprisonment, but escaped to France where he published his great treatise on international law, the *De jure belli ac pacis* in 1625. While in exile he received an irregular pension from Louis XIII before being appointed in 1634 as the Swedish ambassador to France. Grotius' main contribution to philosophy was his unequivocal defence of natural law as a rationally discernible set of principles binding on citizens, rulers and God alike. (*The Concise Encyclopedia of Western Philosophy*; Dzelazainis, 1991; Sommerville, 1991)

Hambden, John (as referred to by Mary Astell and the Earl of Clarendon), see Hampden, John.

Hamilton, James (1606–49), third Marquis and first Duke of Hamilton. After the descendants of James VI, the next in line to the throne of Scotland and, for that reason, used by Charles as his closest advisor on Scottish affairs and appointed commissioner for Scotland in 1638. When the Long Parliament met Hamilton was on good terms with the parliamentary leaders, who advocated alliance with Scotland, and fell out with the King, being reconciled only in 1642. In 1647 with the seizure of the King by the army and the Independents, the Scottish Parliament under Hamilton voted for intervention, leading a disastrous campaign, which resulted in his surrender, trial and execution. Clarendon (*History*, I, p. 119), said of him: 'The Marquis of *Hamilton*, if he had been then weigh'd in the Scales of the People's hatred, was at that time thought to be in greater danger than any one of the other; for he had more Enemies, and fewer Friends, in Court or Country, than any of the other. His interest in the King's affection was at least equal, and thought to be superior, to any man's; and he had receiv'd as invidious instances, and marks of those affections. He had more out-faced the Law in bold Projects and Pressures upon the People, than any other man durst have presumed to do, as especially in the projects of Wine and Iron.' (*DNB* and Clarendon, *History*)

Hampden, John (1594–1643). Statesman. Born in London, he matriculated from Magdalen College, Oxford, in 1610, and in 1613 studied at the Inner Temple. He is described in famous character sketches by Clarendon, in his *History* (I, p. 147; II, p. 205), Astell's source, as a wealthy Buckinghamshire squire, and believed to be a first cousin of Oliver Cromwell. From the beginning of Charles I's reign, Hampden associated himself with the opposition to the court both in and out of Parliament. In 1627 he was jailed for almost a year in Hampshire for failing to pay a forced loan. In the Parliament of 1621 he sat as the Member for Grampound, and in the first three Parliaments of Charles I he represented Wendover. He studied parliamentary law and was a member of nearly all the committees of importance in the third Parliament of Charles I. In 1637 Hampden brought a test case against the Crown over its levying of ship money. Although decided in favour of the Crown, the case resulted in a greater public reluctance to pay the tax, and increased Hampden's personal standing. Clarendon (*History*, I, p. 53) remarked of his accomplishment: 'it was at last (upon the refusal of a Private Gentleman to pay twenty or thirty Shillings as his share) with great solemnity publickly Argued before all the Judges of *England* in the Exchequer Chamber, and by much the major part of them, the King's right to Impose asserted, and the Tax adjudged Lawful; which Judgement proved of more advantage, and credit to the Gentleman condemn'd (*Mr Hambden*) than to the King's service'. Hampden represented Buckinghamshire in the Short Parliament of 1640 and led the opposition to the King's demand for twelve subsidies in exchange for the abandonment of ship money. Hampden was also very influential in the Long Parliament, where he was noted for his debating skills, and he zealously supported the Grand Remonstrance. He was one of the parliamentarians impeached along with Pym in 1642, on charges including encouraging the Scots to invade England and levying war against the King. They escaped before they could be arrested, however, and Hampden shortly afterwards moved a resolution giving control of the militia and the Tower to Parliament. When the King refused this demand, war became inevitable and Hampden was appointed as a leading member of the Committee of Safety to defend Parliament. Hampden worked to keep order among his unruly soldiers, and, determined not to settle for peace on unsatisfactory terms, resisted Charles' early overtures for peace. In 1643 he was mortally wounded in a skirmish with Prince Rupert near Oxford. (*DNB*; Clarendon, *History*; *New Encyclopaedia Britannica*)

Harrington, Sir James (1611–77). Political theorist. He devoted himself to study, taking no active part in the Civil War. He was made a groom of the bedchamber of Charles I, and accompanied Charles to the Isle of Wight where they discussed political and other questions. Although a republican in principle, he seems to have been attracted by Charles, and was shocked by his execution. Harrington returned to his studies and in 1656 produced the controversial *Commonwealth of Oceana*, which described his model of a commonwealth. In 1659 he formed the Rota Club for political discussions, but it was closed the following year when the Restoration became a certainty. In 1661 Harrington was committed to the Tower, but was later transferred to Plymouth where his health declined. (*DNB*)

Harrison, Thomas (1619–82). Nonconformist divine. Born in Yorkshire, he was taken by his parents to New England where he was trained as a minister. After being dismissed as chaplain to the Governor of Virginia, he returned to London where he gained some fame as a preacher. In 1657 he accompanied Henry Cromwell to Ireland, living with the Cromwell family and preaching at Christ Church, Dublin. At the Restoration he returned to England, preaching to large congregations in Chester until he was silenced by the Act of Uniformity. Following this, he went back to Dublin where he founded a flourishing Congregational (*q.v.*) church. He graduated as a DD but there is some doubt as to whether this was at Cambridge or Dublin. He was highly regarded as a preacher, and his writings include the publication of a sermon on the death of Oliver Cromwell, *Threni Hibernici, or Ireland Sympathizing with England and Scotland in a Sad Lamentation for the Loss of their Josiah*, preached at Christ Church, Dublin (London, 1659), to which Mary Astell refers in *An Impartial Enquiry* (p. 14). (*DNB*)

Hickes, George (1642–1715). Nonjuring bishop. Born near Thirsk, he was educated at Oxford University, gaining an MA from Lincoln College in 1665. The following year he was ordained as a priest and he tutored at Lincoln College until 1673. After travelling in Europe he returned to Oxford, receiving the degree of BD in 1675. In 1676 Hickes became chaplain to the Duke of Lauderdale, and accompanied the Duke, who was High Commissioner to Scotland, when he went to

Scotland. Hickes took the degree of DD in 1679, and was quickly promoted to chaplain to Charles II in December 1681, and Dean of Worcester in 1683. Hickes strongly opposed James II's 1687 Declaration of Indulgence, but retained his loyalty to the monarchy, and refusing to take the Oath of Allegiance to William and Mary in 1689, was deprived of office shortly afterwards. In May 1690 Hickes went into hiding, spending some time with White Kennett. In 1693 he went to St-Germain and was received by the exiled James II, who approved of his appointment as a suffragan to the nonjuring Archbishop Sancroft. Hickes cautiously reentered England where he was consecrated as Bishop of Thetford in 1694. Hickes remained in hiding until 1699 when proceedings against him were dropped, but he meanwhile wrote many pieces in defence of the nonjurors' position. In 1713 Hickes himself consecrated other nonjuring bishops in his own private chapel in St Andrew's Holborn. (*DNB*)

High Churchmen The term High Churchmen refers to that group within the Church of England which stresses its historical continuity with the Catholic Church. It places high importance on the authority of the Church, the claims of the episcopate and the nature of the Sacraments. Some of the earliest of the High Churchmen resisted the attacks of the Puritan reformers during the time of Elizabeth I. The actual term did not come into use until the late seventeenth century however, when Laud and others argued the doctrine of the divine right of kings. Those High Churchmen who were more eminent in piety and learning found their position compromised by the crowning of William III, most of them becoming nonjurors. Those who remained with the established Church were excluded from ecclesiastical preferment as tainted with Jacobitism, and largely fell into obscurity. (*The Oxford Dictionary of the Christian Church*)

Hoadly, Benjamin (1676–1761). Whig divine. Son of a New England pastor, though born in Kent, Hoadly was educated at Catherine Hall, Cambridge, where he worked as a college tutor until he took holy orders in 1701. His mentors were Bishop Compton of London, the only bishop in the Lords to sign the invitation to William of Orange in 1688, William Sherlock, Dean of St Paul's, and the Whig William Fleetwood (Bingham, 1947, 155). In 1703 Hoadly took part in the conformity controversy, strongly opposing the bill against Occasional Conformity on the grounds that occasional communion would lead to union. His treatise, the *Reasonableness of Conformity to the Church of England*, minimized doctrinal differences between conformists and Dissenters, a subject he debated with Edmund Calamy. In 1704 he obtained the rectory of St Peter-le-Poor in Broad Street, and the following year preached a famous sermon, *The Measures of Submission to the Civil Magistrate Consider'd*, before the Lord Mayor and aldermen in which he argued that the teaching of St Paul in Romans 13 'only amounted to a charge to obey rulers who governed for the good of their people'. This offended the High Church party, and led him into another war of words, this time with Atterbury, whose reply to Hoadly, we know from Ballard (*Memoirs of Several Ladies*, p. 387), he submitted to Astell for comment (see Introduction). Astell early divined that Hoadly was an important adversary. By 1709 he was known as a champion of the latitudinarians and the Whig party, campaigning against hereditary right and passive obedience in preparation for a Hanoverian succesion, and publishing a collection of twelve political works in support of 'revolution principles'. Following the Queen's death in 1715, he was made royal chaplain. In that same year he published a treatise which downplayed the power of the Church hierarchy and was rewarded by promotion to the bishopric of Bangor. In 1716 Hoadly published *A Preservative against the Principles and Practices of the Non-jurors both in Church and State*, in which he argued that a person's 'title to God's favour cannot depend upon his actual being or continuing in any particular method, but upon his real sincerity in the conduct of his conscience and of his own actions under it'. This doctrine, being a direct affront to the High Churchmen, was repeated in a sermon before King George I, and led to the 'Bangorian controversy', a bitter and prolific outpouring of publications, including several from Dr Sherlock. Hoadly was now in 'the highest favour at court', and in 1721, he was translated to Hereford. Here he wrote several letters condemning his old opponent, Atterbury, who faced a charge of high treason. For such calumnies Astell took the trouble to insert his name into the fourth edition of *Reflections upon Marriage* (p. 45), listing him among 'Advocates of Resistance'. In 1723, Hoadly was translated to the see of Salisbury and in 1734 to the rich see of Winchester, where he spent his remaining years. (*DNB*; Bingham, 1947)

Hobbes, Thomas (1588–1679). Philosopher. Born in Malmesbury, Wiltshire, Hobbes showed early talent in classical languages and was admitted to Magdalen Hall, Oxford, in 1602, graduating with a BA degree in 1608. There followed a period in which he was tutor to the Cavendishes in Derbyshire, during which he travelled abroad and perhaps met Paolo Sarpi, the Venetian. In 1623 Hobbes acted as amanuensis to Francis Bacon, providing a conduit for English scientific ideas to Sarpi and the Venetians. In 1629 his translation of Thucydides was published. His continental links were strengthened by sojourns abroad, and from 1635 he was associated with Mersenne, Gassendi and French philosophers in Paris, including Descartes, to whose *Meditations* Hobbes provided written *Objections*. In 1642 his *De cive* was published in Paris, where he sat out the Civil War, returning to England in 1652, a year after the publication of *Leviathan*. Hobbes was excluded from the court of the future Charles II from 1651 and from 1666 lived under the threat of prosecution for atheism, on which he wrote several works with the intention of exonorating himself. In 1679 he drafted a manuscript on the Exclusion Crisis for the third Earl of Devonshire's son, supporting a moderate Whig position. He died at Hardwick Hall in 1679. (*DNB; Leviathan*, ed. Richard Tuck, 1991)

Holland, first Earl of, see **Rich, Henry**.

Hooper, George (1640–1727). Bishop of Bath, Wells and, briefly, of St Asaph. Son of a Worcestershire gentleman, George Hooper was educated at Westminister, winning a King's scholarship to Christ Church College, Oxford. He graduated with a BA degree in 1660 and DD in 1677, having studied Hebrew, Syriac and Arabic under the renowned orientalist, Edward Pococke Hooper was reputed to be fluent in these tongues, as well as Greek and Latin, his fame as an antiquarian prompting Archbishop Selden to engage him as his chaplain. Upon the marriage of Princess Mary to the Prince of Orange, Hooper went with her to The Hague in 1677 as almoner, incurring the displeasure of the Prince, who leaned towards the Dissenters, by persuading the Princess to read Hooker and Eusebius. Hooper was twice offered, and twice declined, the Regius Professorship of Divinity at Oxford, was chaplain to Charles II in 1685, Dean of Canterbury in 1691, and prolocutor of the Lower House in 1701. In the same year he declined the primacy of Ireland, but accepted the see of St Asaph in 1703, resigning it in the same year in favour of his friend, the deprived Bishop Ken, to take the diocese of Bath and Wells, which he held until his death in 1727.

Hooper produced a number of historical and antiquarian works, ranging from contemporary Church–state relations, to a comparative study of 'Attic, Roman and Jewish' weights and measures, and studies of the controversy between Tertullian and Valentinian, including the *De Valentinianorum haeresi, quibus illius origo ex Aegyptiaca theologia deducitur* (1711). Among his numerous published sermons, many addressed to a royal or parliamentary audience, is to be found the commemorative sermon for Charles I, preached to the two Houses of Parliament on 31 January 1703/4, to which Astell elliptically refers in *An Impartial Inquiry* (p. 16). Astell's double-edged remarks about Hooper, in company with Binckes and Sherlock, preaching 'upon this Day such antiquated Truths as might have past upon the Nation in the Reign of K. *Charles* II. or in Monmouth's rebellion', were prescient, for Hooper went on, in 1706, to preach against the union of England and Scotland, to defend the cause of the Scottish Episcopal Church and to defend the relentless High Church Tory, Henry Sacheverell, against impeachment. (*DNB*)

Howe, John (1630–1705). Puritan divine. A graduate of Christ's College, Cambridge, his 'platonick tincture' was ascribed by Edmund Calamy to his knowledge of Cudworth and his long-standing friendship with Henry More. During his chaplaincy at Magdalen College, Oxford from 1652 to 1655, he was admitted on 'Catholic terms' to the President's church meeting. He faced the Presbyterian issue during his prelacy at Great Torrington, Devonshire, where his predecessor Lewis Stukely had been an Independent; and he acquitted himself well by conciliating the parties. At the instigation of a friend, and upon passing the challenge of preaching for two hours before Cromwell, Howe was made domestic chaplain to the Protector. Here, too, he was a moderate influence. After Cromwell's death Howe went back to Torrington, later publishing sermons from this period. In 1670 he left for Dublin as domestic chaplain to Viscount Massereene, of Antrim Castle, where he became an organizer of the Presbyterian movement in Northern Ireland. He moved to London in 1676 and in 1677 his tract on predestination written at the instigation of Robert Boyle, caused controversy. Howe was attacked as an Arminian by Theophilus Gale in the conclusion of his *Court of the Gentiles*, but defended by Andrew Marvell. Protestant feeling following the Popish Plot of 1680 led to renewed efforts to incorporate the Nonconformists. On 11 May 1680, Stillingfleet, then Dean of St Paul's, preached against schism, to which Howe replied, in the words of Stillingfleet, 'like a gentleman'. Calamy reports that Tillotson was reduced to tears by Howe's remonstrations. In 1685, following difficult years in which his followers were arrested, Howe moved to Utrecht, preaching there in the English church where Gilbert Burnet preached. He returned to London in May 1687, after James II's declaration for liberty of conscience, and after consulting with William of Orange but, despite pressure from James, refused to give Nonconformist sanction to the royal dispensing power. When asked by William Sherlock, then Master of the Temple, what he would do if offered the mastership, Howe delighted him by replying that he would take the post but turn over the emolument to the legal proprietor. In 1688 Howe headed the London Nonconformist ministers who welcomed William III. In the ensuing decade he worked for the amalgamation of Presbyterians and Congregationalists, effected in 1690 with wide acceptance of the 'heads of agreement', largely drafted by Howe and published the next year. Peace did not prevail for long, however, and the outbreak of a controversy between Tobias Crisp and Richard Baxter drew out Crisp's opponents, the Arminians and Socinians. Howe once again sought to conciliate, in 1694 and 1695 publishing tracts in the Socinian controversy. His participation in the controversy over Occasional Conformity, which he had urged as a friendly resort by Nonconformists to the parish churches for worship and the sacraments, began in 1701, when Sir Thomas Abney (1640–1722), Lord Mayor of London, an open Occasional Conformist and member of Howe's congregation, drew attention to the issue. Daniel Defoe, who opposed any conformity, had fired the first shots in the round with his pamphlet on the matter, *An Enquiry into the Occasional Conformity of Dissenters*, of 1698. In 1701 he reissued it with a new Preface to Howe, to which Howe responded, courteously as always. It is conjectured that when William III summoned Howe shortly before his death, it was to question him on this matter, as well as 'about his old master Oliver'. It is said that Howe approved the scheme of non-synodical Presbyterianism advocated by Edmund Calamy in his *Defence of Moderate Nonconformity* (1704), shortly before he died, 'quite worn out' from it all. (*DNB*)

Hyde, Edward (1609–74). First Earl of Clarendon. He obtained a BA at Oxford in 1626, began work as a barrister in 1633 and soon gained a good reputation. He began his political career as a member of the popular party. Church questions, however, soon led Hyde to separate himself from the popular party, and the King urged him to persist in the Church's defence. He opposed the Grand Remonstrance and composed the King's reply. With Falkland and Colepeper he managed the King's parliamentary affairs. He joined Charles I in York in 1642, and for three years drew up all his declarations, advising him to adhere to law and constitutional methods while refusing further concessions. He was expelled from the House of Commons in August 1642, but in the following spring he was admitted to the Privy Council and knighted, and soon after was appointed Chancellor of the Exchequer. He was prominent in negotiations between the King and Parliament, particularly at Uxbridge in January 1645, and refused real concessions while attempting to win over opposition leaders by personal offers. In December 1643 he recalled the Oxford Parliament as a counterpoise to that of Westminster. Hyde accompanied Prince Charles to Jersey, where Hyde remained when the Queen insisted that Prince Charles join her in France. While in Jersey Hyde began writing his *History of the Rebellion*, an authoritative source for Tory historians of the eighteenth century and frequently cited by Astell. Hyde clashed with the Queen on important issues such as her wish to give concessions to the Scots and plans to use foreign armies. Following the execution of Charles I, Hyde was retained by his son, Charles II, against the Queen's advice. He was made Lord Chancellor in January 1658, and both the Papists and Presbyterians petitioned for his removal. Hyde opposed concessions to Presbyterians, Romanists and isolated movements in England, but favoured negotiations with the Levellers. His aim throughout was to restore the monarchy, not just the King. As Chancellor and a member of the secret 'Committee of Six' he became the virtual head of government in 1660. In November of that year he was given the title of baron, and at the coronation in 1661 was further given the titles of Viscount Cornbury and Earl of Clarendon. Clarendon was opposed to severe treatment of Nonconformists, and pressed for the passing of the Act of Indemnity. He was however, firm in enforcing the Act of Uniformity in 1662. He had played important roles in the settlement of Scotland and Ireland, and was prominent in the establishment of a permanent system of administration for the colonies. Clarendon had, however, by 1667, succeeded in alienating not only the House of Commons and the courts, but also the King who was tired of his 'reproofs and remonstrances'. His opposition to the policy of toleration incensed the King. Charles II dismissed him as Chancellor in 1667, but Clarendon's enemies were not satisfied, and the House of Commons impeached him on seventeen counts, including one of high treason. After first protesting his innocence, Clarendon was forced to flee to France, where he died seven years later. (*DNB*)

Independents Members of the system of ecclesiastical polity in which each local congregation is believed to be a church independent of any external authority. The term independency prevailed in England in the seventeenth century, but was not favoured in New England, where the term for the same movement was Congregationalism. (*OED*)

Jacobites Those who supported James II and later, his son James III, as rightful heirs to the throne.

Johnson, Samuel (1649–1703). Whig divine. Born in Staffordshire or Warwickshire, he was educated at Trinity College, Cambridge, although he did not graduate. He took holy orders and was made rector of Corringham in Essex in 1670, and also domestic chaplain to Lord William Russell. In 1679 he preached a sermon against Popery, and in 1682 he published a work entitled *Julian the Apostate* which portrayed Popery as a modern paganism and which boldly argued against unconditional obedience on constitutional grounds. Following the discovery of the Rye House Plot, and Russell's execution, Johnson was imprisoned for this work, but he was released on payment of a fine. He continued to publish tracts against Popery, and in 1685 entered into a paper war with Sir Roger L'Estrange. In 1686 he published *An Humble and Hearty Address to all the English Protestants in the present Army*, which made a great impression, and led Calamy to observe that Johnson was thought by many to have done more towards paving the way for King William's revolution than any other. Johnson was again arrested, charged with great misdemeanours and condemned to be removed from the priesthood and publicly tortured. Despite this, he maintained his pamphlet agitation until the Revolution. In 1689 Parliament resolved that the judgement against him in 1686 had been illegal and cruel, and he was restored to the priesthood. He was however, disappointed in his hopes to obtain a bishopric, and survived on a pension from William. He expressed admiration for Mary Astell, who cited his works. (*DNB*)

Jones, Lady Catherine According to Bridget Hill's introduction (1986, 9), the Lady Catherine Jones Astell refers to is the daughter of the Earl of Ranelagh. She was prominent in court circles and entertained George I at Ranelagh Gardens in 1715. According to the *British Biographical Archive*, Catherine Boyle (d. 1691) married Arthur Jones, Viscount of Ranelagh, so becoming Lady Catherine Jones, the Countess of Ranelagh. These must have been Lady Catherine's parents, about whom little is known. Lady Catherine Jones, Mary Astell's patron, was the dedicatee of the correspondence between John Norris and Astell, the *Letters Concerning the Love of God*; and the addressee of Mary Astell's *magnum opus*, *The Christian Religion as Profess'd by a Daughter of the Church*. (DNB)

Kennett, White (1660–1728). Bishop of Peterborough and ecclesiastical biographer. Born in Dover, he graduated from Oxford University in 1684. Having taken holy orders he worked as a curate, and his dislike of James II's ecclesiastical policy soon modified his political views. He preached against Popery and openly supported the Revolution. He returned to Oxford as tutor and Vice-Principal of St Edmund Hall, and in 1691 was made a lecturer. He received a BD in 1694 and a DD in 1700. He acquired a reputation as a historian and antiquarian, topographer and philologist, and was known to Mary Astell, as she states, as 'a Writer in the Convocation Controversy' (*An Impartial Enquiry*, p. 3). In a sermon on 31 January 1703–4, Kennett stated that there had been some errors in the reign of Charles I, due to a 'popish' queen and a corrupt ministry, 'whose policy tended in the direction of an absolute tyranny'. This sermon was printed, with 'exaggerations corrected', in 1704, but it still elicited many angry replies from his High Church opponents, Mary Astell's being the most celebrated. In 1706 he published the third volume of a series of works on English history, *The Compleat History of England*. This exposed him to renewed attacks from his Jacobite enemies which only served to increase his popularity at court, and he was appointed chaplain in ordinary to Queen Anne. He became Bishop of Peterborough in 1718. (*DNB*)

latitudinarianism, see **Low Church**.

Laud, William (1573–1645). Archbishop of Canterbury. Born at Reading, he was educated at St John's College, Oxford, graduated with an MA in 1598, and was ordained as a priest in 1601. In 1606 he preached a sermon which contained Popish opinions, and with the general feeling of increasing antagonism to Calvinism, he was offered many preferments. In 1607 he became the vicar of Stanford in Northamptonshire, and in 1608 he graduated as DD and was made chaplain to Bishop Neile. In 1611 Laud was elected, despite opposition from the Calvinists at court, to the presidentship of St John's College. In 1614 Bishop Neile gave Laud the prebend of Buckden and, in 1615, the archdeaconry of Huntingdon. The following year James I promoted him to the deanery of Gloucester. In 1621 he was installed as prebendary of Westminster, and the King also gave him the bishopric of St David's. With the death of James in 1625, Laud's real predominance in the Church of England began. Shortly after his accession, Charles I asked Laud to recommend members of the clergy who were suitable for promotion, and Laud used this opportunity to remove his opponents. Laud magnified the King's authority in the state as well as in the Church, and by 1626 had come to be regarded by the House of Commons as hostile to civil liberty and religious truth. Charles, in his gratitude, nominated Laud as Bishop of Bath and Wells in 1626 and made him Dean of the Chapel Royal; appointed him as a Privy Councillor in 1627; and presented him with the bishopric of London in 1628. On Laud's advice, Charles, in 1628, prohibited controversial preaching and declared that all questions of the external policy of the Church were to be decided by convocation. When Parliament was dissolved the following year Laud came to dominate the ecclesiastical situation through his influence with Charles. In 1629 Laud was elected Chancellor of the University of Oxford, and was appointed Archbishop of Canterbury in 1633. In 1635 he was placed on the Commission of the Treasury and on the Committee of the Privy Council for Foreign Affairs. He continued to enforce strict conformity in ecclesiastical affairs, and in 1639 the first 'Bishops' War' erupted, with the Scots resorting to arms to resist his unwelcome religious innovations. For stressing the importance of decorating churches and separating the communion table from the congregation, both of which were reminiscent of Roman Catholicism, Laud was suspected by some of intending to facilitate a reunion with Rome. Although far from Laud's Arminian attitudes, any hint of such an intention was enough to unite the diverse elements of Protestant reform against the threat of Popery. Laud used the prolonged sittings of convocation in 1640 to pass a new body of canons expressing the doctrine of the divine right of kings, which implied that bearing arms against the King was an offence against God. By tying the establishment of his church system to absolutism in the state, however, Laud subjected himself to ridicule and hatred, and was forced to repeal the act. Shortly afterwards the House of Commons impeached Laud of treason and he was imprisoned in the Tower. After a lengthy trial, and in spite of a pardon by the King, Laud was beheaded in January 1645, still protesting the charge of the 'bringing in of popery'. (*DNB*; *New Encyclopaedia Britannica*)

Leslie, Charles (1650–1722). Nonjuror and pamphleteer. Born in Dublin, he graduated with an MA from Trinity College in 1673, studied law, and took holy orders in 1680. Through the good auspices of his patron, the Earl of Clarendon, he was made Chancellor of Connor in 1686. His loyalty to James II remained unshaken, and when he refused to take the oaths to William and Mary, he was removed from this post, finding employment as chaplain to Clarendon, and later officiating at Ely House, a magnet for nonjurors. In 1692 he commenced his series of controversial pamphlets in which he attacked the King, the Whig divines, Quakers, Deists, Jews and Dissenters. His *New Association of those Called Moderate-Church-man* (1702), is cited by Defoe in *A Brief Explanation of a Late Pamphlet* (1703) as one of the provocations which inspired Defoe's *The Shortest Way with the Dissenters* (1702), the work which began the round of pamphlet warfare on Dissent to which Astell contributed. Addressed to the pamphlet, *The Danger of Priestcraft to Religion and Government* (1702) by John Dennis (1657–1734), Leslie's *New Association* responds to Lockian ideas, inveighing against 'that *Whig-Principle* (strenuously Asserted in this *Pamphlet*) That all Men are Born *Free*' (Leslie, p. 10). Leslie's *Cassandra. Num. I* (1704–5), opens by declaring 'The Root and Foundation of all our *Republican Schemes*, and Pretences for *Rebellion* is this suppos'd Radical Power in the *People*, as of Erecting *Government* at the beginning, so to *Overturn* and *Change* it at their Pleasure.' In *The New Association, Part II* (1703), Supplement, p. 4, one of the first published critiques of the *Two Treatises* (1690), he makes arguments foreshadowed by Astell in the first edition of *Reflections upon Marriage* (1700) and made more explicit in her 1706 Preface. In Leslie's case these arguments are made with direct reference to 'The Great *L—k* [who] in his *Two Discourses of Government*, makes the *Consent* of every *Individual* Necessary.' So close were the views of Astell and Leslie on these matters that she was forced to subtitle her work *A Fair Way with the Dissenters and their Patrons* ...

Not Writ by Mr L—y, or any other Furious Jacobite, to ensure that it did not suffer the fate of *Moderation truly Stated*, taken to be the work of Leslie. In 1704 Leslie began publishing the periodical *The Rehearsal* in opposition to Defoe's *Review*, while continuing to carry on his 'ecclesiastico-political' warfare. A warrant was issued in 1710 for his arrest following the publication of a pamphlet which supposedly maintained that the Queen was a usurper. Leslie escaped to St-Germain in 1711, and in 1713 accepted a place in the Pretender's household at Bar-le-Duc. After the suppression of the rebellion, Leslie accompanied the Pretender to Avignon and Rome. Leslie tried to obtain a letter from the Pretender which would promise to maintain as inviolate the rights and privileges of the Church of England, should he be restored to the throne. In 1721 Leslie returned to Ireland where he died the following year. (*DNB*)

Lessius, Leonard (1554–1623). Jesuit theologian. A native of Brecht, he taught philosophy at Douay from 1574 to 1581, and at Louvain from 1585 to 1600. He played a prominent role in the theological controversies then raging on the nature of grace, and had many of his works censured. His principal work on the subject of grace was *De gratia effacaci*, published in 1610, and he also wrote extensively on moral theology. (*The Oxford Dictionary of the Christian Church*)

L'Estrange, Sir Roger (1616–1704). Tory journalist and pamphleteer. Born in Norfolk, he was an ardent Royalist and probably studied at Cambridge. In 1639 he accompanied Charles I and his army to Scotland. He planned to recapture the town of Lynn, which had fallen to the parliamentarians, but was betrayed, arrested and jailed for four years. On his release in 1648 L'Estrange went to Kent and began planning a Royalist uprising. The Royalists in London, however, viewed his impetuous actions unfavourably, and he found it 'politic' to flee to Holland. While abroad, it seems he was employed by Clarendon in the service of Charles II. He returned to England in 1653, and published attacks on Lambert and the leaders of the army in 1659, wrote pro-monarchy pamphlets in 1660 and, in 1661–2, blamed the Presbyterians for the Civil War and for Charles I's death. He also advocated a more stringent censorship of the press, and in 1663 his loyalty to the Crown was finally rewarded. He was appointed first surveyor of the printing presses and a licenser of the press. In this capacity, in 1663, he drew up a list of seditious works, approved by the King and later the basis for the burning of the books at Oxford, 21 July 1683. Among the grounds for sedition were Whig distinctions between 'the king's two bodies', which would allow resistance to the 'person', but not to his authority (Schwoerer, 1993). L'Estrange also published his own period-icals, the *Intelligencer* and *The News* between 1663 and 1666. In 1679 he published pamphlets attacking Shaftesbury for his criticisms of Charles II and his government. By examining the evidence for the Popish Plot, L'Estrange brought suspicion upon himself and he fled England. On his return in 1681, he again continued with his attacks on the Dissenters and Whigs in his periodical *The Observator* and James II acknowledged his services. He was elected MP for Winchester in March 1684–5, and was knighted in April 1685. However, with the Revolution he was deprived of his office of licenser, and imprisoned briefly in 1688 and 1691, and again for fourteen months in 1695–6. (*DNB*; Schwoerer, 1993)

Levellers The Levellers, led by the charismatic John Lilburne, were the first democratic political movement in modern history, urging the adoption of a new compact between ruler and ruled. In 1647 they drafted the first of three versions of an Agreement of the People, which called for the reform of Parliament through elections based upon a broad franchise, and the frequent sittings of Parliament for fixed terms. The Levellers also wanted radical reform of the Church, with the com-plete disestablishment of the Church, the abolition of the tithes which supported parish ministers and complete freedom of conscience and worship. Law reform was also on their agenda, as they made the follow-ing demands: that the law be equal for all; that court proceedings be performed in English rather than Latin or Norman-French; that there be no imprisonment for debt; and that capital punishment be abolished for comparatively petty thefts. They were influential amongst the rank and file of the parliamentary army and in the journeymen and craftsmen of London. In 1647 the Levellers' ideas were debated in the General Council of the Army. Cromwell and the conservative officers rejected their pleas, and two mutinies, one in 1647 and a more serious one in 1649, were sternly repressed by Cromwell. The Leveller movement never recovered from this defeat. (Smith, 1984; *New Encyclopaedia Britannica*)

Lilly, William (1602–81). Astrologer. Born in Leicestershire, he obtained work in London as a domestic servant in 1620. He first turned his attention to astrology in 1632, and went on to teach it and publish almanacs. When a rival almanac-maker who happened to be a staunch Royalist criticized his works in 1645, Lilly promptly became a parliamentarian, 'in order to answer him with better effect'. The argument was continued in the many pamphlets that were published by them in 1647 and subsequent years. In 1651 Lilly published his *Monarchy and no Monarchy*, in which he asserted that 'England should no more be governed by a king.' At the Restoration, Lilly was taken into custody, and was thoroughly examined by a committee of the House of Commons about his knowledge of the details of Charles I's execution. Although freed, he was directed to attend the trials of many of the regicides. (*DNB*)

Locke, John (1632–1704). Philosopher. Born in Somerset, he was educated at Christ Church, Oxford, where he obtained an MA in 1658. He was appointed lecturer on Greek in 1660, lecturer on rhetoric in 1662 and censor of moral philosophy in 1663. Locke rejected both Aristotelian philosophy, then dominant at Oxford, and the Puritan dogmatism of his upbringing. From his *Essay on the Roman Republic*, written around 1666, and the *Essay on Toleration*, written in 1667 but published only in 1690, we know that Locke was almost as anticlerical as Thomas Hobbes, admiring the civic religion of Rome and advocating the toleration of all religions. Most of his friends had Royalist sympathies. In 1666 Locke took up residence with his Oxford acquaintance, Ashley Cooper, and his family. He acted as Ashley Cooper's physician as well as managing his affairs. Cooper, created first Earl of Shaftesbury in 1672 and Lord Chancellor later in the same year, made Locke Secretary of Presentations, responsible for Church affairs under the Chancellor's care and required to appear with him on state occasions. It was in this capacity that he assisted Shaftesbury on the occasion of his famous speech *Delenda est Cathargo*, reported by Mary Astell (*An Impartial Enquiry*, p. 41). In 1673, Locke became Secretary to the reconstructed Council of Trade until it was dissolved in 1674–5, when Locke went to France, returning to Shaftesbury's service in 1679. Locke's *Two Treatises of Government*, written between 1679 and 1681, constantly revised and secretly guarded until their release was safe after 1689, belong to this period. With Shaftesbury's dismissal in 1680 and his escape to Holland in 1682, Locke found himself implicated in Shaftesbury's plotting, and he was expelled from England in 1683. Living quietly in Holland under the threat of extradition, Locke became associated with Limborch, the Amsterdam theologian, and Le Clerc, later his biographer. He returned to England after the 1688 Revolution and accepted William III's offer to become Commissioner of Appeals, a post he held till his death. In 1691 he went to live in the household of Sir Francis and Damaris Masham, in Essex. His work *An Essay Concerning Human Understanding* was published in 1690 and Locke immediately became the leading philosopher of his time. (Astell makes reference to vol. II, Chapter 33, 'On the Association of Ideas', in *An Impartial Enquiry*, p. 40, to refute Kennett.) *Two Treatises of Government*, followed in the same year, canonizing Whig political theory for the next century. In 1695 Locke's *Reasonableness of Christianity* was published and attacked by John Edwards and John Norris, Astell's patron, among others. Locke replied to both Edwards and Norris, the first at length in *A Vindication of the Reasonableness of Christianity* , *etc., from Mr Edwards Reflections* (1695), the second briefly in *Remarks Upon Some of Mr. Norris's Books, Where he Asserts P. Malebranche's Opinion of Seeing All Things in God*, written in 1693. The debates which Locke's religious writings instigated occasioned Astell's magnum opus, *The Christian Religion*. In 1696 Locke was appointed member of a new Council of Trade on which he worked diligently until poor health forced his retirement in 1700. He wrote little else before his death in 1704. (*DNB*; Laslett edn of Locke's *Two Treatises*, 1988)

Low Church This term refers to the group within the Church of England which placed little importance on the claims of the episcopate, priesthood and sacraments. The beliefs of Low Churchmen generally approximated to those of Protestant Nonconformists. The term dates from the early eighteenth century, but was originally used to refer to the latitudinarian or liberal group within the Church of England. (*The Oxford Dictionary of the Christian Church*)

Major, John (1469–1550). Historian and Scholastic divine. Born in Scotland, he studied at Cambridge and in 1493 went to the University of Paris where he obtained an MA in 1496. He taught in arts and Scholastic philosophy there, and graduated as DD in 1505. He then lectured in Scholastic divinity at the Sorbonne before returning to Scotland in 1518 to occupy the post of principal regent or professor of philosophy and divinity at the University of Glasgow.

In 1521 his *History of Greater Britain, both England and Scotland*, was published; the first history of Scotland written in a critical spirit. In it he strongly advocates the union of the two kingdoms. In 1522 Major moved to the University of St Andrews where he taught logic and theology. In 1525 he returned to the University of Paris, where he did much writing, including a commentary on the four gospels which attacked the heresy of Lutheranism. He was highly regarded as 'the prince of Paris divines'. In 1531 he returned to St Andrews and was made Provost of St Salvator's College in 1533. Here he lectured in theology, taking little or no part in the events that preceded the Scottish Reformation. Major was a liberal in politics and as a churchman, he strongly maintained Gallician principles. He urged the reform of ecclesiastical abuses, but held fast to the doctrinal system of Rome. (*DNB*)

Malebranche, Nicolas (1638–1715). French philosopher. Born in Paris, he completed an arts degree before studying theology at the Sorbonne. In 1660 he entered the Oratory, and was ordained in this congregation in 1664. He spent his life in meditation and in writing. While the Platonist orientation of his congregation depended in large measure on St Augustine, Malebranche strongly integrated this patristic doctrine with the scientific ideas of Descartes. Malebranche's doctrine centred on a theory of reason as immutable and eternal and part of God's wisdom. Thus, Malebranche argued that reason is superior even to faith, as faith will pass. He believed that God, as part of the rational universe, is revealed by knowledge. (*European Authors, 1000–1900*)

Mancini, Hortense (1646–99). Duchess of Mazarin. Born in Rome, Hortense was the fourth daughter of Lorenzo Mancini, and apparently the favourite niece of Cardinal Mazarin. She went to Paris where she attracted much attention for her beauty. The Cardinal arranged her marriage to the Duc de Meilleraye, insisting that in return for an enormous fortune, the Duc must assume the name of Mazarin. The marriage however, was not a happy one, and she fled disguised as a man. In 1675 she accompanied the Duchess of York to England. King Charles II admired her greatly, and possibly even considered marrying her. But Hortense was so charmed by the Prince de Monaco, then in England, that Charles angrily suspended temporarily the pension he had provided for her. William III continued her allowance, however, and she lived a comfortable life of exile in Chelsea where she stayed till her death. She amused herself by playing bassette and hosting dinners for her aristocratic literary circle of friends. Her celebrated divorce produced a spate of publications in defence of both parties, mostly ghosted and of uncertain provenance. It was this divorce literature that prompted Mary Astell's *Reflections upon Marriage*, as she freely confesses (1706, Preface, pp. i, 1). (*British Biographical Archive*; Hill, 1986)

Mariana, Juan de (1536–1624). Spanish Jesuit. Within seven years of joining the order in 1554, Mariana was a professor at the College of Rome, as a New Testament scholar. He taught also in Sicily, and Paris, where he lectured on Aquinas, before retiring to Toledo for health reasons where he lived and wrote for fifty years. Among his numerous works is a History of Spain in twenty-five books (1592), later expanded to thirty (1603), which won him the title of 'the Spanish Livy'. Mariana earned notoriety for his bold defence of popular sovereignty and the right to resist in *De rege et regis institutione libri tres* (1599). It is this work to which Astell (*An Impartial Enquiry*, p. 28), following Foulis (*History of the Romish Treasons*, pp. 80–1), makes reference. Mariana's attack on the changes to the coinage proposed by Philip III earned him imprisonment. The Italian edition (1628) of his account of *Errors in the Government of the Jesuits*, which appeared in French in 1624, was placed on the Index. (*The New Schaff-Herzog Encyclopedia of Religious Knowledge*)

Masham, Lady Damaris (1658–1708). Theological writer. Born at Cambridge, daughter of Ralph Cudworth, she was educated under his care. About 1682 she became acquainted with John Locke, and under his direction studied divinity and philosophy. In 1685 she married Sir Francis Masham, third Baronet, of Oates, Essex. In 1690 John Norris, the English Platonist, dedicated to Masham his *Christian Blessedness, Or Discourses upon the Beatitudes of our Lord and Saviour Jesus Christ*, to which Norris' critique of Locke, 'Cursory Reflections upon a Book Called, An Essay Concerning Human Understanding' was ironically appended. Masham and Norris remained on friendly personal terms until 1691 when John Locke came to live with the Mashams at Oates, but in the controversy occasioned by the publication of Locke's *Reasonableness of Christianity*, Lady Masham supported Locke's views and broke with Norris. In 1696 she published, anonymously, *A Discourse Concerning the Love of God*, directed at Norris' criticisms of Locke and sharply critical of the Astell–Norris correspondence published as *Letters Concerning the Love of God* (1695). It also answered some theories put forward by Norris and Mary Astell in Norris' *Practical Discourses on Some Divine Subjects* (1691). Mary Astell replied to this work in *The Christian Religion* (1705). Around 1700 Lady Masham wrote *Occasional Thoughts in Reference to a Vertuous or Christian Life*, published in 1705, in which she appealed to women 'to study intelligently the grounds of their religious belief'. (*DNB*; Perry, 1986, p. 91)

Mazarin, Duchess of, see **Mancini, Hortense**.

Milton, John (1608–74). Poet. Born in London, he graduated with an MA from Cambridge University in 1632. Although he had been educated with a view to taking orders, Milton was alienated by the Church policy which became dominant under Laud and worked instead as a teacher. In 1641 Milton produced three pamphlets which vehemently attacked episcopacy on historical grounds. He took no active part in the Civil War, and in 1643 married a seventeen-year-old girl. The marriage only lasted one month, however, and led Milton to write on the need for divorce, which angered the clergy and gained him much notoriety. In 1647 Milton gave up teaching to concentrate on writing. He continued his work on the *History of Britain*, but was recalled to public affairs by the events which led to the execution of Charles I. His *Tenure of Kings and Magistrates*, which argued in favour of the right of the people to judge their rulers, appeared immediately after the King's death. The newly formed Council of State promptly invited Milton to become their Latin Secretary. Despite his eyesight failing in 1650, he continued this work, with assistance, until the Restoration. Pamphlets written by Milton in this period show that he was inclined towards a strict republicanism, favouring a complete separation between the Church and the state, and the permanent rule of the Chiefs of the Army and the Council. In 1650 Milton was commissioned to write a reply to Salmasius' attack on those who were responsible for the King's death. In 1660 Milton was arrested for this work, entitled *Pro populo Anglicano defensio*, but was relieved of his fines by the Indemnity Act. Between 1658 and 1663 he wrote his most famous work, *Paradise Lost*, and in 1671 one of his last poems *Paradise Regained*, was published. He died of gout in 1674, and is regarded as one of the greatest English poets. (*DNB*; Filmer, *Patriarcha*).

Montagu, Lady Mary Wortley (1689–1762). Writer. Lady Mary demonstrated her intellectual abilities at an early age and is thought to have taught herself Latin. She was encouraged by, amongst others, Bishop Burnet, to whom she submitted a translation of Epictetus' *Encheiridion* in 1710. She entered into correspondence with Edward Wortley Montagu, MP for Huntingdon, and brother of her friend Anne, who became a keen suitor. When Lady Mary's father, Lord Kingston, rejected Edward's proposal for his daughter's hand, Lady Mary went against her father's orders and married Montagu. In 1714 Montagu's cousin Charles Montagu (Lord Halifax), was made First Lord of the Treasury in George I's ministry, and Montagu was appointed Commissioner of the Treasury. Lady Mary was popular at court and became well known to all the wits, including Pope. With the death of Halifax the following year, Montagu lost his position, and was made ambassador to Constantinople in 1716. Lady Mary, while in Adrianople with her husband, noticed the practice of inoculation against smallpox, and introduced this custom to England on her return in 1718. Lady Mary became a leader in London society, her *Letters* revealing a keen appetite for the scandal of the times. She continued her correspondence with Pope, who confessed his adoration, but her rejection of his love led him to publish several attacks upon her character. In 1739 she travelled unaccompanied to Europe, although her reasons for doing so are not known. In 1758 she settled in Venice, but returned to England on her husband's death in 1761. Lady Mary died the following year. Her published works included *Town Eclogues*, privately published as *Court Poems* in 1716, and *Letters from the East*, for which Mary Astell wrote a Preface in 1724, but which were not published until 1763. (*DNB*)

Morton, Charles (1627–98). Puritan divine. Born in Cornwall, he graduated with an MA from Oxford University in 1652 and was also incorporated at Cambridge University in 1653. His sympathies were originally with the Royalist views of his grandfather, but he reconsidered his opinion on discovering that the laxest members of the University were attracted to that side, and became a Puritan. In 1655 Morton was appointed to a rectory in Cornwall, but was ejected with the Act of Uniformity in 1662. After spending some years in London he went to Stoke Newington, the chief school of the Dissenters, to teach and Defoe was one of his pupils. Samuel Wesley, one of his students, in *Letter from a Country Divine* (1703, p. 7), records the use of scientific method and the presence of 'air-pumps, thermometers, and all sorts of mathematical instruments' at Newington Green Academy. Morton, upset by the processes of the bishops' court, took his family to New England in 1686. He was made Vice-President of Harvard College, where his *Compendium Physicae* and *The Spirit of Man* (1693) remained on the curriculum for many years. The first was a work that introduced the findings of Descartes, Gassendi, Harvey, Newton and Boyle to students. Philosophy lectures given in his own rooms offended the governing body and he was requested to refrain from giving them. In 1686 he was solemnly inducted as a minister of the first church in Charlestown, New England, and he died there in 1698. (*DNB*; Backscheider, 1989, 13–20)

Nalson, John (1638?–86). Historian and Royalist pamphleteer. Possibly educated at Cambridge, he took holy orders and became rector of Doddington in the Isle of Ely. In 1678 he took the degree of LLD. He was an active pro-government polemical writer during the latter part of the reign of Charles II, and wrote several treatises vindicating the King's prerogative in Church and state against the aspersions of the Dissenters. Although jailed for a month in 1678 for one such pamphlet, he continued to write. He was made prebend at Ely in 1680, and died there six years later. (*DNB*)

Nicholls, William (1664–1712). English divine. Born in Buckinghamshire, he was educated at Magdalen Hall, Oxford, graduated with a BA degree from Wadham College, was admitted as a probationer-fellow of Merton college in October 1684 and completed his degree of MA there in 1688. About that time he entered into holy orders, became chaplain to Ralph, Earl of Montagu, became rector of Selsey, near Chichester in Sussex, in 1691, was admitted as a BD in 1692 and a DD in 1695. It appears from a letter he wrote to Robert Harley, Earl of Oxford, that he was disappointed that he did not receive, as promised by the Queen, the prebend of Westminster. He also complained to Oxford that he was 'forced on the drudgery of being the editor of Mr. Selden's books for a little money'. He wrote around twenty major works, which included his *magnum opus*, the *Comment on the Book of the Common Prayer, and Administration of the Sacraments* (1710); *Defensio Ecclesiae Anglicanae* (in English and Latin, 1707, 1708); and *The Duty of Inferiours towards their Superiours, in Five Practical Discourses* (1701).

This work discussed the duties of subjects to their princes; of children to their parents; of servants to their masters; of wives to their husbands; and of parishoners and the laity to their pastors and clergy, attacking Hobbes and Hobbists, among others who would deny natural hierarchies. Internal evidence would suggest it to be the source for Astell's comments in *Reflections upon Marriage* (as Hill, 1986, 71, observes), but the date seems too late for the first edition, where the remarks also appear. (*DNB*; *British Biographical Archive*)

Nonconformists The word Nonconformist was first used in the penal Acts following the Restoration of the monarchy in 1660. It is a term which was used to denote any English Protestant who did not conform to the doctrines or practices of the established Church of England. Hence, it was generally applied in England and Wales to describe any Protestants who had dissented from Anglicanism, or Dissenters, such as Baptists, Congregationalists, Presbyterians and Unitarians, and also to independent groups such as the Quakers. (*New Encyclopaedia Britannica*)

nonjurors The term nonjurors refers to those churchmen who refused to take the Oaths of Allegiance to William and Mary after the Revolution of 1688, because they had previously taken similar oaths to James II. Even the death of James II in 1701 did not release them from their obligation as they had sworn to be faithful not just to James II, but also to 'his heirs and lawful successors'. An Act of Settlement was passed soon after William's accession, which required the nonjurors 'to abjure the pretended Prince of Wales', whom they believed was the lawful heir of James II, and to acknowledge William III and each of his successors. The Oath of Allegiance was altered, with the words 'rightful and lawful' being omitted, so that those who were not willing to recognize the new sovereigns as *de jure* rulers, could at least acknowledge them as *de facto* sovereigns. Anyone who refused to take this altered oath was deprived of his post, whether lay or clerical. Only Archbishop Sancroft, five bishops and around four hundred clergy chose to do so. However, there is another characteristic which the nonjurors shared. Nonjurors also insisted on the independence of the Church from the monarchy and/or state in matters of spiritual authority. Hence, by excluding nonjuring bishops from practising, and replacing them with bishops appointed by the civil power, the monarchy had intervened in an area which it had no right to intervene in, and the schism within the Church of England was formed. By denying the monarch's divine and indefeasible right, however, the nonjurors made themselves susceptible to claims that they were in fact Papists. Such claims were incorrect however, as non-jurors were uncompromising opponents of Romanism. (Overton, 1903)

Norris, John (1657–1711). Divine. Born in Wiltshire, he graduated from Exeter College, Oxford, in 1680. Described as an excellent scholar, he was a student of Platonism, and soon became a prolific author. He was a decided churchman, opposed to both Whigs and Nonconformists. He obtained an MA in 1684, and was soon afterwards ordained. In 1692 he became rector of Bemerton, near Salisbury. He attacked the Quakers for their 'gross notion' of the inner light, criticized Locke's *Essay Concerning Human Understanding* (1690), and corresponded with Mary Astell and Damaris Masham. At his instigation his correspondence with Astell was published under the title, *Letters Concerning the Love of God* (1695), attracting a critical response from Lady Masham in her anonymous, *A Discourse Concerning the Love of God* (1696). His major work, *Essay Towards the Theory of an Ideal and Intelligible World* was published in two volumes in 1701 and 1704. Norris was a disciple of Malebranche, expounding the doctrine of the vision of all things in God, and refuting the philosophy of Locke. His views attracted a written response from Locke in two works, *An Examination of P. Malebranche's Opinion of Seeing All Things in God*, written about 1694–5, and *Remarks Upon Some of Mr Norris's Books Where he Asserts P. Malebranche's Opinion . . .* In the latter Locke briefly scrutinized Norris' 'Cursory Reflections Upon a Book Called, An Essay Concerning Human Understanding', appended by Norris to his *Christian Blessedness: Or Discourses upon the Beatitudes* (1690); and *Reason and Religion: Or, the Grounds and Measures of Devotion* (1689). (*DNB*)

Occasional Conformity Occasional Conformity was a practice adopted to circumvent the restrictions placed on Nonconformists. It involved Nonconformists attending an Anglican service once a year and receiving a certificate of attendance from the vicar, which then qualified them for public office. In the Parliament of 1702–5 three Occasional Conformity Bills were introduced by the High Tory commoners, but all were defeated. It was not until the Tories gained power in 1711 that the Occasional Conformity Act, which forbade the practice, was passed. The Act was later repealed by the Whig-dominated Parliament in 1719. (Hill, 1986; Worden, 1986; *New Encyclopaedia Britannica*)

Owen, James (1654–1706). Presbyterian minister. Born in Carmarthenshire, Wales, he was grounded in classics by James Picton, a Quaker. About 1672 he took a course in philosophy and, although he looked forward to the ministry, was undecided about conforming. He finally decided in favour of Nonconformity, and in 1676 he became a chaplain in Shropshire. He took charge of a Nonconformist congregation at Oswestry, and from here travelled to North Wales to give monthly lectures. He was ordained by presbyters in 1677, and in 1690, with the help of money from the London Presbyterian fund, established an academy for training students for the ministry at Oswestry. In 1700 he became minister of High Street Chapel, Shrewsbury, where he continued his academy. His works include a pamphlet written in defence of Occasional Conformity in 1703 entitled *Moderation a Vertue*, to which Mary Astell responded with her *Moderation truly Stated* (1704), at twice the length. Owen replied to a number of his critics, making reference to Astell among them, in his Preface to *Moderation still a Virtue* (1704), to which Astell once again replied in the Postscript to *A Fair Way with the Dissenters* (1704). (*DNB*)

Owen, John (1616–83), Independent divine and theologian. From an old Welsh family, he graduated as DD from Queen's College, Oxford, in 1653, having studied classics, mathematics, philosophy, Hebrew and rabbinical lore. He left the University in 1637 rather than submit to Laud's new statutes, preferring private chaplaincy. In 1643 he launched a trenchant polemic against Arminianism with two tracts (*Theomachia autexousiastike: Or a Display of Arminianism, Being the Discovery of the Old Pelagian Idol. Freewill and the new Goddess Contingency* and *The Duty of Pastors and People Distinguished*). After a thorough investigation of the Primitive Church, he settled for Independency, and covenanted with the House of Lords for the vicarage of Coggeshall, which he ran on Congregationalist lines. In 1648 he resumed his polemic against Arminianism, drawing the criticism of Richard Baxter. Owen became famous for his thanksgiving sermons, preached after victories for the Parliament, beginning with the sermon celebrating the surrender of Colchester to Sir Thomas Fairfax of 27 August 1648, and including the famous sermon of 24 October 1651, celebrating the destruction of the Scots army at Worcester, to which Astell refers in *A Fair Way with the Dissenters* (p. 10). (*DNB*)

Parsons, Robert (1546–1610). Jesuit missionary and controversialist. Born in Somerset, he graduated with an MA from Balliol College, Oxford, in 1572. In 1574 he was made Dean, but shortly afterwards he resigned his fellowship and quit Oxford, travelling to Louvain where he was received into the Roman Catholic Church, going on to study medicine in Padua and becoming a Jesuit in 1575. He soon became influential in the Society of Jesus and in 1580 was appointed, by the Pope, as superior of the mission to England, to campaign against Elizabeth and the Protestant religion. While in England he had made many converts among the gentry, but when his fellow Jesuit, Campion, was taken and executed, Parsons fled to Normandy, where he printed several books in defence of the cause. In 1583 he returned to Rome and was made head of the entire English mission. In 1588 he went to Spain where he established the English colleges of Valladolid and St Omer for the training of English missionaries, and assisted the attempted invasion of England by King Philip, offending the patriotism of the majority of English Catholics. Following the failure of this attempt he turned to preventing the succession of King James I, in 1592 publishing anonymously his *Elizabethae, Angliae reginae haeresin Calvinianam propvgnantis, saevissimvm in Catholicos sui regni edictum* under the pseudonym of Andreas Philopater, to which Astell refers in *An Impartial Enquiry* (p. 26). In 1594 he published *A Conference abovt the Next Svccession to the Crowne of Ingland*, using the name of R. Doleman, a secular priest who hated Parsons as much as Parsons hated him, for this publication. The chief purpose of this work was to support the title of the Infanta against that of King James, by arguing that the authority of the monarchs is derived from the people. A considerable part of Milton's *Defensio* was borrowed from this work which, as Astell notes in *An Impartial Enquiry* (p. 28), was reprinted during both the constitutional crisis of 1648–9 and the Exclusion Crisis of 1679–81. In 1596 Parsons returned to Rome, where he had 'hopes to get him a Cardinals Cap', as Henry Foulis (*History of Romish Treasons*, p. 87) relates, Astell's source for Parsons. However, the Pope had heard many complaints against him and was considering removing the preferments he already had, and so Parsons went to Naples. He returned to Rome after the death of Pope Clement VIII, and was appointed rector of the

English College at Rome in 1597. He remained there until his death. (*British Biographical Archive*; *DNB*)

Philopater, Andreas This is a pseudonym used, it would appear, by two different people. According to the *British Biographical Archive*, Robert Parsons used this name, while the *DNB* credits Joseph Cresswell (1557–1623?) a Jesuit, with publishing a translation under this pseudonym. Mary Astell suspected that it was used by both of these men 'in club'. (*British Biographical Archive*; *DNB*)

Presbyterianism Presbyterianism is a form of ecclesiastical polity wherein the Church is run by presbyters, i.e. ministers and elders. Presbyterian churches are governed by a hierarchy of local and regional courts, the representatives to these courts being popularly elected by the congregations. The supreme legislative and administrative court is known as the General Assembly. The only Presbyterian State Church is the Church of Scotland. All Presbyterian Churches believe that the supreme standard of faith and practice is contained in the Scriptures, and their doctrine is traditionally Calvinistic. Presbyterian worship is simple, orderly and dignified, and emphasizes the hearing and preaching of the Word of God. (*The Oxford Dictionary of the Christian Church*)

Prynne, William (1600–99). Puritan pamphleteer. Born in Somerset, he was educated at Oriel College, Oxford, gaining a BA in 1621. He was admitted to Lincoln's Inn in the same year, and was called to the bar in 1628. A confirmed militant Puritan, he published his first book, a theological treatise, in 1627. This was followed by three other works in the next three years, all attacking Arminianism and its teachers. In 1632 Prynne published a large volume entitled the *Histrio-Mastix*, which argued that stage plays were unlawful and immoral. Unfortunately for Prynne, the Queen herself had taken part in the performance of Walter Montague's *The Shepherd's Pastoral*, and his book was taken as a personal affront to the Queen. He was sentenced to life imprisonment, but while in the Tower he continued to write anonymous tracts against episcopacy. In 1637 Prynne was again sentenced to life imprisonment, in addition to the removal of the rest of his ears not already pilloried in the first sentence, and the branding of his cheeks with the letters SL to stand for seditious libeller. When the Long Parliament assembled in 1640, the House of Commons declared the two sentences against him illegal, restored him to his degree and to his membership of Lincoln's Inn and voted for compensation. On the outbreak of Civil War, Prynne became one of the leading defenders of the parliamentary cause in the press. He argued that the bishops and the King's ministers had acted together to introduce Popery, and gained revenge on Laud, who had shown no sympathy for his earlier plight, by studiously assisting in his prosecution. He produced many pamphlets on the evils of Independency (see Congregationalism), and vehemently opposed both the demands of the Independents for liberty of conscience, and the demands of the Presbyterian clergy for the unrestricted establishment of their system. In 1647 Prynne sided with Parliament, writing several anti-army pamphlets and, as member for Newport in 1648, urged the Commons to declare themselves against the army. As a result, Prynne was shortly afterwards arrested and expelled from Parliament in Pride's Purge. On his release he launched a paper war against the new government, disputing its right to collect taxes. He was again imprisoned, this time for nearly three years without a trial. Once again he continued his pamphleteering when released, this time attacking the Papists, Quakers and Jews, among others. As soon as the Long Parliament was reestablished, Prynne tried several times to regain his parliamentary seat. When finally readmitted in 1660, Prynne asserted the rights of Charles II and accelerated the passage of the Militia Bill. Prynne, as the Member for Bath in the Convention Parliament, argued to restrict the Act of Indemnity so that the regicides would be made to pay dearly for their actions. He was one of the leaders of the Presbyterians in the religious debates, and his opinions on constitutional matters held great weight. Shortly after the Restoration he was appointed as keeper of the records at the Tower. He continued to write however, and he is estimated to have written over 200 books and pamphlets in his lifetime. (*DNB*)

Pufendorf, Samuel von (1632–94). German philosopher. Born in Saxony, Pufendorf studied orthodox theology and Aristotelian philosophy at Leipzig University. In 1656 he went to Jena where he was introduced to the methods of Descartes and discovered the works of Hobbes and Grotius. In 1658 Pufendorf went to Copenhagen to work as a tutor in the home of the Swedish ambassador. With the outbreak of war between Sweden and Denmark, Pufendorf was jailed for eight months, during which time he wrote his first work on natural law, *Elementorum jurisprudentiae universalis libri duo*, which was published in

1660. Following this he was given a chair in natural law at Heidelberg University, where he taught until 1668. His controversial work *De statu imperii Germanici ad laelium fratrem dominum trezolani liber unus*, published in 1667, was a bitter attack on the constitution of the Holy Roman Empire and the house of Austria. In 1668, Pufendorf went to Sweden to accept the chair of natural law at the University of Lund. Here he wrote his major work, published in 1672, entitled *De jure naturae et gentium libri octo*. In this, and an extract from it published in 1673 under the title *De officio hominis et civis juxta legem naturalem libri duo*, Pufendorf argued that every individual had a right to equality and freedom, so that master–servant relationships could only exist on the basis of an agreement. In 1677, after the Danish occupation of Lund, Pufendorf was made royal historiographer in Stockholm. In 1687 he published *De habitu religionis Christianae ad vitam civilem*. In this work Pufendorf argued for the civil superiority of the state over the Church, while at the same time he defended the Church's power in ecclesiastical matters and the individual's freedom of conscience. Pufendorf's views became the basis of the collegial system of church government which, in the eighteenth century, was to form the foundations of Church–state relations in Germany. In 1688 Pufendorf went to Berlin where he worked as historiographer to the elector of Brandenburg. He was made a baron in 1694 and died later that same year. In 1695 his final work, *Jus feciale sive de consensu et dissensu Protestantium*, was published posthumously. This work argued for the formation of a united Protestant Church from the Reformed and Lutheran Churches. (*The New Encyclopaedia Britannica*; *The Encyclopaedia of Philosophy*)

Pym, John (1584–1643). Parliamentary statesman. Born in Somerset, he was educated at Broadgate Hall, Oxford, and in 1602 became a student at the Middle Temple, though he was never called to the bar. He sat in the House of Commons as MP for Calne in the 1614, 1621 and 1624 Parliaments. In the first Parliament of Charles I in 1625, Pym sat as Member for Tavistock, and helped compose the articles against Papists which were adopted with some modifications. In 1628 Pym warmly supported the Petition of Right, which sought to obtain from Charles strict definitions of the limits to arbitrary taxation and arbitrary imprisonment. In the Short Parliament of 1640, Pym began to play the part of unacknowledged leader of the House of Commons. In a long speech summing up the civil and ecclesiastical grievances of the nation,

Pym stopped short of blaming any of the King's ministers. He did however, resist an immediate grant of supply, which led Charles to dissolve the Parliament. Pym then drew up a petition calling for the convening of a fresh Parliament and demanding that Charles' advisors be brought to trial. Pym again represented Tavistock in the Long Parliament, and felt, as did most of his colleagues, that Charles' attempts to establish an arbitrary government were closely connected with a Roman Catholic plot to destroy Protestantism in England. During 1640 he moved the impeachment of Laud and Strafford and in 1641 supported the Root and Branch Bill for the abolition of episcopacy. Fearing an armed intervention, Pym revealed to the House of Lords his knowledge of a plan by Charles to bring the northern army to Westminster, and succeeded in passing bills allowing for Strafford's execution and forbidding the future dissolution of Parliament without its own consent. This made Parliament master over Charles, and he agreed to disband both the English and Scottish armies in the north of England, but refused to acknowledge the supremacy of Parliament by changing his counsellors to ones approved of by Parliament. Aware of Charles' intention to procure armed support, a Committee of Defence was established, of which Pym was a member. Following the news of the Ulster insurrection in November 1641, Pym continued in pushing the Grand Remonstrance which demanded the appointment of ministers which Parliament could trust, and the settlement of Church affairs by an assembly of divines to be selected by Parliament. Presented to Charles on 1 December, he finally rejected it on the 23rd, and on the 30th, Pym moved that guards be stationed to protect Parliament, and that the bishops who had protested their exclusion from Parliament be impeached. Pym and five other Parliamentarians, including Hampden, were charged with complicity in the Scottish invasion but escaped before Charles could arrest them. In July 1642 Pym was one of fifteen members of the newly formed Committee of Safety, which was a rudimentary government acting in the interests of Parliament, and which took on the role of organizing military action once the war had begun. In November 1642 Parliament, under Pym's leadership, seized the power of taxation, and in March the following year Pym introduced to England a new form of impost, the excise. After the initial defeats of the parliamentary armies, he convinced the Parliament of the necessity of an alliance with Scotland, and Pym, along with the other Members of Parliament, began taking the covenant (see Solemn League and

Covenant) in September 1643. Pym died three months later and was buried at Westminster Abbey. His body was removed after the Restoration. (*DNB*)

Rastell, John (1532?–77). Jesuit. Born at Gloucester, the *British Biographical Archive* has as his birth date 1527, compared with the *DNB*'s date of 1532. He was educated at New College, Oxford and was made a perpetual fellow of New College in 1549. He graduated with an MD in 1555, and was ordained a priest about that time. He was unable, according to his conscience, to comply with the religious changes in Elizabeth I's reign, and left Oxford in 1560. He went first to Louvain, then to Antwerp in 1564 and finally to Rome, where he entered the Jesuit novitiate of St Andrew in 1568. He was English penintentiary for a time at St Peter's, Rome, before being sent as confessor and consultor to the house of the Jesuits in Ausburg, and finally to Ingolstadt, where he was appointed vice-rector of the College of Jesuits. He was a determined antagonist of Bishop Jewell, and published several works. (*British Biographical Archive*; *DNB*)

Rich, Henry (1590–1649). First Earl of Holland. Second son of the first Earl of Warwick by his wife Penelope Rich, Holland was a favourite of James I, responsible for negotiating the marriage of Prince Charles with Princess Henrietta Maria of France, for which he was rewarded by being raised to the rank of Earl of Holland in 1624. Holland subsequently used his influence at court, particularly with the Queen, to cabal against the King's ministers. In the Long Parliament he was among those peers supporting the Popular party and opposing Strafford. In and out of royal favour, he publicly declared to the kingdom at large that he found the Court too indisposed to peace and the Papists too powerful for such a patriot as he. But he fell foul of the Parliament as well, after declaring for the King at the onset of the second Civil War, and ended up being executed along with the Duke of Hamilton and Lord Capel on 9 March 1649. Clarendon (*History*, III p. 209), who had defended him in the Privy Council in 1643, said of him: 'He took more care to be thought a good friend to Parliaments, than a good Servant to his Master, and was thought to say too little of his having failed so much in his Duty to him, which most good Men believ'd to be the Source from which his present calamity sprung. He was a very well bred Man and a fine Gentleman in good times; but too much desired to enjoy ease and plenty, when the King could have

neither; and did think Poverty the most insupportable evil that could
befal any Man in this world.' (*DNB* and Clarendon, *History*)

Rich, Robert (1587–1658). Second Earl of Warwick and older brother
of Henry Rich, Earl of Holland. Created Knight of the Bath in 1603,
he became a member of the Inner Temple in 1604 and MP for Maldon
in 1610 and 1614. In 1608–9 a player in Ben Jonson's *Masque of Beauty*,
Warwick soon abandoned court life for planting colonies, in the
Bermudas, New England, Guinea and Virginia, being appointed to
membership of the Virginia Council by the King. From a Puritan
family, however, he gradually became estranged from the King, refusing to subscribe to the forced loan, opposing ship money and associating more closely with his fellow colonialists in the Bermuda and Providence companies, Lord Saye, Lord Brooke, Oliver St John and Pym.
With the dissolution of the Short Parliament in 1640 Warwick was
arrested by the King for his involvement in Scottish affairs.
Vehemently opposed to Laudian Church policy, he appointed Puritan
clergymen to the livings in his gift and was described by Calamy as 'a
great patron and Maecenas to the pious and religious ministry'. In 1646
he was named among the Presbyterians and Scottish party in the House
of Lords, in January 1647 participating in the negotiations for a scheme
of settlement acceptable to the King. But after the Presbyterian riots
of July 1647 he affirmed the independence of Parliament and retired
from his seat in the House in protest. Clarendon's claim that he, like
his brother the Earl of Holland, declared for the King at this point, is
unfounded. In 1648 he was appointed Lord High Admiral by the Parliament and blockaded Charles' ships. But he stopped at abolition of
the monarchy, was relieved of the Admiralty, petitioned unsuccessfully
for the life of Holland, his brother, and played no active role in the
Commonwealth. Clarendon (*History*, II, pp. 159–60) says of him: 'He
was a Man of pleasant and companiable Wit, and conversation; of an
universal Jollity; and such a licence with his Words, and his Actions,
that a Man of less Virtue could not be found out: so that one might
reasonably have believ'd that a Man so qualified, would not have been
able to have contributed much to the overthrow of a Nation, and Kingdom. But with all these faults, he had great Authority and Credit with
that People, who, in the beginning of the Troubles, did all the mischief;
and by opening his doors and making his House the Rendezvous of all
the silenced Ministers, in the time when there was Authority to silence

them, and spending a good part of his Estate, of which he was very prodigal, upon them, and by being present with them at their Devotions, and making himself merry With them, and At them, which they dispensed with, he became the head of That Party; and got the Style of a Godly Man.' (*DNB*; Clarendon, *History*)

Root and Branch Bill During the 1630s an increasing number of Puritan Englishmen had become angry with the growing persecution of Calvinists by Arminian bishops. They believed that the system of episcopalianism was itself faulty, and embraced Presbyterianism or even Congregationalism instead. In December 1640 a petition was presented by 15,000 London citizens to the House of Commons, and was followed by similar mass petitions from nineteen counties. This resulted, in 1641, in a parliamentary debate on a bill calling for the abolition of the episocopacy. The Root and Branch Bill as it was called, provided for the exercise of ecclesiastical jurisdiction by lay commissioners, but despite much debate, no agreement was reached. Although many opposed the Laudian interpretations of episcopacy, the moderate members were not prepared to abolish episcopacy 'root and branch'. Pym was one of those who supported it and Oliver St John helped to frame it. (Smith, 1984; Worden, 1986; *DNB*)

Rutherford, Samuel (1600?–61). A Scottish gentleman, educated at the University of Edinburgh, Rutherford distinguished himself sufficiently to be appointed Regent of Humanities there. The town Council of Edinburgh records in 1626 his dismissal for fornication, a scandal he spent much of his life living down by becoming extremely religious. In 1636 he published *Exercitationes apologeticae pro divina gratia*, a treatise against Arminianism, from a humble pastorate in Galloway. This and his reputation for Nonconformity caused him to be dismissed from his ministry in the same year, and he was exiled to Aberdeen where he continued the controversy. A member of the Glasgow Assembly of 1638, he was rewarded with appointment by that body to the chair of divinity at St Mary's College of St Andrews University. He participated in Covenanting assemblies in subsequent years, in 1642 publishing *Plea for Presbytery*. In 1643 he was appointed a commissioner of the Church of Scotland to the Westminster Assembly, where, for his verbal and published attacks on Independents, Milton named him in the sonnet on 'The New Forcers of Conscience under the Long Parliament'. He published a series of tracts, including *Lex* *rex*, a political treatise, of 1644; *Due Right of Presbyteries*, in the same year; *Divine Right of Church Government*, in 1646. In 1648 he published *A Survey of the Spiritual Antichrist*, an attack on sectaries and Enthusiasts, and again in 1648, *A Free Disputation against pretended Liberty of Conscience*, characterized by a contemporary as 'perhaps the most elaborate defence of persecution which has ever appeared in a protestant country'. These earned him the offer of chairs in divinity in Holland, and at Edinburgh, all of which he declined in favour of the rectorship of St Andrews. In London he joined the rigid Covenanters in opposing the 'engagement' and overturning the government. Charles II paid him a personal visit at St Andrews in 1650, for which he was rewarded with Rutherford's Latin speech instructing him on the duty of kings. Rutherford later joined the western remonstrants who condemned the treaty with the King as unlawful. He was the only member of the Presbytery of St Andrews to take up the remonstrants' position, opposing the resolution to relax the laws against the engagers to permit them to defend the country against Cromwell; a battle that, with its consequences, the restoration of the episcopacy ten years later, consumed the last decade of his life. (*DNB*)

Sacheverell, Henry (1674?–1724). Political preacher. Born in Wiltshire, he was educated at Magdalen College, Oxford, where in 1708 he obtained his DD and was made bursar the following year. His pamphlets and sermons advocated the High Church and Tory cause, and vehemently abused Dissenters, latitudinarians and Whigs. His views were aired in *Character of a Low Churchman* (1701), *On the Association of . . . Moderate Churchmen with Whigs and Fanatics* (1702) and *The Rights of the Church of England* (1705). His sermon preached before Oxford University on 2 June 1702 is among the publications which prompted Defoe's parody, *The Shortest Way with the Dissenters* (1702). His sermons of 1709 at Derby and St Paul's, London, arguing in favour of non-resistance, and condemning toleration and Occasional Conformity, were sufficiently extreme to be declared by the House of Commons as seditious libels on Her Majesty and her government. Sacheverell was impeached, although the feeling of the country was strongly on his side, in proceedings which drew John Toland (1670–1727), John Dennis (1657–1734) and Gilbert Burnet into the debate. During his trial there were riots, meeting houses were attacked and the houses of several leading Whigs were threatened. Although found guilty, his only punishment was a ban on preaching for three years, and such a light sentence was viewed as a triumph for the High Church and Tory party. The Tory victory in the general election in 1710 was recognized as being largely due to the ill-judged impeachment of Sacheverell, although the Tories still despised him. He resumed preaching in 1713 and accepted the Queen's offer of the rich living of St Andrew's, Holborn. He died from complications following an accident. (*DNB*)

St John, Oliver (1598?–1673). Chief Justice under Charles I and Cromwell. Grandson of the first Lord St John of Bletsho, Earl of Bolingbroke and son of Oliver St John of Cayshoe, Bedfordshire, St John was educated at Queens' College, Cambridge, and Lincoln's Inn. He was first employed by the firm of Francis Russell, fourth Earl of Bedford, but according to Clarendon (*History*, I, p. 148), 'he was not taken notice of for practice in *Westminster*-Hall, till he argued at the Exchequer-Chamber the case of Ship-money on the behalf of Mr. *Hambden*'. In 1629 he was sent to the Tower for passing to Bedford Sir Robert Daley's 'Proposition for his Majesty's service to bridle the impertinence of Parliament', and only escaped prosecution by the Star Chamber because of a royal pardon to honour the birth of Charles II. St John married into the Cromwell family twice and was early associated with the Earl of Warwick, Lord Saye, John Pym and other opposition leaders in managing the company for the plantation of Providence. Clarendon says (*History*, I, p. 148), 'he never forgave the Court the first assault, and contracted an implacable displeasure against the Church purely from the Company he kept'. On 29 January 1640 the King, on the proposal of Bedford, made St John Solicitor-General, in the hope that 'he would have been very useful in the present exigence to support His Service in the House of Commons, where his Authority was then great; at least, that he would be ashamed ever to appear in any thing that might prove prejudicial to the Crown' (Clarendon, *History*, I, p. 167). The King misjudged; St John is credited with having framed the Militia Bill and the Root and Branch Bill, and delivered a speech in support of excluding bishops from voting in Parliament. During the Civil War St John was considered, with Sir Henry Vane, one of the leaders of the Independents in the Lower House. But he is said to have disapproved of Cromwell's election to the Protectorate and distanced himself from him for most of its duration. Nor did he support the establishment of Presbyterianism, insisting rather, as an 'Erastian lawyer' on the rights of the state. After the Restoration St John escaped reprisal despite his high office under Cromwell. He lived for a time as a private citizen in Northamptonshire until, it is said, Clarendon's threats to extort his property as the price of his safety drove him abroad in 1662, first to Basle then to Augsburg, where he lived until his death. (*DNB*; Clarendon, *History*)

Sancroft, William (1617–93). Archbishop of Canterbury. Born in Suffolk, he was educated at Emmanuel College, Cambridge. In 1642 he was elected fellow and became a tutor of the College, holding the offices of Greek and Hebrew reader, and in 1644 he was made bursar of the College. In 1658 an English translation of a Latin work of his, *Fur praedestinatus*, was published. It vigorously attacked Calvinism, claiming it was morally subversive. Shortly afterwards, also in 1658, Sancroft published *Modern Policies taken from Machiaval, Borgia and other choise Authors by an Eye-witness*, which was an indictment of the religion and politics of the Commonwealth. In 1657 he travelled abroad, studying at Padua, and hearing of the Restoration when in Rome, returned to England in 1660. He was made chaplain to Bishop Cosin and was employed in the Savoy Conference. In 1661 he was appointed as one of Charles II's chaplains, and the following year he was made DD at Cambridge and master of Emmanuel College. In 1664 he was nominated by the King to the deanery of York and then to the deanery of St Paul's, where he devoted himself to the restoration of the cathedral before, and again after, the Great Fire of London in 1666. In 1668 he was admitted Archdeacon of Canterbury, resigned in 1670 and was made prolocutor of the lower house of convocation of Canterbury. In 1678 Sancroft was appointed Archbishop of Canterbury and in this position he attempted, unsuccessfully, to win back the Duke of York to the English Church. In 1685 James II acceded to the throne but Sancroft refused to take part in the high commission court James had established and subsequently was forbidden to appear at court. He worked diligently in his own see, but came into conflict with the King again when he refused to order the clergy to give up afternoon catechizing, and when he joined the governors of the Charterhouse in refusing to admit a Papist on the King's orders, which were contrary to the law. In 1688 Sancroft, in consultation with other senior clergy, stated that the council's order that all clergy read the King's declaration of liberty of conscience in church, was illegal. Sancroft and the six bishops who had signed the petition against the council's order, were committed to the Tower, and eventually found not guilty of seditious libel. On his release, Sancroft headed a deputation to James which advised him to revoke all his illegal acts. Later in that same year Sancroft, believing James incapable of government, signed a declaration calling on William of Orange to assist in procuring peace and a 'free Parliament', but he favoured appointing William merely *custos regni*, not as King. In 1689 Sancroft excused himself from attending William's coronation. He was suspended later that year and deprived the following year, along with five bishops and about 400 clergy. Soon afterwards Sancroft joined the other nonjuring bishops in circulating a flysheet which denied all sedition or intrigue with France. He appears to have joined in the preparation for the consecration of new nonjuring bishops, and until his death in 1693, would communicate only with nonjurors. (*DNB*)

Shaftesbury, Earl of, see **Cooper, Anthony Ashley.**

Sherlock, William (1641?–1707). Dean of St Paul's. Born in Southwark, he was educated at Cambridge, graduating with an MA degree in 1663. After taking orders he did not have a preferment until 1669, when he went to a rectory in London where he soon gained a reputation as a preacher. His first publication, *The Knowledge of Jesus Christ, and Union with Him* (1674), started a war of words, with Sherlock attacking John Owen, DD, who had argued that divine mercy was known only through Christ. In 1680 Sherlock commenced the DD, and was collated in 1681 to the prebend of St Pancras in St Paul's Cathedral. In 1684 he wrote his *Case of Resistance* in which, on scriptural grounds, he argued for the 'divine right of Kings' and the duty of passive obedience. Yet he declined to read James II's 1687 declaration for liberty and conscience, and continued to attack Papists. He was made master of the Temple in 1685. At the Revolution he opposed alterations in the prayerbook to gain Dissenters, sided with the nonjurors, and encouraged others to refuse the oath to William and Mary. As a result he was suspended from all his preferments. In 1689 Sherlock published the most popular of his works, the *Practical Discourse concerning Death*, but the following year switched allegiances and took the oath to William and Mary. He was promptly rewarded with the restoration of his preferments and in addition was granted the deanery of St Paul's in 1691. Other controversial writings by Sherlock include *Preservative against Popery* (1688), *Vindication of the Doctrine of the*

Trinity (1690) and *Present State of the Socinian Controversy* (1698). (*DNB*; *British Biographical Archive*)

ship money Charles I, in order to raise money for the maintenance of the navy, expanded the collection of ship money, an ancient levy by which revenue was raised for the outfitting of war ships. Ship money was traditionally only collected from ports in times of emergency, but Charles I extended its collection to inland communities, arguing that pirates had become a national menace. Initially the collection of ship money was generally accepted, but as it continued to be levied year after year, discontent rose. In 1637 Hampden challenged the legitimacy of this practice in court, but the royal judges narrowly decided in favour of the Crown. However, legal opinion on the matter varied significantly and revenue from the collection of ship money declined. In 1641 the Long Parliament declared ship money illegal. (*New Encyclopaedia Britannica*)

Socinians, see **Unitarians.**

Solemn League and Covenant The Westminster Assembly of Divines, a committee of more than 100 clergy from all over England, had been formed following the outbreak of war in 1642 to advise Parliament on the 'good government' of the Church. With the parliamentary armies in need of Scottish assistance, the Assembly negotiated the Solemn League and Covenant in 1643. This was an agreement reached between the parliamentary armies and the Scots in which the Scots agreed to bring an army to England to fight against the Royalist forces in return for guarantees of a Presbyterian Church establishment. The Assembly was thus committed to develop a church polity close to Scotland's Presbyterian form. Ultimately, however, religious differences between Scottish Presbyterians and English Independents (see Congregationalists) vitiated the alliance. The 1662 Act of Uniformity officially renounced the Solemn League and Covenant. (*New Encyclopaedia Britannica*)

Steele, Sir Richard (1672–1729). Essayist, dramatist and politician. Born in Dublin, he matriculated from Christ Church, Oxford, in 1690, but left Merton College in 1694 without taking a degree. He joined the army and gained employment in 1696–7 as Lord Cutts' confidential agent or secretary. By 1700, Steele was a captain, and the following year he wrote the *Christian Hero: an Argument Proving That No*

Principles But Those of Religion are Sufficient to Make a Great Man. Steele's military colleagues however, looked unfavourably on this religious piece, and Steele responded by writing *The Funeral: Or, Grief a-la-Mode*, a less moralistic comedy which was performed at Drury Lane late in 1701. This was followed by two less successful productions, *The Lying Lover: Or, the Ladies Friendship*, in 1703 and *The Tender Husband: Or, the Accomplished Fools*, in 1705. In 1706 he was appointed as a gentleman waiter to Prince George of Denmark, and held this position until the death of Prince George in 1708. In April 1709 Steele began his career as an essayist by establishing the *Tatler*, which was to develop into a collection of individual essays on social and general topics. It ceased publication abruptly in 1711, due, it is believed, to the *Tatler*'s satirization of Harley, who had become head of government. Only two months later, however, the even more successful *Spectator* was launched. From 1712 Steele's writings took on a more overtly political tone, and in 1713 Steele openly challenged the Tory paper the *Examiner*, in his new publication the *Guardian*. In 1713 Steele was elected MP for Hampshire, and the following year published a pamphlet entitled *The Crisis*, which reviewed the whole question of the Hanoverian succession. As a result, Steele was accused of seditious libel and was expelled from the House of Commons. With the death of Queen Anne later that year, however, his fortunes changed. Among the rewards King George I bestowed upon him for his loyalty to the Hanoverian cause was the licence of the Theatre Royal of Drury Lane. Shortly after this, Steele published *The Ladies Library* and *Mr Steele's Apology for Himself and his Writings*. In 1715 he was elected MP for Boroughbridge in Yorkshire, and was knighted. He established several short-lived periodicals, the last of which, in 1720, was entitled *The Theatre*. In 1722 he became MP for Wendover in Buckinghamshire, and produced his last comedy, *The Conscious Lovers*, at Drury Lane, which was a great success. Money difficulties led him to retire to Wales in 1724, where he remained until his death in 1729. *DNB* states that Steele, unlike his contemporaries, sought to offer women 'a reasonable service of genuine respect'. (*DNB*)

Stephens, William (1647?–1718). Whig divine. Born in Worcester, he was educated at St Edmund Hall, Oxford, graduated with an MA in 1671, was incorporated at Cambridge the same year, and received a BD in 1678. After preaching near Oxford he was made rector of Sutton in

Surrey, and archdeacon in 1690. He is most remembered for his strong Whig principles. Preaching before the House of Commons in 1700, Stephens offended the Tory house by omitting the prayer for the King and royal family, suggesting that the observance of the anniversary of the execution of Charles I be discontinued and insisting upon the Whig doctrine of the foundation of government on consent. He is mentioned by Mary Astell in *A Fair Way with the Dissenters* (p. 21), along with Prynne, Burton, Bastwick, Tutchin and Defoe, 'a whole Swarm of Wasps from the same hive'. (*DNB*)

Stillingfleet, Edward (1635–99). Bishop of Worcester. Born in Dorset, he was educated at St John's College, Cambridge, where he graduated with an MA in 1656, and was incorporated at Oxford in 1677. From 1654 he worked as a tutor in Nottingham and around this time was ordained. In 1657 he was made rector of Sutton and in 1659 published his first book, *The Irenicum*, which, while arguing against Nonconformity, suggested a compromise between the Church and the Presbyterians. Stillingfleet's later views departed a conciliatory line for a defence of intolerance in his works the *Unreasonableness of Separation* (1680) and *The Mischief of Separation* (1680) (Goldie, 1991, 333, 342). Having graduated as a BD from Cambridge in 1663, and, having gained fame for his writings, he was appointed preacher at the Rolls Chapel in 1664 and rector of St Andrew's, Holborn, in 1665, and was also made reader of the Temple. He was collated to the prebend of Islington in St Paul's Cathedral in 1667, graduated as DD in 1668 and became a canon in Canterbury Cathedral the following year. He soon became a popular London preacher and was made a royal chaplain. He managed to remain on good terms with the Nonconformists despite his finding favour at court. His writings against the Socinians (see Unitarianism) and Romanists were extremely popular, and in 1677 he was made Archdeacon of London. In 1678 he was appointed Dean of St Paul's and was also prolocutor of the lower house of convocation of Canterbury. He was less prominent during the reign of James II, but with the Revolution he again found favour. In 1689 he was consecrated as Bishop of Worcester, and was placed on the commission to consider the revision of the prayerbook and the possibility of 'comprehension'. His views on the duties and rights of the parochial clergy were published in his *Ecclesiastical Cases* in 1695. He spoke frequently in the House of Lords and advised Archbishop Tenison as well as other bishops. Despite his infirmity, Stillingfleet entered into an important controversy with Locke over the doctrine of the Trinity in 1696–7, which went to the heart of Locke's epistemology in *The Essay Concerning Human Understanding* (1690). Mary Astell's critique of Locke on thinking matter in *The Christian Religion*, shows acquaintance with, and perhaps the influence of, Stillingfleet's critique. (*DNB*)

Swift, Jonathan (1667–1745). Dean of St Patrick's and satirist. From a Yorkshire Royalist family, intermarried with the Dryden, Davenant and the Ormonde families, Jonathan Swift was reared in Dublin, where he spent the greater part of his life. Soon after completing an Oxford BA Swift was adopted by the statesman, Sir William Temple, who used him as a go-between with William III. Temple, in 1692, had published an essay which transported to England the debate over the ancients and moderns. Begun in France by Fontenelle and joined by the Englishmen William Wotton, Bentley and Charles Boyle, the debate was the object of Swift's first famous work *The Battle of the Books*, which lampooned Fontenelle's position. Secretly published in 1704 along with *Tale of a Tub*, Swift's work was attacked in turn by Mary Astell, in *Bart'lemy Fair* (p. 110), where she demonstrates knowledge about Swift's authorship not widely known (Swift, *Bickerstaff Papers and Pamphlets on the Church*, 1957 editor's introduction, pp. xxix–xxx). Swift's ridicule of theological pedantry, and of Papists and Dissenters alike, created the suspicion of a wholesale condemnation of Christianity. The impeachment of Whig lords elicited from Swift his *Discourse on the Dissensions of Athens and Rome* (1701), variously attributed to Lord Somers and Bishop Burnet. It caused him to be taken for a Whig, although Swift did not commit himself on the matter and noted that this was the first occasion he had reflected on the differences between Tory and Whig. During the controversy over Occasional Conformity, Swift was persuaded by Somers and Burnet to write on the matter (1703–4), but too late for publication. In 1707 Swift wrote a series of pamphlets ridiculing Deists as well as Papists and Presbyterians, under the pseudonym Bickerstaff, adopted by Steele for the *Tatler*, for which Swift later wrote, numbering among his friends Halifax, Addison, Steele and Congreve. Swift agreed with the Whigs on accepting the principles of the 1688 Revolution, but insisted on state support for the established Church, detesting equally Presbyterians, Dissenters and Jacobites. When in 1710 the Whig ministry was breaking up, after years of fruitless search for preferment, Swift remarked that he had hopes of 'a new world, since [he] had the merit of suffering by not complying with the old'. Swift's equal detestation of Dissenters and Jacobites, typical of an Irish churchman, increasingly distanced him from the Whigs, to the point of open enmity and from 1710 he began a close association with the Tory politicians Harley and Bolingbroke that was to be life-long. When, in 1711 a Whig alliance, to which the Queen was drawn by the Duchess of Somerset, seemed close to passing the Occasional Conformity Bill, Swift penned a character assassination of the Duchess, probably seen by Queen Anne, but which Damaris Masham persuaded him not to publish. From 1711 his Tory sympathies caused a permanent breach with Steele, although he saw Addison occasionally, and he promoted the prospects of Berkeley (later Bishop) and Pope, as White Kennett attests. The collapse of the Bolingbroke government and the death of Anne caused Swift to retire to Ireland, but not to cease the continuous stream of invective and satire which marked his life. From 1720 on he embarked on a new phase as an Irish patriot, writing under the name of M. B. Drapier, producing in the 1730s trenchant critiques of British policy in Ireland. In 1727 Pope engineered the publication of *Gulliver's Travels*, which became an instant classic, but did not improve his prospects overall. He lived out his long life in Ireland, increasingly pessimistic and bitterly satirical, as his writings attest. (*DNB*)

Tory see **Whig and Tory.**

Tutchin, John (1661?–1707). Whig pamphleteer. Tutchin entered the public record with the publication of his *Poems on Several Occasions, with a Pastoral*, in 1685, the year of the Monmouth Rebellion in which he took part and for which he was imprisoned. Upon the accession of William III, Tutchin wrote *An Heroick Poem upon the late Expedition of his Majesty to rescue England from Popery, Tyranny, and Arbitrary Government* (1689). His *Congratulatory Poem to the Rev. John Tillotson upon his Promotion to the Archiepiscopal See of Canterbury* was printed in 1691 and in 1692 he was employed in the royal victualling office, but dismissed in 1695 for embezzlement. His poem of 1700, *The Foreigners*, attacked the King as being the dupe of the Dutch, and was referred to by Defoe as 'a vile abhorred pamphlet in very ill verse', prompting the latter's *The True Born Englishman* (1700, probably first edition) in response. Not content with his attack on William III, Tutchin in 1701 showed his evenhandedness towards the monarchy by publishing the twelve-page *The British Muse: Or Tyranny Exposed. A Satire; Occasioned By All the Fulsome and Lying Poems and Elegies That Have Been Written on the Death of the Late King James*, for which he was arrested. From April 1702 Tutchin commenced publication of *The Observator*, named after Roger L'Estrange's periodical begun in 1681, devoted to promoting the ideals of the country Whigs and attacking the Tories. In response, Charles Leslie commenced publication of *The Rehearsal* on 5 August 1704, the first number named *The Observator*, the fifth, *Rehearsal of Observator*. Both the journals of Tutchin, who is named by Astell in *A Fair Way with the Dissenters* (p. 21), and of Leslie, came to Astell's attention, Leslie's being of special significance as the vehicle of his early critique of Locke's *Two Treatises*, to which Astell's critique in *Reflections upon Marriage* bears such a striking resemblance. Curiously, Tutchin came to the defence of Defoe in his work (attributed to Defoe; Tutchin only supposed author according to the *National Union Catalog*), *A Dialogue between a Dissenter and the Observator concerning the 'Shortest Way with the Dissenters'*, of 1703. Rearrested and once more unsuccessfully tried, this time allegedly for attacking the Papists, Tutchin from 1705 on was jointly attacked with Defoe, although not always agreeing with him. He died in prison in 1707. Edward Ward dedicated his *Secret History of the Calves' Head Clubb* (1703), a club which celebrated the death of Charles I, to his memory. (*DNB*)

Unitarians The basis of Unitarianism is the rejection of the doctrines of the Trinity and the Divinity of Christ in favour of the unipersonality of God. Unitarians have no formal creed but believe in the abiding goodness of human nature, and dispute the orthodox doctrine of eternal punishment. Unitarianism is also referred to as Socinianism, a term which is derived from the Latinized name of two of its founding teachers. (*The Oxford Dictionary of the Christian Church*)

Ward, Edward (1667–1731). Humourist. Born in Oxfordshire, he had little education. He worked as a publican in London entertaining his guests, especially the High Church party, with his stories. Between 1691 and 1734 he published many coarse poems which satirized the Whigs and the Low Church party. In 1705 he was pilloried for one such publication which attacked the government. Although exaggerated, his writings offer an insight into the social life during Queen Anne's reign, and especially on the habits of various classes in London. His works included the *Secret History of the Calves' Head Clubb*. (*DNB*)

Wesley, Samuel (1662–1735). Divine and poet. Born at Dorset, he was sent to London in 1678 to be educated for the Independent ministry before entering Exeter College, Oxford, in 1683 where he graduated with a BA in 1688. In February 1689–90 he was ordained as a priest and obtained a curacy in London. In June 1690 Wesley was instituted to the rectory of South Ormsby, Lincolnshire, where he wrote literary works. In 1695 he became rector of Epworth in Lincolnshire, where due to increasing family responsibilities and many misfortunes, his indebtedness grew. In 1705 he was imprisoned in Lincoln Castle for several months for failure to pay his debts. In 1703 a controversy erupted over the publication of *A Letter from a Country Divine to his Friend in London, concerning the Education of Dissenters in their Private Academies*. Apparently Wesley had written this hostile criticism of the inner life of Nonconformist academies back in 1690, after attending a meeting of the Calves' Head Club. It was written as a letter to Robert Clavel, but was not sent to him by Wesley and was not meant to be published. Clavel had, without Wesley's knowledge or permission, published it anonymously. His later years were spent writing a major work on Job which was not published until after his death. (*DNB*)

Whig and Tory Introduced in 1679, during the heated struggle over the Exclusion Bill, these terms were initially meant as terms of abuse. Whig was used to describe horse thieves and later, Scottish Presbyterians. It connoted Nonconformity and rebellion and was applied to those who claimed the power of excluding the heir to the throne. The term Tory originally referred to Irish cattle rustlers and was later used to suggest a Papist outlaw. It was applied to those who supported the hereditary right of James despite his Roman Catholic faith. The Revolution of 1688 had been a joint achievement and so greatly modified the division in principle between the two factions. Most Tories came to accept something of the Whig doctrines of limited constitutional monarchy rather than divine right absolutism. In the eighteenth century, these terms increasingly came to represent two opposing political parties. Under Queen Anne, the Tories represented the resistance, mainly from the country gentry, to religious toleration and foreign entanglements, and Toryism became identified with Anglicanism and the squirearchy. Whiggism, on the other hand, was associated with the aristocratic, landowning families and the financial interests of the wealthy middle classes. (*New Encyclopaedia Britannica*)

Whiston, William (1667–1752). Divine. Born in Leicestershire, he was educated at Cambridge, graduating with an MA in 1693. Being opposed to the oaths to William and Mary, he insisted on applying only to bishops who had not replaced one of the deprived nonjurors. William Lloyd, Bishop of Lichfield, ordained him deacon in 1693 after which he returned to Cambridge. He was forced to retire from tutoring due to poor health. He was appointed as chaplain to John Moore, Bishop of Norwich, and published his first work, *A New Theory of the Earth, From its Original, to the Consummation of all Things* in 1696. The work, confirming the narrative of Genesis on Newtonian grounds and explaining the deluge by a collision with a comet, was directed against the influence of Descartes, in general, and Thomas Burnet's theories of the earth, in particular. It was submitted in manuscript to Newton, and praised by Locke in his Letter to Molyneux of 22 February 1696; but Whiston appears to be more of Newton's camp than Locke's, defending the Bible and the Mosaic account of the Creation against 'the loose *Deists* and pretended *Socinians* of this Age' (p. 62). In 1701 Whiston was appointed deputy to Newton's Lucasian professorship and succeeded Newton as professor in 1703. He delivered lectures on mathematics and natural philosophy, and was one of the first to popularize Newton's theories. Combining science and theology he wrote, in 1708, to the archbishops arguing that the accepted doctrine of the Trinity was erroneous. As a result he was banned from the University and deprived of his professorship in 1710. He then moved to London where in 1711, he published his major work, *Primitive Christianity Revived.* Convocation voted for his prosecution but the proceedings against him were dropped following the death of Queen Anne. In 1715 Whiston started a society for promoting primitive Christianity which held fortnightly meetings. Whiston also lectured in various English cities on subjects such as meteors, eclipses and earthquakes, which he associated with the fulfilment of prophecies. In 1747, after gradually becoming more uncomfortable with the Athanasian creed used by the Church of England, Whiston joined the Baptists. (*DNB*)

White, Thomas (1593–1676). English Catholic theologian, who wrote under various pseudonyms (Thomas Anglus, Ablius, Bianchi, Blacklow, Candidon). Educated at the English College at St Omer in Valladolid and at Douay, he was ordained in 1617. He subsequently taught at Douay, where he was vice-president in 1650, was president of the English College at Lisbon, living also in Paris and Rome. A fertile theologian, he developed his own system of religious doctrines on freedom, grace and predestination, bringing him into conflict with the Church which proscribed his works. His belief in the authority of the Church to interpret Scripture involved him in controversy with Protestants, and caused him to capitulate to the Church on other doctrinal matters. Among his numerous works are editions of the books of William Rushworth (1654); *Institutiones peripateticae* and *Institutiones sacrae* (1646, 1652), from the latter of which twenty-two propositions were censured by the University of Douay in 1660; *De medio animarum statu* (1653); and *Institutiones ethicae sive staterae morum* (1660). *The Grounds of Obedience and Government* second edition (1655), dedicated to his 'most honoured and best Friend', Sir Kenelme Digby, was a work believed to flatter Cromwell to gain favour for Catholics. While in retirement in London, he and Thomas Hobbes, who held him in high regard, undertook much heated theological discussion, and Hobbes wrote a critique of Thomas White's *De mundo dialogi tres* (1642), which has only recently been translated. (*DNB*; *The New Schaff-Herzog Encyclopedia of Religious Knowledge*)

Wotton, William (1666–1727). Scholar. Born in Suffolk, by the age of five he could read English, Latin, Greek and Hebrew. He attended Catherine Hall, Cambridge, and graduated with a BA in 1679, aged thirteen. He was made a fellow of St John's College, Cambridge, and he graduated with an MA degree in 1683, and a BD in 1691. He was elected a fellow of the Royal Society in 1687. In 1694 Wotton published *Reflections upon Ancient and Modern Learning*, which argued for the moderns in the controversy between Sir William Temple and Monsieur Perrault. It was a document which stated clearly the facts, and as such provides a good summary of the discoveries in nature and physical science up to that time. Wotton, having received preferment, was given in 1691 the living of Llandrill-yn-Rhos in Denbighshire, and became chaplain to Daniel Finch, the second Earl of Nottingham. Shortly afterwards he was made rector of Middleton Keynes in Buckinghamshire.

In 1705 he was given the prebend of Grantham South in Salisbury Cathedral, and in 1707 received the degree of DD. He published several theological works including *A Defence of the Rights of the Christian Church* (1706), and *The Case of Convocation Considered* (1711). (*DNB*)

Index

Cambridge Texts in the History of Political Thought

Titles published in the series thus far

Aristotle *The Politics* (edited by Stephen Everson)

Arnold *Culture and Anarchy and Other Writings* (edited by Stefan Collini)

Astell *Political Writings* (edited by Patricia Springborg)

Austin *The Province of Jurisprudence Determined* (edited by Wilfrid E. Rumble)

Bakunin *Statism and Anarchy* (edited by Marshall Shatz)

Baxter *A Holy Commonwealth* (edited by William Lamont)

Beccaria *On Crimes and Punishments and Other Writings* (edited by Richard Bellamy)

Bentham *A Fragment on Government* (introduction by Ross Harrison)

Bernstein *The Preconditions of Socialism* (edited by Henry Tudor)

Bodin *On Sovereignty* (edited by Julian H. Franklin)

Bossuet *Politics Drawn from the Very Words of Holy Scripture* (edited by Patrick Riley)

Burke *Pre-Revolutionary Writings* (edited by Ian Harris)

Christine de Pizan *The Book of the Body Politic* (edited by Kate Langdon Forhan)

Cicero *On Duties* (edited by M. T. Griffin and E. M. Atkins)

Constant *Political Writings* (edited by Biancamaria Fontana)

Diderot *Political Writings* (edited by John Hope Mason and Robert Wokler)

The Dutch Revolt (edited by Martin van Gelderen)

Early Greek Political Thought from Homer to the Sophists (edited by Michael Gagarin and Paul Woodruff)

Ferguson *An Essay on the History of Civil Society* (edited by Fania Oz-Salzberger)

Filmer *Patriarcha and Other Writings* (edited by Johann P. Sommerville)

Fourier *The Theory of the Four Movements* (edited by Gareth Stedman Jones and Ian Patterson)

Gramsci *Pre-Prison Writings* (edited by Richard Bellamy)

Guicciardini *Dialogue on the Government of Florence* (edited by Alison Brown)

Harrington *A Commonwealth of Oceana* and *A System of Politics* (edited by J. G. A. Pocock)

Hegel *Elements of the Philosophy of Right* (edited by Allen W. Wood and H. B. Nisbet)

Hobbes *Leviathan* (edited by Richard Tuck)

Hobhouse *Liberalism and Other Writings* (edited by James Meadowcroft)

Hooker *Of the Laws of Ecclesiastical Polity* (edited by A. S. McGrade)

Hume *Political Essays* (edited by Knud Haakonssen)

King James VI and I *Political Writings* (edited by Johann P. Sommerville)

John of Salisbury *Policraticus* (edited by Cary Nederman)

Kant *Political Writings* (edited by H. S. Reiss and H. B. Nisbet)

Knox *On Rebellion* (edited by Roger A. Mason)

Kropotkin *The Conquest of Bread and Other Writings* (edited by Marshall Shatz)

Lawson *Politica sacra et civilis* (edited by Conal Condren)

Leibniz *Political Writings* (edited by Patrick Riley)

Locke *Two Treatises of Government* (edited by Peter Laslett)

Loyseau *A Treatise of Orders and Plain Dignities* (edited by Howell A. Lloyd)

Luther and Calvin on Secular Authority (edited by Harro Höpfl)

Machiavelli *The Prince* (edited by Quentin Skinner and Russell Price)

de Maistre *Considerations on France* (edited by Isaiah Berlin and Richard Lebrun)

Malthus *An Essay on the Principle of Population* (edited by Donald Winch)

Marsiglio of Padua *Defensor minor* and *De translatione Imperii* (edited by Cary Nederman)

Marx *Early Political Writings* (edited by Joseph O'Malley)

James Mill *Political Writings* (edited by Terence Ball)

J. S. Mill *On Liberty*, with *The Subjection of Women* and *Chapters on Socialism* (edited by Stefan Collini)

Milton *Political Writings* (edited by Martin Dzelzainis)

Montesquieu *The Spirit of the Laws* (edited by Anne M. Cohler, Basia Carolyn Miller and Harold Samuel Stone)

More *Utopia* (edited by George M. Logan and Robert M. Adams)

Morris *News from Nowhere* (edited by Krishan Kumar)

Nicholas of Cusa *The Catholic Concordance* (edited by Paul E. Sigmund)

Nietzsche *On the Genealogy of Morality* (edited by Keith Ansell-Pearson)

Paine *Political Writings* (edited by Bruce Kuklick)

Plato *The Statesman* (edited by Julia Annas and Robin Waterfield)

Price *Political Writings* (edited by D. O. Thomas)

Priestley *Political Writings* (edited by Peter Miller)

Proudhon *What is Property?* (edited by Donald R. Kelley and Bonnie G. Smith)

Pufendorf *On the Duty of Man and Citizen according to Natural Law* (edited by James Tully)

The Radical Reformation (edited by Michael G. Baylor)

Seneca *Moral and Political Essays* (edited by John Cooper and John Procope)

Spencer *The Man versus the State* and *The Proper Sphere of Government* (edited by John Offer)

Stirner *The Ego and Its Own* (edited by David Leopold)

Thoreau *Political Writings* (edited by Nancy Rosenblum)

Utopias of the British Enlightenment (edited by Gregory Claeys)

Vitoria *Political Writings* (edited by Anthony Pagden and Jeremy Lawrance)

Voltaire *Political Writings* (edited by David Williams)

Weber *Political Writings* (edited by Peter Lassman and Ronald Speirs)

William of Ockham *A Short Discourse on Tyrannical Government* (edited by A. S. McGrade and John Kilcullen)

William of Ockham *A Letter to the Friars Minor and Other Writings* (edited by A. S. McGrade and John Kilcullen)

Wollstonecraft *A Vindication of the Rights of Men* and *A Vindication of the Rights of Woman* (edited by Sylvana Tomaselli)